MW00834311

Recognizing Wrongs

RECOGNIZING
WRONGS

———————

John C. P. Goldberg

and

Benjamin C. Zipursky

THE BELKNAP PRESS OF
HARVARD UNIVERSITY PRESS

Cambridge, Massachusetts
London, England
2020

Library of Congress Cataloging-in-Publication Data

Names: Goldberg, John C. P., 1961– author. | Zipursky, Benjamin C., 1960– author.
Title: Recognizing wrongs / John C.P. Goldberg and Benjamin C. Zipursky.
Description: Cambridge, Massachusetts : The Belknap Press of Harvard University Press, 2020. |
Includes bibliographical references and index.
Identifiers: LCCN 2019029432 | ISBN 9780674241701 (hardcover)
Subjects: LCSH: Torts—United States. | Torts—United States—Philosophy.
Classification: LCC KF1250 .G649 2020 | DDC 346.7303—dc23
LC record available at https://lccn.loc.gov/2019029432

To Julie, Alex, and Matthew, for everything
J.C.P.G.

To Antonia, Emma, Rebecca, and Gillian, for your love and your wisdom
B.C.Z.

CONTENTS

Recognizing Wrongs

Introduction

ANXIOUS LAW STUDENTS ARE OFTEN pleasantly surprised to discover that the required first-year course with the odd name—"Torts"—is in many ways down to earth. True, the assigned judicial opinions often feature memorably exotic facts. But even these convey an idea so familiar and compelling that it is easily taken for granted: One who wrongfully injures another can be held accountable by the victim.

The various torts—negligence, trespass, and products liability, to name just three—all partake of this idea. A physician who commits malpractice (professional negligence) faces the prospect of paying compensatory damages to her patient. A homeowner who builds a shed that extends onto his neighbor's land, if sued by his neighbor, might be ordered by a court to tear it down. A manufacturer that sells a defectively designed drug with devastating side effects faces liability to consumers who suffer them. This is the stuff of Torts courses and tort law, and it is hardly exotic.

Ironically, it is those who spend their time studying tort law who often are least in tune with its commonsensical aspects. For more than a century, in law school classes and in books and articles, leading torts scholars, particularly in the United States, have been prone to insist that tort law is not what it appears to be. If there is any rhyme or reason to the subject, they say, it can only be grasped by locating its hidden economic, historical, philosophical, or political logic. To get a hold on tort requires mastery of microeconomics, of Weber's rationalization thesis, of Aristotle's ethics, or of public choice or critical theory. No

1

wonder the timorous have stayed at home, safely away from the daunting thickets of tort theory.

We are theorists, and this book will present readers with some terminology and concepts that may try their patience. But instead of offering yet another fanciful reconstruction, we embrace our subject's most visible aspects. Tort law is what it looks to be, and what its name once clearly announced—it is a law of wrongs. It is this seemingly simple yet misunderstood idea that we aim to recover, to clarify, and to bring up to date. As our title indicates, the goal is to *re-cognize* (rethink) the field by *recognizing* torts for what they really are: legally *recognized* wrongs of a particular sort.

A book that aspires to take tort law at its word might prompt certain worries. Like any long-standing institution, tort law has at times reflected and advanced values that have rightly been rejected. Concerned as it is with the interactions of individuals and firms rather than, say, grand questions of constitutional design or international human rights, tort law might also seem to be small potatoes. An approach such as ours, one might worry, bespeaks a conservative, complacent, or small-minded outlook.

Whatever our shortcomings, these are not among them. Our account does not preserve tort law in amber, but captures its core features, which include its capacity to respond to, prompt, and guide legal and social change. Likewise, we seek to uncover its statutory and constitutional components. Members of a polity organized on liberal-democratic principles, we argue, have a right to be provided with an avenue by which to obtain redress from those who wrongfully injure them. In this way, tort law implicates basic rights.

* * *

In the remainder of this Introduction we offer orientation for readers in the form of three overlapping previews. First, we highlight core concepts that we will introduce, develop, and deploy to make our case. Second, we identify intersecting planes on which the explanations and arguments of the book operate. Finally, we provide summaries of each chapter. Some readers will welcome the signposting. Others may find it a distracting exercise in carts before horses. The latter can proceed directly to Chapter 1. However, they may find it helpful to consult the remainder of this Introduction as they proceed through the book, or after reading it.

Three Ideas

Three ideas—two substantive and one methodological—will figure prominently in our account of tort law: (1) civil recourse; (2) torts as wrongs; and (3) pragmatic conceptualism.

Civil Recourse

What we refer to as "the principle of civil recourse" can be summarized as follows: A person who is the victim of a legal wrong is entitled to an avenue of civil recourse against one who wrongs her. As should be apparent, this principle is capacious. Indeed, it figures in other departments of law beyond tort law.[1] Regardless, it is central to tort law.

If, by rolling back a used car's odometer from 173,000 to 73,000 miles, someone gets you to pay more for the car than you otherwise would have paid, tort law gives you a way to respond to having been so deceived. Common-law legal systems, including those of Australia, Canada, England, and the United States, comply with the principle of civil recourse by giving you the power to invoke the court system to hold the fraudster accountable. Not just the law of fraud, but the law of torts generally, is organized around the principle that where one person has acted in a manner the law deems wrongful to, and injurious of, another, the victim has a right to be provided with a power to redress the wrong through a civil action. As we will demonstrate, the idea of a victim's right to redress as against a wrongdoer is one instantiation of a broader principle that is recognized in both state and federal law in the United States, is entrenched in our positive political morality, and is entirely defensible as a matter of political philosophy.

Torts as Wrongs

We will begin our analysis of tort law with several chapters discussing civil recourse. There are good reasons for doing so—reasons that will become clearer as we proceed. However, by starting with the remedial or redressive aspect of tort law, we run the risk of obscuring that ours is as much an account of tort law's *substance* as of its remedies. A theory that characterizes the particular type of recourse available to tort plaintiffs

---

1. As we emphasize in Chapters 1, 2, and 4, the principle of civil recourse runs throughout private law, and in some areas of public law as well.

as *redress for wrongs* must give an account of the relevant wrongs. Ours does.

As a moment's reflection will reveal, not all wrongs do or should qualify as torts. There are wrongs that the law does not and should not recognize: it is wrong for a guest to behave boorishly at a wedding, irritating the otherwise happy couple, but this is not a wrong that generates or should generate legal liability. There are also wrongs that, even if appropriately dealt with through the law, do not seem to call for redress. It is wrong for the owner of a convenience store knowingly to accede to a sixteen-year-old's insistent request to purchase a pack of cigarettes. But if the child later decides not to smoke them and instead throws them in the trash, the idea of a victim who has a plausible claim for redress against the owner gains little purchase. Finally, there are wrongs that, even though legally recognized and even though injurious, do not amount to torts. It is a different kind of legal wrong—a crime—to possess certain narcotics. Yet, if a person overdoses in the course of committing this crime, such that he requires emergency care from his community hospital at a cost to it of thousands of dollars, he has not committed a tort against the hospital.

Our second big idea—that torts are wrongs of a particular sort—responds to the need for an account of the distinctive nature of tortious wrongdoing. It has structural, substantive, and jurisprudential components.

With regard to structure, torts are distinctive for being *legally recognized*, *injury-inclusive*, and *relational* wrongs. To commit a tort is to engage in conduct that violates an institutionally entrenched norm or directive—one recognized explicitly or implicitly in judicial decisions or legislation. All torts likewise involve not only the violation of a norm, but a violation that culminates in a setback to another. Moreover, they involve conduct that is wrongful in the particular sense of being wrongful with regard to persons such as the person now complaining of the conduct. The boorish wedding guest imagined above violates a norm, but not a *legally recognized* norm. The convenience store owner does nothing to the minor customer that tort law would count as *injurious* to the customer.[2] The narcotics possessor commits a legally recognized wrong that causes a loss to the hospital that treats him, yet does not commit a wrong *in relation to* the hospital.

---

2. Even if the child could claim a legal entitlement to a refund of the purchase price, that claim would not be for a tort.

By contrast to these wrongs, the torts we have already mentioned in this Introduction—negligence, trespass, products liability, and fraud—all fit the structural account of tortious wrongdoing we have just sketched and that we will develop throughout this book. Consider now another tort: libel. To commit libel is (roughly speaking) to violate a *judicially recognized* directive stating that one must not publish in writing a statement *about another* that is of a sort that tends to harm reputation, and that *has harmed the other's reputation*. As the italicized portions of this description indicate, libel, too, is a legally recognized, injury-inclusive, relational wrong. Like all other torts, it involves the violation of an authoritative directive that requires certain persons to refrain from doing certain injurious things to certain others (or, less frequently, a directive requiring them to do certain things for others to spare them from injury).

Turning from structure to substance, we observe that many of the same directives against mistreatment have long been entrenched in all Anglo-American jurisdictions. Assault and battery, false imprisonment and fraud, and negligence and nuisance are torts in each. We offer an account of why these wrongs have figured so centrally in the common law. Courts and legislatures have also at various times revised the list of torts. We provide an account of how judges have gone about doing so, and should go about doing so.

Here we reach the jurisprudential dimension of our claim that torts are wrongs. Under the label "dual constructivism," we describe how it is possible, simultaneously, for there to be a settled law of torts and for judges to identify new torts (or to add new dimensions to existing torts) through common-law reasoning. In so doing, we take a position on the nature of common-law adjudication that falls between the positivism of H. L. A. Hart and the interpretivism of Ronald Dworkin: a position we believe sits comfortably with either.

Pragmatic Conceptualism

The third leg of our overall approach does not consist of claims about civil recourse or about tort law per se, but instead consists of a general approach to law and legal reasoning. Our label for it—"pragmatic conceptualism"—will strike some readers as oxymoronic, but it is not.

Legal scholars in the United States have tended to follow Oliver Wendell Holmes in associating "pragmatism" with forms of analysis that downplay the significance of law's normative concepts (for example, "tort," "wrong," "duty," "right," "proximate cause," "injury"). A pragmatist, they suppose, is one who focuses on observable realities, and particularly on the points at which the legal rubber hits the road—that is, the moments at which judges and other officials exercise power by ordering people to pay money or undertake certain actions. Holmesians, of course, do not deny that judges speak and write in the language of the law. Rather, they suggest that judges do so out of habit, or for appearances' sake. When a judge reaches a result in a particular case, what is "really" going on—the "life of the law," in Holmes's famous phrase—is not something distinctive called legal reasoning, but standard means–ends reasoning (or perhaps no reasoning at all but instead a mere expression of intuition or preference). An engineer designing a bridge chooses its features in the first instance based on an understanding of what will enable it to serve as part of a transportation system. Judicial reasoning, on a Holmesian view, is similarly a matter of engineering, but the engineering involved is "social" rather than mechanical, and is dressed up in the jargon of the legal profession.

The kind of pragmatism we advocate is quite different. Drawing from the work of early and modern pragmatist philosophers, we argue that law professors who embrace Holmesian jurisprudence have badly misunderstood the main lessons of this philosophical tradition. Law's concepts are no less practical and practice-based than the notion of "policy" of which Holmesians are so fond. There is nothing problematically metaphysical about supposing that law contains norms, principles, and concepts not reducible to the results they generate. To treat them as mere labels or empty vessels is to misunderstand and to fail to apply the law.

To summarize: Tort law is a law of wrongs. More specifically, it is law that defines injury-inclusive, relational wrongs and provides victims of such wrongs with the power to obtain redress from wrongdoers upon proof of the wrong. For lawyers, judges, legislators, and legal scholars, the enterprise of tort law and tort theory is conceptual and pragmatic. Understanding tort law's distinctive features and grasping how they relate to one another is crucial to enabling tort law to do what it is supposed to do.

Modes of Analysis and Domains of Explanation

As we practice it, tort theory simultaneously involves doctrinal analysis, policy analysis, interpretive legal theory, analytic jurisprudence, and moral and political philosophy. As our argument proceeds, it will move back and forth among these.

Doctrine

Tort theory is for us a bottom-up exercise that requires immersion in language, practices, rules, and principles that courts and legislatures have developed, that judges and juries apply, and that lawyers invoke. Our engagement with doctrine has thus been anything but casual. In addition to co-authoring a textbook and participating actively in the American Law Institute's efforts to promulgate authoritative Restatements of tort law, we have written articles on classic doctrinal topics (for example, assumption of risk, causation, the duty of care, emotional and economic harm, and fraud) as well cutting-edge issues (such as mass torts, nuisance, oil spill liability, preemption, and punitive damages). Some of these subjects, as well as others, will be addressed in later chapters. The point is that our theorizing about tort has always stayed—and here again will stay—in close contact with doctrine and history. In turn, we hope that it will have practical value for lawyers, judges, and legislators.

Politics and Policy

The last forty years have seen the rise of "tort reform." That phrase is a euphemism coined by lawyers for businesses, physicians, insurers, and others who have advocated for changes in law that reduce the scope of tort liability. The main opponents of tort reform are plaintiffs' attorneys, consumer advocates, and some progressive academics. Regrettably, in keeping with the tenor of the times, debates about tort reform have tended to proceed along sharply partisan lines. The tort system is portrayed either as a way for whiners, shirkers, and sharks to extract "windfalls" from businesses and professionals, or as the only thing that gives the "little guy" a chance to fight back against the recklessness of the rich and powerful.

Our politics lie off this spectrum, which perhaps ensures that our work will fully satisfy no one. So be it. On our understanding, tort law most immediately serves to identify wrongs and enable victims to obtain redress from wrongdoers. Other goods tend to follow from tort law being and doing this. The fact that injuries caused by products can generate liability under several tort headings (fraud, negligence, products liability) surely incentivizes some manufacturers to take precautions they otherwise might not take, and thereby makes the world a bit safer. Likewise, compensatory damage payments made by manufacturers to tort plaintiffs sometimes will operate as a kind of after-the-fact insurance, taking a victim's acutely felt loss and spreading it around as a minor (and thus to consumers unnoticed) component of the product's price. But the case for having such law does not turn primarily on whether it has these effects.

In one respect, we are with the plaintiffs' lawyers. Tort law is very much about *empowerment*. It provides each of us with a remarkable ability to make demands on our fellow citizens, officials, and firms, including those who, because of their wealth or influence, aren't used to being held accountable. A customer who suffers third-degree burns from a boiling-hot cup of coffee purchased from a fast-food franchise's drive-through window can write a letter to the franchise's multibillion-dollar corporate parent requesting reimbursement for her hospital bills. But letters are easily ignored. Alternatively, she can complain by suing in tort and—if she establishes that she suffered her injuries because the restaurant was negligent or sold her a defective product—can obtain a court order requiring the mega-corporation to pay her damages.[3] "David v. Goliath" is hardly the only tort scenario, or even the standard one. But it dramatically demonstrates an important egalitarian dimension to having a body of law that instantiates the principle of civil recourse.

Where we part ways with pro-plaintiff orthodoxy is in our insistence that the power provided by tort law comes with serious strings attached.[4] One really does have to be the victim of a certain kind of wrong to be authorized to invoke the courts to hold another accountable. And the question of whether such a wrong has been committed—and of what the redress should be, assuming there has been a wrong—is not so open-ended that jurors should be able to conclude that a tort has been committed, and that millions of dollars should change hands, just because they are faced

---

3. Here we refer to the famous "McDonald's coffee case." *See* Liebeck v. McDonald's Restaurants, P.T.S., Inc. (N.M. Dist. Ct. Sept. 16, 1994) (affirming a jury verdict of $160,000 in compensatory damages, but reducing its punitive damages award from $2.7 million to $480,000). The parties later settled for an undisclosed amount. Tort reformers claim that *Liebeck* typifies the pathologies of a system that allows foolish people who injure themselves to extract millions of dollars in damages from businesses. The facts of the litigation do not support this characterization. *See, e.g.,* CARL T. BOGUS, WHY LAWSUITS ARE GOOD FOR AMERICA: DISCIPLINED DEMOCRACY, BIG BUSINESS, AND THE COMMON LAW 19–21 (2001).

4. John C. P. Goldberg, *Tort in Three Dimensions*, 38 PEPPERDINE L. REV. 321, 324–32 (2011) (arguing that progressive calls to treat tort law as akin to an "ombudsman" threaten to delegitimate it by detaching its processes from its substance).

with a sympathetic victim and a wealthy business that has behaved in a less-than-exemplary fashion, or just because it would serve the cause of distributive justice or some other important value.

Our relation to pro-defendant reformers is similarly oblique. Even though Anglo-American tort law's origins date back to the time when Robin Hood was said to be relieving the well-to-do of their wealth, it was not then, and is not now, a scheme designed to take from the rich and give to the poor. But it is a mechanism of accountability. Because of tort law, victims of certain injurious wrongs do not have to rely upon the solicitude of those who injure them or on the beneficence of charitable organizations or government benefits programs. Moreover, because victims are empowered to pursue and obtain redress, they can proceed of their own volition, without first seeking permission from a governmental official.

The reach of tort law can be quite broad. Manufacturers and physicians understandably chafe at this aspect of our system—they are sometimes held liable only because they failed to meet standards of conduct that are difficult consistently to meet. But they are hardly unique in this regard. "Ordinary" people sometimes face tort liability on similar terms. As we explain in Chapter 6, there are good reasons to have a law of wrongs and redress that is unforgiving in certain ways.

The rise of the tort reform movement is, we believe, in no small part the product of an academic failure: specifically, the failure of modern law schools to provide their students with an adequate understanding of the field.[5] Many of today's judges, legislators, and lawyers were taught that tort law is merely a means—and probably a clumsy and expensive means—of deterring unsafe conduct, or of providing insurance against losses associated with injuries, or some of each. The notion that tort law is but an ad hoc regulatory mechanism lacking any real center has in turn given lawyers and judges in the United States a feeling of license, and opinions applying tort law increasingly have become unmoored from its core notions of wrongs, injury, and redress. In such an environment,

---

5. We are no doubt prone to inflate the significance of academia. Still, as the cliché goes—and as even the hardheaded Holmes claimed at the close of his most famous essay—ideas have consequences. Oliver W. Holmes, *The Path of the Law*, 10 HARV. L. REV. 457, 478 (1897). Of course, power politics have also been at work. Daryl J. Levinson & Benjamin I. Sachs, *Political Entrenchment and Public Law*, 125 YALE L.J. 400, 438–41 (2015) (discussing the Republican Party's adoption of tort reform as a conscious strategy to reduce the ability of trial lawyers to fund Democratic Party candidates).

it is hardly surprising that legislators, the media, and the public are prone to debate tort law on the wrong terms, and to want to reform it in perverse ways.

Reform proponents today are largely on the right, whereas its foes (we include ourselves) are mostly on the left. This has not always been so, and isn't always so today: tort law continues to have its detractors from the progressive side and its supporters among conservatives. Our principal political claim is one that should be, and often in the past has been, championed by left, right, and center: The capacity of individuals to use the courts to hold others accountable is a fundamental feature of our legal system, one that we ought not permit to wither.

Interpretive Theory

This book may strike legal philosophers as too conventional or practice-based, even as lawyers and law professors may worry that it is too ethereal. Unsurprisingly, we believe we are operating in the theoretical sweet spot.

Our method, to use fancy words, is "hermeneutic" or "interpretive." We seek to explain how the particulars of tort law—its institutional structure, its rules, and the concepts lawyers and judges use when reasoning about it—mesh with one another to form a reasonably coherent whole. At the same time, we rely on our account of the whole to make sense of its parts. Through this method we aim to develop a usable account of tort law that operates simultaneously at a high level of abstraction, at a high level of detail, and at various planes in between.

In providing an interpretive account, we do not pretend to be neutral or agnostic. Interpretations inevitably carry normative implications. To offer, as we do, a general account of tort law is already to defend it against critics who maintain that it is a jumble. To demonstrate, as we will, that tort law is not hardwired with regressive political commitments is to eliminate an oft-cited ground for skepticism about it. More affirmatively, we will argue that tort law and the principle it embodies fit comfortably within a liberal-democratic framework of government.[6] We do not offer an unqualified

6. Which is not to say that tort law is an inherently liberal-democratic institution, or can only be justified on liberal-democratic grounds. Any such conclusion would be surprising, given that (as explained in Chapter 2) tort law has been a part of Anglo-American law since well before the emergence of liberal-democratic forms of government. *See* JOHN GARDNER, FROM PERSONAL LIFE TO PRIVATE LAW 196–97 (2018) (offering this observation).

defense of existing doctrine or institutions. Instead, we maintain that there is much to be said in support of tort law—certainly a lot more than many law professors seem to suppose.

In sum, this book belongs to a genre of philosophy that aims for a space between apology and critique. We maintain that critics of tort law have failed to understand its structure and its content, and have failed to see how it instantiates and furthers important values to which we generally profess allegiance. A legal system without tort law would be less committed to these values. Whether one ought to favor such a system obviously will depend on the details of its design and implementation, and on judgments about how to make tradeoffs among competing values.

Common Law and Legal Reasoning

Like many analytic legal philosophers, and unlike the majority of our law school colleagues, we reject the notion, associated with Legal Realism, that judicial opinions characteristically involve judges rationalizing decisions made on other grounds. To say the same thing, we think there is a cogent notion of legal reasoning available to judges facing tort cases (and other kinds of cases)—one of which they avail themselves, sometimes despite themselves. Hence our attention to doctrine. We are hardly alone in taking this position, and indeed we expressly rely upon the work of Hart and other critics of Realism. Alas, most torts professors—even those who purport to be agnostic about jurisprudence—have remained attracted to Realism in one form or another. We are hopeful that we might change some minds by providing a book-length treatment that surpasses Realist accounts of judicial decision-making in its veracity, authenticity, candor, and detail.

Though it is both immodest and imprudent to say so, in writing this book we aspire to recapture some of what Benjamin Cardozo brought to the common law and to jurisprudence. It is immodest because Cardozo was one-of-a-kind—our country's greatest judicial expositor of tort law, the leader in his time of the country's most important common-law court, and a well-respected Justice of the United States Supreme Court. It is imprudent because the luminaries of Anglo-American legal theory have generally not looked kindly upon Cardozo's jurisprudential writings, which are sometimes maddeningly elliptical.

On our view, Cardozo's not-quite-elevated status in academia is a symptom of the problem we are trying to address. Holmes's skeptical mindset and austere prose have played better than Cardozo's more stylized approach. Ultimately, however, the two offered quite different accounts of the implications of philosophical pragmatism for a forward-looking, modernist judge. Holmes's pragmatism partakes of reductionism and instrumentalism. He was glad, in the end, to give the keys to the courthouse to the statistician and the economist.

Like Holmes, Cardozo thought it crucial for judges to be aware of what was really going to work for society. But he did not begin with the conviction that the traditional, morally tinged language of the law is claptrap. To the contrary, he saw in it an expression of widely shared but evolving norms and values. Instead of shunning the law's concepts as fictions posing as transcendental truths, Cardozo demonstrated how judges, by paying close attention to the institutional structures of the law, to history and tradition, and to changing social norms, could apply and update them in a principled manner. His approach was thus "constructivist." Both as a methodology of adjudication in the common law and as an account of the relationship between law and morality, Cardozo's constructivism—which bears some obvious affinities to Rawls's notion of reflective equilibrium and Dworkin's interpretivist account of legal reasoning—is superior to Holmes's instrumentalism.

In the law of torts, common-law reasoning is reasoning about wrongs, about how people may and may not (under the law) treat one another. Thus, much of this book—especially Part Two—is an examination of the grounds for believing that such forms of reasoning are defensible and valuable in the very practical domain of the law. If, as we claim in Chapter 8, "dual constructivism" is the appropriate mode for common-law reasoning, we will have also explained how a backward-looking practice can nonetheless allow for the recognition of new wrongs without devolving into crude instrumentalism.

Moral Philosophy

Moral philosophy involves the analysis of concepts such as duty, right, wrong, responsibility, prudence, virtue, vice, honesty, dishonesty, goodness, and so on. Tort scholars and philosophers usually expect that when moral philosophical analysis is found alongside of tort theory, it is there to help guide legal analysis. While we have sometimes found this to be the case, we have found the converse to be true as well. Both here and in prior work, for example, we have illuminated problems of moral luck by considering them through the lens of tort law and theory.[7]

It is possible that the insights provided by civil recourse, dual constructivism, and pragmatic conceptualism cut still deeper, however. This is for at least three reasons. First and foremost, the topic of responsibility within moral philosophy is famously imprecise: questions of culpability, causation, wherewithal to make good, and others are covered by it. Tort law contains a rich institutional, historical, and linguistic context for considering these questions and the interconnections among them. In particular, the idea of civil recourse may offer moral theorists a fresh perspective on responsibility in terms of the appropriateness of someone's being the object of a process of holding to account.[8]

Second, and relatedly, a topic of ongoing (and increasingly visible) importance in moral philosophy concerns the structure of duties, the extent to which duties are agent-relative, and the degree to which it matters whether duties are conceived of as correlative to rights. Much of this book relates to a parallel debate in tort law (specifically, in negligence law). Although we do not maintain that all legal and moral duties are inherently relational in their analytic structure, we do maintain that *tort law's* duties of conduct are relational. This is hardly an accident. The relationality of tort duties is tied to the reasons such duties exist, and it has numerous implications for debates over agent-relativity.

A third aspect of tort theory that may prove illuminating for moral theory relates back to the moral luck comments offered above. At the root of moral luck puzzles is the thought that a person ought not be held accountable for aspects of her conduct over which she lacks significant control. As Bernard Williams and Thomas Nagel long ago observed, however, our speech and practices, and sometimes our deepest intuitions, do not always jibe with this abstract conviction. In everyday life, we sometimes think it appropriate to hold someone responsible "strictly" for an act—i.e., notwithstanding that it was largely beyond her control to refrain from so

---

7. *See* Chapter 6.

8. Here it bears note that Stephen and Julian Darwall, and Jason Solomon, have drawn an affinity between civil recourse theory and Peter Strawson's influential philosophical writings on resentment and responsibility. Stephen Darwall & Julian Darwall, *Civil Recourse as Mutual Accountability*, 39 FLA. ST. L. REV. 17, 38–41 (2011); Jason M. Solomon, *Equal Accountability through Tort Law*, 103 NW. L. REV. 1765 (2009).

acting. Day in and day out, tort law deals with a directly analogous problem. Here, building on our prior work, we offer a principled explanation of "strict liability" in tort, and in so doing, we lay a groundwork for a more nuanced understanding of the connection between control, fault, and responsibility in nonlegal domains.

Political Philosophy

As Samuel Scheffler has argued, a comprehensive theory of justice of the sort that Rawls put forward in A Theory of Justice must provide an account of the institutional framework of a just political state: what Rawls called "the basic structure of society."[9] One who offers such a theory thus faces the question of whether that structure encompasses private law, including law enabling and governing agreements (contracts), wrongful infliction of injuries (torts), and the possession and transfer of things and land (property). Scheffler persuasively argues that Rawls gave an affirmative answer to this question, and really could only have done so. A theory of justice—Scheffler and Rawls agree, and so do we—must have something to say about the law of torts.

This last conclusion will not be surprising to tort theorists, as many have said as much. Arthur Ripstein, whose pioneering reading of Kant perhaps influenced Scheffler, presents his recent book of tort theory—Private Wrongs—as a work of political philosophy.[10] Before him, scholars ranging from Guido Calabresi, Ronald Coase, Richard Epstein, and Richard Posner to Jules Coleman, George Fletcher, John Gardner, and Ernest Weinrib have done the same, albeit sometimes less openly.[11] Whether or not expressly labeled as theories of "corrective justice" and whether or not "justice" is openly invoked, theirs are deep-cutting theories of why a well-ordered state in modern times needs or does well to have a law of torts.

Our own political-philosophical contention about tort law as part of the basic structure is straightforward. Following John Locke, we view tort law as being important to the justness of a state in a manner that parallels the significance of the law's recognition of a privilege of self-defense. There

---

9. Samuel Scheffler, *Distributive Justice, the Basic Structure and the Place of Private Law,* 35 O.J.L.S. 213 (2015).
10. ARTHUR RIPSTEIN, PRIVATE WRONGS (2016).
11. Relevant works by these scholars are cited throughout this book.

are certain forms of vulnerability that a liberal-democratic state cannot fairly require individuals to endure. It cannot require of us, on pain of penalties, to acquiesce to another's attack. And it cannot require us to sit by and do nothing in the face of certain forms of mistreatment. The existence of a system of civil recourse as part of the basic structure of American government partly determines the nature of our interactions with one another. It is part of how we understand ourselves as having responsibilities to one another, and it contributes to the ability of our system of law to claim to be just.

Road Map

This book has three parts, each with multiple chapters. Part One is mainly concerned to define and defend the principle of civil recourse and to give a careful account of the type of wrong that triggers its operation.

Chapter 1 starts off on a deliberately provocative note. *Ubi jus ibi remedium* is an ancient legal maxim that is commonly translated to mean "where there's a right, there's a remedy." Though it tends these days to be regarded as a tautology or platitude, *ubi jus* in fact expresses our legal system's commitment to an important substantive principle: the principle of civil recourse. As we demonstrate, the maxim and the principle hold a special place in American legal history; one that extends beyond tort law to foundational constitutional principles articulated in the Declaration of Independence, *Marbury v. Madison's* endorsement of judicial review, and the Fourteenth Amendment's rights-protective provisions. No less of an expression of *ubi jus* is the modern emergence of liability for workplace sexual harassment. Having identified the salience of the principle of civil recourse to American law generally, and to tort law in particular, the chapter ends on a note more sobering than celebratory. Born in part of academic failures to appreciate the significance of the tradition described in this chapter, our legal system's commitment to *ubi jus* is arguably waning.

Chapter 2 considers and rejects several sacred cows of American torts scholarship that are sometimes taken to render unavailable or uncompelling the type of account we offer in this book. Specifically, the chapter exposes five such shibboleths: (i) that tort law first emerged as a (feeble) response to the carnage generated by the Industrial Revolution and is thus best understood as "accident law"; (ii) that torts are not wrongs in any robust sense but merely behaviors to which courts and legislatures have chosen, for policy reasons, to attach liability; (iii) that a wrongs-and-redress account of tort law is insufficient to capture what makes tort a distinctive department of the law; (iv) that tort law can only be understood and evaluated as law that aims to improve public safety, provide compensation to injury victims, or both; and (v) that the only valid way for judges and scholars to reason about tort cases is instrumentally. Much of our prior work has been devoted to demonstrating the falsity and perniciousness of these bromides. This chapter continues that effort.

Chapter 3 shifts from stage-setting to affirmative argumentation. Specifically, it offers an analytic and interpretive account that isolates the nature and structure of the rights and duties recognized in the common law of torts. The theory we offer—the "conduct-rule theory of rights"— does not take rights *or* duties *or* liabilities to be foundational to tort law. Instead, following a line of reasoning in Hart's work, it takes primary legal *rules*, which we call "directives" or "conduct rules," to be basic.[12] The rules that one must not intentionally touch another person in a harmful or offensive manner, that one must not defraud another, and that one must not enter land possessed by another without permission— these are all examples of conduct rules that courts have adopted as rules of tort law. Because these rules contain relational directives, they in turn generate correlative pairs of rights and duties, such as rights not to be battered, defrauded, or have one's land trespassed upon and duties not to batter, defraud, or trespass. A tort is a contravention of one of these judicially recognized (or legislatively enacted) relational directives, and the contravention of a relational directive is at once both a violation of the victim's right and a breach of the tortfeasor's duty. From within this framework, the *ubi jus* maxim is neither circular nor vacuous. Instead it asserts, substantively, that where there is a contravention of a relational legal directive, the person on whom the directive confers a right against being injured is entitled to a legal power to demand redress from the person on whom the directive imposes a duty not to injure when the duty is breached and the right is violated.

Chapter 4 offers a defense of the principle of civil recourse. It does so by drawing on an approach to justification that runs from John Locke's *Second*

---

12. Law professors are fond of distinguishing well-specified "rules" from fuzzier "standards." In this context, we use the term "rule" to encompass both.

Treatise through Rawls's work to T. M. Scanlon's. Much as adult members of a liberal-democratic polity are entitled to demand the right to vote as a condition of playing by its rules, so too they can demand a state-backed system that empowers them to respond, civilly, to violations of their legal rights. A legal system that (among other things) empowers victims of legal wrongs to use the court system to obtain redress from their wrongdoers does right by its members: it treats them, in relevant respects, equally, fairly, and with due regard for the status of each as an agent.

Chapter 5, the final chapter of Part One, fills out our account of the principle of civil recourse by inquiring into why liability to pay money damages counts as "redress" for wrongful injury. In our parlance, "redress" refers to a special case of civil recourse. It is the fulfillment—*recognition*—of a legitimate demand by an injury victim for responsive action from a wrongful injurer. Our explication of the nature of tort redress provides us with an occasion on which to distinguish our theory from its cousin, corrective justice theory. It also allows us to demonstrate how our theory can illuminate contemporary issues in tort law—here concerning the propriety of punitive damage awards and constitutional limits thereon.

Part Two shifts the focus from civil recourse to wrongs. Chapter 6 sets the table by identifying three particularly salient aspects of tortious wrongdoing, as opposed to other forms of wrongdoing. It does so by dispelling three arguments that are commonly taken to defeat the possibility of torts being understood as wrongs, when in fact these arguments establish only that torts are a particular species of wrong. According to skeptics, the law of torts cannot be a law of wrongs because: (i) it gives dumb luck a large role in determining whether a tort has occurred, and it is not plausible to treat liability so haphazardly imposed as a way of holding persons responsible for their wrongs; (ii) it sometimes imposes strict liability, and strict liability by definition is not wrongs-based; and (iii) it contains a "proper-plaintiff principle" that blocks the imposition of liability even when one person's wrongful conduct injures another in a predictable manner, and no self-respecting law of wrongs would contain such a principle. While these claims are superficially compelling (which is why they have gained some traction), each is unfounded. Given what tort law is all about—identifying wrongs with victims who are entitled to redress—tort law's relative indifference to moral luck, its embrace of a certain kind of strict liability, and its proper-plaintiff principle form defensible and indeed complementary features of this body of law.

With Chapter 6 having cleared the decks, Chapters 7 and 8 attend to tort law's substance. Chapter 7 focuses on accounts of tortious wrongdoing that have long been popular among U.S. legal academics and that, in keeping with the hardheaded orientation of Holmesian pragmatism, proceed from functionalist premises. The key move, articulated in the opening pages of William Prosser's magisterial 1941 torts treatise, is to abandon the effort to provide a conceptual account of what a tort is, and instead to "back out" a description from the "observable" or "bottom-line" features of the tort system. Successful tort suits typically result in damage payments or monetary settlements. It follows that such proceedings are particularly well suited to serve two goals: discouraging undesirable conduct through the threat of liability ("deterrence") and shifting losses from one person to another through monetary payments from defendants to plaintiffs ("compensation"). From here, Prosser argued, a functional definition of the field begins to emerge: Each tort must have two poles or aspects: a *setback* (harm) aspect, and a *socially undesirable conduct* aspect. The law of torts can then be understood as a collection of setback–conduct pairings.

As we discuss below, Prosser's "dual instrumentalist" account of tort law gets one important thing right: namely, that all torts have a conduct aspect and an injury aspect. Yet his instrumentalist rendering of that insight doomed his account to failure. It cannot explain why courts have recognized the torts they have recognized. It also fails to capture how judges reason when applying and revising tort law. Interestingly, some of the savviest instrumentalist scholars—including Judge Richard Posner—long ago recognized these problems and sought to solve them. Their attempted solution, however, went in exactly the wrong direction, as it involved shifting from dual to "singular" instrumentalism—that is, to a form of instrumentalism that focuses on deterrence *or* compensation, rather than both. This attempted cure only makes things worse. The problem with dual instrumentalism is not its dualism, but its instrumentalism. In turn, the key to understanding the wrongs of tort is to capture the two-sided or dual nature of tortious wrongdoing from within a noninstrumentalist framework.

Chapter 8 does just this, substituting for dual instrumentalism an approach that we dub "dual constructivism." Like dual instrumentalism, dual constructivism acknowledges that torts are injury-inclusive wrongs.

Also like dual instrumentalism, dual constructivism offers an account that is practice-based rather than Platonic: the wrongs that count as torts are the wrongs that courts and legislatures have recognized as torts. The trick is to figure out which wrongs have been so recognized, and what they really amount to. This task might seem straightforward, requiring only that one consult standard legal sources to determine the content of tort law in a given jurisdiction at a given time. And yet, as lawyers know, things are not so easy. Legal materials often do not speak unequivocally. Hence the need for judicial construction, and scholarly reconstruction.

When deciding tort cases, judges tend to ask and answer, and ought to ask and answer, the question "Has the defendant interacted with the plaintiff in a way that the law explicitly *or implicitly* recognizes as a mistreatment?" This inquiry involves a mode of reasoning that is "integrative" in seeking to locate instances in which the injurious potential that renders conduct wrongful is realized in injury to a victim; "direct" rather than reverse-engineered from policy considerations; "rectitudinal" in being genuinely concerned with whether a wrong has been committed; and "elucidative" as opposed to legislative. The common-law judge neither follows existing law blindly nor legislates de novo. She *constructs* the law, not in the manner of a builder who builds anew, but (to borrow Blackstone's metaphor) as a renovator charged with remodeling an existing structure. Once tort law is understood as constructed in this sense, one can better appreciate that the recognition of torts by courts is an exercise in identifying and enjoining certain wrongful injurings, an exercise that aims both to protect persons from mistreatment and to provide them with a way to respond to having been mistreated.

Part Three aims to demonstrate the value of our approach for the clarification and resolution of contemporary issues in doctrine, policy, and legal theory. Chapter 9 first sets forth how civil recourse theory and dual constructivism fit together. In doing so, it explains that our view of torts as injury-inclusive, relational legal wrongs goes hand in hand with the recognition that tort law has an equally important public dimension. Second, it explains at a general level how an approach such as ours, even though abstract, can assist lawyers, judges, legislators, and citizens in understanding and reforming law. Third, it addresses complaints that our theory is oblivious to certain realities of modern tort litigation—in particular, the pervasiveness of claims-aggregation, settlement, and liability insurance—and thus has little practical value. We rebut these contentions in part through an extended analysis of mass products liability litigation concerning injuries allegedly caused by the drug Vioxx.

Chapter 10 continues the focus on live and concrete issues in contemporary tort law, proceeding sequentially through problems in negligence, products liability, and defamation. As to negligence, a much-litigated question concerns whether therapists face malpractice liability not to their patients but to *patients' family members*—typically the father of a young female patient—who claim that the therapist has negligently induced the patient to "recover" false memories of parental abuse. Whereas instrumentalist analyses provide only indeterminate balancing tests for these difficult cases, a wrongs-and-redress understanding of tort law, combined with a dual constructivist approach to adjudication, offers meaningful guidance. Turning next to products liability law, we build on Chapter 6's analysis of "strict liability wrongs" to make progress on perhaps the central doctrinal question in the field—namely, what standard or standards the courts should use to determine whether a product contains a design defect, such that its seller will face liability for injuries it causes. The chapter concludes by addressing the hot-button issue of internet defamation. A federal law known as the Communications Decency Act grants protection from liability for defamation to owners and operators of websites and other internet users. Nonetheless, as we explain, courts have misread and misapplied the statute so as to grant a broad immunity that it does not in fact provide, and have done so because of a failure to attend carefully to the structure and substance of the tort of libel. The three topics of Chapter 10 provide a sampling of the analyses we have offered elsewhere. The point of including them here is to demonstrate with greater clarity some of the ways in which our framework can illuminate and help to resolve pressing practical issues.

We close the book on a theoretical note—actually, on three theoretical notes. Although presented as a Conclusion, they are sounded more with the hope of resonance than with a drive for closure. The first relates to what, for want of a better term, might be deemed the "civil society" aspect of our theory. Here we explain that tort law, by entrenching a variety of social norms and crafting enforceable legal rights and duties, contributes to sustaining and reforming a range of valuable relationships and institutions in our society. In helping us to know what to expect of one another, and to know how to live up to those expectations, it helps us to recognize our responsibilities. The second note concerns what Rawls rightly called the first virtue of social institutions—justice. Although we reject the idea that tort law aims in the first instance to ensure that justice is done between victim and injurer, we do think that having a law of torts, at least in a modern liberal democracy, is critical to having a just legal and political system. Tort law is in this way constitutive of justice. Third and finally, we sound once again a note of jurisprudential pragmatism. As we emphasize in the book's opening chapters, ours is the pragmatism of Cardozo, not Holmes. It calls on judges faced with tort cases to reason constructively from legal materials and social norms, rather than formalistically or instrumentally. Whereas Holmes urged modern lawyers to turn away from wrongs, Cardozo marked a better path—the path of recognizing wrongs.

PART I

Civil Recourse

1

Civil Wrongs and Civil Rights

IN THIS CHAPTER we make two claims that stand in some tension with one another. After sketching tort law's basic features, we first suggest that these features reflect a principle that is central to our legal and political traditions. We then explain (in the chapter's final section) how many contemporary legal scholars, as well as the lawyers and judges they have trained, have come to misunderstand tort law and to lose sight of its animating principle.

What Is a Tort? What Is Tort Law?

Just as there are many crimes—murder, arson, burglary, treason—there are many torts. Like the different crimes, each tort has a name and readily recognizable exemplars.

Battery is one tort. For a person to commit a battery is for her intentionally to touch another in a manner that is harmful or offensive. One who punches another commits battery.[1] So does one who kicks, spits on, or fondles another. In the course of deciding lawsuits brought by persons seeking redress for having been punched, kicked, spat upon, or fondled, courts have fashioned the legal rule that gives battery its substantive

---

1. In the language of tort law, one who intentionally touches another in a harmful or offensive manner has committed a "prima facie" wrong. This locution is a reference to the fact that the law recognizes certain justifications for doing things that normally are not allowed (for example, punching another in self-defense to ward off an attack). The existence of such justifications does not affect the points being made in the text.

content. A person who violates this rule in turn incurs a legal vulnerability. He or she can be sued by the victim and, if the lawsuit prevails, will be the subject of a court judgment requiring him to pay money damages to the victim.

Other torts go by names such as "assault," "conversion," "fraud," "libel," "negligence," "outrage"—a particularly evocative name!—"products liability," and "trespass." Like battery, each of these torts sets a rule or rules specifying how one must refrain from mistreating others or, less frequently, identifying steps one must take to protect or rescue another from certain dangers. It also enables persons injured by violations of these rules to obtain a remedy, whether in the form of a damages payment or a court order directing the defendant to take or refrain from taking particular actions.

Some scholars argue that, despite appearances, the various conduct-rules of tort law reduce down to a single *substantive* principle—for example, that each is an expression of the Golden Rule ("Do unto others . . ."). Others argue, oppositely, that tort law is an almost haphazard collection of those instances in which courts happen to have decided that conduct will generate liability. Our view falls in between these two extremes. We do not believe that the wrongs of tort law express a single, foundational principle. Nonetheless, they are united by certain features. Each tort is a *legally recognized wrong.* Each is also an *injury-inclusive, relational wrong,* in that it involves one person wronging another by interfering with an aspect of individual well-being. Finally, each is a *civilly actionable* wrong. Taken as whole, tort law defines *wrongs* and provides an avenue through which victims can obtain *redress.* This book is largely devoted to explaining these ideas. Here it will suffice to offer a few thoughts about each.

The word "tort" was incorporated long ago into English legal usage from French. It means "wrong." Each of the recognized torts is a wrong. It is not merely that courts have used words such as "battery" and "negligence" to identify conduct to which the law attaches adverse consequences. After all, the law regularly attaches such consequences to acts that are *not* wrongs. So far as the law is concerned, there is nothing wrong with buying a car or a bicycle. Still, one who buys a car or a bicycle may be required by law to pay a tax on the purchase. It would be farcical to describe such a payment as "redress" for a "wrong." By contrast, it *is* wrong intentionally to cause someone to believe that they are about to be shot (assault), to spy on a person in her bedroom (invasion of privacy), and constantly to use noisy machinery that keeps one's neighbors up at night (nuisance). None of these is an instance of acceptable-but-taxed conduct. Nor is the injurer's after-the-fact failure to make a compensatory payment what renders these acts wrongful. They are wrongful when done. The same is true even for those parts of tort law that are commonly said to impose "strict liability," including modern products liability law.[2]

The wrongs identified by tort law tend to be familiar. One needs no legal training to know that one mistreats another by defrauding him, defaming him, and so forth. But the reverse is not true. It is obviously wrong to humiliate a stranger at a social event by gratuitously commenting on his obesity. Wrong, but not a tort. Courts have defined the tort of slander to exclude insults and true statements, and for the most part have refused to deem emotionally injurious conduct to be tortious when it is merely insensitive or rude, as opposed to outrageous. To assert that a particular way of interacting with others is a tort is to assert that it is of a type that has been *recognized* as a wrong in an authoritative legal source, such as a judicial decision or legislation, or at least that it is properly deemed to belong to the class of such wrongs. Because the task of interpreting prior judicial decisions and legislation often is not straightforward, the line between wrongs that are legally recognized and those that are not can be difficult to discern. Moreover, the list of torts has changed over time as lawmakers have fashioned new torts and discarded existing ones. And even for a well-established tort such as battery or negligence, there are uncertainties about how it applies to particular cases. These important qualifications notwithstanding, it remains true that for a wrong to be a tort it must be a legally recognized wrong.

Just as there are injurious wrongs not recognized by the law as torts, so too there is conduct marked off as wrongful by bodies of law other than tort law. Possession of narcotics is an example: although the law deems such conduct wrongful, it does so by designating it as a *crime*. In one respect, possession is an unusual crime. Many crimes have tort counterparts—to beat up another person is at once to commit the crime of assault and the tort of battery; to burn down another's house is to commit the tort of trespass to land and the crime of arson. The crime of drug possession

---

2. Under the doctrine of strict products liability, even careful manufacturers are subject to liability for injuries caused by their defective products. Strict liability and products liability are discussed in Chapters 6 and 10.

by contrast, lacks a tort counterpart. That it does so will help us to isolate distinctive features of tortious wrongdoing.

Drug possession lacks an equivalent in tort for a simple but important reason: it is defined such that it is capable of being committed without any injury being inflicted on another person. To be sure, a given instance of drug possession might cause harm to a particular person (for example, one who possesses illegal drugs might suffer an overdose) or even to many. The point is that injury is no part of the definition of the offense. Thus, the crime of narcotics possession is complete as soon as a person exercises the requisite control over the relevant substance with the requisite mental state: no proof of a setback to another is required. The same cannot be said of the legal wrongs that are torts. Every tort involves a person injuring another person in some way, or failing to prevent another's injury: every tort is an *injury-inclusive* wrong.[3] There are some difficult questions about what counts as an "injury."[4] But these difficult questions presuppose the present point. If there has been no injury, there can be no tort.

So, torts are legally recognized and injury-inclusive wrongs. Further, they are *relational* wrongs.[5] Each tort identifies conduct that is not merely wrongful in the sense of being antisocial, but wrongful *as to* a particular person or wrongful as to each member of a defined group of persons. Felling trees located on someone else's property is not merely wrong in a generic sense. It is a wrong to their owner. Knowingly publishing an article falsely asserting that a political candidate takes bribes is not merely antisocial. It is a wrongful injuring of the candidate. Carelessly driving one's car so that it collides with and injures a motorcyclist is not a wrong "in the air."

3. As we observe in the text, some crimes (arson) are injury-inclusive wrongs, others (drug possession) are not. Our point is not that tort law is unique in recognizing such wrongs. Rather, it is that only such wrongs can be torts.

4. Suppose that the careless operation of an industrial plant exposes nearby residents to a carcinogen, and that each resident now faces a slightly greater likelihood that she will contract cancer than persons who have not been exposed. Has the operator of the plant "injured" the residents just by causing them to face increased odds of contracting an illness, even before anyone has actually become sick?

5. As noted in the Introduction, and explained further in Chapter 3, we use the term "relational" to identify conduct that involves mistreatment of another, as opposed to conduct that is antisocial without involving such a mistreatment. As the examples just given indicate, a wrong can be relational in this sense even in the absence of a preexisting *relationship* between injurer and victim. Though relational wrongs often do occur within such relationships (as when a lawyer commits malpractice upon a client), it is perfectly commonplace for a person to engage in conduct that is wrongful as to a stranger.

It is a wrong to the motorcyclist (and an injurious one at that). By contrast, in the eyes of tort law, the same careless car driver commits no tort as to a stranger who happens to witness the collision of car and motorcycle and its gory aftermath from the balcony of his second-floor apartment. This is so even if the stranger is predictably traumatized as a result.

About this aspect of torts, too, we will have more to say. In particular, it will be important to explain what does and does not follow from recognizing the relational structure of tortious wrongdoing. For now, however, we will turn to consider how the features of torts we have thus far identified connect organically to the idea of civil recourse.

When a crime is committed, the offender is vulnerable to certain actions by government officials, including prosecution at the hands of a state or federal official, and punishment by judge and jury. When a tort is committed, a legal power is conferred on the victim to obtain redress from the tortfeasor via a judicial proceeding. This power is conditional: the putative victim's right to redress hinges on her ability to prove that she has actually been the victim of a tort at the hands of the defendant(s) being sued. The point is that the commission of a tort renders a tortfeasor vulnerable not to the state per se but to the victim (or her representative), who in turn can invoke the power of the courts in pursuing her claim. It is the putative victim, not a government official, who decides whether to assert a claim and demand a remedy. It is also the putative victim who decides whether to drop her lawsuit, settle it for a monetary payment, or see it through to judgment.

Today judges and scholars are fond of saying that tort law is a system for compensating injury victims and deterring wrongdoers by the threat of liability. While not entirely off-base, this way of speaking is misleading, for it puts a regulatory cast on law that is at least as much "private." It is true that injury victims often obtain compensation for their injuries through tort suits, and the threat of tort liability probably does deter individuals and firms from injuring others. But compensation and deterrence—understood as aggregate or social goods—are beneficial effects of having tort law. Neither is its purpose. When money changes hands as a result of a tort suit, it is not paid out as part of a public benefits program, nor is it paid out as a fine. It is paid to the victim (or her representative or survivors) as redress. Our claim is *not* that lawmakers who fashion the rules of tort law are indifferent to whether it will affect behavior or benefit injury victims. Rather, it is that tort law is structured such that it guides conduct and protects and empowers victims in a particular way that is not accurately captured by describing it as a scheme of deterrence and compensation.

Civil Recourse as Constitutional Principle

We hope that we have said enough to provide an initial feel for the distinctive features of tort law and for how they hang together. To summarize: A tort is a wrong of a special sort. Specifically, a tort is a legally recognized wrong, an injurious wrong, a wronging of another person, and a wrong that is civilly actionable by a victim who seeks redress for it. These attributes mesh well with one another. Relational, injurious wrongs are wrongs that involve a special kind of victimization and hence are appropriately deemed actionable by means of suits by victims seeking compensation, as well as injunctive relief and other remedies.

In the next section of this chapter we will canvas significant instances in U.S. legal history that demonstrate the centrality of tort law to our legal traditions. Before doing so, however, we wish to take a brief but we hope illuminating detour from tort law to the more general idea of civil recourse. This lesson concerns the centrality to American legal thought—including American constitutional law—of the idea that when a person has suffered a legal rights violation at the hands of another (whether a tort or some other legal wrong), then, ordinarily, she is entitled to recourse against the wrongdoer. In the words of the old legal maxim, *ubi jus ibi remedium*. Where there's a right, there's a remedy.

The importance and breadth of this principle can be grasped by considering the first comprehensive treatise on English law, published on the eve of the American Revolution by William Blackstone. Book 3 of Blackstone's *Commentaries* focuses on "private wrongs" (conduct that amounts to the mistreatment of particular persons), as distinct from "public wrongs" (conduct that amounts to a wrong to the public at large). According to Blackstone, the entire common law of private wrongs (including what we would today call contract and tort law) is the instantiation in law of the "general and indisputable rule, that where there is a legal right, there is also a legal remedy . . . ."[6] Such law is provided, he reasoned, in fulfillment of a political obligation owed to Englishmen by their monarch, who is "officially

---

6. 3 WILLIAM BLACKSTONE, COMMENTARIES ON THE LAWS OF ENGLAND * 23 (1765–69).

bound to redress in the ordinary forms of law" those "wrongs committed in the mutual intercourse between subject and subject."[7]

Modern jurists are prone to dismiss Blackstone's "general and indisputable rule" as empty or circular. We demonstrate in Chapter 3 that they are mistaken. The *ubi jus* maxim is an expression of a substantive principle of law and political morality. We refer to this principle as *the principle of civil recourse*. According to it, a person who enjoys a certain kind of legal right, and whose right has been violated by another, is entitled to enlist the state's aid in enforcing that right, or to make demands in response to its violation, as against the person who has violated it.

The idea behind the principle of civil recourse is straightforward. Our legal system recognizes in various ways that each of us is entitled to be free of certain kinds of interferences (or to have certain things done for us). The more serious government is about enjoining these interferences, and the more serious each of us is about complying with the relevant norms of conduct, the more powerful is the argument that *rights* are at stake. When a right of this sort is violated, the victim should be able to demand certain things from the wrongdoer. Yet a demand of this kind would be hollow if the wrongdoer were simply free to ignore it. Thus, the state renders the victim's demand legally enforceable, so long as it is authenticated through the judicial process. In opening courthouse doors, government gives victims an avenue of *civil recourse*.

The adjective "civil" in the phrase "civil recourse" has several connotations that will be fleshed out in ensuing chapters. For now it will suffice to mention three. First, "civil" stands in opposition to "uncivil" or "barbaric." Recourse obtained under legal rules and through legal processes is a far cry from physical retaliation or enslavement, both of which, in other times and places, have been deemed acceptable forms of recourse. Second, and relatedly, in a system of civil recourse, a victim does not proceed directly against a wrongdoer. Instead she turns to the courts. Third, civil recourse stands in opposition to criminal punishment. Some rights-violators act in a manner that warrants state punishment. But not all. And even when actions warrant state punishment, they may also warrant a separate claim for victim recourse. Fortunately there are legal forms of accountability that

---

7. *Id.* at *115–16. Similar sentiments are expressed in the work of jurists and scholars ranging from Edward Coke and Matthew Hale to Thomas Hobbes and John Locke. *See* John C. P. Goldberg, *The Constitutional Status of Tort Law: Due Process and the Right to a Law for the Redress of Wrongs*, 115 YALE L.J. 524, 531–59 (2005).

do not amount to punishment. A system of civil recourse is one such alternative.

Armed with a preliminary sketch of the principle of civil recourse, let us return to the Founding era. Although the Founders rejected various aspects of Blackstone's thinking, they embraced his treatise as their guiding light on many questions of law and legal theory. Among these was his invocation of the rule that legal rights of a certain sort go hand in hand with legal remedies. Indeed, it turns out that Americans embraced *ubi jus* as a ground for being recognized as Americans. This we know from the Declaration of Independence. Our point is not that the Declaration should be a fixture in Torts classes or treatises. Instead it is that the form and content of this foundational document attest to the grip that the principle of civil recourse exercised on the thinking of the Framers, even when the topic at hand was momentous political events rather than personal injuries.[8]

To a greater extent than John Adams, James Madison, or other Founders, Thomas Jefferson was steeped in the law.[9] Under the tutelage of George Wyeth, and in his eight years of law practice, Jefferson not only studied the writings of Edward Coke and Blackstone, he prepared detailed reports of cases from the English courts. As a result, he was quite familiar with "tort" complaints—that is, actions alleging wrongful injury brought under the old English writ system.[10] Of the opinions that he studied and copied, Jefferson took special note of decisions issued by John Holt, Chief Justice of the King's Bench, that upheld claims by private citizens against government officials for injuries caused by breaches of their official responsibilities. In such cases, Jefferson wrote, "an action will lie against [the official] . . . qua tort-feasor."[11]

That Jefferson understood perfectly well what it means to be a "tort-feasor," and that government officials, like private citizens, could commit and be held accountable for torts, allows us to appreciate just how correct

8. Our depiction of the Declaration of Independence as an assertion of a legal right to redress is derived largely from John C.P. Goldberg, *Tort Law at the Founding*, 39 FLA. ST. L. REV. 85, 88–95 (2011).

9. Matthew Crow, *Thomas Jefferson and the Uses of Equity*, 33 LAW & HIST. REV. 151, 169 (2015).

10. David T. Konig, *Whig Lawyering in the Legal Education of Thomas Jefferson*, in THE LIBRARIES, LEADERSHIP, & LEGACY OF JOHN ADAMS AND THOMAS JEFFERSON 97, 104–06 (Robert C. Baron & Conrad Edick Wright eds., 2010). We have more to say about the relation of tort law to the trespass writs in Chapters 2 and 8.

11. *Id.* at 112 (quoting Jefferson's notes).

Garry Wills was to assert that Jefferson modeled the Declaration of Independence on a *complaint*—the legal document that a plaintiff files in court to commence a civil lawsuit such as a tort suit.[12] Again, the Declaration is no ordinary legal document.[13] A private citizen commences a tort suit by filing a complaint in court asserting that another person has physically attacked, defrauded, defamed, or otherwise wrongfully injured her. The Declaration was issued on behalf of an entire people, through which they announced the commencement of a revolution and sought to justify the creation of a new and democratic nation.[14] Yet the core of the document—its case for the legitimacy of the former colonists' forthcoming experiment in democratic self-rule—consists of a claim that the English king had committed the legal wrong of tyranny against them, for which wrong they were entitled to a special form of recourse.

There are crucial, salient differences between a personal wrong such as trespassing on another's land and the political wrong of tyranny. This is why one will not find "tyranny" listed in a law treatise as a legal wrong, or as providing its victims with what lawyers refer to as a cause of action cognizable in a court of law. And yet the Declaration is premised on the idea that they are not entirely different creatures.[15] Trespass and tyranny, Jefferson supposed, both involve the wrongful infliction of injury on their victims, and both generate in those victims a right of redress. A person who trespasses wrongfully interferes with another's possessory rights. In response, the victim is entitled to redress from the trespasser. Likewise, a monarch who systematically oppresses his own citizens interferes with their rights to life, liberty, and the pursuit of happiness. In response, such persons, under certain conditions, are entitled to formal recognition as the "people" of a new nation; one entitled to equal standing with other nations.[16]

---

12. GARRY WILLS, INVENTING AMERICA: JEFFERSON'S DECLARATION OF INDEPENDENCE 57–64, 334–36 (1978).

13. Nor was Jefferson its sole author, though he of course wrote the initial draft. On the democratic significance of the Declaration being the work of multiple contributors, see DANIELLE ALLEN, OUR DECLARATION: A READING OF THE DECLARATION OF INDEPENDENCE IN DEFENSE OF EQUALITY (2014).

14. ALLEN, *supra* note 13.

15. Jefferson's willingness to extend tort-like treatment to tyranny was part and parcel of his recognition that tort law, and law generally, is as much about empowerment and revision as it is about constraint and conservation. Crow, *supra* note 9, at 170–71.

16. ALLEN, *supra* note 13, at 121.

There is more to the comparison. Jefferson's characterization of tyranny as a wrong entitling its victims to redress was a sophisticated bit of political theory. But it was also a claim about the colonists' *legal* rights. England's courts had long ago declared that violations of an individual's property rights are impermissible—against the law. They had further empowered victims of such violations to obtain legal redress in the form of a compensatory payment from the wrongdoer. Likewise, claims the Declaration, the unwritten English constitution and the law of nations had long ago forbidden tyranny. It, too, is against the law. And to tyranny's victims the law provides redress in the form of recognition of their status as the people of a new and independent nation. On this point—the assertion of a *legal* right to independence—Jefferson and his fellow Founders broke decisively with English constitutionalists, including Blackstone, who had supposed that any such right could only be political, not legal.

Jefferson's tort analogy went one step further still. A tort victim's legal right to redress is contingent on the victim filing a complaint, proving her allegations in court, and obtaining a judgment ordering the defendant to pay damages or otherwise remedy the wrong. This notion of redress is, as we have noted, an expression of the principle of civil recourse. That principle in turn presupposes institutions, procedures, and rules—a civil justice system—through which redress can be pursued and obtained in a suitably rule-bound and regulated manner. Indeed, the principle embodies a political (and, in the United States, a constitutional) duty on the part of government to provide citizens with such institutions, procedures, and rules. Remarkably, the Declaration demonstrates an appreciation of this core feature of tort law, and offers an ingenious analogue appropriate to the distinctive legal wrong of tyranny.

In 1776 a claimed violation of the English constitution and the law of nations could not be adjudicated in a courtroom. But it did not follow, according to Jefferson, that there was no forum in which such a complaint could be adjudicated. English subjects claiming to have been tyrannized were instead required to assert their independence, to prove to the satisfaction of *other nations* that they were actual victims of tyranny rather than merely rebellious subjects, and to demonstrate their intention and ability to constitute themselves as a democratic nation.[17] Hence the Dec-

17. The Declaration dutifully observes that the former colonists had fulfilled a prior procedural step to legitimate revolution by petitioning the king for relief, which relief had not been (and showed no signs of being) granted.

laration's list of the "long train of abuses and usurpations" perpetrated against the colonists, and its "solemn" assertion of the colonists' commitment to organizing themselves as a people. As Wills observed, Jefferson would later describe the Declaration as "an *appeal* to the *tribunal* of the world," with the word "appeal" referring not merely to a remonstrance but to the initiation of a formal legal proceeding to be adjudicated by a "tribunal."[18] Nor was the notion of the "world" sitting as a tribunal fantastical. The Declaration was a complaint lodged with other nations (especially France, Holland, and Spain) in their capacity as stewards of the law of nations, and hence with jurisdiction to adjudicate whether the colonists' claim to being entitled to be recognized as a people was valid under applicable legal standards.[19] The eventual decision of these European powers to *recognize* the "United States of America" as an independent nation—and the concomitant obligation it placed on England to also recognize it—constituted the granting of recourse to the former colonists on their claim of having suffered the legal wrong of tyranny.[20]

The Declaration of Independence demonstrates that the principle of civil recourse is built into our national identity. As Danielle Allen puts it, the document stands for a liberal-democratic notion of equality "in which, when one person does injury to another, the other person can push back and achieve redress . . . ."[21] No less than the right to speak one's mind, the right to practice one's faith, or the right to be free of arbitrary arrest, the right to civil recourse is at the center of our legal and political traditions.

Consider now another well-known moment from the Founding era—one that finds Jefferson playing a very different role. By means of a "midnight" appointment from the outgoing Adams administration, William Marbury was named a federal justice of the peace. Although his commission had been executed, it was never delivered. Marbury brought suit in the United States Supreme Court seeking an order directing James Madison, Jefferson's secretary of state, to hand over the commission. Here again we are looking at a claim that clearly falls outside the domain of tort. Marbury

---

18. WILLS, *supra* note 12, at 335 (quoting Jefferson's papers) (italics added).

19. MIKULAS FABRY, RECOGNIZING STATES: INTERNATIONAL SOCIETY AND THE ESTABLISHMENT OF NEW STATES SINCE 1776, at 25–33 (2010); David Armitrage, *The Declaration of Independence and International Law*, 59 WM. & MARY Q. 39, 45 (2002).

20. This is not to deny, of course, that the Declaration was also a performative political document. ALLEN, *supra* note 13, at 265.

21. *Id.* at 254. Chapter 4 discusses this notion in more detail.

was seeking a "writ of mandamus," not redress for having been the victim of a tort.[22] Yet we are also again looking at a claim that gave rise to an important invocation of the principle of civil recourse.

Invoking Blackstone, Chief Justice Marshall's 1803 opinion for the Supreme Court in *Marbury v. Madison* proclaims that "the very essence of civil liberty . . . consists in the right of every individual to claim the protection of the laws, whenever he receives an injury," and that "[o]ne of the first duties of government is to afford that protection." It added: "[t]he government of the United States has been emphatically termed a government of laws, and not of men. It will certainly cease to deserve this high appellation, if the laws furnish no remedy for the violation of a vested legal right."[23] Marbury had a legal right to his commission. In accordance with *ubi jus*, he was entitled to a court-ordered remedy—in this case, the remedy would consist of an order directing that the commission be delivered.

As every law student knows, *Marbury* ends with a cruel twist for the complainant. Notwithstanding its endorsement of Marbury's entitlement to a remedy, Marshall's opinion proceeds to deny Marbury any relief. The problem, according to Marshall, was not substantive but jurisdictional: Article III of the Constitution allows the Supreme Court to hear only certain kinds of lawsuits, and Marbury's was not among them. Congress's attempt to give the Court the authority to provide Marbury with the redress to which he was entitled was unconstitutional.

Many understandably regard *Marbury*'s outcome as attesting to the impotence of the *ubi jus* principle. Yet what is remarkable about the decision is that Marshall used it as an occasion to take a swipe at Jefferson.[24] The

---

22. Roughly speaking, a suit for a writ of mandamus seeks a court order that commands a government official to perform some act the official is duty-bound to perform.

23. Marbury v. Madison, 5 U.S. (1 Cranch) 137, 163 (1803).

24. Even under the best of circumstances, the application of *ubi jus* to allegations of official wrongdoing is complicated. Richard H. Fallon Jr. & Daniel J. Meltzer, *New Law, Non-Retroactivity, and Constitutional Remedies*, 104 HARV. L. REV. 1731, 1781 (1991) (noting exceptions to the *ubi jus* maxim, especially with respect to suits alleging official wrongdoing). And *Marbury*, of course, was decided at a moment when the fledgling federal judiciary was vulnerable to being decimated by the anti-Federalists. *See, e.g.*, BRUCE ACKERMAN, THE FAILURE OF THE FOUNDING FATHERS: JEFFERSON, MARSHALL AND THE RISE OF PRESIDENTIAL DEMOCRACY 163–98 (2005); Richard H. Fallon Jr., Marbury *and the Constitutional Mind: A Bicentennial Essay on the Wages of Doctrinal Tension*, 91 CAL. L. REV. 1, 18 (2003); Jed Handelsman Shugerman, Marbury *and Judicial Deference: The Shadow of* Whittington v. Polk *and the*

easier and more straightforward course would have been for Marshall to rule on the jurisdictional issue first, thereby avoiding the need to discuss whether Marbury had a legal right, the violation of which would give rise to a claim for redress.[25] Instead, the Chief Justice wrote an opinion that called out the president of the United States for not delivering the commission, and for effectively rendering *ubi jus*—cast as a fundamental legal principle—nugatory in the case at hand. He did so knowing that this was a serious charge of wrongdoing that would and did rankle Jefferson.[26]

Civil Rights, Civil Wrongs, Civil Recourse

We began this chapter with a sketch of tort law. We then briefly described the principle of civil recourse that tort law embodies and suggested that this broad principle, which extends well beyond tort law, was regarded as a fundamental legal and political principle in the Founding era. We now bring the two topics together by considering prominent instances in which lawmakers, judges, and scholars have emphasized the importance to our legal system of both the *ubi jus* maxim and its particular instantiation in *tort law*. In our history, the phrase "civil rights" often has served as an expression of these commitments.[27]

We can start with the 1866 Civil Rights Act and the Fourteenth Amendment. Both were adopted in part to enable freed slaves to avail themselves of the common law of tort, contract, and property on the same terms as white citizens. The drafters of both believed that to confer the status of "citizen" on a person is, among other things, to afford persons legal rights

---

Maryland Judiciary Battle, 5 U. PA. J. CONST. L. 58 (2002); Michael J. Klarman, *How Great Were the "Great" Marshall Court Decisions?*, 87 Va. L. Rev. 1111, 1163–64 (2001).

25. As Jed Shugerman has demonstrated, when resolving a comparable issue just months prior to the Supreme Court's decision in *Marbury*, the judges of the Maryland General Court reached a similar result on less confrontational grounds. Shugerman, *supra* note 24, at 80–83.

26. Louise Weinberg, *Our Marbury*, 89 VA. L. REV. 1235, 1274–75 (2003). Marshall's manner of proceeding also left open the possibility, later realized, that a future Marbury might find relief in another court. Fallon & Meltzer, *supra* note 24, at 1782, n. 268.

27. Here and elsewhere, our historical analysis aims to be descriptive, not starry-eyed. For a people with our past, it is impossible to emphasize a principle's historical pedigree without observing that its realization has often been spotty, and has been shamefully distorted by prejudice. In this respect, the principle of civil recourse is no different from the principle of free speech or of equal citizenship. At the same time, one need not fall into cynicism. Our history is a dark tale, but it also at times attests to the progressive power of ideals.

against being mistreated in certain ways, and to enable them to respond to wrongs through legal process.[28]

To be sure, although it sought to guarantee all citizens access to tort law, the Fourteenth Amendment was not designed to constitutionalize (and thus federalize) tort law, or to require the states to adhere to particular tort doctrines or procedures. Rather, it aimed to guarantee equal access to laws that the states had long provided on a discriminatory basis, on the assumption that states would continue to provide such law more or less as they always had. This assumption was not merely predictive, but normative. Echoing Blackstone, the Supreme Court, in the course of a humdrum opinion, gave succinct expression to the relevant norm: "It is the duty of every State," the Court observed, "to provide, in the administration of justice, for the redress of private wrongs."[29] The Fourteenth Amendment requires states to perform this duty evenhandedly.

The postbellum Congress also took steps to provide freed slaves with the ability (in principle) to respond to a particular kind of mistreatment—namely, mistreatment at the hands of persons acting under color of law. Given *ubi jus*, the recognition in federal law of a right against such mistreatment went hand in glove with the recognition of a right to redress. Thus the first section of the Civil Rights Act of 1871—the provision that would give rise to what lawyers today call "1983 actions"—stated that:

> any person who, under color of any law, statute, ordinance, regulation, custom, or usage of any State, shall subject . . . any person within the jurisdiction of the United States to the deprivation of any rights, privileges, or immunities secured by the Constitution of the United States, shall . . . be liable to the party injured in any action at law, suit in equity, or other proper proceeding for redress . . . . [30]

---

28. George Rutherglen, Civil Rights in the Shadow of Slavery: The Constitution, Common Law, and the Civil Rights Act of 1866 40–57 (2013).

29. Mo. Pac. Ry. Co. v. Humes, 115 U.S. 512, 521 (1885). The prevailing view today among U.S. constitutional lawyers is that the Fourteenth Amendment's guarantees do not require states to adopt or enact particular laws, but instead require them to apply equally the laws that they choose to enact or adopt. This is a departure from mainstream mid-nineteenth-century views, which took the states to be under a political obligation, and perhaps even a legal obligation, to enact or adopt various laws, including law for the redress of wrongs. For an overview of the evolution of views on the constitutional status of tort law, see Goldberg, *supra* note 7.

30. 17 Stat. 13 (1871).

A century later, in the *Bivens* case, the Supreme Court was confronted with the question of whether the same link between wrongs and redress would hold when federal (rather than state) officials violate individual rights bestowed by the federal Constitution, even in the absence of a statute providing for redress. Invoking *ubi jus* and *Marbury's* assertion that "'[t]he very essence of civil liberty certainly consists in the right of every individual to claim the protection of the laws, whenever he receives an injury,'" the Court concluded that the Fourth Amendment right against unreasonable searches and seizures is properly interpreted to confer on individuals a right against mistreatment, and hence a legal power to respond through court action.[31]

Bivens's recognition of a right of action implicit in constitutional rights guarantees was foreshadowed by earlier decisions adopting a similar approach to the interpretation of federal statutes. When federal statutes specifying safety regulations first emerged at the turn of the twentieth century, the Supreme Court faced the question of whether violations that resulted in injury give rise to a claim for redress even in the absence of an explicit indication from Congress that it had intended for them to be actionable. The Justices concluded that if particular conduct-regulating statutory provisions were best read to define injury-inclusive, relational wrongs (i.e., statutory torts), then they should be construed to authorize a remedy. Thus, invoking *ubi jus*, a 1916 decision interpreted federal statutes requiring safety devices on railway cars to create a strict duty owed by railroads to their employees, the breach of which generated a right to redress for injured employees.[32] In the 1960s the Court likewise derived rights of action for victims of securities fraud from a statutory and regulatory scheme aimed at protecting investors' rights.[33] Indeed, the Court not only embraced this idea but later expanded it significantly, thereby setting the stage for the modern securities fraud class action.[34] Even the Roberts Court, which has been described as the most pro-business Court in our

31. Bivens v. Six Unknown Named Agents of Federal Bureau of Narcotics, 403 U.S. 388, 397 (1971). As we note below, since about 1980, the Court has reversed course and largely refuses to find implied rights of action in the federal Constitution and federal statutes unless required to by *stare decisis*.

32. Texas & P. Ry. Co. v. Rigsby, 241 U.S. 33, 39–40 (1916).

33. J. I. Case Co. v. Borak, 377 U.S. 426, 430–31 (1964).

34. Basic v. Levinson, 485 U.S. 224, 247 (1988) (recognizing the fraud on the market doctrine).

nation's history, has reaffirmed this particular and expansive application of the principle of civil recourse.[35]

Other federal civil rights laws also give expression to the *ubi jus* maxim by recognizing new tort claims. The modern law of workplace sexual harassment provides an illuminating example. Title VII of the 1964 Civil Rights Act states that it is unlawful for employers "to discriminate against any individual with respect to his compensation, terms, conditions, or privileges of employment, because of such individual's race, color, religion, sex, or national origin . . . ."[36] Fifteen years after the law's enactment, Catherine MacKinnon published a groundbreaking book on workplace sexual harassment, arguing that it is a form of gender discrimination.[37] Her work, along with that of other scholars and activists, had an enormous impact. In its 1986 *Vinson* decision, the Supreme Court permitted a woman who had been sexually harassed at work to hold her employer liable.[38] Later, in the 1991 Civil Rights Act, Congress modified the 1964 Act by authorizing victims of workplace discrimination to receive (subject to certain limits) compensatory damages for "pecuniary losses, emotional pain, suffering, inconvenience, mental anguish, loss of enjoyment of life."[39]

One might think that sexual harassment litigation is fundamentally "public" rather than "private" in at least two senses: (i) it is an effort to reshape society rather than to provide for the redress of personal wrongs; and (ii) it expresses a public-law principle of equal treatment or equal protection. Sexual harassment law certainly does have these dimensions. Indeed, they were central to MacKinnon's understanding of her project, which is why she argued *against* classifying workplace sexual harassment as a (mere) tort. In part she worried that, were harassment so characterized, courts would regard it as too novel to be recognized within a precedent-based system. More fundamentally, she believed that sexual harassment has to be seen as a systemic, structural problem that calls for a systemic, structural response. Tort law, on her view, could not play this role because, as a species of private law, it merely responds to isolated instances of misconduct by compensating victims on a one-off basis.[40]

---

35. Erica P. John Fund, Inc. v. Halliburton Co., 563 U.S. 804 (2011).

36. 42 U.S.C. §2000e-2(a)(1) (1964).

37. CATHARINE A. MACKINNON, SEXUAL HARASSMENT OF WORKING WOMEN (1979).

38. Meritor Savings Bank, FSB v. Vinson, 477 U.S. 57, 66 (1986).

39. 42 U.S.C. §1981a(b) (1991).

40. MACKINNON, *supra* note 37, at 172.

Thanks in part to MacKinnon's efforts, things have turned out differently than she predicted. Of course, the particular terms on which courts have come to define workplace sexual harassment can be criticized.[41] Nonetheless, workplace harassment today is a legally recognized, injury-inclusive, relational wrong for which victims are entitled to obtain redress through a court action—it is, in effect, a statutory tort. In recognizing this new tort, Congress and the courts have shown themselves willing to recognize additional categories of conduct as wrongful and additional kinds of setbacks as injuries. Indeed, the Supreme Court went out of its way in the *Harris* case to emphasize that the injury at the heart of a so-called hostile-work-environment claim is neither physical injury nor emotional trauma, but the fact of being burdened in one's workspace by the oppressions and distractions of ongoing, pervasive sexism.[42]

The scope of conduct that counts as harassment now extends well beyond the case of women being dominated by men within patriarchal structures. Men can prevail on harassment claims, and same-sex harassment is also actionable.[43] Title VII has not been expanded so far as to create a "general civility code."[44] But it does guarantee a broad right to be free of adverse and differential treatment on the basis of gender. An employee who is subjected to harassment of this sort suffers a legal-rights violation, and is entitled to sue to obtain redress. This sort of development is characteristic of tort law. The recognition of particular instances of mistreatment as tortious naturally invites claimants to make related claims, in turn inviting courts to draw general, principled descriptions of the wrongs in question, for which recourse will be made available.

In retrospect, MacKinnon was quite correct to observe that the treatment of harassment as a tort casts it as in some sense a private wrong—a mistreatment of one person by another. Yet she was too quick to dismiss the connection between judicial recognition of such wrongs and larger reform agendas. When courts allow a tort claim, they are not merely censoring a particular individual, nor merely seeing to it that compensation is

---

41. For example, some argue that courts have adopted an unduly narrow conception of the circumstances under which a firm can be held liable for creating a hostile work environment. *See, e.g.*, Sandra F. Sperino, *The Tort Label*, 66 FLA. L. REV. 1051 (2014).

42. Harris v. Forklift Systems, Inc., 510 U.S. 17, 22 (1993) (quoting *Vinson*, 477 U.S. at 66).

43. Oncale v. Sundowner Offshore Servs., Inc., 523 U.S. 75 (1998); Newport News Shipbuilding & Dry Dock Co. v. EEOC, 462 U.S. 669, 682 (1983).

44. *Oncale*, 523 U.S. at 81.

paid to a particular victim. They are also announcing or applying a norm of interpersonal interaction. These announcements and applications are articulations, in law, of social norms. The shaping of norms of acceptable and unacceptable private interaction has an obvious public dimension. To treat harassment as a tort is to set a generally applicable standard of conduct, the observation of which will effect—and in this case obviously has effected—systemic, structural change. It is to recognize a wrong.

Our whirlwind tour has to this point focused on *federal* civil rights laws. That focus is in a way misplaced. The states have always borne primary responsibility to provide tort law. This is in part what makes federal-law invocations of *ubi jus* particularly noteworthy. But this should not lead us to lose sight of the presence of the principle of civil recourse in state law. That presence is in a sense entirely transparent. The existence of a right to sue for having been wrongfully injured is the bread and butter of state common law. A consumer injured by a defective product, a patient rendered paraplegic by a poorly executed medical procedure, a person whose image is used commercially without her consent—all of these victims can invoke state tort law to seek redress for their injuries. In each state and the District of Columbia, the judiciary enjoys broad authority to recognize private rights of action to redress wrongs. That capacity lies at the core of the common law of torts. Federal courts are not today regarded as having comparable powers. When, starting around 1980, the Supreme Court took itself out of the business of finding implied private rights of action in federal statutes, it did so in part on the understanding that federal courts possess a much more limited authority to fashion common law.

Just as state courts are the primary forums for redressing injurious wrongs, they also remain the most important forums for defining the wrongs for which redress is available. *Bivens* violations, securities fraud, and sexual harassment are injury-inclusive, relational wrongs that have been identified by the Supreme Court through the interpretation of the Constitution and federal statutes. But there is a far broader range of wrongs that have been recognized in state tort law. It includes not only torts of ancient lineage, such as battery and trespass to land, but newer torts such as invasion of privacy and infliction of emotional distress (which emerged in the 1940s and 1950s), as well as strict products liability (which emerged in the 1960s and 1970s). Today the frontiers of state tort law involve suits for consumer fraud, medical monitoring, and internet harassment, among others.

The right to redress wrongs is not merely a basic feature of state common law. In almost every state, it is enshrined in constitutional law as well. Each state has a constitution, and overwhelmingly these documents—through right to remedy, open courts, due process, separation-of-powers, and jury trial provisions—recognize that individuals have a right of access to the courts to seek remedies for wrongs done to them. Many of these trace back to Sir Edward Coke's interpretation of chapter 29 of Magna Carta, with its familiar admonition that justice must not be delayed, denied, or sold. Here is Coke's rendition of that provision:

> [E]very Subject of this Realme, for injury done to him in *bonis, terris, vel persona* [goods, lands, or person], by any other Subject, be he Ecclesiasticall, or Temporall, Free, or Bond, Man, or Woman, Old, or Young, or be he outlawed, excommunicated, or any other without exception, may take his remedy by the course of the Law, and have justice, and right for the injury done him, freely without sale, fully without any deniall, and speedily without delay.[45]

State constitutional provisions of the sort just mentioned are not merely hortatory. With the emergence of the modern tort reform movement, courts have been asked to decide whether legislative curtailments of tort rights and remedies unduly burden rights to redress recognized in state constitutions. Unsurprisingly, they have reached varying conclusions depending on the reform and the constitutional provision in question. Overall, reforms have more frequently been upheld than struck down.[46] This pattern is in part a reflection of judgments about the aggressiveness with which courts should enforce different constitutional rights.[47] In some instances it has also been a reflection of the degree to which courts are increasingly losing sight of tort law's animating principle. It is on this topic that we will conclude this chapter.

---

45. Sir Edward Coke, The Second Part of the Institutes of the Laws of England: A Commentary upon Littleton 55–56 (1642).

46. Victor E. Schwartz & Leah Lorber, *Judicial Nullification of Civil Justice Reform Violates the Fundamental Federal Constitutional Principle of Separation of Powers: How to Restore the Right Balance*, 32 Rutgers L.J., 907, 939–51 (2001) (cataloguing court decisions).

47. Lawrence Gene Sager, *Fair Measure: The Legal Status of Underenforced Constitutional Norms*, 91 Harv. L. Rev. 1212 (1978).

Losing Our Way

A century ago—even fifty years ago—our claims about tort and its animating principle might have been considered humdrum. Times have changed. Today tort law is the target of political attack. Meanwhile, *ubi jus*, and the idea of torts being a law for the redress of wrongs, are dismissed as unhelpful or out of sync with modern conditions.

American law professors have long prided themselves on being "pragmatists." We are among those who do. Unfortunately, many are also attracted to the further thought that pragmatism goes hand in hand with a morally skeptical approach to law. As we noted in the Introduction, Oliver Wendell Holmes was a particularly powerful exponent of this view. Holmes honed his thinking primarily through an engagement with common law, and particularly the law of torts. While he acknowledged that the language of wrongs, redress, duties, and rights abounds in tort law, he dismissed it as window dressing. When courts order damages payments, he insisted, they are not enabling the victim of a wrong to obtain redress. They are instead presiding over a governmental system that allows certain persons who suffer losses to require others—namely, those who were in a position to avoid causing them but didn't—to pick up the tab. And the so-called duties of tort law, Holmes claimed, are really not duties at all. In practice, when a lawyer advises a client that the client has a legal duty to refrain from a particular action, she is likely to do so by explaining to the client that the failure to refrain could result in the adverse legal consequence of civil liability. When judges in tort cases specify "duties" to refrain from injuring others, they are doing the same thing.

Ironically—given his radically revisionary thoughts about tort law—Holmes has set the tone for torts scholarship in U.S. law schools.[48] Of course, there are many different takes on the subject. But two have been particularly important, and both are grounded in his particular version of pragmatism. The first—the law-and-economics school—has been particularly influential among academic elites. The second, which, for lack of a better label, we dub the "social welfare school," has been more broadly embraced, and figures prominently in some leading torts casebooks and treatises.

---

48. Thomas C. Grey, *Accidental Torts*, 54 VAND. L. REV. 1225 (2001).

The law-and-economics school, led by the likes of Guido Calabresi, Ronald Coase, Richard Posner, and Steven Shavell, treats Holmes's skeptical comments about legal duties as the foundation of a social-scientific approach to torts. In their view, tort law—or at least the parts of it that are today most visible, including negligence and products liability—does not actually set norms of conduct. Nor does it provide redress to victims. Instead it consists of liability rules that set prices on conduct. Tort law, on this rendering, does not tell us what we must and must not do, but instead informs us that if we engage in certain conduct that produces certain consequences, we may find ourselves having to pay for those consequences. In short, it is a government-created incentive scheme no different from a scheme that uses taxes or fees to incentivize behavior. The only difference is that the "tort tax" is paid to victims, thus allowing tort law to spread losses in addition to deterring them.

By harnessing the tools of microeconomics, members of the law-and-economics school purport to enable lawyers and jurists to reason more rigorously than is possible through the supposedly muddled language of the law. They also purport to explain tort law's value in terms of the social benefit it promises to deliver. If she has done her job well, a judge who deems a product manufacturer liable to a consumer injured by its product has concluded that this and other similarly situated manufacturers are well positioned to take precautions against future injuries of this sort, and to do so at a cost that is lower than the expected benefits (in terms of injury-related losses avoided) of the precaution.

The law-and-economics approach has been hugely influential, and its practitioners are sought out for appointments at prestigious law schools. Still, many academics—and judges and lawyers more so—have criticized it on the ground that it is artificially narrow. There is more to tort law, the critics rightly suppose, than figuring out how to minimize the cost of accidents. Courts care, and should care, about other things, including broader notions of social welfare, as well as fairness. For these and other reasons, members of the social welfare school differ from the economists by supposing that judicial decisions fashioning tort rules do turn, and should turn, on a range of considerations rather than the single consideration of efficiency, and hence must be balanced in a manner that calls as much for the application of common sense as for sophisticated microeconomic (or cognitive-psychological) analysis.

45

One way to get a feel for the substance—and the influence—of the social welfare approach, is to appreciate how Torts classes tend to be taught to first-year law students. More often than not, professors do not present the subject as a coherent field. Instead, students are taught that tort law is a grab bag of instances in which courts have been presented by litigants with the opportunity to address social problems such as medical errors, drunk driving, gun violence, workplace injuries, climate change, and so on. In turn, when courts, or at least high appellate courts, decide tort cases, they operate like mini-legislatures or agencies. For an appellate court to rule in a tort case is for it to make a broad policy decision—to consider the full array of social costs and benefits (including administrative costs associated with adjudicating future cases)—so as to determine whether, on balance, it will be better for society to allow or disallow liability in the case at hand and others like it. Torts courses are thus understood as occasions on which to introduce students to the promise and pitfalls of judicial regulation.

Whatever insights they may have generated, the economic school and social welfare school are both off-base. And they go astray for the same reason: namely, their Holmesian unwillingness to take the language of tort law at face value and to recognize the concepts of wrong, right, and duty within it.

For a judge to identify conduct as tortious is not for her to legislate on a question of social policy. It is instead for her to adjudicate whether the defendant's conduct amounts to a legally recognized wrong of the relevant sort. Our opponents will here accuse us of embracing a discredited formalist conception of adjudication, but the charge is baseless. We readily acknowledge that contestable judgments often must be made in determining whether a plaintiff has a valid tort claim. We further concede that in the course of clarifying and refining existing law, courts might sometimes legitimately consider the consequences of adopting different possible interpretations of that law. Neither of these concessions entails that judicial decisions in tort cases are legislative rather than adjudicative in nature. (More on this in Chapter 8.)

Likewise, the imposition of liability is not, at its core, a forward-looking decision about who should be incentivized to take precautions for the benefit of society. It is, in the first instance, a backward-looking judgment that the plaintiff is entitled to redress because the defendant wrongfully injured her—that is, failed to comply with a legal duty that required him to avoid injuring a person such as the plaintiff through conduct of a certain sort. A law-and-economics scholar will worry that our insistence that torts are wrongs, and that tort law specifies genuine duties, is a manifestation of a pernicious tendency among philosophically trained legal scholars to read their favored moral theories into legal doctrine. This envisioned charge is also false. We argue for taking tort law at face value as lawyers, and as adherents to a strand of pragmatism that calls for analysis that takes legal concepts seriously.

These brief and perhaps cryptic remarks cannot help but raise many questions. A number of them will be pursued in subsequent chapters. We will close this chapter by briefly entertaining and sketching answers to two. The first question is, Why has the skeptical, Holmesian brand of pragmatism been so influential? Our explanation is multifaceted. There is the towering figure of Holmes himself. There is the now-standard—though quite erroneous—narrative fashioned by American Legal Realists in the 1920s, 1930s, and 1940s, according to which moralism and conceptualism in legal thinking are ineluctably tied to "*Lochner*-ism" and the harsh laissez-faire politics of classical liberalism.[49] And there is the rise of the administrative state and modern civil rights law and, with it, a sense that the "really" important issues in law are matters of public rather than private law.

Other factors have been at work. For centuries, tort law primarily addressed and responded to instances of individuals mistreating other individuals. Today, by contrast, the defendant (and often the plaintiff) is likely to be an entity, such as a business corporation. And even when the defendant is an individual, her role in the litigation might well be minimal because she will rely on her liability insurance company to defend the case, and to pay whatever settlement is reached or damages are awarded.

Of course, the law has long treated entities as persons, at least in certain respects. And there is nothing weird about attributing actions and responsibilities to entities. While no doubt irritating to some, the statement "the New England Patriots have won six Super Bowls" is entirely cogent. (Its cogency is what gives it the capacity to irritate.) Still, the idea of law that enables victims of wrongs to hold to account those who have wronged them arguably applies effortlessly to individuals in a way that it does not to

---

49. For a debunking of this guilt-by-association argument, see John C. P. Goldberg & Benjamin C. Zipursky, *The Moral of* MacPherson, 146 U. PA. L. REV. 1733 (1998).

firms. While certainly recognizable as a kind of accountability, the imposition of liability on a corporation for wrongs committed through the agency of perhaps-departed managers and employees seems a step removed from accountability as between and among natural persons. This aspect of modern tort practice has invited some to jump to the conclusion that tort law is out of place in our mega-corporation, global-economy, big-data world.[50]

Perhaps as important as any of the foregoing explanations is the nature of tort law and common law more generally. The law of torts consists of an imperfect, socially constructed set of norms of personal interaction. Although we do not have a comprehensive shared morality in our society, nor a shared religion, we do have widely shared norms as to what constitutes mistreatment, as well as an institutional structure for enforcing them. Just because of the kind of law that it is, tort law is almost annoyingly conventional, middle-of-the-road, and unexotic. For the most part, it stands ready to hold us to familiar and widely acknowledged responsibilities. These features of tort law are among its strengths. Indeed, they have played an important part in enabling it to function as genuine law notwithstanding its lack of codification and its decentralized articulation and administration in courts around the country. Academics, however, often equate critical inquiry with the idea of getting beyond commonplaces. They tend to suppose that they have not really explained something until they have shown it to be quite different from what it appears to be. Such was certainly Holmes's mindset. Likewise, Holmes-inspired tort scholars seem to have prided themselves on their ability to explain how it is that, despite all appearances, tort law is not really a law of wrongs and redress.

Now to the second question: What, if anything, is at stake in getting tort law right? Interpretive accuracy is a good in itself. But it is also of practical importance. In particular, to characterize tort law as a scheme of efficient deterrence, and to characterize judicial applications of tort law as acts of legislation, is to render tort law vulnerable to criticisms to which it would not be vulnerable if it were seen for what it really is.

Nor is this vulnerability merely hypothetical. As we noted in the Introduction, for nearly forty years now tort law has been under sustained attack. Of course, Holmesian thinking long predates this attack. Tort reform, one might say, is the flowering of intellectual seeds planted long

---

50. We respond directly and indirectly to this line of thought in Chapters 9 and 10.

ago. All that was required was the arrival of conditions that enabled them to blossom.

In the mid-1970s, businesses, the medical profession, and their insurers began targeting tort law for aggressive criticism. By 1990, tort reform was adopted as a central plank of the Republican Party platform.[51] According to the reformers, tort liability—particularly liability for negligence and for defective products—has given rise to an onslaught of frivolous litigation, has come to threaten the viability of entire industries and professions, and has enabled plaintiffs' attorneys to "extort" settlements from deep-pocketed firms and insurers.

Reform at the federal and state levels has come in both obvious and subtle forms. Obvious measures include legislation and court decisions capping damages or foreclosing entire theories of liability. Subtler measures include the imposition of heightened procedural barriers or evidentiary burdens. The U.S. Supreme Court has been particularly—indeed, stunningly—active in this process. Although in 1938 the Court forswore the authority to craft substantive tort law, by the 1960s it was finding in the federal Constitution new substantive limits on liability for defamation.[52] Since the 1980s it has turned its attention to other aspects of tort law. For example, in applying the constitutional clause stating that federal law trumps conflicting state law (the "Supremacy Clause"), the Court—admittedly in an uneven fashion—has held that if products such as cars, drugs, and medical devices go through federal regulatory review for safety, their manufacturers cannot be subject to certain kinds of tort liability even if consumers are later injured as a result of defects in the products.[53] At the same time, the Justices have also recast the role of the federal courts as protectors of civil rights, largely abandoning their previous openness to the identification in federal laws of implied private rights of action.[54] They have also crafted new immunities that leave victims of official wrong-doing without remedies, and have set limits on the procedures through

51. Daryl J. Levinson & Benjamin I. Sachs, *Political Entrenchment and Public Law*, 125 YALE L.J. 400, 438–41 (2015) (discussing the Republican adoption of tort reform as a strategy to reduce the ability of trial lawyers to fund Democratic candidates).

52. New York Times Co. v. Sullivan, 376 U.S. 254 (1964).

53. *See, e.g.*, Pliva, Inc. v. Mensing, 564 U.S. 604 (2011) (generic drugs); Riegel v. Medtronic, 552 U.S. 312 (2008) (medical devices); Geier v. American Honda Motor Co., 529 U.S. 861 (2000) (automobiles).

54. *See, e.g.*, Bush v. Lucas, 462 U.S. 367 (1983); Touche Ross & Co. v. Redington, 442 U.S. 560 (1979).

which, and the amounts in which, state courts may award punitive damages in tort cases.[55]

There is no shortage of explanations for this pattern of decisions and arguments. Tort liability did expand in the late twentieth century, sometimes in ways that pushed the limits of plausible notions of responsibility for wrongdoing. Lawyers, particularly plaintiffs' lawyers, have never enjoyed a favored place in the popular imagination. Though largely unsupported by empirical studies, claims about the unsustainable burdens imposed by the tort system have struck a chord in an age of anxiety about America's continued status as a global economic power. Perhaps most importantly, tort reform proponents have pursued a well-financed, well-organized, and sustained public relations campaign to discredit the tort system, often relying on memorable but misdescribed anecdotes of abuse.

Another factor—and the one that hits closest to home for us—is the rise to dominance in the American legal academy of "demoralized" notions of tort law. We are not so delusional as to suggest that tort reformers have been moved to embrace reform by reading law journal articles. Rather, we mean to suggest that over time, as Holmesian ideas have taken root and have served as the basis for Torts classes, treatises, and casebooks, judges and lawyers have begun to lose their sense of the field. If one understands tort law as a law of wrongs and redress, one can understand why it belongs as a mainstay of legal education and our legal system. Conversely, when it is instead viewed as judicial policy-making, or a scheme to incentivize precaution-taking, it is difficult to see why it is fundamental. Indeed, once so understood it becomes particularly vulnerable to deregulatory impulses. After all, regulation by tort liability is imposed haphazardly by inexpert judges and juries in particular cases, and without the legitimacy that duly enacted legislation and even agency regulations tend to enjoy within our democratic system.

Tort law today has a target on its back in part because it has for decades been miscast by those who treat it as a form of regulatory law. The need for revision—even massive revision—is almost an inevitable consequence of this mischaracterization. Of course, even when tort law is properly characterized, criticism and revision might still be warranted. But the

---

55. On immunities, *see, e.g.,* Harlow v. Fitzgerald, 457 U.S. 800 (1982). On punitive damages, *see, e.g.,* Philip Morris USA v. Williams, 549 U.S. 346 (2007); State Farm Mut. Auto. Ins. Co. v. Campbell, 538 U.S. 408 (2003); BMW of N. Am., Inc. v. Gore, 517 U.S. 559 (1996).

spirit and the scope of modern tort reform bespeaks an entirely different and far more destructive inclination.

*　*　*

The chapters that follow are an extended effort to blend the obvious with the sophisticated, and to do so in a manner that illuminates one important legal domain, the law of torts. Our hope is to make this area of law clearer, in part so that it can be more sympathetically and accurately appraised. More broadly, we aim to establish that law is better understood when we take care to unpack rather than dismiss its constitutive elements, including concepts of wrongs, rights, duties, and redress.

2

Against the Grain

<hr>

WE MAINTAIN THAT tort law is law for the redress of wrongs, and that, as such, it embodies the principle of civil recourse, which runs deep in our law and our traditions. As we suggested at the end of Chapter 1, each of these claims goes against the grain of contemporary U.S. torts scholarship.

Because in this book we aim for a systematic statement of our views, and because we have elsewhere provided critiques of conventional academic wisdom, we will not dwell extensively on the work of others. However, it may be helpful to address initially certain broad objections that torts sophisticates are likely to have. With respect to some objections we offer a rebuttal. For others we outline ways in which subsequent chapters will address them. In providing these responses, we make a number of claims that help to explain where we are "coming from." Nonetheless, readers in a hurry to get to our more overtly affirmative arguments may wish to proceed to Chapter 3.

Trespass and Tort

We claim that tort law has deep roots in our legal history. Scholars with a historical bent may greet this claim with skepticism. The use of the word "torts" to refer to a field or department within our legal system is of relatively recent origin.[1] Indeed, the publication of the first treatises devoted

---

1. And yet Jefferson's awareness of the term "tort-feasor" (Chapter 1), Congress's conferral of jurisdiction on federal courts in the 1789 Judiciary Act to hear claims by aliens sounding in

by name to tort law coincided with the start of the Civil War,[2] and now-prevailing usage of the word "torts" solidified only toward the end of the nineteenth century.

Do these facts undermine the thought that tort law is a venerable institution? The simple answer is no. Tort law was not discovered or invented in 1860. What we today call "tort law" was for centuries part of a broader category known in medieval times as the law of "trespass" and in early modern times as the law of "civil wrongs" or "private wrongs."

Already by the mid-1300s, English royal courts had recognized two general pleading forms, or "writs," through which suits for wrongfully inflicted injuries would typically be brought—the writ of trespass *vi et armis* ("trespass") and the writ of trespass on the case ("case"). Issued by the Chancery at the request of a complainant, these writs ordered local officials to summon a defendant to court to answer the complainant's allegation of having been mistreated by the defendant.[3] When a suit commenced by the issuance of either kind of writ was successful, the defendant would be held liable to the complainant for damages.

By its terms, the trespass writ was limited to injuries caused by the use of force in violation of the king's peace. (Famously, however, this did not stop clever lawyers from pleading certain nonforcible wrongs, such as veterinary malpractice, as if they involved force.) It thus authorized suits for, among other things, physical beatings and detentions, removals of trees from a person's land, and certain accidents resulting in physical injury.

"tort," see John C.P. Goldberg, *Tort Law at the Founding*, 39 FLA. ST. L. REV. 85, 95–99 (2011), and William Blackstone's use of the word "torts" as a synonym for wrongs in his Commentaries suggest that lawyerly usage of the term "tort" in the late 1700s and early 1800s was hardly esoteric. *See* 3 WILLIAM BLACKSTONE, COMMENTARIES ON THE LAWS OF ENGLAND *117 (1765–69).

2. C. G. ADDISON, WRONGS AND THEIR REMEDIES, BEING A TREATISE ON THE LAW OF TORTS (1860); FRANCIS HILLIARD, THE LAW OF TORTS OR PRIVATE WRONGS (1859). Addison seems to have treated breaches of contract as a distinct kind of tort; hence he wrote of torts grounded in contracts. ADDISON, *supra*, at 5. Hilliard, by contrast, appears to have treated contract and tort as conceptually distinct categories, though he also emphasized points of overlap, particularly between contract and fraud. HILLIARD, *supra*, at 1–3.

3. Royal writs initially consisted of executive orders summarily resolving disputes (*praecipe* writs). From these gradually emerged a different kind of writ, exemplified by the writ of trespass *vi et armis*—namely, the *ostensurus quare* writ. The latter kind of writ was issued by the king at the behest of a complainant, and instead of peremptorily resolving a dispute, summoned an alleged wrongdoer to account for his treatment of the complainant—to appear before a judge and "show why" he should not be held to account. JOHN H. LANGBEIN, RENÉE LETTOW LERNER, & BRUCE P. SMITH, HISTORY OF THE COMMON LAW: THE DEVELOPMENT OF ANGLO-AMERICAN LEGAL INSTITUTIONS 88–91 (2009).

The "case" writ, meanwhile, allowed claims on a more fluid basis. Essentially, a complainant invoking this writ was required to show that she had been injured by conduct that, under the circumstances, was wrongful. Eventually plaintiffs were allowed to sue in case for fraud, malpractice, and nuisance, among others. It was also the mechanism through which litigants could pursue claims that today fall under the heading of breach of contract.

While today lawyers use the word "trespass" in a narrower sense to refer only to wrongful interferences with property rights, as it was used in medieval times the word meant something close to what we today mean by "tort"—a wrongfully inflicted injury giving rise to a claim by the victim against the wrongdoer. "Battery" and "false imprisonment" are today the names of torts. In medieval and early modern times they were the names of trespasses. A claimant who obtained a writ of trespass *quare clausum fregit* complained of the wrong that we today call trespass to land. A "case" action for *malapraxis* alleged that a professional had injured the plaintiff or his property through a failure to exercise the competence expected of members of the profession.

One need look no further than the Lord's Prayer to locate the substance of the old notion of trespass: to trespass was to transgress against another. Hence the need to seek forgiveness from God and victim. Through rulings in suits initiated via the two trespass writs, courts identified ways of interacting with others that were transgressive in the particular sense of wrongful and injurious. It is no surprise, then, that when the first analytic English law treatises were written in the 1600s and 1700s by the likes of Matthew Hale and William Blackstone, they collected the various forms of conduct the courts had recognized as actionable under the headings "civil wrongs" or "private wrongs." Judicial decisions holding a defendant liable in a trespass action for battery had recognized certain bodily contacts as legal wrongs committed by one person against another (hence "private"), and as giving to the victim a power to demand redress from the wrongdoer through an action at law (hence "civil"). Likewise when, around 1500, the common-law courts began to allow plaintiffs to proceed with "the action on the case for words," they were recognizing a new civil or private wrong—the wrong of publishing injurious, defamatory remarks about another—that we today know as the wrong of defamation (i.e., libel and slander).

The language of "private wrongs" was hardly esoteric. It not only provided the name for the third book of Blackstone's *Commentaries* (which, for Anglo-American lawyers, was a go-to legal treatise in the period from roughly 1775 to 1875), it also served as the subtitle of Hilliard's 1860 Torts treatise. Nonetheless, as the nineteenth century wore on, usage of both that phrase and "trespass" in its older sense gave way to modern usage of the term "tort." This change in terminology came about as jurists were increasingly inclined to split the category of private wrongs into subcategories. In particular, they came to distinguish wrongs involving breaches of agreed-upon legal obligations from those involving breaches of legal obligations not defined by agreement.[4] Agreement-generated obligations were treated under the new heading of *contract*. This in turn invited use of the word *tort* to refer to the remainder of the category of private wrongs. Thus emerged the standard modern definition of torts as private or civil wrongs other than breaches of contract.

So the modern category of tort is a subset of the older categories of trespass or private wrongs. But this hardly defeats the claim that torts are legally recognized wrongs for which victims are entitled to obtain redress from wrongdoers through the courts. Quite the opposite: to recognize that tort law was once housed within these categories is to recognize that torts are and, in our legal tradition, always have been, wrongs.

It should perhaps go without saying that political, social, economic, and intellectual conditions today bear little resemblance to those of England circa 1350. Likewise, the law of relational, injurious, legal wrongs has seen many changes in both substance and procedure. We neither deny nor downplay these obvious facts. Instead, we mean only to point out that, amid this record of transformative change, there are some significant continuities. Compare, for example, certain aspects of criminal and contract law. For centuries now, Anglo-American law has embraced the notion that a person accused of a crime is entitled to due process, and that certain kinds of agreements are enforceable through the courts. These very basic ideas have stuck with us even as the world has been made over, and even as they have been expressed in a variety of institutional arrangements and

---

4. The recognition of a distinction within civil wrongs between those that involve a breach of agreement and those that do not was, of course, hardly unprecedented. Ancient Roman Law had distinguished between wrongs *ex contractu* and wrongs *ex delicto*. Blackstone's Commentaries mentions a version of this distinction. *See* 3 BLACKSTONE, *supra* note 1, at *117 ("Personal actions are such whereby a man claims a debt, or personal duty, or damages in lieu thereof; and likewise whereby a man claims a satisfaction in damages for some injury done to his person or property. The former are said to be founded on contracts, the latter upon torts or wrongs . . .").

practices. The same is true of the notion that law ought to define relational, injurious wrongs and provide victims of those wrongs with the opportunity to obtain redress from those who have wrongfully injured them.

Torts and Contracts; Plaintiffs and Relators

One might complain that our attempt to find continuity over time and across different torts succeeds only at a superficial level. Our description of tort as a law of wrongs and redress, this argument suggests, is insufficiently robust to capture what tort law is and what it is *not*. Most notably, it fails to distinguish the law of torts from the law of contracts. It also fails to distinguish torts from what are sometimes called "equitable wrongs."[5]

If torts are legal wrongs for which the law provides redress, what are breaches of contract? Do they not fall within the same description? If so, have we failed to offer a theory sufficient to isolate what makes tort law a distinctive department of the law? To put the question even more sharply: Isn't the standard textbook definition of torts—civil wrongs, other than breaches of contract, for which the law provides redress—an admission that tort law lacks any unifying principle and is instead a grab bag of liabilities that have been fashioned by different judges for different purposes?[6]

Our response involves a set of modest concessions. First, as noted in Chapter 1, we do not claim, as some other theorists have, that there is a deep underlying *substantive* unity to tort law—that, despite their surface differences, all the torts recognized by the courts turn out to express the same principle, whether it be Calabresi's cheapest cost avoider principle or Kant's principle of equal freedom.[7] We think tort law hangs together, but not on this basis. What unites torts is that each is a legally recognized, relational, injurious wrong for which redress through the courts is available. This means in part—as we explain in Chapter 8—that torts always will involve conduct that interferes with aspects of individual well-being, such as bodily integrity, liberty of movement, reputation, and privacy.

Second, as we have already indicated, we grant that the principle of civil recourse is the animating principle (or an animating principle) of

5. John Gardner, *Torts and Other Wrongs*, 39 FLA. ST. L. REV. 43 (2011) (pressing a version of this objection).

6. Thomas C. Grey, *Accidental Torts*, 54 VAND. L. REV. 1225, 1240 (2001).

7. The latter is the claim of ALLAN BEEVER, A THEORY OF TORT LIABILITY (2016). Chapter 8 offers a nonreductive, positivistic, and pragmatist account of the substance of different torts.

areas of law other than tort law. Recall Chapter 1's discussion of *Marbury v. Madison*: Marbury sought an order that his commission be delivered via a writ of mandamus, not damages on a claim of trespass. Still, he was entitled, in principle, to recourse through the courts for the (nontortious) legal wrong done to him. Nothing in this concession, however, entails that our rendition of tort law as a law of wrongs and redress fails to distinguish it from other bodies of law that instantiate the principle of civil recourse, as brief consideration of the relationship of tort to contract will demonstrate.

Tort and contract stand in close relation to one another, and not simply because they are both required courses for first-year law students. To repeat a point made above, before about 1800 English and American lawyers tended to treat breach of contract on a par with batteries, libels, and trespasses to land—that is, as one legally recognized private wrong. This is hardly surprising. A contract breach is a relational legal wrong—that is, a failure to heed a legal obligation, owed to another, to conduct oneself in certain ways with regard to that other, which failure generates in the victim a right of action. Still, there are important differences that separate the two fields.

In the first instance, contract law is a set of rules that enables persons and firms to define for themselves the terms on which they will interact (insofar as their interactions fall within the scope of the agreement).[8] What is wrong, in this domain, is thus by and large determined by the agreement. Even when tort duties arise by virtue of a contractual agreement or by some other voluntary interaction between persons, the wrongs of tort—its conduct-guiding directives and violations thereof—are "in the law."[9] When a doctor treats a patient in exchange for compensation, there is a contractual relation between the two, but this does not leave them free to contract out of the tort-law requirement that the doctor refrain from injuring the patient though incompetent treatment.

Moreover, arguably the core breach-of-contract claim—in which one party sues another for nonperformance and seeks the benefit of the bargain—is not felicitously captured by the idea of a suit seeking *redress* for a

8. Contract law also sets modest constraints on the set of agreed-upon obligations that courts will enforce. A murder-for-hire agreement, for example, is unenforceable.

9. MacPherson v. Buick Motor Co., 111 N.E. 1050, 1051 (N.Y. 1916) (emphasizing that a manufacturer's duty not to injure consumers through the sale of a carelessly made product is not contractual but "has its source in the law").

wrong. Instead, such suits are efforts to enlist a court's assistance in seeing to it that the defendant perform the obligation(s) that she agreed to perform (or, if that is not feasible, to provide an equivalent to such performance). In other words, contract law often (and perhaps prototypically) empowers the plaintiff *to secure that which the contract entitles her to receive.* Tort law hardly ever empowers a plaintiff to secure performance of a duty of conduct that the defendant owed her, or a close substitute. By the time of tort litigation, it is usually too late for that. Instead, tort law enables plaintiffs to obtain *responsive* conduct that stands apart from the conduct that the defendant was obligated to avoid or undertake, and that is thus more cogently described as *redress* for the wrong done.[10]

Again, these differences do not entail that contract law *must* be seen as a department of private law distinct from tort. But they are more than sufficient to support the prevailing modern view that the two fields stand apart from one other. The ability of civil recourse theory simultaneously to explain how contract and tort bear a close connection yet can be pulled apart is, in our view, all to its credit.

Other legal actions depend upon neither breaches of contract nor torts. If your business partner, in the course of activities related to the partnership, takes for herself an economic opportunity that was rightly an opportunity for the partnership, you may be able to obtain a court order requiring her to share with you some of her profits. This is but one of many examples of cases in which individuals can use the civil litigation system to obtain relief from another, but that would not be classified by lawyers as "tort" (or "contract") cases. Yet they might seem to fit the abstract idea of law for the redress of wrongs. Does our account permit us to capture what separates tort law from the body or bodies of law comprised of cases such as these?

Our answer is again equivocal, and again we are inclined to think that its being so reflects well on our account. Many suits of the sort just described historically fell within the jurisdiction of "equity" rather than

---

10. Contract claimants sometimes seek and obtain other forms of recourse, such as "reliance" damages, which more closely resemble tort damages. For example, a claim by a couple whose wedding reception is ruined by their caterer's last-minute breach probably is not best understood as seeking performance or a substitute for performance. Instead, it seeks reliance damages as a form of redress. Notably, reliance damages are often described as a fallback, to be awarded only when expectation damages are inadequate or incalculable. And yet, as noted in the text, we are not particularly troubled by the thought that, in cases such as this one, there is an overlap between tort and contract.

"law." Actions that sound in equity are fundamentally different from tort actions, in two respects.[11] First, in a tort suit the plaintiff asserts an *entitlement* to relief based on proof that another has violated her legal right against mistreatment. A claim in equity is not grounded in such a right. Rather, it is more akin to a petition or request for assistance that a court has some discretion to accept or reject.

Second, and relatedly, as Henry Smith has most forcefully articulated, equitable relief is derivative of or parasitic on law, in that it is predicated on an injustice generated through the operation of law.[12] A complaint alleging an equitable wrong, in other words, is one alleging abuse of legal right, misuse of legal powers, or some other misfiring of law, for which the claimant seeks judicial intervention that may or may not be forthcoming depending on whether the court from which relief is sought concludes that the balance of the equities in the particular case is such that it ought to invoke its powers to rectify the injustice.

Third, even though in some respects equity reaches more narrowly than tort, in other respects it extends further. In particular, equity sometimes allows for the granting of relief to plaintiffs who have not suffered any setback or injury. For example, the beneficiary of a trust who discovers that the trustee has failed to exercise reasonable care in managing the trust's assets can seek equitable relief that might include an order that the trustee be removed even without any showing of loss or other injury. For all these reasons, "equitable wrongs," in their pure form, are distinct from torts.

Like tort and contract, tort and equity have historically interacted in complicated ways. Sometimes, for example, when equity courts have granted relief in certain recurring scenarios, law courts have responded by recognizing new torts—new legal rights and wrongs—covering these same scenarios. In such instances, discretionary, second-order equity is supplanted by the recognition of a new, first-order legal right against mistreatment.[13] To make things more complicated still, the courts' law and

---

11. John C. P. Goldberg & Benjamin C. Zipursky, *From Riggs v. Palmer to Shelley v. Kraemer: The Continuing Significance of the Law-Equity Distinction*, in PHILOSOPHICAL FOUNDATIONS OF THE LAW OF EQUITY (Dennis Klimchuk, Irit Samet, & Henry Smith eds., forthcoming).

12. Henry E. Smith, *Fusing the Equitable Function in Private Law*, in PRIVATE LAW IN THE 21ST CENTURY 173 (Kit Barker, Karen Fairweather, & Ross Grantham eds., 2017).

13. A famous instance of this phenomenon in U.S. law is the development in the early twentieth century of the tort of "misappropriation of likeness," based in part on equity courts having granted relief to petitioners complaining about unauthorized uses of their images.

equity jurisdictions were "fused" in the late nineteenth and early twen-tieth centuries. As a result, claims that once were heard in different courts under different procedural and remedial rules are now usually heard in the same courts under more or less the same rules. Thanks in large part to a combination of supplantation and fusion, the line between torts and equitable wrongs is blurry and shifting. But there is still a line. And thus it is still cogent and helpful to define tort law as a law of relational wrongs— violations of legal rights—that *entitle* victims, upon proof of the wrong, to the assistance of a court in obtaining certain kinds of responsive action from the wrongdoer.

A final variant on the type of criticism we are contemplating in this section—namely, that our account is too thin or capacious to capture the distinctiveness of tort law—points to laws that grant private rights of action to person who are *not* victims of wrongs. Consider the False Claims Act, a federal statute that authorizes private citizens to bring lawsuits against pri-vate actors that defraud the U.S. government (for example, by overcharging for goods provided to the military). These suits are sometimes referred to as "*qui tam*" actions, a name that refers to a Latin phrase that translates in part as "he who sues for the king as for himself." If a *qui tam* suit prevails and damages are awarded, the citizen who brings it is entitled to keep a percentage of the damages. Here we see an instance in which law confers a private right of action for a wrong, but there is no requirement of identity as between the person wronged and the person bringing suit. Private rights of action, it turns out, are not unique to tort, and do not always consist of a means by which victims of mistreatment can respond to those who have mistreated them.

This envisioned criticism is also wide of the mark. We have not set out to provide a theory of private rights of action, but instead a theory of torts in which rights of action figure prominently. We fully accept that legisla-tures (and perhaps courts) can confer on individuals the power to bring lawsuits and to recover damages for reasons other than fulfillment of the obligation to provide victims of legal wrongs with an avenue of civil re-course against wrongdoers. Our point is merely that *in tort law* private rights of action are a mechanism of redress, which is why they are con-ferred only on persons who have suffered legally recognized mistreat-ments. Other laws confer private rights of action for other reasons.

In the case of the False Claims Act, Congress sensibly concluded that the federal government could not effectively enforce anti-fraud rules by relying exclusively on officials to commence enforcement proceedings. Thus it "deputized" private citizens to sue civilly to vindicate the government's interests, and conferred on them a share of the damages owed to the government to incentivize them to bring suit. That private rights of action, in this context, are not about civil recourse is evidenced by the fact that claimants are styled "relators" rather than "plaintiffs." Relators are empowered to sue because they are in a position to relate—bring to a court's attention—facts relevant to *another's* legal claim. It is no accident that tort suits are brought by plaintiffs, not relators. In tort, private rights of action are conferred only on tort victims.[14]

Modernity and Morality

We place wrongdoing at the center of tort law. Here it would seem we are on solid ground. To repeat: the word "tort" means "wrong." Yet, since about 1880, when Holmes questioned the linkage of torts and wrongs, academics have been inclined to insist otherwise.

In the opening chapters of *The Common Law*, Holmes offered a striking narrative of the development of criminal and tort law.[15] In both fields, he noted, the rules applied by judges were thick with moral language. For example, courts had defined the crime of murder as a killing done out of "malice." Likewise, claims brought via the two trespass writs, and later for the tort of negligence, tended to involve allegations of "fault." Yet Holmes insisted that this language should not be taken at face value.

---

14. Where the victim is deceased or has no legal right to sue, the law authorizes others to assert the victim's rights on her behalf, as in the case of a survival action brought by the estate of a person tortiously killed, or in the case of a suit brought by the parents of a minor who is tortiously injured. Although the person suing is not the victim, the point of the proceeding is to vindicate the victim's rights.

As we discuss in Chapter 6, by statute, survivors of a family member who has been tortiously killed can bring claims against the tortfeasor seeking to vindicate certain of *their own interests*, including their expectation of continued economic support from the decedent. From the time they were first recognized, "wrongful death" claims of this sort, though obviously predicated on tortious wrongdoing, were recognized not to be tort suits, strictly speaking. Rather, they are "derivative" actions that allow persons who have not themselves been the victims of legally recognized mistreatment to obtain compensation for harms they have suffered as a result of the mistreatment of another. As is true with regard to *qui tam* actions, our theory in no way counsels against the recognition of wrongful death claims. Instead, it merely emphasizes—as was once widely understood—that such claims are not, strictly speaking, tort claims.

15. OLIVER W. HOLMES JR., THE COMMON LAW 2–5, 37–38, 51–57, 107–08 (1881).

At one time, he allowed, words like "malice," when used in law, meant what they seem to mean. But that was back in the days when criminal law was understood to serve the quasi-religious function of punishing evil or sinful people. Similarly, in medieval times the old trespass actions focused on "fault" because they were initially predicated on the "primitive" thought that law should empower victims of wrongs to wreak vengeance. Distrustful of moralism, and imbued with a secular and scientific spirit, Holmes maintained that there is no place in modern law for notions of evil or vengeance. Law for the modern world, he insisted, is a purely secular instrument of state control. Its function is to set the ground rules for the Social-Darwinian struggle, leaving individuals more or less free to pursue their own ends as best they can.

Quietly but inevitably, Holmes argued, Anglo-American law had come to reflect this shift from premodern to modern conceptions of law and governance. To be sure, when judges applied inherited doctrine, they continued to deploy the old terminology. But that was only because the common law's emphasis on precedential reasoning encouraged them to mask change within traditional concepts and categories. Thus, even though judicial opinions concerning the crime of murder continued to mention "malice," that concept, *as actually applied*, extended beyond instances in which a killing was done with ill will toward the victim. Indeed, as courts had come to define it, a death caused "maliciously" was merely a death that was *avoidable* and hence potentially deterrable—a death that a reasonable person in the position of the defendant would have foreseen causing, and could have avoided causing. The question of whether the killer had acted in a sinful, culpable, or blameworthy manner had quietly become irrelevant. And this was as it should be. Criminal law had left behind the task of punishing sinners for their sins and was instead in the business of discouraging individuals from unduly interfering with others' lives. Without changing its key terms, criminal law had morphed from a law of punishment into a law of deterrence, and as such had come to hinge the imposition of sanctions on the failure of the defendant to meet an objective standard of conduct set by the law.[16]

According to Holmes, a close study of judicial opinions applying tort law revealed a similar tectonic shift. Most notably, in applying the law of negligence, courts had settled on an "objective" notion of fault. Liability

16. *Id.* at 46.

for negligence would attach so long as the plaintiff's injury resulted from the defendant's failure to act with the care demanded by the law, regardless of whether the defendant was culpable for the failure. In tort no less than in crime, notions of blame and vengeance had become irrelevant. The focus instead was on the tangible fact of the victim's loss and the conditions under which that law should permit its transfer to another or others. In a Darwinian, every-man-for-himself polity, losses ordinarily ought to lie where they fall, but even a libertarian state allows losses to be shifted from victim to injurer when resulting from conduct by the injurer falling below the standard set by the state to protect the liberty of all. Without changing its key terms, tort law had morphed from a law of vengeance into a law of localized distributive justice.[17]

Holmes's narrative—including, crucially, his inference from the objectivity of negligence law's fault standard to the conclusion that tort law's moralistic terminology is mere veneer—is now a centerpiece of conventional academic wisdom. For present purposes it will suffice to note two challenges that it presents to a view such as ours. First, while historicism and Social Darwinism have gone the way of phlogiston theory, Holmes was on stronger ground in arguing that it is a mark of civilized societies that their laws suppress and supplant vengeance. That blood feuds and clan warfare are largely absent from our daily lives is a good thing. From this perspective, a wrongs-and-recourse approach to tort law might seem archaic and faintly barbaric. After all, we claim that tort law empowers victims to obtain redress from those who have wrongfully injured them. Redress through law is not vengeance, but there is enough of a resemblance to raise the question of whether we are committed to legitimating base impulses that society has done well to delegitimize and suppress.

Second, Holmes was also correct to observe that negligence and other torts set standards under which conduct can be deemed wrongful even though not culpable in a robust sense. Tortious conduct consists of the failure to act in conformity with certain rules or standards, many of which are quite unforgiving. As a result, considerations that would defeat or substantially mitigate blame or completely or partially excuse wrongdoing in other settings often do not suffice to defeat or even reduce liability for negligence and other torts.

17. *Id.* at 79.

To take a familiar example, imagine a homeowner who builds a fence, having every reason to believe that its location falls within the boundaries of his property. As it turns out, the public records on which the home-owner reasonably relied contain a mistake, and the fence actually sits on his neighbor's property. The homeowner has committed the tort of tres-pass to land. The fact that he acted reasonably—indeed, the fact that it was effectively impossible for him to avoid committing the trespass once he decided to build the fence—does not excuse his trespass. Given that the building of a fence under the foregoing conditions counts as wrongful, and that fault in negligence is defined objectively rather than subjectively, there is some reason to worry that contemporary tort law's moralistic lan-guage is window dressing. Is not a tort such as the envisioned trespass a "wrong" only in the nominal sense of identifying conduct to which lia-bility attaches?

Though superficially impressive, neither of these Holmes-inspired ob-jections holds water. To see why requires a more careful elaboration of what it means, in the tort context, to commit a wrong and to obtain re-dress. We will provide that elaboration in ensuing chapters. By way of preview, however, we offer a few observations.

Like Nietzsche and other intellectuals of his time, Holmes associated the coming of modernity with what Max Weber referred to as "disen-chantment." Traditional notions of wrongdoing, Holmes supposed, were bound up with prescientific, superstitious, or religious worldviews. Yet it is only within certain hyperstylized intellectual frameworks such as Holmes's that notions of wrongdoing appear primitive or puzzling. A parent who instructs his child that it is wrong for the child to hit her sibling, or that the child should be careful not to run into her sibling, is not doing or be-lieving anything mysterious. The same is true of a lawyer who advises a corporate client that it would be wrong to misrepresent the company's fi-nances to investors, or to discriminate against a job applicant on the basis of race or gender. And one need not believe that law's business is to ensure the salvation of citizens' souls to accept that law should (among other things) articulate and enforce certain standards of conduct. Tort law elab-orates, reinforces, and at times revises familiar obligations that we owe to one another—obligations, for example, to refrain from appropriating an-other's property, or to take care against injuring others. There is nothing about modernity that requires skepticism as to the intelligibility and pro-priety of this sort of enterprise.

At the same time, being serious about wrongs need not lead to the valorization of vengeance. Holmes supposed that objectively defined wrongs are not really wrongs—that notions of wrongdoing are necessarily bound up with robust notions of culpability or blame—and that redress must be a form of revenge. A central aspiration of this book is to demonstrate that the particular notion of wrongdoing at work in tort law is attractive in part because it is *not* tied to notions of retribution or vengeance. One can cogently describe conduct, including the "innocent" trespass described above, as "wrongful" even when the standard against which conduct is judged is objective, highly demanding, and insensitive to a range of justifications and excuses. This less red-blooded conception of wrongdoing-as-conduct-rule-violation permits the imposition of liability in a range of cases in which it would otherwise be inappropriate. But it also comes with a less freighted conception of accountability. Redress for wrongs such as these is *civil* recourse, not criminal punishment, much less the wreaking of vengeance. Or so we will argue.

Public and Private

We maintain that tort law, like contract and property law, is in crucial respects a species of private law. In particular, it specifies duties owed to individuals and firms (rather than duties owed to government) and it confers on beneficiaries of those duties a private power to respond to breaches.[18] A central theme of this book is the importance of recognizing and preserving these private dimensions of the law of torts.

Our emphasis on the private-law aspects of tort law flies in the face of a core tenet of progressive legal theory, at least among law professors in the United States. Perhaps the central plank in their platform is the rejection of the public–private distinction. To appreciate that "all law is public law"—the thought goes—is to take the first step toward legal wisdom. (Here again we see Holmes's influence. Law, he emphasized, is a creature of the state. How, then, can any law be private?) Relatedly, modern academics tend to suppose that notions of private law go hand in hand with a regressive commitment to the protection of a vast private sphere of interaction,

---

18. As we explain in Chapter 3, this is *not* to say that the state is somehow absent from private law. It is very much present, but present in a particular way. Also, government can sometimes occupy the role of a private actor—as, for example, in its capacity as the owner of property.

along with an unrealistic and equally regressive emphasis on the place of individual autonomy within interpersonal interactions.

Proof of the regressive valence of private-law conceptions of tort is said to reside in nineteenth-century tort law's sorry record for handling the surge in accidents that accompanied the rise of railroads and other mechanized industries. Relying on doctrines such as contributory negligence, assumption of risk, and the fellow servant rule—and with them a false picture of the degree to which individual workers should be deemed responsible for their own injuries—the courts of this time too often denied claims brought by injured laborers and their dependents against employers.[19] Through the adoption of the so-called privity rule, the same courts also limited the scope of manufacturers' liability for product-related injuries, leaving consumers only the false hope of protecting themselves through contract.[20] In sum, tort law in the period from roughly 1840 to 1900—a period in which most lawyers thought of tort law in old-fashioned (pre-Holmesian) terms as a species of private law—set insufficient constraints on action, even action that had disastrous social consequences. This constellation of historical facts purportedly tells us that any private-law conception of tort law is inherently linked to an every-man-for-himself version of classical liberalism.[21]

Progressives, of course, recognize that tort law did not stop developing in 1900. As they are fully aware, courts soon overturned or scaled back the aforementioned doctrines, thus permitting broader forms of liability. Nonetheless, in keeping with their insistence that anything like a private-law notion of torts is inherently regressive, they offer a particular narrative of these later developments. Unsurprisingly, it links the emergence of "better" tort law to a fundamental intellectual breakthrough: namely, the recognition, sometime around the turn of the twentieth century, that tort law, despite appearances, is really public law.[22]

The New York Court of Appeals' 1916 decision in *MacPherson v. Buick* is often held out as a landmark in the emergence of this new public-law and

---

19. JOHN FABIAN WITT, THE ACCIDENTAL REPUBLIC: CRIPPLED WORKINGMEN, DESTITUTE WIDOWS, AND THE REMAKING OF AMERICAN LAW 22–29, 51–70 (2004).

20. Winterbottom v. Wright, 152 Eng. Rep. 402 (Ex. 1842).

21. LAWRENCE M. FRIEDMAN, A HISTORY OF AMERICAN LAW 467–68 (2d ed. 1985) (arguing that tort law emerged as classical liberalism's pathetic response to the accident "epidemic" brought about by the Industrial Revolution (and that, happily, it died off with the emergence of more progressive forms of liberalism)).

22. Leon Green, *Tort Law Public Law in Disguise (I)*, 38 TEX. L. REV. 1 (1959).

progressive conception of tort.[23] In a justly celebrated opinion penned by Benjamin Cardozo, *MacPherson* eliminated the privity rule (mentioned above), thus recognizing a broad duty of care on manufacturers and clearing the way for consumers to bring negligence actions (and later, strict liability actions) for product-related injuries. Prominent scholars, including William Prosser and Leon Green (in the mid-twentieth century) and Robert Rabin and G. Edward White (later in the century), have held up *MacPherson* as illustrative of the potential for more progressive liability rules.[24] As noted, these efforts have gone hand in hand with a claim that tort law's progressive potential was unlocked only when insightful judges such as Cardozo came to recognize that tort law could operate as a form of public law.

True, a tort suit such as MacPherson's still took the *form* of a plaintiff leveling allegations of mistreatment against a defendant in a legal proceeding presided over by a judge. But Cardozo, it is said, perceived that the real value of tort suits resides in the fact that they give judges occasions to use tort damage awards to achieve certain public ends. In particular, by authorizing awards of damages, they can provide compensation to those in need of it while also discouraging the defendant and other similarly situated actors from engaging in the sort of injury-producing conduct in which the defendant engaged.[25] Understood as public law, tort law could function, progressively, as a mechanism of compensation and deterrence.

The recasting of tort law as public law, progressive scholars claim, is exactly what happened in *MacPherson*. When Cardozo dispensed with the old privity rule, he not only rejected a particular rule of negligence law, he entirely reconceptualized the tort of negligence and tort law more generally. On this reading, the import of *MacPherson* is not merely that it expanded the class of persons to whom product manufacturers owe a duty of care but also that it did so on the basis of a new understanding of that

---

23. 111 N.E. 1050 (N.Y. 1916).

24. WILLIAM L. PROSSER, HANDBOOK OF THE LAW OF TORTS § 83, at 677–78 (1941); G. EDWARD WHITE, TORT LAW IN AMERICA: AN INTELLECTUAL HISTORY 12–16, 125–26 (expanded ed. 2003); Green, *supra* note 22, at 9–10 (1959); Robert L. Rabin, *The Historical Development of the Fault Principle: A Reinterpretation*, 15 GA. L. REV. 925, 936–38 (1981).

25. Thus, in the opening pages of his 1941 treatise, William Prosser unabashedly asserts that tort law is a means of fairly allocating losses that inevitably attend a crowded, industrialized society, and in that sense is a judicial exercise in "social engineering." PROSSER, *supra* note 24, at 8, 15–18.

duty. What had previously been understood as a private-law duty running horizontally to other persons was transformed into a vertical public-law duty owed to no one in particular, or to government, or to the world. By this reframing, Cardozo took off the table a question with which courts had previously struggled when adjudicating negligence claims: the question of *to whom*, and *under what circumstances*, a duty of care was owed. After *MacPherson* (the argument goes), negligence law's duty of care is owed by all to all—there is no one to whom a negligence defendant can point and say: "I did not owe it to *her* to be careful."[26] In sum, according to the dominant progressive narrative, Cardozo's *MacPherson* opinion revealed tort law's untapped potential only because it was penned by a visionary judge who—without letting on what he was doing—embraced an entirely new vision of the particular tort at issue in the case before him and of tort law more generally.

In explaining why an approach such as ours runs against the grain, we have been observing that political progressives have tended to suppose that tort law can be a force for good *only if* recast as a species of public law. *Whether* it can actually be so recast is a question that has in fact divided progressives. We noted in Chapter 1 that in her early writings on workplace discrimination, Catherine MacKinnon was anxious that harassment *not* be cast as a (mere) tort. This anxiety, we can now see, reflected her doubts about the extent to which tort law really can operate as public law. Even though she was writing sixty years after *MacPherson*—a period that saw the emergence of various liability-expanding doctrines—MacKinnon was still not confident that judges applying common-law tort principles could free themselves from what she took to be its traditional focus on a highly circumscribed (and gender-biased) list of wrongful injuries. More fundamentally, she worried that the sustained mid-twentieth-century scholarly effort to recast tort law as public law had not fully liberated tort law from its private-law roots, and hence the treatment of harassment as a

---

26. As it turns out, courts did not cease issuing "no duty" decisions in 1916 or thereabouts—a highly inconvenient fact for those who read *MacPherson* as recognizing a duty of care that, by definition, is always present and hence can never not be owed. The standard progressive reading of *MacPherson* thus must be embellished, typically by means of a claim that "no duty" decisions are not what they appear to be, but instead rest on other, unstated grounds, such as an implicit policy judgment by the courts that there will be "too much" liability in the relevant class of cases.

tort would inevitably suggest that harassment was but a private wrong to be addressed on a one-off basis through individual lawsuits. Even when progressive judges apply tort law, she supposed, they cannot help but think in terms of individual responsibility. Soon enough, they will find themselves making fine-grained determinations as to whether a given individual (or entity) in a given circumstance can be held answerable to another for having wronged her (or it). Hardwired into this focus is the acceptance of an implicit limitation on state action: that the state may legitimately respond to social problems only by attending to individual misconduct. Thus, whereas optimistic progressives such as Green and Prosser believed that judges could and would come to embrace fully the idea of tort law as a public-law, regulatory regime, MacKinnon in her early writings on gender discrimination was more pessimistic.[27]

Our position stands in opposition to both the optimistic and the pessimistic strands of progressive conventional wisdom. Yet it does not stand in opposition to progressivism. We hold no candle for classical liberalism. Rather, we reject the assumption that a wrongs-and-redress conception of tort goes hand in glove with laissez-faire, and that progressivism in tort law requires (or even stands to benefit from) the embrace of a purely public-law conception of the field.

Tort law is indeed individualistic.[28] But it hardly follows that, on this understanding, it is destined to be regressive, or that tort liability must be narrowly cabined. On our account, a tort is always a "doing unto" another (or a failure to "do for" another), and a tort suit is always an effort by the person unto whom injury has been done to hold a wrongdoer answerable to her. Government, we argue, provides tort law in fulfillment of a duty it

27. MacKinnon arguably modified her views as to the potential value of tort law as a tool of progressive public policy. In the early 1980s, she and Andrea Dworkin famously developed and advocated for the adoption of anti-pornography laws. These laws included provisions that would have deemed tortious certain pornography-induced physical harms. Specifically, they would have enabled a victim who suffers physical injury at the hands of another person as a "direct" result of that other person's exposure to pornography to hold liable the author(s) and distributor(s) of the relevant pornography. *See* American Booksellers Ass'n v. Hudnut, 771 F.2d 323 (7th Cir. 1985) (striking down on First Amendment grounds an Indianapolis ordinance adopting these provisions), *aff'd*, 475 U.S. 1001 (1986) (mem. op.).

28. Just to be clear, when we speak of tort law as "individualistic," we do so on the conventional understanding that business firms and other entities can count as persons in the eyes of the law, and that multiple persons, whether acting in concert or independently of one another, can sometimes be held responsible for the wrongful infliction of a single injury.

owes to individuals to provide a law of wrongs and redress. It fulfills that duty by empowering them to hale alleged wrongful injurers into court for a certain kind of proceeding—one that aims in the first instance to vindicate certain of the putative victim's interests, rather than those of the state or the public.

Other aspects of modern government and law appropriately embody different principles. For example, programs that aim to provide a social safety net are animated in part by the idea that members of an affluent polity *collectively* are responsible for ensuring that other members have access at least to necessities. The operative idea here has less to do with how one is obligated to conduct oneself toward others, which is why individual duties associated with this kind of responsibility can be discharged through participation in a governmental tax-and-transfer system. And this kind of responsibility obviously calls for a different sort of state apparatus than the provision of courts as dispute resolvers and law articulators.

The foregoing contrast notwithstanding, it is wrong to associate tort law's individualism with atomism or libertarianism. Atomistic conceptions of society envision a social world made up of citizens who share little beyond a physical space, and who occasionally interact, for better or for worse, as they pursue individual projects. The law of tort, by contrast, presupposes and reinforces *recognizable* (broadly shared) norms as to what counts as the mistreatment of one person by another. Tort is all about the ways in which one must adjust one's own conduct in light of the interests of others—adjustments that often include not merely refraining from undertaking certain actions but also taking affirmative measures to avoid injuring (and even to assist or protect) others. This is one reason professionals, business owners, and others complain about tort law's burdensomeness.

Libertarian political theory supposes that the government acts legitimately only insofar as it protects certain basic individual rights, such as the right to security of person and property from invasion by others. The state's job, on this view, is to create a safe space for competent adults to make the arrangements they wish to make. Tort, by contrast, imposes obligations as a matter of law, around which individuals usually are not permitted to contract. And even though the modern welfare state might in some instances supplant or render superfluous certain applications of tort law, there is nothing about tort law that suggests it is incompatible with modern, egalitarian liberalism. To assert the obvious, the common law of tort has for decades operated as a well-integrated part of the modern welfare states of Britain, Canada, and the United States. To repeat: tort notions of responsibility are individualistic, not libertarian.

Returning to *MacPherson*, we heartily agree that it is a landmark in American law. However, we reject the contention of Prosser and others that its significance resides in its repudiation of a wrongs-and-redress conception of tort. Indeed, as we demonstrated in our first co-authored article, the standard account is deeply flawed. It completely fails to engage what Cardozo's *MacPherson* opinion actually says.[29] And the claim that, after *MacPherson*, negligence law's duty of care should be understood as a public-law duty owed to the world runs into an insurmountable problem. In New York and elsewhere it remains standard for courts to reject negligence claims on the ground that the defendant owed no duty to the plaintiff. And, contrary to the claims of Prosserians, these decisions really are decisions about duties, not policy-driven decisions about proper levels of aggregate liability.

Most fundamentally, the standard progressive reading fails to capture what it is about *MacPherson* that was progressive. Cardozo concluded, of course, that the duty to exercise care to avoid injuring life and limb is not merely a creature of contract. But he still regarded this duty as running from one person (or firm) to another. Roughly speaking, Buick owed a duty to take care not to injure MacPherson because MacPherson was among those whom a manufacturer in Buick's position should anticipate physically endangering were it to go about its business carelessly. MacPherson's status as a person whose life and limb were foreseeably endangered is what entitled him to the exercise of care by Buick, and what rendered him a proper plaintiff to sue Buick. The key breakthrough in *MacPherson*—foreshadowed by earlier English and American decisions—is the recognition that, while duties in the law of torts are relational in their analytic structure, relationality in the requisite sense is present as between an actor and a potential victim when physical injury to the victim is a sufficiently foreseeable consequence of an actor's careless actions. This is the moral of *MacPherson*. And this is why, *MacPherson* notwithstanding, courts continue to issue cogent no-duty rulings in negligence cases. Both can be made sense of only when negligence law and tort law more generally are understood as, in important respects, private law.

29. John C. P. Goldberg & Benjamin C. Zipursky, *The Moral of* MacPherson, 146 U. PA. L. REV. 1733 (1998); *see also* ANDREW L. KAUFMAN, CARDOZO 272–73 (1998).

To insist, as we do, that tort law is private law is not to deny that tort law's operation has public dimensions or that its operation has implications for public policy. As we have already noted, one component of tort law consists of a rule of law and positive political morality that imposes on government an obligation to provide institutions that permit the realization, in practice, of the principle of civil recourse. Moreover, tort suits are in many instances a way for accident victims to get needed monetary assistance, and the threat of tort liability at times deters unsafe conduct. These are not unimportant facts, nor ones to which courts should blind themselves. The progressive critic goes several steps further, however, asserting that if tort law is to be progressive, judges dealing with tort claims must understand themselves to be operating a program for compensating injury victims and/or deterring antisocial conduct and therefore ought to craft doctrine so as to make tort law the best compensation and deterrence system it can be, given practical constraints.

Courts are sometimes in the situation of needing to craft tort law with an eye on the aggregate consequences of its operation. Still, we see no reason to suppose that an inquiry into such consequences is central to the adjudication of tort cases, much less exhaustive of it. We would also suggest that progressive critics who insist on a public-law conception of tort adjudication are themselves relying on an outdated understanding of tort law's place in our legal and political system. At the turn of the twentieth century, the administrative state barely existed, health insurance was spotty at best, and notions of rights to workplace safety and consumer protection were in their infancy. In these circumstances, a progressive judge who thought the state should be doing more to assist accident victims might have reasonably concluded that liability-expanding decisions in certain tort cases provided a rational and legitimate path toward that end. Even at midcentury, a judge who saw a need for greater regulation to improve product safety might have been warranted in applying stricter standards and permitting higher damages in suits brought for such injuries.

Today, however, it is unlikely that these are the most effective routes to expand compensation for accidents or to incentivize safe practices. We now have in place elaborate regulatory, market-based, and blended mechanisms for insurance and regulation. While each has its share of problems, it is widely agreed that tort law tends to be a particularly inefficient and haphazard device for achieving these goals by itself, though in operation it may sometimes complement (and may at other times impede) these other mechanisms. In sum, preoccupation with tort law's potential to perform public-law functions is today not so much a sign of progressivism as a symptom of nostalgia for a moment when courts might operate at the leading edge of the regulatory state.

Finally, modern progressive critics have, in our judgment, made a serious miscalculation by insisting on a public-law conception of tort law. As we emphasized at the end of Chapter 1, a private-law, wrongs-and-redress conception reflects basic commitments to equality and liberty. The *ubi jus* maxim at the core of tort law has long been an anchor for claims of individuals to enjoy a certain political and legal status, and a concomitant power to hold others accountable to them. We see this today not only in constitutional tort litigation and gender discrimination cases. The idea of a right to redress wrongs is arguably at or near the core of the modern international human rights movement. The notion that courts stand ready to provide remedies to the victim of wrongs is an idea of equal rights. This is why access to courts has long figured centrally in notions of the rule of law. In tort law, actors, even powerful private and state actors, must in principle confront the prospect that they will be held accountable for their mistreatment of others. Wrongs and redress, institutionalized through courts by means of a legal process initiated and substantially controlled by complainants— these are not inimical but central to a progressive vision of law.

Realism and Pragmatism

We have considered some historical and political objections to our project. Other objections are philosophical in nature. As noted in Chapter 1, these primarily come out of the American Legal Realist tradition. Our insistence that tort law is built upon concepts of wrongs and redress runs counter to the anti-conceptualist spirit of Realism and, more generally, to the instrumentalism of the version of pragmatism that Holmes brought to law. This is not the place to mount a full-fledged critique of either Realism or instrumentalism, but it will be useful to discuss certain jurisprudential pieties against which we seem to be pressing, to explain the extent to which we are doing so, and to defend our approach.

As a particular instantiation of pragmatism in law, Legal Realism is anti-formalistic in at least two ways. It is skeptical of the value of conceptual analysis and thus advocates instead an instrumentalist approach. Relatedly, it insists that legal scholarship must shift its attention from law-in-the-books (statutory texts, judicial opinions, treatises) to law-in-action. If a student or scholar wants to know something about tort law, she should not waste her time figuring out the meaning of concepts such as "duty," "right," "injury," "ordinary prudence," "malice," "scienter," "necessity," "proximate cause," and the like. She really only needs to understand that these concepts are unhelpfully indeterminate. Instead she should record, or learn from those who record, the outcomes of tort cases: when money changes hands and in what amounts. If all goes well, social-scientific scrutiny of the data will reveal patterns that can serve as the basis for predicting future outcomes and for rational law reform. Or she should think about how rationally self-interested actors (or real human beings) are likely to respond to different patterns of sanction. For their part, judges should acknowledge that their decisions in all but the most straightforward cases do not rely on "legal reasoning" but instead involve instrumental (means–ends) judgments as to which outcomes in which cases will promote deterrence, compensation, or some other goal without generating too many undesirable side effects.

We reject these facets of Realism and instrumentalism. We do so, however, on the basis of a shared commitment to pragmatism. In short, we reject as unduly narrow their understanding of what is entailed in being a pragmatist about law. Pragmatists believe that language and concepts have the content they do by virtue of their connection with human practices in which they are used. This core insight lies behind the Realist rejection of both Langdellian formalism and of a strict, source-bound conception of what counts as law. In these respects we are at one with Realists. Realists, however, tend not to take the lessons of pragmatism fully to heart. Their justified anti-formalism typically generates an unjustified acceptance of reductive instrumentalism. Similarly, their laudable insistence that we understand law as it operates in practice often leads to a dogmatic embrace of an external, social-scientific approach to understanding law. Properly understood, pragmatism in law points in very different directions.

On our view, the possibility of legal knowledge and legal truth is best understood through the lens of the brand of philosophical pragmatism developed by twentieth-century scholars including Wilfrid Sellars, W. V. O. Quine, Hilary Putnam, Richard Rorty, and Robert Brandom. Theirs is, of course, a family of overlapping positions within philosophy. Yet, as a close cousin of the later work of Ludwig Wittgenstein and the contemporary work of Jürgen Habermas, the general approach that they developed was hardly idiosyncratic. Moreover, the philosophical pragmatism we are countenancing is not a mere bait-and-switch on the term "pragmatism." It traces back to the work of Holmes's colleague and fellow Metaphysical Club member, Charles Sanders Peirce.[30] Finally, given Quine's stature as perhaps the most illustrious American logician and philosopher of language of the twentieth century, this brand of pragmatism surely cannot be accused of being soft-headed.

Quine famously took a key insight of turn-of-the-century philosophy of language and extended it to a more ambitious conclusion. According to it, language connects with the world not sentence by sentence, but language by language, or whole theory by whole theory. This sort of holistic view carried forward ideas originally offered by Peirce. When fleshed out in greater detail, pragmatism of this sort maintains as one of its central tenets that the meaning of propositions cannot be separated from the role they play in drawing practical and speculative conclusions from various inputs. In terms that can be associated equally with the progenitors of artificial intelligence and high-end software, on the one hand, or twentieth-century semantic theorists on the other, the content of any given proposition cannot be adequately identified or explained atomistically.

Quine's self-consciously dry and neatly presented pragmatism provided a more linear presentation of ideas also developed by Wittgenstein. The content (or meaning) of an assertion, they both believed, derives simultaneously from how that assertion is used, practically, in the world and how its acceptance meshes with the web of belief of those who say or hear it. The catchphrase "meaning is use," notwithstanding its banality, emphasizes that this view really does deserve to count as a form of pragmatism. For these thinkers—as for the founding American pragmatists—usage, social practice, and human activity are far more basic to understanding difficult philosophical problems than are grand abstractions.

Holmes recognized in the burgeoning pragmatist movement of which he was a founding member the possibility of solving some of the jurisprudential problems facing command theorists such as John Austin when

---

30. On the relation between Peirce and later pragmatists, as well as the relation between the work of these thinkers and the form of legal pragmatism offered here, see Benjamin C. Zipursky, *Legal Pragmatism and Legal Pragmaticism*, in PRAGMATISM, LAW AND LANGUAGE 237 (G. Hubbs & D. Lind eds., 2013).

trying to make sense of the very un-command-like body of law known as the common law. But the past century has generated new ways of thinking about where pragmatist insights can and should lead. What we are suggesting is that there is another way of thinking about pragmatism and the common law. We have labeled this view "pragmatic conceptualism."[31]

The "conceptualism" part of the phrase "pragmatic conceptualism" is deliberately provocative, for Holmesian pragmatism is expressly committed to a reductive as opposed to a conceptualistic approach to understanding legal vocabulary. The Holmesian rejection of conceptualism typically stems from an outdated and insufficiently pragmatic view of what is involved in explaining concepts. If one thinks of conceptual analysis as a detached examination of abstract entities or meanings that happen to appear in law, then it does seem arid and unpromising. But once one recognizes that concepts exist only within structured social practices that involve using language—doing things with it—the elucidation of concepts can be understood as a genuinely pragmatic undertaking. For lack of a better term, it involves a "second-order" practice of trying to observe, grasp, teach, revise, adjust, and order aspects of the underlying social practices. Even though the concepts, ideas, and principles cannot be fully detached from the practices in which they are embedded, it is entirely possible to reflect upon, refine, and critique them.

Ironically, it is perhaps easiest to grasp the tenets of pragmatic conceptualism by considering how the common law actually operates. Common law is quite plainly an integrated, rule-and-principle-driven system of doing and saying. For example, legal usage contains concepts that describe what a plaintiff's lawyer must do to commence a case, to establish that a contract has been formed, or to prove the elements of a tort. Lawyers also know what questions judges are likely to ask about the cases before them, and how judges will process answers to those questions. They understand the various linkages within the system between inputs (pleadings, evidence, and such) and outputs (dismissals, denials, trial, verdict, and such). Unlike the motion of an automobile, law's outputs are not the result of mechanistic processes. In law, inputs lead to outputs only through the use of language, concepts, and rules. The same holds true for legal acts and events that occur outside the courts. For pragmatic conceptual-

---

31. Benjamin C. Zipursky, *Pragmatic Conceptualism*, 6 LEGAL THEORY 457 (2000).

ists, the goal is to illuminate these patterns of human activity by gaining a clear understanding of the usages that drive these practices.

Anti-conceptual, instrumental versions of pragmatist legal analysis are guided by a particular conception of what makes an explanation valuable. They aim to explain which goals are being served when a set of norms and their associated concepts are being engaged. Reductive instrumentalism not only tries to depict the significance of what results from the operation of this system in these goal-serving ways; it also tries to explain how the rules and concepts within them fit together by depicting the various parts in terms of their ultimate contributions to the achievement of these goals. This is an appealing approach to law for numerous reasons. To public officials charged with applying the law, it seems to offer criteria by which to guide their decisions. And to the public it seems to offer criteria for deciding whether the system is worth having. Finally, it seems to give a practical handle on the various bits and pieces of doctrine that float around while also inviting the use of empirical methodologies to assess the efficacy of the system.

Two sorts of reasons ultimately ground our rejection of a reductive instrumentalist explanation of the inferential norms of the common law of torts. One has to do with the value of *authenticity*. The other has to do with the value of *respecting institutional roles*. With regard to authenticity, we believe that it ignores the reality of tort law's inferential norms to treat them, separately and collectively, as thoroughly consequentialist. Some legal concepts—such as the antitrust concept of an unreasonable restraint on trade as developed by the U.S. Supreme Court—plausibly do reduce to a consequentialist inquiry (in this case, about competitiveness). Others—such as the concepts of intent in battery, or actual causation in negligence law—quite plainly do not. A lawyer, judge, or student who is thinking, inferring, and reasoning like a lawyer and who knows antitrust law might find a largely instrumentalist analysis of "unreasonable restraint" to be a reliable and illuminating guide to that concept that aids her efforts to apply that body of law. By contrast, the actual causation concept—given how it is used and the role that it plays in the analysis of negligence cases—must be understood to include a backward-looking inquiry into necessary conditions, sufficient conditions, and the like. Many contemporary tort scholars have been keen to argue that all, or almost all, of tort law's key concepts— duty, reasonable care, product defect, proximate cause, and so on—are best understood as inviting consequentialist inquiries akin to the antitrust inquiry envisioned above. For reasons presented at length in the coming chapters, these instrumentalist reconstructions simply fail to grasp these concepts accurately.

Our other reason for rejecting instrumentalist reconstructions of tort law relates to a set of views on political legitimacy and institutional authority. On our account, the norms that ground courts' patterns of inference actually constitute the common law of torts. It follows that judges whose job it is to apply tort law have a prima facie duty to decide cases in a manner that faithfully engages those norms and that draws inferences about liability from within them. Why not decide cases in a manner that better attains the good consequences that the application of the norms typically accomplishes? The answer is this: If the common law just is the pattern of norms, and that pattern, under its own internal structure, pushes in a different way than is called for by instrumentalist analysis, then the instrumentalist judge would not be faithfully applying the law. Common-law judges, of course, have authority to change the law, especially in incremental ways. But they are not lawmakers in the sense that legislatures are lawmakers. And of course judges have the raw power to ignore or distort the language and the concepts of the law. But their obligation is to apply the law, not to advance the best policy that can be advanced under the guise of heeding law's concepts, rules, and structures.

Happily, tort concepts are often sufficiently open-textured to allow for extensions that simultaneously conform to the normativity built into the inferential practices of the law *and* improve the capacity of the law to realize important social goods. It is one thing, however, to be open-minded and sensitive to the differences in consequences that will flow from different available interpretations. It is another thing to suppose that the only question to consider is the question of consequences. One can, like Cardozo, accept a pragmatism of the first sort without abandoning the judicial duty to apply the law.

When we apply our pragmatic conceptualist methodology to tort law, we find ourselves not only rejecting the instrumentalist route but turning 180 degrees away from it. It is not just that we reject studiously amoral, reductive accounts of tort law. It is that we are of the view that the best accounts of tort law act will actually feature a number of morally rich ideas.

Holmes's effort to craft a pragmatic reconstruction of tort law and common law was hobbled from the start. For him, the problem with the common law's status as law was not simply the absence of a legislative process, the absence of any privileged text, the absence of a clear command from the sovereign, and uncertainties as to what courts would do in various circumstances. Another problem—in some ways the key problem—was his moral skepticism. He despaired of the idea that our moral ideas hang together in a coherent and defensible manner. To the extent that he could imagine moral ideas of a noninstrumentalist sort working within a set of practices, he was persuaded that those practices would be of a "primitive" sort that members of a modern society simply could not embrace.

Why Holmes came to associate pragmatism with moral skepticism (and moral skepticism with liberalism of a sort) raises fascinating questions of intellectual history and biography. Regardless, it is clear that he was an outlier among his fellow pragmatists and their intellectual descendants. Indeed, a central tenet of most versions of pragmatism is that other philosophical theorists go badly astray in positing hard-and-fast distinctions between fact and value, reason and passion, and science and morality. Yet, instead of attacking moral skepticism head on, it may be more fruitful to explain why even certain kinds of moral skeptics should be open to our account, especially moral skeptics who, like Holmes, claim the mantle of pragmatism.

Our contention is that, even apart from questions about whether various propositions about duties, rights, and wrongs are true, or known, or even possible objects of knowledge, the common law of torts operates on the basis of such propositions. We come to the job of explaining the common law somewhat like one trying to explain how the members of a community use their language. The goal is to make explicit the various patterns of thought and conduct that animate this area of the law. If it turns out that many of the concepts and principles utilized in this area have the same character as, or a character very similar to, those which are utilized in nonlegal discourse about how one ought (morally) to conduct oneself—indeed, if it turns out that some of the concepts are identical—that is something to be acknowledged, not hidden from view. We do not think that the reality of what the law is involves a set of transcendental norms. Nor do we think it is some privileged set of discoverable sources. We think that in identifying principles and concepts, we are essentially highlighting certain aspects of the legal practices of courts, litigants, and legal actors more broadly.

Let us call these sorts of explanations *embedded* moral explanations of the common law. It is plausible that Holmes would have—and actually did—reject even these as an aspiration for legal explanation. Likewise, some early twentieth-century philosophers were so deeply skeptical of moral language that they regarded as a sham the practices of reason-giving in moral discourse. This view has been widely discredited. Indeed, even those today who, like Simon Blackburn and Allan Gibbard, reject the possibility of truth for moral utterances, nonetheless contend that cogent and defensible patterns of reason-giving and justification exist in the moral domain. More generally, most of today's leading pragmatists—whether because they endorse a modest conception of truth or otherwise—do not relegate moral discourse to second-class citizenship. Holmes turns out to have been a dogmatist about morality, and dogmatism is not a substitute for philosophical argumentation.

Candor requires that we address four remaining aspects of our philosophical perspective. Some readers will want to know whether our commitment to the pragmatic reconstruction of legal practices involves an embrace or a rejection of legal positivism. Our account, we believe, is compatible with both positivist and anti-positivist conceptions of law. Legal positivism is, of course, frequently depicted as insisting on a separation of law and morality. But the great majority of positivists are content to acknowledge the presence of moral concepts in law and legal reasoning. Their larger concern is whether a given rule's status as a legal rule can be determined in part by moral criteria. This book is not about that issue.

Second, although the great bulk of our account is about the embedded moral concepts in the law of torts, we do not limit our moral-philosophical arguments in this book simply to embedded accounts. As we have already indicated in Chapter 1, for example, we think the principle articulated in the *ubi jus* maxim is defensible from within a contractarian version of liberal-democratic political theory. More generally, we do not shy away from offering normative arguments of a nonconsequential sort. Nonetheless, the core of this book is the presentation and explanation of what we have called tort law's embedded moral principles.

Third, some readers—if only out of (justified) suspicion of those who bandy around the term "pragmatism"—might criticize us for presenting two quite different versions of non-Holmesian pragmatism, and for conflating them. These readers would be half right. There are two different kinds of anti-Holmesian pragmatism at work here, but we have not conflated them. We have presented them together because we use them both and we are (believe it or not) anxious about imposing too many distinctions on our readers.

One form of pragmatism is, broadly speaking, related to truth and knowledge. It typically goes hand in hand with labels like "anti-foundationalism," "holism," "coherentism," or "internal realism." (We suggested in the Introduction that Rawls's epistemology in moral and political philosophy is pragmatist in this anti-foundationalist way.) We are philosophical pragmatists about law in this respect.[32] Yet at the same time, the label "pragmatic conceptualist" also aims to express a view about the respect in which inferential practices of judges and lawyers constitute the particular kind of law known as common law.

In principle one could be a philosophical pragmatist about knowledge and truth in law while rejecting our view of the common law, and in principle one could endorse pragmatic conceptualism as to the common law while rejecting an anti-foundationalist approach to law in general. To avoid further forays into these niceties in the remainder of the book, we here provide notice that the term "pragmatic conceptualist" may be used in what follows to refer to one or both of these views.

Finally, we are not only pragmatic conceptualists in both of the foregoing respects, we are "pragmatic" in the nontechnical sense of that term, too. Part of our inquiry into various aspects of the common law—part of any academic's question in a large study—is whether having such a law is worthwhile, and whether there are ways it should be revised. In this inquiry, the consequences of tort law's operation must figure significantly.

32. It is an interesting question whether our mentor in jurisprudence, Ronald Dworkin, was a philosophical pragmatist about law in this respect. One of us has argued that the answer is "no, not quite." Zipursky, *supra* note 30, at 248–50 (suggesting that, in light of his extraordinary focus on adjudication and the foundational role of first-order morality in his jurisprudence, Dworkin is closer to being a nonfoundationalist in moral epistemology but a natural lawyer in jurisprudence).

3

Rules, Duties, Rights, and Rights of Action

WE MAINTAIN THAT the *ubi jus* maxim captures an idea central to tort law. But what does it really mean to say: "Where there's a right, there's a remedy"? American lawyers and law professors pride themselves on being down to earth. And *ubi jus* is the sort of lofty notion that seems to cry out for deflation. According to the deflationary or "no-nonsense" view, what it means for a person to have a legal right is that she has a legal remedy. On this view, *ubj jus* is circular.

In this chapter we explain why the circularity objection and the no-nonsense view are not compelling. More affirmatively, we offer an account of legal rules, legal duties, and legal rights that illuminates the structure of tort law. Building primarily on the work of H. L. A. Hart, we begin with some *conceptual* claims about what it means to be under a legal duty and to have a legal right.[1] We then fuse these conceptual claims with *interpretive* claims about the type of rules one actually finds in American law. Specifically, we maintain that tort law contains an array of rules, including the rules that define the various torts and thereby generate *relational duties* that are owed by some persons to others. These are typically duties to refrain from acting upon others in certain ways, and the rules that

---

1. Although we use something very close to Hart's conception of a legal duty here, the theory of legal rights we offer is quite different from (and probably inconsistent with) Hart's general theory of legal rights. The reasons for the difference have largely to do with our different aspirations for what a theory of legal rights should try to achieve, and these differences do not warrant discussion here. As we note below, our argument also invokes the distinction between claim rights and powers most famously articulated by Wesley Hohfeld.

generate them simultaneously generate rights against being so acted upon. It is the existence of these rules, and these rights and duties, that renders the *ubi jus* maxim substantive. To invoke the maxim is to assert as follows: Where there are legal rules that specify certain kinds of duties owed to others and rights enjoyed by those others, and where such a duty has been breached and such a right violated, the right-holder is entitled to an avenue of civil recourse against the duty-bearer. In tort law—which will be the focus of this chapter—the duties in question are typically duties to refrain from wrongfully injuring certain others, and the rights are rights against being so injured.

Notwithstanding the overall affirmative cast of this chapter, the no-nonsense view and the circularity objection will figure prominently in what follows. A challenge for any account that, like ours, claims to be revealing an apparently obvious truth about its subject is to explain why, if the truth is obvious, so many have missed it. Thinking about the circularity objection will lead us to confront a dominant approach to duties and rights that has led legions of legal thinkers to dismiss or downplay *ubi jus*, notwithstanding its apparently fundamental status. As is the case for several other facets of our account, our principal foil is Oliver Wendell Holmes.

Holmes on Rights and Duties

The beginning of confusion about legal rights and duties in American jurisprudence is Holmes's celebrated essay "The Path of the Law." Written as an address to law students, the essay famously contains some cautionary advice about how to understand references within law to notions of right and duty.

> ... The primary rights and duties with which jurisprudence busies itself ... are nothing but prophecies .... [A]s I shall try to show, a legal duty so called is nothing but a prediction that if a man does or omits certain things he will be made to suffer in this or that way by judgment of the court;—and so of a legal right.
>
> ....
>
> Take again a notion which as popularly understood is the widest conception which the law contains;—the notion of legal duty, to which already I have referred. We fill the word with all

the content which we draw from morals. But what does it mean to a bad man? Mainly, and in the first place, a prophecy that if he does certain things he will be subjected to disagreeable consequences by way of imprisonment or compulsory payment of money.[2]

It is easy to see why Holmes's account caught on. In these passages he seems to be offer a grounded, jargon-free account of what law is "really" about. And there is an appealing practicality to the warnings he conveyed to his student audience. Clients do not retain lawyers to be lectured on their moral duties. They do so, at least in part, because they desire information about the likely consequences of different courses of action.

At the cost of spoiling Holmes's elegant prose, we will pry out of it several propositions. We can begin by distinguishing two types of contentions contained in this passage: *analytic* contentions—that is, contentions about what makes it *true* that a person has a legal duty to refrain from performing a certain act; and *interpretive* contentions[3]—that is, contentions about what lawyers are typically aiming to communicate when they say that a person has a legal duty to refrain from performing a certain act.[4] Each of these types has an affirmative and a negative variant.

For analytic contentions, the affirmative and negative variants are:

(1a) (affirmative) What makes it true that a person has a legal duty to refrain from doing A is that, if the person does A, then the person is subject to liability.

---

2. Oliver Wendell Holmes, *The Path of the Law*, 10 Harv. L. Rev. 457, 458, 461 (1897). We will assume that Holmes was asserting claims about the nature of legal duties, rather than merely suggesting to his audience that it would be a good corrective to their overly moralistic legal education for them to go through the exercise of *supposing* that legal duties boil down to predictions about legal sanctions.

3. We here sharply distinguish analytic and interpretive contentions for purposes of clear exposition, not because we are committed, philosophically, to the thought that the two constitute hermetically sealed categories.

4. It is important to emphasize that, in what follows, we use the term "act" to refer not merely to voluntary bodily movements (for example, walking) but also to injurious conduct (for example, knocking someone down). This usage is by no means idiosyncratic. Both in and out of law, the term "act" sometimes refers only to voluntary bodily motions detached from any consequences but at other times incorporates the results of such actions. Thus, a perfectly cogent response to the question "What did you do?" might be: "I broke the mirror" or "I accidentally hit him." *See* Benjamin C. Zipursky, *Two Dimensions of Responsibility in Crime, Tort and Moral Luck*, 9 Theoretical Inquiries L. 97 (2007).

(1b) (negative) Whatever makes it true that a person has a legal duty to refrain from doing A, it is *not* that doing A is morally wrong.

For interpretive contentions, the two variants are:

(2a) (affirmative) What a lawyer means when she advises a client that the client is under a legal duty to refrain from doing A is that the client will be subject to liability for doing A.

(2b) (negative) Whatever a lawyer means when she advises a client that the client is under a duty to refrain from doing A, the lawyer does *not* mean that the client has a moral duty to refrain from doing A.

Needless to say, these four propositions have received a great deal of scholarly attention. (1b) and (2b) have been the focus of debates over legal positivism and the separation of law and morality. (2a) stands at the heart of American Legal Realism. Our interest, however, is principally in contention (1a) and its extension to the idea of a legal right.

According to Holmes, what it means for a person to have a legal duty to refrain from doing something is for it to be the case that acting in that manner will subject the person to legal sanction in the form of criminal punishment or civil liability. Importantly, on Holmes's view, rights are correlative to duties. (This is why the first paragraph quoted above from "The Path of the Law" ends with the phrase "and so of a legal right.") Given the correlativity of rights and duties, to say that Yolanda has a legal right that Xander not defraud her is equivalent to saying that Xander has a legal duty not to defraud Yolanda. And because, according to Holmes, Xander's having a legal duty means nothing more than that Xander faces liability if he defrauds Yolanda, it follows that Yolanda's right that Xander not defraud her is constituted by Xander facing liability if he defrauds Yolanda. Thus, analytically, what makes it true that Yolanda has a legal right against Xander's defrauding her is that, if Xander defrauds Yolanda, Yolanda will have a legal remedy against Xander.[5] It follows, on the Holmesian view, that "Where there's a right, there's a remedy" really is vacuous—an analytic truth.

The connection between (1a) and (1b) is significant for at least two reasons. The most obvious is that (1a) offers a way of giving legal words meaning

---

5. Here we are assuming that liability to Yolanda is the only legal "sanction" that Xander might face (i.e., that there will be no criminal punishment or regulatory sanction).

without relying on moral ideas. It thus undermines the thought that legal duties and rights are connected analytically to moral duties and rights. But the larger aim of Holmes's project generally, and of "The Path of the Law" in particular, is to show that there is something fallacious about the inference from moral duty to legal duty, and from moral right to legal right. To the students whom he addressed, Holmes sought to make clear that they cannot and should not make judgments about legal liability merely on the basis of moral intuitions or judgments. "Where there's a right, there's a remedy" would be noncircular if the word "right" referred to moral rights and the word "remedy" referred to legal liability. Once we see, however, that the word right refers to "legal right," then (Holmes claimed) we must concede that the maxim is circular.

Leading tort scholars within the law-and-economics movement, including Guido Calabresi, Richard Posner, and Steven Shavell, all adopt frameworks descended from Holmes's, and their frameworks all lead to the same place, jurisprudentially. Consider Calabresi. Legal rules, he and Douglas Melamed famously argued, almost all fall within one of three kinds: property rules, inalienability rules, and liability rules.[6] Under a property rule, no one may act upon or remove the entitlement of another without her consent. Under an inalienability rule, even consent is ineffective to remove an entitlement. Under a liability rule, an actor may unilaterally choose to interfere with another's entitlement, but then will be subject to liability for having done so. Tort law, Calabresi insists, is overwhelmingly a scheme of liability rules. To be under a rule of tort law stating that one must not do A is to be under a rule according to which one will be liable if one does A. Here, too, the *ubi jus* maxim is rendered circular.

Hart's Alternative

As we embark on our critique of Holmes's analysis of legal duties and rights, we want to be clear that our position is entirely compatible with his insistence on separating legal duties and rights from moral duties and rights. More succinctly, our analysis in this chapter is perfectly compatible with legal positivism, though one need not be a positivist to adopt it. Indeed,

---

6. Guido Calabresi & A. Douglas Melamed, *Property Rules, Liability Rules and Inalienability: One View of the Cathedral*, 85 YALE L.J. 1089 (1972).

the principal source of our anti-Holmesian analysis is Hart, a self-described positivist. Hart famously criticized the predictive theory of law and Holmes's analysis of legal duties. More importantly, Hart offered a framework that establishes the cogency of treating legal duties as a species of obligation comparable to, yet distinct from, moral obligations.

Hart's critique of Holmes has several components. We will focus on two: the argument against the predictive theory of legal duties, and the argument from the obliged / obligated distinction.

In an effort to account for the ordinary parlance of duty—what it means for a speaker to assert that X is under an obligation to refrain from doing A—Holmes proposed to treat such statements as predictions that liability will follow if X does A. Hart's most concise response to this claim observes that people obviously can and often do mean something distinct from predicting the onset of disagreeable consequences when they assert that they are (or someone else is) under a legal obligation. Indeed, it is perfectly coherent to assert both that someone is subject to an obligation and that she is under no risk of sanction:

> If it were true that the statement that a person had an obligation [to someone] meant that *he* was likely to suffer in the event of disobedience, it would be a contradiction to say that he had an obligation, e.g. to report for military service but that, owing to the fact that he had escaped from the jurisdiction, or had successfully bribed the police or the court, there was not the slightest chance of his being caught or made to suffer. In fact, there is no contradiction in saying this, and such statements are often made and understood.[7]

Additionally, Hart pointed out that assertions about obligations obviously can carry some content other than predictive content. In particular, he observed that Holmes's "predictive" analysis cannot account for judicial speech about obligations.

Perhaps the most memorable negative argument in *The Concept of Law* against the Holmesian conception of obligation is in some ways the subtlest. Holmes maintained that having a legal duty (or obligation) to do A is roughly analogous to being told by a threatening gunman that one must do A. Such a person would be obligated to do A on pain of a sanction that

7. H.L.A. Hart, The Concept of Law 84 (2d ed. 1994).

the more powerful party is in a position to inflict. In law, it just so happens that the more powerful party is the state.

Hart responded that Holmes's picture runs roughshod over a distinction between being "obliged" and being "obligated." The addressee in the gunman example might accurately describe himself as "obliged to do A." But if the threat were the only reason provided to him to do A, then it would not be correct to describe the addressee as under an obligation to do A: "There is a difference . . . between the assertion that someone was obliged to do something and the assertion that he had an obligation to do it."[8] The former is a psychological statement referring to the beliefs and motives with which the action is done. "But the statement that someone had an obligation to do something is of a very different type . . . ."[9] It connotes that there are or may be mandatory reasons applicable to that person in light of which he ought to do A. Holmes's account of duties runs roughshod over this distinction.

We now turn to the affirmative side of Hart's critique. A large subset of laws, on Hart's view, consists of what he calls "duty-imposing rules." The force of these rules is to enjoin, direct, or demand conduct of a certain form. "Car headlights are to be used after dusk, or when it is raining" is such a rule, directing persons who drive cars to turn on their headlights under certain circumstances. Duty-imposing rules, in the law, are a subset of rules of conduct more generally. "The fork and knife should be put on the plate when one is finished eating" is a rule of conduct too, albeit a rule of etiquette and not a duty-imposing rule. In other words, some forms of rule—legal and moral, for example—impose obligations, whereas other forms of rule—rules of etiquette, for example—do not.

Hart argued that three features separate domains in which socially recognized rules are understood as imposing obligations from those in which they are not. First, "[r]ules are conceived and spoken of as imposing genuine obligations when the general demand for conformity is insistent and the social pressure brought to bear upon those who deviate or threaten to deviate is great." Second, and partly explaining the social pressure, in the

---

8. *Id.* at 82. In our view Hart rested his argument too heavily on a claim about the ordinary-usage meanings of the terms "obliged" and "obligated." However, even if he was wrong in his claims about usage, his larger point stands. The distinction between acting in order to avoid a threatened harm and acting in fulfillment of an obligation is perfectly familiar.

9. *Id.* at 83.

domain of obligations the rules "are believed to be necessary to the maintenance of social life or some highly prized feature of it." Third,

> it is generally recognized that the conduct required by these rules may, while benefiting others, conflict with what the person who owes the duty may wish to do. Hence obligations and duties are thought of as characteristically involving sacrifice or renunciation, and the standing possibility of conflict between obligation or duty and interest is, in all societies, among the truisms of both the lawyer and the moralist.[10]

Hart, of course, believed that legal systems are among those systems whose primary rules do impose obligations. His recognition that the primary rules of law have these three features is coupled with his analysis of obligations as particular to rules enjoying these features. The result is that he is able to offer an interesting explanation of what it means to say that the law imposes obligations, beyond saying that it has rules that enjoin conduct.

A person has a legal duty to refrain from doing A, according to Hart, as long as there exists a valid legal rule applicable to him that enjoins him not to do A. To assert that a person has a legal duty to refrain from doing A is not to predict that he will be sanctioned if he does A. It is to assert that there exists a relevant legal rule that says, in effect, "Do not do A." It is often a consequence of such a rule that the legal system will also empower someone to impose a sanction or liability for the failure to live up to it, but asserting that there is a primary rule directing an actor to refrain from doing A *is* not predicting what will or might happen if the actor does A. We will refer to what Hart described as primary, duty-imposing rules as "legal conduct rules" or "legal directives."

A citizen's capacity to recognize legal obligations is, in part, a capacity to grasp that there is a legal rule that speaks to a certain situation, and that directs her to act (or not act) in a certain way in that situation. In "The Path of the Law," Holmes advised that the good lawyer focuses on the legal sanctions that may follow if certain conduct is undertaken. Hart, by contrast, emphasizes a lawyer's or layperson's capacity to glean information about the content of the law's directives concerning what a

10. *Id.* at 87.

person is permitted or not permitted to do.[11] Critically, however, Hart's account is every bit as positivistic as Holmes's. For Hart, it is a matter of fact—of positive law—whether there is or is not a legal rule enjoining certain conduct.

We recognize, of course, that many Holmesians are skeptical of the distinction drawn above. Indeed, if readers will pardon the anachronism, it is fair to say that Holmes himself was attracted to the view that nearly *all* legal norms of conduct were in some sense mere liability rules and that, therefore, a richer, Hartian conception of legal duty was illusory:

> Take again a notion which as popularly understood is the widest conception which the law contains;—the notion of legal duty, to which already I have referred . . . . But what does it mean to a bad man? Mainly, and in the first place, a prophecy that if he does certain things he will be subjected to disagreeable consequences by way of imprisonment or compulsory payment of money. But from his point of view, what is the difference between being fined and being taxed a certain sum for doing a certain thing? . . . You see how the vague circumference of the notion of duty shrinks and at the same time grows more precise when we wash it with cynical acid and expel everything except the object of our study, the operations of the law.[12]

Hart's discussion of the internal aspect of rules and the internal point of view provides powerful (though hardly uncontested) answers to these questions. For the moment a brief response will suffice. Hart was willing to concede, at least for the purposes of argument, that there is a possible bad-man perspective on law generally and on the particular laws of a legal system. He insisted, however, that there is another possible perspective, which might be called the "generally law-abiding citizen perspective." Oversimplifying, Hart used the phrase "the external point of view" to

---

11. This contrast is somewhat overstated. Holmes, unlike his Legal Realist followers, maintained that lawyers could and should make their predictions about judicial sanctions on the basis of their readings of standard legal sources such as cases and statutes, as opposed to psychological or sociological facts about the relevant parties or the judge(s) who might decide the matter at hand.

12. Holmes, *supra* note 2, at 461–62.

refer to the bad-man perspective and the phrase "the internal point of view" to refer to the law-abiding citizen perspective.[13]

Hart argued that there are many persons in a legal community at any given time who occupy the internal point of view. Relatedly, he argued that legal rules have an *internal aspect*—they must be such that there is a way of seeing them as the generally law-abiding citizen does. Although it is a matter of controversy whether Hart believed that some or most ordinary members of society *must* occupy the internal point of view if there is to be an actual, functioning legal system, it is clear that he did not think all members of society needed to do so. Conversely, however, it appears that Hart did believe that legal officials—in particular, judges—must see the law from the internal point of view.[14]

On the basis of the assumption that it is possible for persons to occupy an internal point of view with respect to legal norms—i.e., to understand the law as enjoining them to comply with certain standards of conduct— we will proceed with the idea that legal duties need not be understood in Holmesian terms. We further assume that a jurisprudential thinker committed to distinguishing legal duties from moral duties need not adopt a Holmesian analysis of legal duties. Instead, it is possible to see legal duties as existing whenever there are conduct-enjoining rules that have the status of valid laws within a legal system. As did Hart, we will assume that a great many of these conduct-enjoining rules qualify as valid not because of the moral justifiability of their substance but because they came to be law through a process that the legal system treats as validity-conferring. For example, the validity of a statutory provision requiring that each automobile owner in a state carry $50,000 in liability insurance turns on whether the state legislature properly enacted the statute, not on whether it is morally justifiable. On this account, the existence of a legal duty consists in the existence of a valid duty-imposing legal rule.

---

13. HART, *supra* note 7, at 90 ("What the external point of view, which limits itself to the observable regularities of behaviour, cannot reproduce is the way in which the rules function as rules in the lives of those who normally are the majority of society. These are the officials, lawyers, or private persons who use them, in one situation after another, as guides to the conduct of social life, as the basis for claims, demands, admissions, criticism, or punishment, viz., in all the familiar transactions of life according to rules. For them the violation of a rule is not merely a basis for the prediction that a hostile reaction will follow but a *reason* for hostility.")

14. Scott Shapiro has argued persuasively that this claim was one of the centerpieces of Hart's theory of law. SCOTT J. SHAPIRO, LEGALITY 79–117 (2013).

The Conduct-Rule Theory of Rights

Having generated an option for understanding legal duties as distinct from moral duties without understanding them as liability rules, we now turn to the task of generating an account of legal rights that will pave the way for a substantive, noncircular rendering of the *ubi jus* maxim.

The crucial move here is to distinguish two kinds of legal directives: those that are "simple" and those that are "relational." Simple legal directives require persons to perform certain acts or enjoin persons from committing certain acts. Laws requiring persons to purchase liability insurance for their cars or to register for the military draft, and laws enjoining persons from polluting or conspiring to sell narcotics, contain simple legal directives. A simple (negative) directive has the following form: *Each member of the class of persons C must refrain from doing* A.

Relational legal directives, by contrast, enjoin persons to treat or to refrain from treating other persons in a particular way. Directives specifying that a parent is required to care for his children, or that enjoin a physician from incompetently treating her patient, or that prohibit eavesdropping on another, are all relational legal directives. Respectively, they require a parent to attend to *her child*, a physician to avoid injuring any of *her patients* through incompetent care; and each person to refrain from eavesdropping *on any other person*. Though they thus differ in scope—in terms of both the class of persons to whom they are addressed and the class of persons whom they protect—relational directives (of a negative sort) all share the following form: *Each member of the class of persons C must refrain from doing A to each member of the class of persons P.*

The distinction between simple and relational legal directives generates a distinction between two kinds of legal duties. To say that a person has a "simple legal duty" to refrain from doing A is to say that the person is subject to a simple legal directive enjoining A. To say that a person has a "relational (or dyadic) legal duty" to refrain from doing A is to say that there is a relational directive under which doing A to another person or other persons is identified as legally required or prohibited. Insofar as there are legal rules against polluting and conspiring to sell narcotics, violations of these rules are breaches of simple legal duties. Insofar as there are legal rules against child neglect, medical malpractice, and eavesdropping, violations of these rules are breaches of relational legal duties.

It may be illuminating to compare the distinction between simple and relational directives to the distinction between intransitive and transitive verbs. To use a transitive verb correctly, one must specify or imply a direct object that is being acted upon (e.g., "Dan injured Pam"). To use an intransitive verb correctly does not require the identification of an object (e.g., "Dan burped"). In a similar manner, relational directives identify how an actor must conduct herself *in relation to other persons*, whereas simple directives identify how an actor must conduct herself, full stop.

Importantly, the distinction between simple and relational directives, and simple and relational duties, is *not* a distinction between directives and duties that are personal, particular, or specific (on the one hand) and those that are impersonal, abstract, or general (on the other). Relational directives—such as the directive not to defraud any other person—can be quite broad. Likewise, although relational directives and duties are at the heart of tort law, the simple/relational dichotomy does *not* map neatly onto the distinction between tort law and other bodies of law, such as criminal or regulatory law. Tort law's substantive directives are all relational—they always enjoin certain actors from doing certain things *to* certain others, or to do certain things *for* certain others. It is not true, however, that criminal law's directives are all simple. Some are ("Do not possess narcotics") but others are not ("Do not murder another"). At this juncture we are making a claim about the *analytic structure* of different directives and different duties. We are not yet advancing an interpretive claim about tort law, though we will advance such a claim below.

With the ideas of relational legal directives and relational legal duties before us, we can fairly quickly proceed to the recognition of a certain kind of legal *right*. By identifying a class of duty-bearers whose duties consist of *obligations to refrain from acting upon certain other persons*, relational directives at the same time identify a class of *rights-bearers*. Yolanda has a legal right against Xander's doing A to her (for example, carelessly injuring her) if and only if Xander has a relational legal duty to refrain from doing A *to* her. Because relational legal directives are the source of relational legal duties, it follows that *Yolanda has a legal right to have Xander refrain from doing A to her if and only if there is a relational legal directive requiring Xander to refrain from doing A to her.*[15]

---

15. The same analysis applies with respect to affirmative relational directives. For example, a legal directive that requires all hotel owners to take reasonable steps to provide first aid to

The point can, of course, be enlarged from the case of relational duties owed by one particular person to another particular person. Yolanda has a right not to have *anyone* do A to her if and only if there is a relational legal directive enjoining the class of *all persons* not to do A to her. And all persons have a right not to have anyone do A to them if and only if there is a relational legal norm enjoining the class of all persons not to do A to any other person.

We have provided the foregoing analytical apparatus in part to allow for the flexibility that any theory of legal rights and duties will need. It is not simply that some rights are rights to be treated in certain ways while others are rights to be free of certain kinds of mistreatment. It is also that many rights are rights as against a significant subset of persons, while other rights are as against everyone, and other rights still are as against only one (or one kind of) person. A legal right to have one's confidences kept exists as against one's lawyer, one's doctor, or one's clergy person, but perhaps not as against a reporter or a stranger. A legal right not to be punched in the nose exists as against everyone.

For present purposes, we will concede that it is not always easy to decide whether a particular legal directive is simple or relational, that it is not always clear who the rights-holders are under such directives, and that it is not even clear what criteria are to be used to ascertain the existence and content of such a directive. We will further accept, in the spirit of Hohfeld, that there are at least some legal rights—e.g., the right to vote—that are best conceived at least partly as legal powers, which in turn suggests that some legal rights do not correspond to duty-imposing directives. None of these concessions undermines the plausibility of our claims that (i) there is a cogent distinction to be drawn between simple and relational directives, and (ii) there is a cogent notion of legal rights and duties that can be derived from the notion of a relational directive.

Consider, for example, what many would take to be archetypical legal rights: namely, the rights guaranteed by the federal Constitution's Bill of Rights. It counts in favor of the intelligibility of our account that many of these rights fit the model we have offered. The Eighth Amendment, for example, states that "excessive bail shall not be required, nor excessive

---

guests who are injured on their premises generates a duty for hotel owners and operators that corresponds to a right enjoyed by guests.

fines imposed, nor cruel and unusual punishments inflicted."[16] Given that only governments set bail and inflict punishment (and bracketing the question of whether the government in question is the federal or a state government), one may fairly paraphrase the Amendment as follows: "government shall not require excessive bail of anyone, or impose excessive fines or inflict cruel and unusual punishment on anyone." So put, this is plainly a relational legal directive. The Eighth Amendment imposes a legal duty on officials not to set excessive bail *for anyone,* and not to impose excessive fines or inflict cruel and unusual punishments *on anyone.* At the same time, it confers on each person covered by its protections a right not to be subjected to these mistreatments. The commonplace notion of a person "asserting her Eighth Amendment rights" conveys effortlessly the connection we are describing between legal rule, legal duty, and legal right.

Legal rights are hardly confined to the Bill of Rights. Many of these other rights also fit our model. Consider Vermont's Fair Credit Reporting statute, which provides consumers with a right to obtain their credit scores as follows:

(a) A credit reporting agency shall, upon request and proper identification of any consumer, clearly and accurately disclose to the consumer all information available to users at the time of the request pertaining to the consumer, including:

    (1) any credit score or predictor relating to the consumer, in a form and manner that complies with such comments or guidelines as may be issued by the Federal Trade Commission;

    (2) the names of users requesting information pertaining to the consumer during the prior 12-month period and the date of each request; and

    (3) a clear and concise explanation of the information.[17]

This provision contains a relational legal directive that confers rights upon consumers and duties upon credit-reporting agencies. We mention it not because it is remarkable, but because it is completely unremarkable. State law and federal law are shot through with relational directives, relational legal duties, and corresponding legal rights.

---

16. U.S. Const. amend. VIII.
17. 9 V.S.A. § 2480b(a).

The Hartian framework we have provided solves the challenge we set for ourselves of identifying a way to separate legal rights and duties from moral rights and duties without requiring the adoption of a bad-man, liability-rule view. Hart argued that legal rules enjoy their status as valid law by virtue of facts that obtain independently of whether the rules are morally justifiable.[18] Such rules, he maintained, are valid because they are properly enacted, adopted, or recognized. Because their content is essentially injunctive and because they exist within a system that at least some members—as a matter of sociological fact—cogently understand to impose obligations of conduct, it is proper to speak of them as "duty-imposing" legal rules. Moreover, the courses of conduct they purport to require are plausibly described as "legal duties."

Imagine, for example, that a credit reporting agency has just begun doing business in Vermont. It receives a letter from a Vermont consumer requesting his credit score. If the letter were forwarded to an in-house lawyer, and if she were knowledgeable about the situation, she might well communicate to the relevant company officials that the company is under a legal duty to provide the consumer with the requested report. What she would mean by saying this is that a valid Vermont law exists that is applicable to the company. *The lawyer is neither telling the company what it ought to do, morally, nor offering a prediction as to its risk of facing a legal sanction. Instead, she is identifying that the company is subject to a valid legal rule that requires that it act in a certain manner in relation to consumers.*

To get to our claim about rights requires just one more step. Returning to our imagined in-house lawyer, one could just as easily envision her advising the credit reporting agency as follows: "Under Vermont law, a consumer has a legal right to the release of his credit scores. Indeed, Section 2480b of volume 9 of the state statutes indicates that we are required to send him a copy of his credit report within 30 days of his request." Obviously the lawyer is once again looking at the same duty-imposing rule. But because the rule contains a *relational* rather than a simple legal directive, it is no less natural for the lawyer to describe the legal situation facing the agency in terms of the consumer's right as in terms of the company's

18. Hart famously shared the inclusive positivists' qualification of his separation thesis by recognizing the possibility that a legal system might, as a matter of social fact, adopt criteria for legality or validity that depend on whether putative laws satisfy certain moral criteria.

duty. Relational legal directives are simultaneously duty-imposing and rights-conferring.

The general point is that for a certain kind of legal right to exist in a given legal system is for a particular kind of legal rule to be valid in that system. Of course, there can be difficult interpretive questions of how to identify which legal rules are valid and what they mean. But interpretive difficulties of this sort were not Holmes's principal concern in "The Path of the Law," nor Hart's in *The Concept of Law*, and they are not our principal concern in this chapter. The issue is whether there is a way to make sense of the statement that someone has a legal right against someone else without saying that someone else faces liability to them, and without saying that the right in question is a moral right. We now see that there is a way to answer yes to this question. A person has a legal right that another not treat her in a certain way if there is a valid legal rule that enjoins the other not to treat her that way.

We shall call the foregoing account the "conduct-rule theory of legal rights."[19] It captures the idea that certain rights exist by virtue of the existence of valid legal directives within a legal system that require some set of persons (including the set of all persons) to treat some set of persons (including the set of all persons) in certain ways, or that enjoin some set of persons from treating some set of persons in certain ways. These relational legal directives or legal norms are conduct rules.

While we have not shied away from giving our account a fancy label, our aspirations for it are modest. We do not claim that this was Hart's account of legal rights; the truth is otherwise. Nor do we claim that it is wholly original; Neil MacCormick arguably offered a similar view.[20] And we do not here contend that it is an alternative to interest-based rights theories (like Bentham's or Raz's), choice theories (like Hart's or Feinberg's), or trump theories (like Dworkin's), or as an instance of any one of them.[21] Finally, as mentioned above, we do not suppose that it is able to accommodate all of the senses of the term "right" that Hohfeld famously

---

19. The theory of legal rights put forward here is derived largely from Benjamin C. Zipursky, *Rights, Wrongs and Recourse in the Law of Torts*, 51 VAND. L. REV. 1, 55–70 (1998).

20. D. N. MacCormick, *Rights in Legislation*, in LAW, MORALITY, AND SOCIETY: ESSAYS IN HONOUR OF H. L. A. HART 189 (P. M. S. Hacker & Joseph Raz eds., 1977).

21. *See generally* MATTHEW H. KRAMER, N. E. SIMMONDS, & HILLEL STEINER, A DEBATE OVER RIGHTS: PHILOSOPHICAL ENQUIRIES (1998); THEORIES OF RIGHTS (J. Waldron ed., 1984).

teased apart.[22] What we do mean to suggest is that the conduct-rule theory enables us to explain what is meant by the maxim "Where there's a right, there's a remedy." Admittedly, an account of a concept that has plausibility in explaining only one maxim would hardly be a serious account, but—as the remainder of this book will show—that is not true of the conduct-rule theory. It has the capacity to capture the concept of a legal right throughout private law.

Rights, Rights of Action, and Remedies

We are almost in position to understand how it is that the *ubi jus* maxim is substantive, not circular. To get there, however, requires the introduction of one additional concept: the concept of a *right of action*.

Though familiar in legal discourse, the phrase "right of action" is hard to pin down. It is sometimes understood to refer merely to a right to file a claim. But this rendition is too thin. Pretty much anyone can file a claim: court clerks rarely refuse to accept complaints, even complaints that will be dismissed promptly on jurisdictional or other grounds. A right of action is a more robust legal power. In the elegant language of an old New York decision, it is "the right to prosecute an action *with effect*."[23] In other words, it is a Hohfeldian power: a power to file a claim and, upon proof of claim, to obtain judicially ordered relief that corresponds to a liability in the person(s) against whom suit has been brought.[24]

Needless to say, the power to pursue and obtain a court-ordered remedy is subject to various conditions, and requires for its exercise the acts of others.[25] A claim must be filed, and evidence put forth. In addition, legal actors such as judges and jurors, while bound by procedural and substantive rules, often enjoy substantial discretion in determining the validity of

22. Wesley N. Hohfeld, *Fundamental Legal Conceptions as Applied in Judicial Reasoning*, 26 YALE L.J. 710 (1917).

23. Patterson v. Patterson, 59 N.Y. 574, 578–79 (N.Y. 1875) (emphasis added).

24. On our use of the right-power distinction, see Chapter 5; see also John C. P. Goldberg & Benjamin C. Zipursky, *Hohfeldian Analysis and the Separation of Rights and Powers*, in THE LEGACY OF WESLEY HOHFELD: EDITED MAJOR WORKS, SELECT PERSONAL PAPERS, AND ORIGINAL COMMENTARIES (Shyam Balganesh, Ted Sichelman, & Henry E. Smith eds., forthcoming).

25. This is hardly an uncommon feature of legal powers. The legal power to marry requires the participation of various actors beyond the power-holder, including an official charged with issuing marriage licenses, and a person authorized to conduct marriage ceremonies.

a claim. Other legal rules specify the menu of remedies available to a successful claimant. These qualifications notwithstanding, where there is proof of valid claim (and no applicable affirmative defenses), it is not within the discretion of a judge or jury to deny the claimant a remedy to which she is legally entitled.

Armed with the idea of a right of action, it is now possible to see how the conduct-rule theory of legal rights generates a noncircular interpretation of the *ubi jus* maxim. Plaintiffs invoke the maxim when they believe they can establish that a right of theirs has been violated and are seeking a remedy—typically damages, but sometimes court-ordered performance—for the rights-violation through a court proceeding. The phrase "where there's a right, there's a remedy" means that a person is entitled to be provided with a remedy by a court for having suffered a certain kind of rights violation. More precisely, the maxim posits a linkage between the legal rights (and corresponding duties) generated by relational legal directives and rights of action. *Ubi jus* thus can be restated as follows: Whenever a person has been wronged by another through a violation of a relational directive, that person is entitled to be provided with a right of action by the state.

That this formulation is *not* circular can be seen by returning to our example of the Vermont credit reporting statute. Readers can know—and did know, after reading our discussion of it—that consumers have a right to obtain from credit reporting agencies their credit scores and the names of others who have requested it. Crucially, readers gained this knowledge *in the absence of any information about the legal consequences that follow from a violation of that right.* Of course, one would expect that a legislature that goes to the trouble of enacting a law conferring this right would make provision for its enforcement. And one might complain that a law without any such provision would be toothless. But a law that fails to provide for the adequate enforcement of a right it confers is readily distinguishable from a law that confers no right at all.

In any event, even if one were to equate a toothless law with a law that confers no legal right—that is, to insist that the right to credit information provided by the Vermont statute cannot count as a legal right unless there is a meaningful enforcement provision—it does not follow that *ubi jus* is circular. After all, there are mechanisms of enforcement other than private rights of action. Indeed, Vermont's statutory scheme expressly empowers state officials to impose civil penalties on actors who violate the

99

statute.[26] If this were the statute's exclusive enforcement mechanism, the proper description of the legal right it confers would be a *right without a remedy*. There would be no remedy for this legal right because a violation of it would give rise only to an official enforcement action, not a victim-initiated court proceeding that promises recourse.

As it turns out, the actual Vermont statute authorizes both public enforcement and private rights of action. Section 2480f(b) reads as follows: "A consumer aggrieved by a violation of this subchapter . . . may bring an action in Superior Court for the consumer's damages, injunctive relief, punitive damages in the case of a willful violation, and reasonable costs and attorney's fees."[27] Obviously this section refers to something more than a right to file a claim. It confers a legal power to obtain a remedy upon proof of claim in a court proceeding. The Vermont statute, in other words, conjoins a legal right against mistreatment with a remedy for violations of that right. In doing so, it instantiates the *ubi jus* maxim.

Another example will help elucidate our rendering of *ubi jus*. It concerns a century-old U.S. Supreme Court decision that we mentioned in Chapter 1. In *Texas & Pacific Railway v. Rigsby*,[28] the plaintiff, a switchman employed by the defendant railroad company, was descending a ladder on the side of the defendant's railroad car. Because the ladder had a loose or missing handhold, he fell and was injured.

At the time of the accident, the railroad was subject to directives set out in two federal statutes known as the Federal Safety Appliance Acts, one enacted in 1893, the other in 1910. Section 2 of the 1910 Act required railroads to equip their cars with secure handholds. Under Section 4 of the same Act, a railroad operating with noncompliant cars was subject to a penalty of $100 per violation, payable to the U.S. Treasury.

Pointing to the railroad's violation of Section 2, Rigsby claimed an entitlement to damages for the injuries he suffered as a result of that violation. His claim prevailed in the lower federal courts, and the Supreme Court affirmed. In the process, the Court rejected the railroad's argument that the suit was unauthorized because the Safety Appliance Acts—unlike the Vermont credit statute—nowhere explicitly stated that persons harmed as a result of violations of the Acts' directives were authorized to obtain

26. 9 V.S.A. § 2461(a) (providing for civil penalties for statutory violations).
27. *Id.* § 2480f(b).
28. 241 U.S. 33 (1916).

damages or other relief. (As noted, the Acts stated only that violations would result in a fine payable to the federal government.) The Court instead reasoned that the Acts were best interpreted to have *implicitly* conferred a right of action on persons such as Rigsby. Invoking *ubi jus* in support of its interpretation, and quoting an English decision, the Court reasoned that when a statute "'enacts or prohibits a thing for the benefit of a person, he shall have a remedy upon the same statute for the thing enacted for his advantage, or for recompense of a wrong done to him contrary to the said law.'"[29]

Both *Rigsby* and the Vermont credit reporting statute point toward the substantive, noncircular rendering of *ubi jus* that we are providing. The Vermont statute shows how a legislature can link a legal right (a right to obtain credit information from a credit reporting company) to a certain kind of legal power (a right of action to obtain a remedy through a court proceeding). *Rigsby* does the same thing, but in a context in which judicial interpretation was required in order to establish the relevant linkage. *Rigsby* is in this respect particularly illuminating because the Court's judgment that workers such as Rigsby were entitled to a remedy under the Safety Appliance Acts turned in large part on its determination that the Acts were best read to contain a relational directive generating a right in workers such as Rigsby to be free of injuries caused by their employers' use of unsound equipment. *In other words, the presence of a relational directive within the 1910 Act—and, with that directive, a legal right against certain forms of mistreatment enjoyed by railroad workers as against their employers—was taken by the Court as a decisive reason to regard the workers as having rights of action, even though the Acts were silent on that precise question.*[30] Note that there is nothing circular about this chain of reasoning. The Court was not engaged in the bootstrapping exercise of asserting that

29. *Id.* at 40 (quoting *Anonymous*, 87 E.R. 791, 791 (1703) (Holt, Ch. J)). As reported in the English Reports, the relevant portion of Holt's opinion reads: "for where-ever a statute enacts anything, or prohibits anything, for the advantage of any person, that person shall have remedy to recover the advantage given him, or to have the satisfaction for the injury done him contrary to law by the same statute . . . ."

30. One might object to our characterization of the Acts as identifying forms of "mistreatment" on the ground that liability under the Acts was strict, such that a railroad could be held liable for worker injuries caused by defective equipment even if it exercised due care to ensure the equipment was not defective. As we explain in Chapter 6, the notion of mistreatment at work in tort law is entirely compatible with certain kinds of strict liability, including the kind at work in the Safety Appliance Acts.

Rigsby had a right to sound safety equipment because it (the Court) was prepared to hold the defendant liable for his injuries. Quite the opposite, it was asserting that Rigsby was entitled to a remedy because the 1910 Act conferred on him a right to be free of certain kinds of mistreatment at the hands of his employer. The bearer of a certain kind of legal right is one who, by virtue of being a bearer of that right, also enjoys a related legal power. This is *ubi jus* in its substantive, noncircular rendition.

As was the case in the previous section, our claims here are modest, at least in certain respects. We do not purport to have established on the basis of these two examples that U.S. law consistently adheres to the *ubi jus* principle. Likewise, the extent to which the maxim admits of qualifications or exceptions is a separate question. So too is the question of whether its converse holds—that is, whether, in the absence of the requisite kind of legal right, one cannot have a right of action.

Finally, we have put to one side the question of how *ubi jus* operates and should operate within our federal system of government, and whether it holds or should hold for federal courts in the same way that it does for state courts. Although we have invoked a Supreme Court decision (*Rigsby*) to illuminate our account, knowledgeable readers will recognize that there is something ironic about our having done so, just as there was something ironic about our focus on federal law in Chapter 1. This is because since the late 1970s the Supreme Court—based on a substantially different understanding of the jurisdiction conferred on federal courts by Article III of the Constitution than is expressed in *Rigsby*—has concluded that federal courts should *not* find implied rights of action in federal statutes, even statutes containing relational directives that generate relational duties not to mistreat others and correlative rights against mistreatment.[31]

31. *See, e.g.*, Touche Ross & Co. v. Redington, 442 U.S. 560 (1979). Although on a somewhat different timeline, a similar transition has played out on the question of whether the federal courts should be guided by *ubi jus* in their interpretation of the rights-conferring provisions of the U.S. Constitution.

In the *Bivens* case, the Court displayed an openness to finding implied rights of action in the guarantees of the Bill of Rights. Bivens v. Six Unknown Named Agents of Federal Bureau of Narcotics, 403 U.S. 388 (1971). Federal agents raided Bivens's residence and arrested him. Both the search, which was conducted without a warrant, and the arrest, which lacked probable cause and involved excessive force, violated Bivens's Fourth Amendment right against being subjected to an unreasonable search and seizure.

Bivens brought suit seeking monetary damages from the agents. He claimed to be entitled to pursue his action in federal court because his claim was grounded in federal law—i.e., in a

Our own view is that there are important differences between the jurisdictions of the federal and state courts, and that these differences may
well warrant the federal courts in taking a different approach to implied
rights of action than state courts, even if not the precise approach favored
by a majority of the current Justices. However, the important point to emphasize here is that our claims about relational legal directives, relational
legal duties, legal rights against mistreatment, rights of action, and remedies stand quite apart from the position one takes on whether and how
federal courts should locate implied rights of action in the federal Constitution and federal statutes. Our goal from the outset of this chapter has
been to articulate a substantive, noncircular rendering of *ubi jus* that
can shed light on how tort law connects rights and remedies. We have
used examples of statutory rights of action—express and implied—to help
make that argument. But the argument stands independently of those
examples.

The Common Law

Even a Holmesian with patience enough to have come this far might
balk at the examples we have relied upon to vindicate a substantive rendering of *ubi jus*. Holmesian thinking, one might suppose, begat "realism" (i.e., skepticism) about the cogency of maxims such as *ubi jus* in
large part because Holmes himself was first and foremost a student of
the common law. Yet the relational legal directives or conduct rules that
we have thus far invoked are embedded in authoritative, enacted texts.
Thus, the patient Holmesian might claim, whatever life has been

---

right conferred on him by the federal Constitution. Lower courts dismissed the suit, reasoning that, although the Fourth Amendment identifies a right that individuals enjoy against
the federal government, it neither explicitly nor implicitly confers a *right of action* on persons
who suffer a violation of that right.

The Supreme Court reversed, holding that a person whose Fourth Amendment right is
violated by federal officials is "entitled to redress his injury through a particular remedial
mechanism normally available in the federal courts"—namely, a suit for damages. *Id.* at 397.
In other words, once it was recognized that the Fourth Amendment conferred on Bivens a
right against mistreatment by federal officials, it should also be understood to confer on him a
power to bring a claim for those violations that, if proven, would entitle him to a remedy.

Bivens thus stands as a constitutional analogue to *Rigsby*. And it has met a roughly similar
fate in subsequent decisions. Indeed, the Court has made clear that it no longer is inclined to
find rights of action implicit in the guarantees of the Bill of Rights. *See, e.g.,* Minneci v. Pol-
lard, 565 U.S. 118 (2012).

breathed into the *ubi jus* maxim by reference to legal directives will be of no help when it comes to making sense of the law of torts, which is largely judge-made.

The first problem with this objection is that it seems to suppose that legal rules can exist only by virtue of having been codified. Hart long ago showed that this view is incoherent for any number of reasons, not the least of which is that there will inevitably be appeals to uncodified law to distinguish valid from invalid constitutional enactments; that is, the notion of a valid legal rule in the constitutional context presupposes the notion of an unwritten rule.

A more subtle concern brings us back to the circularity objection, but now in a more qualified form. The worry is not that all law necessarily boils down to liability rules, but rather that *tort law*, because it is a branch of the common law, boils down to liability rules. This is the view that we earlier associated with Calabresi. Even though it could have been otherwise, the objection runs, the rules of tort law are best understood as liability rules, not conduct rules.

Our response to this argument begins with a piece of black-letter negligence law. It strongly cuts against the supposition of a sharp divide between written constitutions and statutes (understood to be capable of containing genuine directives) and common law (understood to be a scheme of liability rules).

The tort of negligence, which applies to car accidents, slips-and-falls, and the provision of professional services, is a mainstay of modern tort litigation. To prevail on a claim of negligence, a plaintiff typically must prove that the defendant injured her through conduct that was careless. In turn, whether someone has acted carelessly is usually assessed by reference to what a reasonably prudent person would have done under the circumstance. Thus, to prevail, a negligence plaintiff must establish not only that the defendant injured her, but that he did so by means of conduct that fell below this standard of care.

The question of whether a defendant has or has not acted in the manner of a reasonably prudent person is usually for juries. Yet almost every U.S. jurisdiction also recognizes the doctrine of "negligence per se." According to this doctrine, if a negligence plaintiff proves that the defendant injured her by means of conduct that violated a statutory standard of safe conduct, there is no need for the plaintiff to establish that the defendant fell short of the common-law standard. The statutory violation is deemed to count as legal carelessness in and of itself.[32]

For example, suppose a pedestrian lawfully standing on a city sidewalk is struck and injured by a person riding his bicycle on the sidewalk. Suppose further there is an applicable statute requiring cyclists to walk their bikes when on sidewalks. Under the doctrine of negligence per se, if the pedestrian sues the cyclist, the pedestrian can establish carelessness simply by proving the statutory violation. Jurors hearing the case would be required to deem this cyclist careless, even if, left to decide the question on their own, they would deem the cyclist to have behaved as a reasonably prudent person (for example, by riding slowly on the sidewalk in uncrowded conditions while using a loud whistle to warn the occasional pedestrian of his presence).

Importantly, not every statutory violation will have this significance for a negligence claim. This is because the courts have set certain threshold requirements for the application of the negligence per se doctrine. Suppose, for example, another unfortunate pedestrian is struck by a car that is being driven *carefully*. (Sometimes accidents happen even when everyone is being careful.) It turns out, however, that the careful driver had failed to renew his expired driver's license, in violation of a state statute. Courts typically do not treat the violation of licensure statutes as establishing careless conduct, because licensing statutes are usually best understood as administrative rather than substantive. In other words, only statutes that contain relational directives, and hence that generate duties to take care against injuring and rights against being injured, provide the basis for the application of the negligence per se doctrine.

Finally, to take a third example, suppose a state statute requires homeowners whose properties include an in-ground swimming pool to install fences around their pools. Suppose also that a homeowner fails to install a fence around his pool, and that, because of the absence of the fence, a thirty-year-old man who is in the process of robbing the home falls into the pool and drowns. If the robber's estate were to bring a negligence action against the homeowner, and were to argue that the homeowner's statutory violation establishes the owner's carelessness, a court might well

---

32. Even the few U.S. jurisdictions that do not recognize the doctrine of negligence per se treat violations of an applicable statutory standard as evidence of carelessness.

reject the argument on the ground that the statute was not meant to protect criminal trespassers but instead was meant to protect persons on the property by permission, as well as young children who trespass more or less innocently. Unlike in the preceding car–pedestrian example, a court reasoning in this manner would be acknowledging the existence of a statutory rule of conduct, applicable to the homeowner, that generates relational duties and rights. Yet the court would also be concluding that the putative victim—the robber—was not among the class of persons owed a duty and provided with a right under the statute.

As readers perhaps will have already noticed, the inquiry called for by the negligence per se doctrine closely resembles the implied-right-of-action inquiry conducted by the Supreme Court in the *Rigsby* case. (Indeed, some have argued that *Rigsby* is best understood as an application of the negligence per se doctrine.) In both instances, a court is trying to determine whether there is an applicable rule that generates a duty/right couplet, such that a breach/rights-violation generates a right of action. While negligence per se operates on the borderline between statutes and common law, it strongly attests to the idea that negligence—a judicially created tort—is not simply a collection of liability rules, but instead connects duties and rights to rights of action in the manner we have been describing. Negligence law sets a conduct rule that generates a relational duty (roughly, the duty not to injure another through carelessness) and a right (roughly, the right not to be injured by another's carelessness), and confers a right of action on those whose rights have been violated.

The common law is easy to deride because it may seem like it involves nothing other than the words, concepts, and the social and institutional practices of those who use it. But this is hardly a good reason to think there is no substance to its rules. Words, concepts, and practices constitute so much of our lives that they cannot simply be shunted aside as inherently insubstantial. Rather, one must attend to them carefully to capture their meaning.

As we have noted, the linkage between torts and wrongs is etymological. But it goes well beyond that. Courts conceptualize and describe tortfeasors as "wrongdoers" not only in their description of various actors but also in the crafting of the law itself. Consider the following passage from a mid-twentieth-century judicial decision. It rejects the argument that a defendant should be spared liability just because the plaintiff could not identify how much of its losses were attributable to the defendant's actions, as opposed to another, innocent source:

> . . . when one of the two contributing factors is not the result of an actionable fault . . . the single tortfeasor cannot be allowed to escape through the meshes of a logical net. *He is a wrongdoer; let him unravel the casuistries resulting from his wrong.*[33]

This passage was penned not by a moral philosopher who snuck onto the bench but by Judge Learned Hand—he of the economist's beloved "Hand Formula"—in the course of deciding a humdrum admiralty case.

Beyond judicial rhetoric and lawyerly nomenclature, the language of duties, rights, and wrongs is part of tort doctrine, through and through. "Duty" is of course the anchoring element of the tort of negligence, and the law requires the plaintiff to prove that the defendant breached a duty of care that he or she owed to the plaintiff in order to obtain relief. As already noted, negligence law also requires juries to decide whether the defendant acted as a reasonably prudent person would have acted, and it does so in the context of an understanding that we require people to live up to this standard of conduct. Trespass and nuisance law expressly invoke notions of right, referring to "the right to the exclusive possession" of one's land and "the right to use and enjoy" one's land. Privileges throughout tort law—self-defense in battery and the privilege of fair comment in libel law are two examples—cut back on what otherwise would be duties by noting that sometimes defendants are entitled to conduct themselves in certain ways under certain conditions, even if normally such conduct would be a legal wrong.

Lawyers, too, understand torts as legal wrongs that they and their clients have legal duties to refrain from committing and from which they have legal rights to be free. There are no doubt some "bad-man," "bad-woman," and "bad-company" clients, but there is no reason to suppose *all* clients are "bad" in the Holmesian sense.

Here it is important to recall that the alternative to the "bad" client is not the angelic client, but the client who wants to know what the relevant legal obligations actually are. Previously we imagined an in-house lawyer

---

33. *Navigazione Libera Triestina Societa Anonima v. Newtown Creek Towing Co.*, 98 F.2d 694, 697 (2nd Cir. 1938) (Hand, L.) (emphasis added).

seeking to determine her company's statutory duties. That same lawyer will, of course, want to know the company's common-law duties as well. For example, she will want to be able to tell her client what sorts of credit reports might count as defamatory, what sorts of representations to consumers or third parties would count as fraudulent, and so on. To be sure, clients might not expect their lawyers to invoke the language of "legal duty" or to inform them of such putative duties if there really is no conceivable prospect of legal accountability. And lawyers appreciate from the outset that their clients are bottom-line oriented. But that is a far cry from saying that they only give, and are expected only to give, predictions of sanctions. They are informing clients of the standards of conduct the law has set, whether through legislation, regulation, or judicial decision, and there is no reason to suppose they are always (or even typically) separating out these sources.

The liability-rule view of tort law is inadequate in more formal and visible ways than those discussed so far. The institutions and procedures of tort law make little sense on a view that deems tort law to be a taxation scheme or a pricing mechanism. Defendants (or their insurers) do not simply pay a tax or activity fee after the fact. Liability-rule accounts work hard to patch together stories about why our system would make a special place for the victim as prosecutor of the case and recipient of the relevant activity "tax." In doing so, they flagrantly violate the principle of Occam's Razor.[34] Courts hear tort cases because plaintiffs come to them seeking redress for wrongs committed upon them by tortfeasors. It is not that our system incentivizes complainants to come to court so that risky activities are properly priced, as Judge Posner would have it. They are open to people who demand the state aid them in holding accountable someone who has wronged them. Our point, for the moment, is not that the structure of tort suits *cannot possibly* be explained by exponents of the pure-liability rule view. It is that they have a ridiculous amount of explaining to do. Exponents of the view that tort law is about wrongs, duties, and rights are not the ones who should be on the defensive.

Again we emphasize, as we have throughout this chapter, that our arguments have been made on terms that should be amenable to someone as morally skeptical as Holmes and as committed to legal positivism as Hart. The duties, rights, and wrongs of tort law, on our account, are the duties,

---

34. Jules L. Coleman, *The Structure of Tort Law*, 97 YALE L.J. 1233 (1988); Ernest J. Weinrib, *Understanding Tort Law*, 23 VAL. U. L. REV. 485 (1989).

rights, and wrongs that are entrenched in the *legal* directives that make up this field of law, and they of course vary somewhat across common-law jurisdictions. In nineteenth-century Ohio, for example, it was a tort to seduce another's fiancée; today it is not. In nineteenth-century New York, it was not a tort to play a vicious practical joke on someone so as to traumatize him; today it is. Disclosing intimate details of the personal life of a lawyer to the other lawyers in his 500-member firm is not a tort today in New York, but it very likely is a tort in Colorado and California, and indeed most American jurisdictions. We say these things not as moralists who are moralizing but as lawyers describing the law in these various jurisdictions.

American tort law in any given jurisdiction is found not in a code but primarily in a body of decisions that is expressly self-referential and linked to developed common law in other jurisdictions as well as treatises such as the American Law Institute's Restatements. Notwithstanding the variations mentioned above, judges and lawyers in virtually all jurisdictions know that battering someone is a tort, that negligently injuring someone is a tort, that defrauding someone is a tort, and so on. To know these things is of course to know that persons are subject to liability for such conduct. But this is only part of the story. It is also to know that the law has *rules about* not hitting others, not injuring others through carelessness, not tricking others out of their money, and so on—that courts consider persons who violate these norms to be, in the words of Hand, "tortfeasors" or "wrongdoers," and will treat them accordingly.

There is no denying Holmes's rhetorical flair, but his unsound approach to legal rights and duties has imposed high costs on American law and legal discourse. His understandable disdain for the pedantic moralist unfortunately led him to pose a false dilemma between the pedant and the bad man. Missing from his analysis is the ordinary person, the lawyer who counsels this person, and the judge who understands, applies, and crafts the law imagining that her legal community expects her to take this perspective seriously. These actors see the law, including the law of torts, as containing legal duties, legal rights, and legal wrongs. They understand the law to tell them not to hit others, carelessly injure them, libel them, defraud them, and so on. Never mind whether, as a matter of justice, the legal system should tell them this—it does. Like Holmes, they recognize that such standards may not be the measure of a man's or a woman's moral worth. But what the law lacks in transcendental significance it makes up for in pragmatic relevance.

On this view, which is of course the view we urge our readers to entertain, the law of torts in any given state is comprised in significant part of legal directives like those found in the Eighth Amendment or Vermont's consumer reporting statute. True, these directives are for the most part not written down in one place and were not enacted at a particular moment in time, but are instead to be found explicitly or implicitly in a body of judicial decisions. They are nonetheless legal norms of conduct that impose relational legal duties on persons not to mistreat others and simultaneously confer legal rights on persons against being mistreated.

*   *   *

Our aim in this chapter has not been to produce *the* analytically correct account of rights. Rather, we have aimed to ascertain whether there is *a* cogent way to understand rights that renders meaningful the principle with which we began this book: the principle embedded in the *ubi jus* maxim. We have shown that there is such a theoretical perspective and that it so nicely aligns with Hart's jurisprudence that it is safe for use by those with positivistic proclivities regarding the importance of separating law and morality (as well as those who have anti-positivist instincts). When a plaintiff comes to court demanding that a defendant be held liable to her and asserts a tort claim as the basis for that demand, she is saying that the defendant *legally wronged* her and that, therefore, she is entitled to a remedy.

Even though we take satisfaction in offering an understanding of legal rules, rights, duties, and rights of action that permits a robust rendition of *ubi jus*, we concede that there is a cost to having done so. The question now facing us is *why*—since it is not true by definition—a person whose legal right has been violated is entitled to a remedy. In other words, even one who accepts that we have rendered *ubi jus* cogent can still ask whether it articulates a *defensible* legal or moral principle. We turn to this question in Chapter 4.

4

The Principle of Civil Recourse

A Defense

Tort law exists by virtue of court decisions and statutes that
recognize or enact rules of a distinctive type.[1] These rules identify
actions that are wrongful and injurious, thus generating legal rights against
mistreatment and legal duties not to mistreat. For example, a long line of
decisions addressing claims for battery, taken together, embody a directive
specifying that a person must not intentionally touch another in an offensive or harmful manner. They thereby generate a right not to be so touched
and a duty to refrain from so touching. An intentional offensive or harmful
touching is a legally recognized, injury-inclusive, relational wrong committed by the duty-bearer upon the right-holder.

The substantive rules of tort law and the type of legal wrong they generate are distinct from other types of legal rules and wrongs. As we mentioned in Chapter 1, crimes such as narcotics possession are legal wrongs
that are neither relational nor injury-inclusive. Likewise, imagine a regulation issued by the federal Department of Transportation that requires
truck manufacturers to equip their vehicles with alarms that sound when
the vehicle is shifted into reverse and that specifies fines payable to the

---

1. As previously, we use the word "rule" and its cognates (as well as "directive") to encompass both specific norms of conduct and more open-ended norms, which are sometimes referred to as "standards."

agency for failures to comply. A manufacturer's failure to so equip its trucks is a legal wrong that is neither relational nor injury-inclusive.

In addition to defining rights and wrongs, tort law specifies legal consequences that follow from the commission of a tort. A tortfeasor is subject to liability to her victim(s). Of course, a claim to be a tort victim is not self-validating. The right of action conferred on a tort plaintiff is, in the first instance, a power to initiate a legal proceeding by alleging, with suitable specificity, conduct that, if proven, constitutes a tort. In turn, the defendant is required to accede to or contest these allegations. If there is litigation and the plaintiff prevails under applicable rules, the court will enter judgment, which typically generates for the tortfeasor a legal obligation to pay damages to the victim as redress for the wrong.

Two additional features of tort law merit emphasis here. The first concerns the nature of the linkage of tort law's right/duty pairings and its power/liability pairings. An injury victim's power to obtain redress stems from her being able to demonstrate that her right was violated. By the same token, an injurer's liability arises from her having breached a duty to the other. As we explained in Chapter 3, these connections are *substantive*, not analytic. A legal system that recognizes relational, injurious wrongs but does not confer rights of actions on victims of such wrongs would be deficient, not incoherent.[2]

The second feature also relates to the connection between tort law's substantive and remedial aspects, and it brings us to the topic that will be the focus of this chapter. To observe that a person who has been tortiously injured enjoys a right of action is not only to identify a legal power conferred on her by the law. It is also to identify, implicitly, a second-level right/duty pairing. This pairing is "second-level" because the right and duty in question do not concern how individuals must behave toward one another. At issue instead is the right of each person subject to the authority of a government to have it provide her with a right of action when she is the victim of a violation of a (first-level) right/duty pairing. This second-level right/duty couplet is embodied in the *principle of civil recourse*. According to this principle, certain persons—including those whose legally recognized rights against injury have been violated by a

---

2. John C. P. Goldberg & Benjamin C. Zipursky, *Hohfeldian Analysis and the Separation of Rights and Powers*, in The Legacy of Wesley Hohfeld: Edited Major Works, Select Personal Papers, and Original Commentaries (Shyam Balganesh, Ted Sichelman & Henry E. Smith eds., forthcoming).

breach of a corresponding legal duty of noninjury—are *entitled* to have the state provide them with civil recourse against wrongdoers.[3]

The principle of civil recourse is part of our positive law. It also has a counterpart in political morality. In granting to the victims of injurious legal wrongs a right of action—i.e., a legal power to sue the wrongdoer civilly and to obtain a suitable remedy upon proof of claim—government complies with the political principle of civil recourse. This chapter offers an explication of this principle and, with it, a defense of its adoption in our law.

Before proceeding with that defense, we begin with some remarks on our approach to justification, along with an outline of our somewhat complex argument. First, while we accept that descriptive and normative claims differ, we caution against drawing too sharp a distinction between them. If our descriptive (or interpretive) analysis of tort law is sound, then we will already have defended it against certain criticisms (for example, that it is a hodgepodge, or a feeble effort at safety regulation or insurance) and hence will have begun to justify it. We will have also given legal actors, particularly judges—who are bound by role-based obligations to apply the law—reasons to adjudicate tort cases in a particular way. And even though legislatures have greater authority to reform the law, we will have established that there are better and worse ways to go about reform.

Second, and relatedly, to grant that tort law and the legal principle it embodies, like any facet of our legal system, is open to normative assessment, is not to suppose that it must be justified *de novo*. Consider in this regard the principle of free speech (whatever its exact contours might be). Free speech is a principle of our positive law. Yet an observer of our system would fail to appreciate its significance if she were to understand it as a bit of enacted law that we could just as easily take or leave. It is a pillar of our liberal democracy. The point is not that observance of the principle of civil recourse is as important to the maintenance of a just system of government as is observance of the free speech principle. It is that the principle of civil recourse has a comparable status: it figures both in our positive law and in our positive political morality and, as such, has a claim to prima facie legitimacy.

---

3. We say "including" because, as we explain below, the principle of civil recourse calls for the state to provide rights of action to persons other than those seeking redress for injurious wrongs.

As we observed in Chapter 1, the Declaration of Independence, *Marbury v. Madison*, the Fourteenth Amendment to the U.S. Constitution, and the Civil Rights Acts of 1866, 1871, and 1964 all attest to the centrality of the principle to our political self-understanding, as do the "open courts," "right to remedy," and "due process" provisions contained in many state constitutions. Moreover, tort law itself (along with contract law and other branches of private law) is a particularly salient, visible, and deeply rooted embodiment of the principle of civil recourse. Developed in a largely self-conscious fashion over centuries through innumerable court proceedings, as well as through acts of legislation, it has also been subjected to extensive analysis, critique, and reform. In general, it has tracked and continues to track prevailing norms—norms that adults routinely seek to instill in their children, and that govern how we relate to one another in our day-to-day interactions. While there are also long-standing criticisms of the tort system, our sense is that there are few who find something problematic in the general idea that law should, among other things, prohibit basic forms of mistreatment and enable victims to hold accountable (in some way) those who have mistreated them. One does not have to be a Burkean to suppose that rules and institutions that have been self-consciously maintained and revised for centuries, and that track social norms, contain a certain amount of wisdom, generate a certain amount of justified reliance, and carry an initial claim to validity. In turn, this suggests that the principle undergirding them carries a certain plausibility.

Third—and again in keeping with the foregoing remarks—our mode of normative argument belongs to the anti-foundationalist tradition associated with pragmatists such as Quine and Sellars in epistemology, and Rawls, Rorty, and Walzer in political philosophy. We reject the idea that justification, in a context such as this one, involves reasoning from self-evident or intrinsically justified premises to robust substantive conclusions. Rather, we will be content to show that the principle of civil recourse meshes well with values and commitments that have long been regarded as central to our liberal-democratic polity, yet have also been subjected to, and revised in light of, serious critical reflection. In the manner of innumerable political theorists over the past fifty years, we believe it illuminating to articulate a justification for certain features of our political and legal order by arguing that its acceptability and legitimacy depend on its having these features.

Fourth, the point of this chapter and of this part of the book, is to establish the nature and justifiability of rules and corresponding institutions that connect the commission of a certain kind of wrong—an injury-inclusive, relational legal wrong—to a certain kind of power—the power of the victim of such a wrong to commence a civil action against the wrongdoer, and (if she prevails) to obtain court-ordered redress. At this juncture we are not immediately concerned to provide—and for the argument to proceed, need not be concerned to provide—an account of the particular wrongs that a legal system does or ought to recognize. We will have more to say about that topic in Part Two.

Finally, the outline. We start by reprising some of the opening moves in John Locke's *Second Treatise of Government.* Locke, it turns out, was quite well attuned to the significance of civil recourse for a (small-'l') liberal form of government. However, the next section does an about-face, acknowledging that his social-contract approach is not promising if given either a natural rights or an instrumentalist cast. To avoid this dead end, we suggest, following the likes of Rawls and Scanlon, that Lockean insights are better captured from within a reasons-based, contractarian framework.[4] In sum, our defense of the principle of civil recourse turns on an assessment of what members of a liberal-democratic polity can reasonably demand of their government as a condition of recognizing its authority.

The contractarian argument for the principle of civil recourse proceeds in two stages. First we explain why rights to sue that reflect our legal system's recognition of the *ubi jus* maxim correspond to a political right to private rights of action against others. Second, we explain why, specifically, the latter right plausibly encompasses a right to law that enables victims of injurious wrongs to obtain redress by holding wrongdoers accountable.

At the core of the first-stage argument is an analogy to voting rights. In certain instantiations, the right to invoke the legal system to sue others is closely akin to the right to participate in the selection of officials and the formation of policies. Both rights consist of the conferral on individuals of legal powers that, in a liberal democracy, they are entitled to have provided

---

4. John Oberdiek has outlined a contractarian approach to normative tort theory. *See* John Oberdiek, *Structure and Justification in Contractualist Tort Theory,* in PHILOSOPHICAL FOUNDATIONS OF THE LAW OF TORTS 103 (John Oberdiek ed., 2014).

to them. Thus, both are powers that members of such a polity can reasonably demand as a condition of recognizing government's authority to exercise coercive force. To clarify why it would be unjust for a liberal-democratic government to leave individuals without rights of action, we offer examples in which a person enjoys a legal right to the performance of some action by another, yet lacks any means of enforcing that right. Values of equality, fairness, and independence all require that the government not leave individuals in this vulnerable position, and hence justify the provision of a law of civil recourse.

We then turn to the second stage and to the particular form of recourse that consists of redress for injury-inclusive, relational legal wrongs. Though in some ways distinct from recourse that involves judicial enforcement of legal duties of performance, the power to obtain civil redress for such wrongs is also required as a condition of just liberal-democratic governance. Equality and fairness, it turns out, are no less relevant to redress than to other forms of civil recourse. Moreover, as Locke long ago recognized, a distinct value—that of individual sovereignty—further underwrites the right to redress wrongs through legal proceedings.

Locke on Civil Recourse

The beginnings of an argument for the principle of civil recourse, particularly as it applies to wrongfully inflicted injuries and claims arising from them, can be found in the work of seventeenth- and eighteenth-century English political theorists including Hobbes, Locke, and Blackstone. We will focus on Locke, both because the *Second Treatise* offers an elegant statement of the view and because Locke was a significant influence on the Framers of our constitutional order.[5] Just as it is no mere coincidence that Jefferson modeled the Declaration of Independence on a tort complaint, it is no coincidence that a political and legal regime shaped in part by Locke's writings is one in which the principle of civil recourse figures prominently.

Locke aimed to provide a justification for governmental authority suitable to a society that lacks a notion of natural rank or status. He did so, of course, by describing a pre-political state of nature—a condition in which

---

5. 3 THE RECEPTION OF LOCKE'S POLITICS: FROM THE 1690S TO THE 1830S (Mark Goldie ed., 1999).

humans relate to one another as creatures of the "same species and rank."[6] In this condition, none can claim that her desires, interests, and prospects inherently deserve greater consideration than those of another. From these egalitarian premises arises a scheme of duties and rights. Each of us is bound "*to preserve himself*, and not to quit his Station willfully," and is also bound to preserve "*the rest of Mankind*." Correlative to these duties are two natural rights: the right of self-preservation and the right to preserve mankind.[7]

The right to preserve mankind confers on each person a privilege to act so as to "preserve the innocent and restrain offenders." Wrongdoing often consists of threats to life and liberty, or to the rightful possession of things needed for self-preservation. Any wrong committed against a particular person is also a flouting of the rules, and hence a "trespass against the whole Species." In the state of nature, therefore, each person, by virtue of the right to preserve mankind, is entitled to punish any other person's wrongdoing, though only in proportion to the wrong, and only in the service of preventing future wrong.[8]

The right of self-preservation, meanwhile, entitles individuals to take certain self-protective measures. If another person sets upon me in an effort take my horse and coat, Locke explains, I am entitled to resist.[9] The same is true of someone who attempts to take away my liberty. All such persons have, in effect, declared war against me. Absent a special justification (such as the need to protect oneself or third parties from my wrongdoing), it is not permitted for another to cause or threaten me with death or serious harm.

According to Locke, the right of self-preservation not only authorizes actions that aim to ward off certain wrongfully inflicted injuries. It further authorizes certain responses to completed wrongs. A victim of an assault or a theft is naturally entitled to obtain "reparation" from the wrongdoer, understood as "satisfaction for the harm he has suffered."[10]

---

6. JOHN LOCKE, *The Second Treatise of Government*, in TWO TREATISES OF GOVERNMENT 265, 269 (Peter Laslett ed., 1998) (1690).

7. *Id.* at 271. Insofar as we are describing and interpreting Locke's own claims, we will follow his use of "man" and "mankind."

8. *Id.* at 271–72.

9. Indeed, he suggests that I may resist with deadly force because it is reasonable to believe that one who sets upon me to steal property then in my possession is one who is prepared to take my life. *Id.* at 280.

10. *Id.* at 273.

Indeed, Locke goes so far as to say that a victim may (in the state of nature) respond to attacks or thefts by appropriating "the goods and services" of the wrongdoer.[11]

Crucially, Locke draws a distinction between reparation and punishment. Punishment is a manifestation of the right to preserve mankind. Thus, anyone may administer it upon any offender, so long as he does so on appropriate terms and for the right reasons. The point of punishment is to promote public safety by inflicting harm on offenders so as to deter future offenses. By contrast, a victim's claim to reparations is a claim by him, for him. Obtaining reparations from a wrongdoer is thus, on Locke's view, continuous with acting in self-defense.[12] Both are instances of what he termed "self-preservation."

According to Locke, the state is formed, and the state of nature left behind, when individuals reasonably delegate to officials many of the prerogatives associated with the two natural rights. But the state's legitimacy is, of course, conditional on its credibly undertaking to improve on the state of nature. Government's basic charge is thus threefold. First, it must set rules that clarify what counts as wrongdoing and must install officials who will apply these rules impartially. Second, it must enforce these rules by punishing rule violators. Third, it must ensure that victims of mistreatment can obtain satisfaction from those who have mistreated them. A state that fails to do these things—especially a state that takes the powers granted to it and uses them to inflict on individuals the very sorts of wrongs from which they sought to escape through the establishment of the state— is illegitimate.

While the social contract involves a transfer from individuals to government of prerogatives enjoyed (as liberties) under each of the two natural rights, certain differences between them, noted above, carry over in the transition from the state of nature to civil society. Each person delegates *entirely* (or almost entirely) his right to preserve mankind. So long as it is operating legitimately, government determines what counts as a wrong, who shall be punished, and on what terms. For this reason it is open to an appropriate government official to pardon a wrongdoer if, for example, there is reason to think the punishment will not accomplish anything.

11. *Id.* at 274.
12. Though, according to Locke, the right to preserve mankind entitles persons other than the victim of a wrong to assist the victim in obtaining reparations from the wrongdoer.

An individual's delegation of the right of self-preservation is more qualified. The individual cedes to the state the job of determining what counts as a wrongfully inflicted injury. Moreover, where the state has set up processes that enable a victim to obtain satisfaction from a wrongdoer, the individual further generally cedes the right to pursue reparations via self-help. Even then, an important aspect of the individual's right to reparations remains. For whereas the state alone has discretion to decide when and how to punish, the discretion to press a claim for reparations remains with the victim.

> ... [T]he Magistrate, who by being Magistrate, hath the common right of punishing put into his hands, can often, where the publick good demands not the execution of the Law, *remit* the punishment of Criminal Offenses by his own Authority, but yet cannot *remit* the satisfaction due to any private Man, for the damage he has received. That, he who has suffered the damage has a Right to demand in his own name, and he alone can *remit*: The damnified Person has this Power of appropriating to himself, the Goods or Services of the Offender, by *Right of Self-Preservation*, as every man has a Power to punish the Crime, to prevent its being committed again, by the *Right he has of Preserving all Mankind* . . . .[13]

A legitimate state can decide for itself how to wield the power that derives from each individual's right to preserve mankind. But only the wrongfully injured individual has the authority to decide whether to press her claim to reparations. In this respect, too, the right to reparations is continuous with the right of self-defense. After the establishment of the polity, each individual retains her privilege to use defensive force against another in certain circumstances. She likewise retains her power to obtain and demand satisfaction from a wrongdoer, whether by state-established processes or self-help.

As noted, Locke was by no means an outlier among English liberal political theorists in identifying a fundamental continuity between an individual's right to defend himself against mistreatment and his right to obtain, upon demand, satisfaction from a person who mistreats him. The same thought, expressed in different ways, can be found in Hobbes before

13. *Id.* at 273–74.

him and Blackstone after him.[14] All supposed that a liberal state is, among other things, one that leaves it to individuals to take certain *self-preservative* measures in relation to mistreatments at the hands of others.

Updating Lockean Theory: False Starts

Arguments such as Locke's are sometimes cast as efforts to justify governmental institutions and authority on the consent of the governed. However—as Rawls and others have demonstrated—social contract arguments are better understood as thought-experiments that help to isolate the terms on which a coercive political order must operate in order to warrant members of that order in accepting (at a general level) its authority. Our claim is that, for individuals in a liberal-democratic political state such as ours, the justifiability of the state's claim to authority depends, in part, on its recognition and implementation of the principle of civil recourse. The point is not to show that the principle of civil recourse is true. It is to show that its embrace by our courts and political community is eminently justifiable.

It will help isolate our approach by contrasting it with two related approaches that can claim roots in Lockean theory, both of which face serious problems. The first of these amplifies certain individualistic aspects of Locke's account. Specifically, it adds the provocative claim that individuals in the state of nature have a natural right to *retaliate with the use of force* upon the person or possessions of those who mistreat them. Because the political entity created by the social contract justifiably outlaws these unilateral acts of aggression, and because there is a pre-political natural right to engage in them, it follows (on this view) that the state incurs an obligation to provide a replacement. Rights of action would thus be justified as providing a substitute for the right of victims to avenge, forcibly, wrongs done to them.[15]

---

14. John C. P. Goldberg, *The Constitutional Status of Tort Law: Due Process and the Right to a Law for the Redress of Wrongs*, 115 YALE L.J. 524, 541 n. 79 (2005) (Hobbes); *id.* at 545–59 (Blackstone).

15. Some of our earlier writings in tort theory have—perhaps understandably, but mistakenly—been construed as adopting this position. *See, e.g.,* John Finnis, *Natural Law: The Classical Tradition*, in THE OXFORD HANDBOOK OF JURISPRUDENCE AND PHILOSOPHY OF LAW 1, 56–58 (Jules Coleman & Scott Shapiro eds., 2002); Emily Sherwin, *Interpreting Tort Law*, 39 FLA. ST. L. REV. 227, 231–36 (2011).

The main difficulty with the natural rights rendition of social contract theory resides in an equivocation about the putative natural right to retaliate. If the "right" is a raw liberty—if it marks off things that no one is duty-bound to refrain from doing yet also not something that others are duty-bound to permit one to do—then claims as to its existence in the state of nature gain plausibility only at the cost of failing to support the conclusion they are said to support. A raw liberty to inflict harm on others is not the sort of thing for which the state, once formed, is obligated to provide a substitute.

The natural rights rendition of Locke's argument would be more persuasive if it posits a claim-right to retaliate, rather than a mere liberty. The provision of an avenue of civil recourse would then be something like a *quid pro quo* for the right's elimination once the state is formed and issues a ban on most forms of self-help. However, this more robust natural right claim is indefensible if put in terms of a moral privilege to inflict harm intentionally upon another whenever the other invades one's moral rights against being wrongfully injured. Even if, in the state of nature, a person is not obligated to turn the other cheek, it hardly follows that it is morally permissible (always, or even typically) for her to respond forcibly. Here it helps to keep in mind that, in morality no less than law, many wrongfully inflicted injuries are unintentional, and some are even generated by persons acting in good faith—hardly the stuff of justified retaliatory use of force (even assuming that there is such a thing as justified retaliatory use of force).

An instrumentalist recasting of Locke's ideas fares no better. It is not crazy to suppose (though also not obviously true) that society will be more peaceful and productive if individuals who are blocked by the state from avenging wrongs are permitted to sue wrongdoers. From this perspective, whether tort law gives expression to an actual natural right is irrelevant. It is justified because of a proneness among human beings to harbor and act on vengeful dispositions. Hence the value of having a legal safety valve that spares us from a world of Hatfields and McCoys.

The problem with this keep-the-peace justification is that it establishes, at most, that society stands to benefit from the provision to individuals of an avenue for redress, not that individuals have an *entitlement* to that avenue. Moreover, it leaves open many questions about whether various alternatives would be better at achieving peace and harmony, just as it overlooks the possibility that litigation fosters conflict rather than quelling it.[16]

Unlike instrumentalist defenders of private rights of action, we do not suppose that injury victims so consistently harbor strong and lasting vindictive dispositions that a government must provide them with rights of action in order to maintain civil peace. And unlike certain natural rights theorists, we do not posit a pre-political moral right of forcible retaliation, such that the state owes each of us a substitute when it blocks the exercise of that right. This is not to say that all considerations of political legitimacy are post-political. Locke was correct that a political order might or might not have a justifiable claim to authority, and that the standards for assessing such a claim need not implicate instrumentalism or vicious circularity. But it is a mistake to think that only a natural rights foundation can supply such standards. Theorizing about political authority in terms of fair and reasonable terms of cooperation is an option too—one that becomes especially attractive when a coherentist (or reflective equilibrium) approach to justification is recognized as philosophically cogent. To the extent that such a framework leads readers to associate us with Rawls and Scanlon, we would consider ourselves in good company, but nothing in the account hinges on the acceptance of their particular accounts of justice or morality.

Civil Redress as a Kind of Civil Recourse

Before getting further into our Locke-inspired contractarian argument, it will be useful to emphasize a distinction between the terms "recourse" and "redress," as we use them.

Rights of redress are a (proper) subset of rights of recourse. In a world in which governments claim, within their sphere of authority, a monopoly on the legitimate use of coercive force, an individual's lack of authority to use force against others creates problems in a wide range of scenarios.

---

16. There is much more to be said about interpretive private law accounts that emphasize the importance of fostering cooperation by limiting retaliation, as Nate Oman has shown in his highly original and illuminating monograph placing a version of civil recourse theory at the foundations of contract law. *See* NATHAN B. OMAN. THE DIGNITY OF COMMERCE: MARKETS AND THE MORAL FOUNDATIONS OF CONTRACT LAW (2016). Because our object of study is tort law, and because we do not believe retaliation-limitation is central to the conceptual core of tort law, we leave commentary on Oman to other occasions.

Only some of these involve a person who has been wrongfully injured by another. Others involve disappointed promisees or dispossessed property owners. Still others involve victims of breaches of trust, or those who face a not-yet-concrete prospect of being wronged in the future.

In each of these cases, a person is left with insufficient control over something she is entitled to have some control over, and in each the state thus provides an avenue of civil recourse by providing a private right of action. Just as tort law provides recourse in the form of redress for victims of certain wrongs, other bodies of law provide other forms of recourse for scenarios such as those just described. Contract law confers rights of action that often enable disappointed promisees to enforce promised performances, or to obtain their equivalents.[17] Via the law of restitution, owners can sue to secure the return of tangible property or intangible assets. Suits for breach of fiduciary duty can result in the disgorgement of wrongfully held gains. And so forth.

The right to be provided by the state with an avenue of civil recourse in all of these different situations arises from the unacceptability of leaving a person powerless, in various contexts, where the possibility of providing such a power exists. It is *civil* recourse because the state's dispute-resolution mechanisms supplant the ability an individual might or might not possess to engage in self-help. In a complex modern society—as opposed to a tight-knit, clan-based society, where informal modes of response may suffice to empower individuals to work through these predicaments—courts, lawyers, and the law provide the means through which individuals can vindicate their rights.

Because "civil recourse" rather than "civil redress" was the phrase we chose two decades ago to characterize rights of action in tort, and the language has more or less stuck, we will not depart from it now. We recognize here, however, that there is both a narrow sense of the phrase, which refers specifically to the right to redress legal wrongs of the sort instantiated in tort law, and a broad sense, which refers to a right to respond to or act against others civilly, through the exercise of a private right of action, in light of some predicament or problem one faces because of something another has done or failed to do. At times in this book, as in most of our prior work, we

17. For treatments of contract law as instantiating a notion of civil recourse, see Andrew Gold, *The Taxonomy of Civil Recourse Theory*, 39 FLA. ST. L. REV. 65 (2011); Nathan B. Oman, *Consent to Retaliation: A Civil Recourse Theory of Contractual Liability*, 96 IOWA L. REV. 529 (2011).

use the phrase in its narrower sense to refer specifically to civil redress. In this chapter, however, we will typically be invoking the broader notion.

To avoid confusion, it is also important to emphasize that a private right of action against another person is *not* itself a right to civil recourse or redress. It is a legal power. Whether in the narrower or the broader sense, the "right to civil recourse" refers to a particular kind of triangular right—a right, good against the state, to the provision of a mechanism that allows one person to proceed against another, and in this respect a right to be empowered by the state against another, correlative to a duty owed by the state.

Furthermore, as noted in Chapter 2, governments sometimes provide individuals with private rights of action for reasons other than the observance of the principle of civil recourse (even in its broad version). Some rights of action—such as those found in *qui tam* statutes—are conferred on individuals to aid the government's enforcement of other legal duties (such as the duty of a government contractor to refrain from defrauding the government). In other instances, as in federal antitrust or antiracketeering statutes, private rights of action are supplied to individuals both in recognition of a right to redress and to enhance deterrence, enforcement, and accountability for public-oriented reasons.

Finally, we of course accept that the obligation imposed on government by the principle of civil recourse does not deprive it of the authority to set various conditions and limitations on the ability of individuals to pursue and obtain recourse, in part out of the need to ensure that those who are alleged to have committed wrongs have a fair opportunity to defend against such allegations. Jurisdictional requirements, limitations periods, evidentiary rules, and substantive privileges all may be vulnerable to criticism in their particulars. But there is nothing in the principle of civil recourse that prohibits lawmakers from setting reasonable conditions and limitations on the exercise of rights of action. Scholars including Alan Calnan have thus been right to insist that theoretical accounts of tort law must leave room for a great deal of doctrine pertaining to a defendant's entitlement to be free of liability absent proof that he or she committed a legal rights violation.[18] However, this observation counts in favor of civil recourse theory, not against it, because our account permits a theoretical explanation of various limitations on plaintiffs' rights of action.

18. Alan Calnan, The Right to Civil Defense in Torts (2013).

Rights of Action and the Right to Vote

Our core normative claim is this: Law that instantiates the principle of civil recourse belongs as part of the basic structure of a just society organized on liberal-democratic principles. In this respect, a right of action—a right to sue another person civilly to vindicate one's legal right—is like the right to vote. This analogy, which we will now explore, is only an analogy. There plainly are important differences between the two. Some would argue, for example, that the right to vote is inalienable, whereas the right to a law of civil recourse is not. But the basic point stands. The principle of civil recourse sounds in liberal-democratic notions of equality, fairness, and individual independence and sovereignty.

We begin with a point of commonality between rights of action and the right to vote. Only persons of a certain age can vote. The same is true for the filing of civil actions. "Infants," to use the legal term, are not entitled to sue in their own name. Instead, suit must be brought on their behalf by a parent or guardian.

There is an abundance of reasons for this rule. Among them is the recognition that suing, like voting, is the exercise of a power conferred by our political system. Because it is the exercise of such a power, it— like the right to vote—is conferred only on persons who have reached an age that corresponds (roughly) to the attainment of a threshold of maturity. This is true even though an individual's rights against mistreatment are not age-sensitive. One who batters or falsely imprisons a child, or negligently runs her down, breaches a legal duty owed to the child to refrain from so injuring her, and violates the child's legal right against being so injured. Indeed, it is valuable to distinguish primary rights from enforcement powers precisely because the universe of those not to be mistreated is larger than the universe of those entitled to redress for the mistreatment.

As its name suggests, and as its historical instantiations in various "civil rights" laws indicates (see Chapter 1), the principle of civil recourse concerns a particular set of civil rights. So does voting. However, assertions regarding civil rights contain several levels of meaning, so we must proceed with care.

Consider the following assertion: "Jamie Jones, an adult U.S. citizen and resident of the borough of Manhattan, in the City of New York, in New York State, has a right to vote in federal, state, and local elections."

Among the meanings one might attribute to this statement, three are particularly salient. First, it can be construed as a statement of positive law asserting that Jones's attributes are such that she is actually eligible to cast a ballot in certain elections: that when she shows up at the relevant polling station, she will be able to cast a vote. Second, it could be a different kind of assertion of positive law, one that states that Jones's attributes render her eligible to vote, under the law, even if she does not in fact enjoy that power. A person who is prevented from voting only because of her failure to pay an unconstitutional poll tax has a legal right to vote in this second sense: her being denied the opportunity to do so is illegal. Third, the proposition could be understood to assert that Jones, given her attributes, has a right as a matter of political morality to have the state supply her with a legal power to vote regardless of whether the positive law imposes on government a legal duty to supply her with that power.

When advocates speak of the right to vote as a civil right, they usually are speaking of it in its third, political sense. For example, when suffragettes insisted on the right of women to vote, they were not making false statements about positive law. They were making a normative claim about the duty of government to enfranchise citizens regardless of gender as part of a critique of an oppressive caste system. Their complaint was partly about the lack of evenhandedness in the treatment of men and women, but it was also founded on a claim of individual right—that, in a democracy, each competent, adult citizen is entitled to participate in the selection of officials and in certain other political decisions. This goes hand in hand with, but is not identical to, the idea that all individuals should have the same basic political power.

Much like an assertion of the right to vote, a claim that a person has a right to sue civilly has several variants.[19] To speak of a right to sue might

19. It might appear that we are confusing the question of capacity to sue with the question of whether there is a right of action at all—the latter being a matter of substantive law. We are not. Rather, we are deliberately utilizing what are most easily identified as capacity questions as an abbreviated way of talking about a range of rights to bring—and, upon marshalling of the necessary proof, prevail on—a claim that culminates in a judgment and liability. One might, in the same way, discuss specific issues like voter registration rules and gerrymandering as concrete ways of discussing the right to vote. There is now a voluminous scholarly literature on how various voting methods and procedures constitute better or worse instantiations of the abstract idea of the right to vote. While there is surely great value in scholars assessing, empirically and analytically, the differing effects of adopting alternative voting regimes, it hardly follows that the concept of a right to vote dissolves into a purely instrumental question about which voting mechanisms (if any) will produce the most desirable policy outcomes.

be to speak of a power that a person actually enjoys under the law to press a lawsuit and (if she prevails on the claim) to demand certain responsive conduct from the person(s) against whom suit has been brought. Alternatively, to say someone has a right to sue might be to say that the state is under a positive-law duty to provide a legal power to sue, whether it actually has or not in fact provided such a legal power. When, for example, plaintiffs claim that legislative limits on the ability to pursue tort claims, or to obtain certain remedies, violate a right guaranteed to them under state constitutional "open courts" or "due process" provisions, they are invoking this second sense of a right to sue. Finally, to assert there is a right to sue could also be to assert that, as a matter of political morality, the state has a duty to provide the person with a right to sue.

Normative claims about the (political) right to sue are in crucial respects like normative claims about the (political) right to vote. Equal treatment of citizens requires recognition of this right in all persons of sufficient maturity, but there is more to the right than a demand for equal treatment. Just as members of a liberal democracy have a political right to have input on governance (or a right to a fair chance to form governing majorities), so too they have a political right to use the power of the legal system to respond to certain setbacks or quandaries generated by others. Part of what makes it reasonable to accept being subjected to laws and state control—and thus to be barred from doing many things one might wish to do, as well as from responding in certain ways to problems that one faces—is the enjoyment of a right to participate, on fair terms, in decisions about who governs and what policies will be pursued. This is a fundamental tenet of a democratic theory. Another part of what makes it reasonable to accept governmental authority is being granted a certain degree of power to respond to problems generated by others.[20] This is a

---

20. It is important to recall (as discussed above) that there are two sides to the provision of rights of action as a way of complying with the principle of civil recourse. Rights of action are legal powers correlative to legal liabilities. Although the provision of rights of action may itself constitute compliance with the principle of civil recourse, the creation of a range of liabilities to the power of private parties itself creates new hazards and quandaries. In short, there is a reciprocity constraint on the form and content of powers to sue that must be satisfied if the provision of such powers is to satisfy the principle of civil recourse in a manner that is plausibly justifiable. As we have argued extensively in the past (and will discuss in Parts Two and Three of this book), rules and institutions that affect the exercise of rights of action—including procedural, evidentiary, and remedial law, substantive defenses, principles of equity, and the jury system—have been crafted in part to accommodate concerns such as these. To acknowledge these, and the constraints they embody, is not to hedge on the importance of the right to

fundamental tenet of liberal democracy qua *liberal* democracy. The font of the legitimacy of a state's exercise of coercive power lies in the reasonable conditioning of acceptance of its authority upon its compliance with conditions of equality, fairness, and respect for the individual.

The right to vote is rooted in a principle holding that a person is entitled to have input on and control over those who exercise political power. Rights of action are similarly grounded in the principle of civil recourse. We say this not to invite upon ourselves the burden of explaining why members of a democracy are entitled to have a certain kind of say in politics. To the contrary, the right to vote is an entitlement that we think few are or should be prepared to abandon. There is mutual supportiveness between the existence of a (political) right to vote and a principle of democratic political control. The right to vote might be epistemically more basic, but the right to some form of contribution to the political authority of one's community is normatively more fundamental.[21]

In the same manner, the (political) principle of civil recourse lies behind the existence of a legal right to pursue certain forms of civil litigation against others. We recognize a right to use courts to empower a person against others in various ways. Even if one were not to take "where there's a right, there's a remedy" as a starting point, one would still recognize in our system a range of rights to bring claims as a matter of positive law, and, indeed, a range of constitutional duties of states to provide this power to individuals. The principle of civil recourse, at root, is a normative principle about the entitlement to a certain kind of power within a political and legal system that is, in innumerable ways, duty-imposing and liberty-restricting.

It will bolster our analogy to shift from theory to civics. In particular, it will help briefly to recall how the Amendments to the U.S. Constitution adopted in the aftermath of the Civil War went about the task of

---

recourse, any more than one would be hedging on the importance of the right to vote by noting that it must be constrained in various ways—for example, it must be distributed in accordance with a one-person, one-vote principle—if it is to serve as part of a just scheme of liberal-democratic government.

21. In other words, while the claim that there is a right to vote might function as the sort of concrete proposition that forms one side of the oscillation between the particular and the general within a process of reflective equilibrium, that process is likely to reveal that a right to contribute to the political authority of one's community is a deeper, more general principle undergirding the right to vote.

abolishing slavery. The Thirteenth Amendment, of course, directly eliminates enslavement as a possible legal relation: no person within the United States can have legal ownership of another person. Section 1 of the Fourteenth Amendment further bars the states from abridging the privileges and immunities of any U.S. citizen, from depriving them of life, liberty, or property without due process of law, and from denying them the equal protection of the laws. Whatever the full meaning of these provisions, there is little doubt that some or all of the phrases "privileges and immunities," "due process," and "equal protection" were intended to convert what had been a political-but-not-legal obligation of the states to make basic forms of law available to all citizens— including the law of civil recourse—into a legal obligation.[22] Finally, of course, the Fifteenth Amendment guaranteed that a citizen's right to vote shall not be denied or abridged on the basis of race, color, or prior servitude.[23]

As even this cursory reference to a crucial and complex moment in American history demonstrates, we have been, if anything, somewhat restrained in suggesting that there is an analogy between the right to vote and the right to recourse. As a matter of our positive constitutional law and of the political theory underwriting it, the idea of being a full-fledged member of a liberal-democratic polity clearly has long been bound up with the enjoyment of these two basic legal powers. A free person—the opposite of a slave—is, among other things, one who is not left vulnerable

22. Goldberg, *supra* note 14, at 564–68; Robert J. Kaczorowski, *Revolutionary Constitutionalism in the Era of the Civil War and Reconstruction*, 61 N.Y.U. L. REV. 863, 922–24 (1986).

23. As noted above, suffragettes and others rightly argued—before, at, and after the time of the Amendment's enactment—that the denial to adult women of a comparable guarantee violated a political right basic to liberal-democratic forms of government. JILL LEPORE, THESE TRUTHS: A HISTORY OF THE UNITED STATES 321–22 (2019).

There is another interesting parallel between the Fourteenth and Fifteenth Amendments' rights guarantees. As noted in the Introduction, on contemporary understandings the former does not require states to maintain a system of tort law (or contract or property law). Rather, it prohibits them from denying members of certain groups access to such law when such law is made available to others. Likewise, the latter does not affirmatively guarantee a right to vote, but instead prohibits that right from being provided on discriminatory terms. (The same is true of the Twentieth Amendment's guarantee of the vote to women.) As was also noted in the Introduction, both Amendments were adopted on the assumption that states would continue to provide the type of law at issue (tort law, voting law) to at least some of their citizens, in large part because states were understood at the time to be under a political obligation to do so.

to the exercise of power by a government over which she has no say. She is equally one who is not left powerless to respond to violations of rights granted to her by law.

Enforcement Rights

It is unacceptable for a liberal-democratic state to purport to monopolize the legitimate use of force and to impose an array of duties and limitations on individuals, without providing them with an avenue of civil recourse against others, at least in certain scenarios. To flesh out this point, we will offer examples of two such scenarios, each of which involves a person who is left powerless to secure from another a performance to which she is legally entitled.

Suppose Wilma White promises to build a table for Bella Blue and to deliver it to her, and in return Bella Blue promises to pay Wilma $1,000. Wilma builds and delivers the table, which Bella now possesses. Bella, however, does not keep her promise to pay for it. Wilma is unable to force Bella to return the table, and even if she could force its return, Wilma would still have a disappointed legitimate expectation of receiving the benefit of their bargain. Meanwhile, governmental officials with the power to hold Bella to her promise decline to get involved. Finally, imagine that Wilma has no right to sue, because the legal system does not allow women to sue. Wilma now faces a quandary. Unless Wilma happens to know someone with power or influence over Bella who would agree to act on her behalf, there is nothing she can do.

Alternatively, suppose that Gina Green loans her horse to Bella Blue with the understanding that it will be returned. In the past Gina has borrowed things from Bella and returned them, and Bella has borrowed things from Gina and returned them. This time, however, Bella—who has been ill—has kept the horse beyond the time at which it should have been returned. Gina is without something that she owns and wants back. However, Bella's family members have made clear that they will not allow Gina to retrieve the horse herself. If we again imagine that the relevant officials are indifferent and that Gina has no right to sue and no connections to persons with sway over Bella, then she (Gina) is in a predicament comparable to Wilma's.

Both Wilma and Gina are stuck—powerless to respond to the situations they face. As to each, it would be accurate to say she has no recourse.

Each depends on Bella acting a certain way, and Bella is not prepared to undertake those actions. Both examples have a financial aspect, but that is not their most important aspect. Or one could change the examples to make this aspect less important. (Instead of Bella failing to fulfill a promise to pay for a table, imagine that she does not deliver on a promise to provide Wilma with needed medicine. Alternatively, imagine a case in which Bella borrowed, then failed to return, Gina's sentimentally valuable annotated Bible.)

Our actual legal system deals with these types of problems by providing Wilma and Gina with the right to sue. Wilma can sue Bella for the $1,000 she is owed, and Gina can sue Bella for the return of her horse. Wilma and Gina are not left powerless because each is provided by law with an avenue of civil recourse. We have gone so far as to suggest that the state's provision to Wilma and Gina of this avenue is an entitlement comparable to their entitlement to vote. Despite being "low stakes" in a sense, these examples help us to understand the force of that analogy.

Several considerations support our account: equality, fairness, and independence will be central, but in the backdrop are ideas about liberty and the efficacy of certain legal institutions. We will start with the backdrop, and with an anticipated criticism of our argument. The Wilma hypothetical, it might be suggested, cannot get off the ground without an institutionalized practice of promising, and such a practice is tantamount to a private law of contract. On this view, Wilma's situation is a genuine predicament only if one grants the existence of contract law; yet it is incoherent to suppose that a law of contract can exist without someone such as Wilma enjoying a right to sue for breach. The force of this critique (assuming its soundness) is not to undermine the argument that disappointed promisees should be able to sue but instead to undermine the argument that *the right to sue* has some sort of deontological foundation. Any normative defense of the right to sue, it reasons, turns on the overall benefits to society of a set of legally entrenched promising practices. It therefore fails to supply the kind of defense of the principle of civil recourse that our account requires, and for which Chapter 3 purported to pave the way.

As a matter of both political and legal theory, this critique fails. It fails because it relies upon the premise that an institutionalized, legally entrenched practice of promising is incoherent without private rights of action. That is not so. If breaches of promise were sanctioned by informal disapproval or, conversely, subject to punishment by the state, the institution of promising and promise-keeping presumably could thrive. There would be rather straightforward reasons for reliance and for performance. Enforceability and accountability may well be key to the institution of promising, but these do not necessarily require the conferral of private rights of action on disappointed promisees.

Attending to this critique is nonetheless valuable, because it raises another sort of challenge that is also unfounded yet instructive. The Wilma example supposes that it is a sufficiently realistic possibility that the Bellas of the world will breach their agreements and that the Wilmas would want their legal and political system to provide them with a way of responding. But why would we suppose this? More particularly, why wouldn't the Wilmas be at least as interested—or even more interested— in a regime that could guarantee in advance that promisees won't be stiffed by promisors? To put the point more generally, why assume that nonperformance of contracts is a significant fact of life to be confronted in advance, if we instead could design the state's enforcement arm to secure nearly perfect compliance? Wouldn't severe and consistently enforced punishments for breaches prevent the Wilmas from being disappointed promisees, and therefore preempt the need for private rights of action?

The public-enforcement option, as we shall call it, is problematic for two reasons. First, not all breaches of contract are willful. Thus, not all could be eliminated even if promisors were highly motivated by the threat of sanctions to avoid breaching their agreements. Even in a maximum-enforcement regime, then, the Wilmas would still face disappointments and would still have occasions to seek responsive action from the Bellas. Second, even if draconian enforcement would substantially shrink the rate of breach, there would be good reason for the Wilmas to reject this solution. Indeed, part of what we want of a *liberal* state—a state that allows for and protects liberty—is *less* criminal enforcement. A state where routine contractual breaches are met with state-ordered punishment is not likely to be a liberal state.

This last point prompts us to emphasize again (as we did above) the contextual nature of our argument. Our defense of a right of civil recourse is not intended to cut across all polities, just as Rawls's two principles of justice are not. Rawls began with the understanding that no single comprehensive conception of the good life will gain universal assent. This understanding was not driven by moral skepticism, but by the recognition of seemingly durable conditions associated with modernity, including the fact of religious disagreement. Similarly, we recognize that, in principle, breaches of contractual promises could be met with criminal punishment, and that in fact some tight-knit political communities might find ways to diminish Wilma's insecurity without private rights of action. That is not our situation, however. It is part of the project of constructing a legal system for a people such as us that it will work for a large and diverse population without an excessively liberty-diminishing criminal law.

Now we come to the most realistic alternative to a scheme that includes rights of action for persons such as Wilma (and Gina)—a situation in which a combination of informal sanctions (from within the domain of social practices that reinforce positive morality), criminal enforcement, and state-run, noncriminal regulatory enforcement together provide enough support for the practice of promise-keeping to sustain it even in the absence of private suits for breach. This is hardly an unrecognizable or necessarily tyrannical state of affairs. So what would be wrong with it?

Equality is a big part of the answer. In the hypothetical world just described, Bella's compliance or noncompliance will turn on many factors. Whom Bella and Wilma happen to know will matter. Whether Bella needs to please or displease Wilma and whether Wilma can make Bella's life difficult if she fails to pay—these will be significant too. Regarding criminal or regulatory enforcement, a great deal may hinge on who populates the offices that bring enforcement actions. And the extent to which Bella and Wilma are in a position to influence private and public actors will make a difference too. In this world, Wilma has no *right* to make an enforceable demand for the $1,000, even if she can prove the broken promise. As such, it is a world that is likely to see radical differences as to which promisees will obtain compliance from promisors. Given that all persons in the position of Wilma are equally entitled to performance, substantial differences in who will obtain performance constitute a troubling kind of inequality. Conversely, if all of the Bellas should be equally vulnerable to demands for performance but are not, that is a problem of equality too.

For law professors who claim to be relatively down-to-earth to write the foregoing paragraph might seem culpably naive, not because it misdescribes how things would work in the hypothetical world it imagines, but because it seems oblivious to how similar that hypothetical world is to the real world. For there is no denying that, *even with private rights of action,* there are vast inequalities with respect to who can effectively bring a law-suit and who can effectively defend against one.

In fact, nothing in this observation undercuts our account. The question is not whether the current civil justice system complies perfectly or even roughly with the demands of equality. It is whether the value of treating the members of a political community equally can plausibly be deemed to lie behind the principle of civil recourse, as applied to those who have failed to fulfill their contractual commitments. Indeed, to critique our current system for failing to deliver equal access to justice is to confirm that this part of our justice system is aiming, in part, to secure a kind of equality.

Providing rights of action is part of the equal treatment to which members of a polity such as ours are entitled. A more localized problem—one that operates between Wilma and Bella in particular—sounds less in equality (as just described) and more in a notion of fairness. As between them, it would be unfair for Bella to get the benefit of Wilma's performance while Wilma is forced to go without what was promised to her. Wilma's resentment and disappointment in having worked for nothing, despite an agreement to the contrary, contrasts with Bella's having her cake and eating it too. Providing Wilma with civil recourse against Bella fundamentally alters the situation. In principle, at least, Wilma is no longer stuck on the losing end of a one-sided transaction. At least as importantly, when a system of recourse is in place, the Bellas of the world know that the Wilmas have available an option to invoke the legal system to hold them accountable. The *vulnerability* of Wilma to Bella—and (in principle) all Wilmas to all Bellas—is thereby diminished. The Wilmas of the world are entitled to a scheme that is fair in the sense of being committed to enabling victims of certain skewed interactions to remedy them.[24]

Finally, following Arthur Ripstein, we maintain that the state, in providing Wilma with an avenue of civil recourse, affirms and affords a liberal notion of independence.[25] True, the power to sue is in a sense depen-

---

24. That Bella gained something in the transaction with Wilma is not essential to there being an unfairness, in our sense of that term. Fairness is not about restoring some sort of equilibrium by "lowering" Bella and "raising" Wilma. It is about granting Wilma a legal power that leaves her less vulnerable to Bella.

25. ARTHUR RIPSTEIN, PRIVATE WRONGS 103 (2016). Ripstein also uses the word "freedom" to convey this idea. We are not claiming that civil recourse is inherently connected to a notion

dent, rather than independent—it is dependent on the state's provision of a court system. In another sense, however, having an avenue of civil recourse is crucial to independence. Freedom involves, among other things, the capacity to make and execute plans and projects. Wilma's capacity to do these things depends, in part, upon Bella's compliance with the terms of their agreement. Government takes Wilma's independence seriously if there is something she can do to secure the result she had relied upon obtaining. In this way, providing her with an avenue of civil recourse reflects a commitment to the independence of each.

The equality and fairness arguments for recourse apply equally to the case of Gina and the unreturned horse, but the independence argument is especially clear in that case. Perhaps Gina does things with her horse—she goes places she wishes to go, and maybe she earns money with it. She can no longer do these things if Bella has not returned it. But providing persons such as Gina with control over whether her property is returned—providing her with a legal power to ensure she is largely in control over her possessions—again seems critical for a state that aims to treat each person as independent in Ripstein's sense.

The analysis of rights of action in these simple examples leads to a clearer picture of the ways in which the right to sue is like the right to vote. Like a right to vote, a right to sue (and recover upon proof of claim) pertains to the allocation of power. The state's being powerful is a problem, from the point of view of an individual who values her liberty, and it is mitigated by the right to determine who shall occupy positions through which governmental power is exercised. Hence the right to vote. But the exercise by the state of its power over individuals is not the only thing about which to be concerned; each of us is vulnerable to private power, too. The state empowers each of us to use the court system as a way to protect against the private power that others might exercise over us, to some degree ameliorating pre-political inequalities and unfair terms of interaction. To the extent that institutions like contract and property law enhance independence, their doing so is more fully realized in a system that provides an avenue of civil recourse to aggrieved promisees and dispossessed property owners.

---

of individual autonomy or freedom. Rather, our claim is that it *can* serve to recognize, protect, and vindicate autonomy, and hence meshes well with the basic commitments of a liberal-democratic polity.

Redressing Wrongs

The examples of Wilma and Gina share several important features. Both women face a problem stemming from the fact that there is something they are legally entitled to have Bella do for them that she is not prepared to do, and both are powerless to get her to do that thing. In each case there is an institutionalized form of private norms that lies in the backdrop: in Wilma's it is the practice of promising and in Gina's it is the institution of property. Both, we have argued, are entitled to an avenue of civil recourse against Bella. And both in fact enjoy such an avenue as a matter of positive law.

Standard tort scenarios are different for a basic reason, one that we will discuss further in Chapter 5. Wilma and Gina both enjoyed a particular kind of legal right against Bella—namely, a legal right that she do something for (or in relation to) them. Generally speaking, tort suits do not have this characteristic: they are not instances in which the plaintiff asks a court to enforce a legal right that the defendant do something for her, or deliver something to her.[26] Instead the court is asked to *impose* a new legal obligation on the defendant—an obligation to pay damages—because of the defendant's having breached a duty owed to the plaintiff to refrain from wrongfully injuring her. This is why, in the introduction to this chapter, we described our argument as proceeding in two stages. Even if we have made a case for the political right to civil recourse for those instances in which a person is demanding the performance of a legal duty owed to her, the question remains whether a tort victim can claim a right to civil recourse for the breach of a duty that can no longer be performed.

Suppose Paula Purple books a room on the second floor of an inn run by Bella Blue. The lobby features a roaring fire in a large fireplace. At one point Bella removes the fireplace screen to add a log, and forgets to replace the screen. Near the fireplace are many flammable rugs, pillows, and pieces of furniture. Compounding her carelessness, Bella retires to her own bedroom while the fire is in full force, and during the night sparks from the fire ignite in the lobby. The fire spreads, damaging the inn and injuring Paula. Indeed, Paula is badly burned, suffers great pain, and is partially

---

26. Certain standard kinds of suit for breaches of contracts share this characteristic with tort suits.

paralyzed after falling through the floor of her bedroom, which collapsed as a result of the fire. Paula's personal belongings (a knapsack and the hiking clothes inside it) are also destroyed. The "good" news, such as it is, is that Paula's health insurance will cover the cost of her hospitalization, and her partial paralysis will not inhibit her career as a journalist. Moreover, Bella will not charge Paula for her night's stay, and has voluntarily reimbursed Paula in the amount of $400 to cover the cost of replacing her possessions. In addition, Bella has sent Paula a sympathy card that explains that nothing like this has ever happened before at the inn, and that expresses genuine regret and sorrow over what has transpired. Meanwhile, Bella's property insurance will cover the cost to her of repairing the inn.

In a legal system that does not provide an avenue of civil recourse for tort victims, Paula would face a quandary that is in some ways akin to Wilma's and Gina's. Certainly it is easy to imagine that Paula would not be satisfied that Bella has apologized, made amends of a sort, and explained that this was an isolated incident. Likewise, Paula might not take much comfort in the fact that she will be able to continue in her profession and is not facing out-of-pocket losses. While these features of Paula's situation make it less bad than it might have been, Paula might still want to hold Bella to account, somehow, for what Bella has done to her. Indeed, she might believe that she is entitled to do so. And in fact, under our legal system Paula is entitled to hold Bella to account—to obtain redress from Bella for the wrong Bella did to her. That is why Paula is provided with a right of action that enables her to recover damages upon proof of a claim of negligence against Bella.

As we have already indicated, however, there is nonetheless an important difference between Paula's quandary and those of Wilma and Gina. Wilma and Gina were seeking a way to force Bella to do what she was legally required to do for them. Paula's negligence suit would *not* be an enforcement action of this sort. To be sure, Bella's mistreatment of Paula generates a moral duty to Paula—one that Bella perhaps discharged by doing what she did in the aftermath of the fire. But just by virtue of having carelessly injured Paula, Bella did not incur a legal duty to pay damages. That duty kicks in only after judgment is entered for Paula in her negligence suit against Bella. That suit might mean many different things. It might be a way in which Paula can better understand and come to terms with what has happened to her. It might allow her to gain some sort of public acknowledgment of her claim to have been mistreated by Bella. Most likely, it would allow her to obtain money damages. Regardless, it is not about Bella making good on an existing legal obligation to pay a debt or to hand over property. (Recall that all of Paula's out-of-pocket losses have already been addressed.)

The comments above are meant to pull the reader away from the idea that Paula's right to civil recourse depends on an underlying right to the return of her property or to the performance of a legally binding promise. It would be similarly tempting—but equally unavailing—to suppose that Paula's right to sue Bella has a different kind of promissory basis. We can grant that there was in Paula's case an implicit promise from Bella to provide safe and suitable accommodations, which promise was breached. Still, unlike in Wilma's case, in which the promise, or a version of it, could still be performed—and hence a conferral on Wilma of a right to sue could empower her to obtain performance—here there is no way for Bella to act in the manner in which she promised she would.

In sum, the central feature of Paula's case that distinguishes it from Wilma's and Gina's is that Paula is seeking a right to sue because of what Bella *did to her*, not because of actions *Bella can take, and is legally obligated to take, but has not yet taken.* In this respect (though not others), Paula's tort suit is like a criminal prosecution. It seeks accountability for a wrong having been committed. Of course, accountability in a tort suit typically takes the form of a payment of damages, but the quandary the plaintiff faces is not about having been denied a payment she is owed, or having been denied an apology that is due. In criminal law, the power-holder—the public, through the prosecutor—pursues the putative offender in order to hold her to account for her offense. Punishment is a particular kind of holding-to-account for the commission of a public wrong. Criminal liability is the vulnerability to such punishment. Being required to pay tort damages to a person whom one has wronged is a different kind of holding-to-account—the accountability is to one's victim, for the commission of a wrong as to her. Tort liability is vulnerability to such accountability.

Notwithstanding the distinctiveness of Paula's case from Wilma's and Gina's, the considerations of equality and fairness that we highlighted in our analysis of their cases apply here too. Recall that the equality concern in Wilma's case related to power dynamics. In particular, the worry was that Bella's attitude toward performance of her contract would depend heavily on differentials of physical ability, wealth, connections, and the like: wealthy and powerful Wilmas are much less likely to be stiffed than impoverished Wilmas. As to the notion that public accountability through state-enforced criminal sanctions could be made consistent and pervasive enough to deal with the insecurity of the weak Wilmas, we deemed such a possibility to be implausible and in any event inconsistent with liberal-democratic constraints on the ways in which the state can legitimately enforce certain kinds of interpersonal obligations. Regulatory solutions, meanwhile, leave victims in the hands of regulators who face various incentives—some salutary (such as a focus on broader considerations of public welfare), and some pernicious (such as "capture" by those subject to regulation)—that might leave them indifferent or even ill-disposed toward alleviating the difficulties that particular victims face.

Without private actionability, compliance with the relational directives of tort law might happen, but there is no reason whatsoever to believe that compliance would be even roughly evenhanded. That is a large part of the reason why the right of a woman or a member of a minority group to sue is as basic as their right to vote. Given that we do not and should not allow public prosecution to an extent that would come close to ensuring broad compliance with civil obligations, respect for a person's right not to be wrongfully injured will often depend upon the potential tortfeasor knowing that they cannot do so without repercussions—that victims have the power to hold them accountable for having done so. The legal right to sue is provided, in part, as a recognition of a political right. It is a right to the state's assistance in seeing to it that legal rights are not violated in a manner that respects the equal claim of each person to be free from wrongful injury at the hands of another. This is very much part of what was meant when the framers of the Fourteenth Amendment guaranteed to all citizens the "equal protection" of the laws.

The fairness argument stands apart from the equality argument. Whereas the latter invites a comparison of Paula's situation to that of other Paulas—some rich, some poor; some Paul, some Paula; some well-connected, some not—the fairness argument looks at Paula's situation in relation to Bella's. In a regime with no private rights of action, Bella is down the cost of a greeting card and $400, while Paula has suffered a devastating setback because of what Bella did to her. Absent a right of action, Paula is powerless to address this disparity, just as she was powerless sleeping in her bedroom while Bella neglected the fire. After the fire, we cannot insist that Paula is entitled to be completely able-bodied, because that is not something that can happen. But we can insist that Paula not be powerless to redress the wrong done to her: government *does* have the capacity to ensure that Paula is not powerless in this sense. It can do so by providing a right of redress to Paula. It is part of the political morality of liberal democracy that individuals reasonably demand that the state not require them simply to endure this sort of unfairness as between victim and wrongful injurer.

In the examples of Wilma and Gina, we mentioned a third liberal-democratic value instantiated in a system of civil recourse: the value of independence. We enlisted this broad term, borrowed from Ripstein, in part to recognize and accommodate a set of values that are more or less internal to other bodies of private law, including contract (in Wilma's case) and property (in Gina's). Gina's was simpler: part of being able to own something is being able to do things that one otherwise might be unable to do; to go places, learn things, accomplish tasks, connect with others, and so forth. Ownership comes with a kind of security, and, as scholars from Locke to Ripstein have emphasized, that security is lacking without private enforcement powers of a certain sort. Because the value of property ownership turns partly on the value of independence and because ownership is incoherent without security, the value of independence that is central to property law plays an important and intrinsic justificatory role in explaining the availability of an avenue of civil recourse when it comes to retrieving possessions unlawfully in the hands of others. A similar argument was suggested with respect to Wilma's demand for Bella's promised payment.

Tort law of course protects personal property, real property, and bodily integrity, among other things. Thus, it is not implausible to assert that tort law also plays a role in securing the value of independence. Yet it is highly implausible that the various torts are all, in one way or another, about setbacks of a sort that prevent us from pursuing our projects and goals. A person mangled by a defective machine, defamed by a malevolent journalist, or duped by a fraudster may not have to change her projects or be hindered in reaching her goals; he may just be living with more pain, shame, or economic need than before.

The point we are making here is one that will resurface in Parts Two and Three of this book: torts are wrongs or mistreatments, not wrongfully caused losses. We put this forward, generally, as an interpretive claim, but its role in this chapter is different. If torts were always about losses, then our defense of the principle of civil recourse in the form of redress for wrongs would be in some ways easier. We would add to the equality and fairness arguments the independence argument that applies to the vindication of the sort of property and contract rights at work in the cases of Wilma and Gina. Alas, that is not so. Although many torts result in losses, and although some torts require proof of loss as a condition of liability, it is by no means the essence of a tort that the victim suffered something rightly described as a loss. Harmless trespasses, harmless batteries, and many other injurious wrongs are torts without losses. To be sure, there are *injuries* in all of these cases. (Recall that we are the ones who insist that there are no torts without injuries.) But the type of injury at issue is a rights-deprivations without any accompanying material setback. Rights-deprivations in and of themselves can sometimes interfere with projects and plans. Often, however, they do not. Thus, while many torts do involve interferences with the victim's independence, many do not, which is why the provision of the particular form of recourse at work in tort law—redress for injurious wrongs—cannot be justified on the ground that it consistently vindicates independence.

And yet it turns out that there is, after all, a third value (apart from equality and fairness) that underwrites the particular form of recourse one finds in tort law. This value is not independence but something closer to what Locke perhaps had in mind when he connected the right to reparation to a notion of self-preservation.

Without a private right of action against Bella, our legal system would simply require of Paula that she endure Bella's injuring of her and be content with the card and the $400 she received. If there are criminal or regulatory requirements for innkeepers, and if Bella violated those, Bella might face some kind of governmentally imposed sanction for having acted as she did. But it is not Paula's business to determine what will happen on that front. In this envisioned world without civil recourse, Paula is essentially left with no response. And while this state of affairs might seem unjust—and while we believe it is unjust—the matter is hardly self-evident. Indeed, it is not that difficult to conjure up a superficially plausible argument against this conclusion. There are many misfortunes that one is left to deal with on one's own—think of a sudden storm that crushes a person by causing a large tree to fall on and crumple the car in which she is sitting. Paula's situation, one might suppose, is just another of these. She was unlucky for having been in the wrong place at the wrong time, but she was also in some ways quite lucky: to have survived, to have health insurance, and to be able to continue in her career. For Paula to demand a right of redress beyond the resources already available to her, and in addition to the state's enforcement power over Bella, is for her to demand more than justice requires. So the argument would go.

By way of response, and at the risk of going too far afield, we invite readers to dwell momentarily on the much-touted value of "the rule of law." Often what is meant when politicians harp on this idea is that no one should be able to evade penalties and punishments if they have in fact broken the law. In addition, they are often referring to the notion that wrongdoers should be held accountable for their wrongs. Jurisprudence scholars, legal theorists, and many others are characteristically ambivalent about such pronouncements, and rightly so. In a constitutional tradition such as ours, rule-of-law values also involve compliance with due process norms that may conflict with the law-and-order tendencies of the politicians most often proclaiming themselves to be rule-of-law defenders. Moreover, heavy-handed state efforts at punishment are often (or more often) a foe than a friend of liberty. The pervasiveness and aggressiveness of the state qua prosecutor and enforcer against those who commit injurious wrongs is practically inconsistent with a broad understanding of liberty, especially if the notion of a wrongful injury is understood capaciously. Yet under-enforcement creates a problem of equality and fairness. And if it means that wrongdoers are left unaccountable, then those who have been wronged by unaccountable wrongdoers are being given short shrift by the state.

The legal accountability of wrongdoer to victim serves as a solution to the political problem just described. Having consequences for committing legal wrongs is important for deterrence reasons, and an argument can be made that wrongs do not count as legal wrongs unless the legal system attaches negative consequences to their commission. Yet there is another aspect to the need for legal consequences—an aspect that words like "accountability," "answerability," and "responsibility" help to capture. When those from the law-and-order camp demand accountability for those who have broken the law, they are typically expressing a kind of *indignation* that some people are getting away with breaking the law when they shouldn't.

There is something more than (and perhaps deeper than) indignation at the root of the demand for accountability, something that is most acutely felt when the victim herself is outraged that a wrongdoer has escaped accountability. The philosopher Peter Strawson suggested in his classic article "Freedom and Resentment" that indignation in response to moral wrongdoing can be understood as a third-person version of the resentment felt by the victim of the wrong.[27] His basic empirical or sociological claim was that a person who is injured by another naturally (and instinctively) resents the injurer. A philosophical claim arguably implicit in Strawson's account is that the notion of responsibility supplies the conceptual apparatus for the rule-governed activity of gauging the appropriateness of such resentment. When a community deems a person responsible for having wrongfully injured the victim, it is deeming the victim's resentment appropriate.[28]

As has been suggested by Jason Solomon, and by Stephen and Julian Darwall, Strawson's framework sheds light on civil recourse theory, though not exactly in the way they have proposed.[29] In the Paula example as we initially imagined it, Bella—in a world without law for the redress of wrongs—escapes all legal consequences. This is a problem on many levels, but one pertains to accountability. An observer might well be indignant that negligent injurers such as Bella can proceed with their lives as if they had not wrongfully injured another. But the deeper problem relates to Paula herself. If Bella was demonstrably careless and Paula's injuries were a realization of that carelessness, then Paula would be entitled to nurse a grudge against Bella or to be resentful of her. Our point is not that there is a psychological need for civil recourse or that there is a moral entitlement to forcible retaliation. It is instead that if there is no state-provided mechanism for holding Bella accountable for what she has done to Paula, then the state is not taking Paula as seriously as it should. It is

27. See P. F. Strawson, *Freedom and Resentment*, 48 PROCEEDINGS OF THE BRITISH ACADEMY 1 (1962).

28. It is far from obvious that the coherence and legitimacy of such a practice of gauging resentment turns on the truth or falsity of metaphysical claims about human freedom (this is part of why Strawson's article is a classic in theoretical debates about determinism; it purports to show that much of what is philosophically and morally rich in our thoughts about responsibility exists quite apart from metaphysical questions concerning determinism).

29. Stephen Darwall & Julian Darwall, *Civil Recourse as Mutual Accountability*, 39 FLA. ST. L. REV. 17, 38–41 (2011); Jason M. Solomon, *Equal Accountability through Tort Law*, 103 NW. L. REV. 1765 (2009).

failing to respect her as a right-holder, as someone not to be wrongfully injured, as a member of a political community with legal norms regarding how others must be treated. Paula's resentment is not itself the problem, just as citizens' indignation in the rule-of-law/law-and-order context is not the problem. Both are aspects of an affectively intense *apprehension* of the actual problem, which is Paula's victimization at the hands of Bella.

We are not arguing that it is critical that Bella have legal consequences visited upon her. Rather, we claim that it is critical that Paula be in a position to decide (within various constraints) whether Bella has certain legal consequences visited upon her. The political requirement of accountability in this context does not require that Bella actually be forced to pay compensation, much less that she be held accountable in a manner that conveys to the public confirmation of Paula's claim to have been mistreated. The requirement is that Bella *be* accountable—that she *is subject to being held to account or deemed responsible by Paula*. A lack of accountability in this sense is unacceptable because it constitutes a sort of neglect of and indifference to the rights of victims not to be mistreated and the duties of wrongful injurers not to mistreat them. Again, part of the promise of a liberal-democratic legal system is not only protection, but *equal* protection. Forgoing criminal liability for Bella (or some class of down-ticket wrongdoers) is, in a sense, what we demand of a liberty-protective constitutional order. But doing so without providing in-principle private accountability is protecting Bella *at the expense of Paula*.

These considerations bespeak a concern for the values of equality and fairness that we have already discussed. Yet neither of those values seems to capture fully the reasons why potential accountability, at the discretion of the victim, is so important. As with the right to vote, the right to sue modifies what is otherwise a dramatic relinquishment of power over oneself; it secures what might be called "individual sovereignty." To repair back to a Lockean frame, by "entering into" civil society, each of us renders herself vulnerable to a range of mistreatments even as we accept, in principle, significant state-imposed limitations on what we can do to prevent or respond to such mistreatment. We have already explained why this situation is *not* fruitfully described as involving the relinquishment of a natural right of forcible retaliation. Rather, it is one in which the individual incurs a risk that she will not be given adequate concern and respect. None of us can legitimately demand that government attend scrupulously, on an individualized basis, to all of our needs. But each of us can legitimately demand (among other things) a different kind of solicitude: namely, that we not be required merely to "lump it" when treated by another in a manner that marks us *in the eyes of the law* as a victim of wrongful injury. A government that would disempower an individual to the point where she cannot lawfully respond even to officially recognized forms of mistreatment fails to give adequate consideration to the legitimate claim of each individual member of the polity to matter.

Individual sovereignty complements the independence Ripstein emphasizes; both might be viewed as aspects of self-determination. We harbor no illusions that such values are neutral or fundamental in a way that transcends liberal theory; without question, the notion of individual sovereignty we are invoking is characteristic of the liberal political theory undergirding modern Anglo-American common law, a framework that has garnered its fair share of criticisms. Still, the equality, fairness, and individual sovereignty values illuminating the principle of civil recourse deserve our endorsement when given their proper place, as does the principle of civil recourse itself.

*　　*　　*

Readers would not be off base to detect in this chapter a "Goldilocks" argument for private rights of action to redress certain legal wrongs. For such wrongs, we have claimed, criminal prosecution and punishment is inapt, in part because it promises to render the state illiberal, while regulatory enforcement will be driven by considerations that are likely to render accountability haphazard or selective. Yet we also claim that a complete lack of legal accountability is unacceptable, in that it asks too much forbearance of each of us. Private rights of action that render those who breach legal duties of noninjury liable to those whose rights are violated thread the needle—they are just right.

Though this description is in some ways apt, we are reluctant to embrace it because it too readily lends itself to being construed as a functional argument about what the state must do to ensure that there is enough law enforcement, but not too much. Ours is not an instrumental argument of this sort; it is instead contractarian in nature. The question is what kinds of reasons each of us has for accepting private rights of action as a solution to a cluster of political problems. Civil recourse theory provides a particular kind of answer to this question: reasons of equality, fairness, and individual sovereignty support the existence of a legal power to hold accountable those who wrongfully injure us. If this is correct, then the provision of private rights of action to those who have been wronged— where there's a right, there's a remedy—is not circular. Individuals who have been legally wronged not only enjoy a legal power to redress the wrong, and not only have a legal right to enjoy such powers. There are reasons sounding in political morality according to which individuals are entitled to have an avenue of civil recourse against those who have committed legally recognized wrongs upon them. Just as members of a liberal democracy have a right to vote—in the sense of that phrase invoked by suffragettes and civil rights advocates—they have a right to a remedy.

5

Damages as Redress

W E MAINTAIN THAT TORT law empowers persons to obtain redress from those who, in the eyes of the law, have wrongfully injured them. Even sympathetic readers might worry that our account will run out of steam at a critical moment. Ask a practicing lawyer or trial judge what tort law is all about and she might well give a one-word answer: "Money." Plaintiffs and their attorneys seek damages payments and monetary settlements; defendants and liability insurers aim to pay as little as possible as slowly as possible. The idea of civil recourse seems too abstract or rarified to account for the "life blood" of the tort system.

Our imagined skeptic need not deny that there are questions about money and damages that a scholar might fruitfully pursue. Her point instead might be that the relevant questions are for policy analysts, not philosophically minded lawyers. For example, since the late 1970s, state courts and legislatures have adopted a variety of measures designed to control juror discretion to set damages awards, including flat dollar caps. Whether the stated need for these measures is real (for example, whether, without them, doctors will be driven out of practice, or liability insurance will become prohibitively expensive), and whether these measures actually address the need, are questions for policy wonks.

The prospect of money changing hands does indeed motivate and guide the resolution of tort suits. For this reason, it is crucial to "follow the money," in the sense of keeping track of its role in the operation of the tort system. It is nonetheless erroneous to suppose that the centrality of damages or settlement payments to tort law somehow undercuts the value of philosophically oriented accounts. Money means different things in different contexts. Paying for a product or service is one thing. Giving a gift is another. Stimulus packages, campaign contributions, fines, fees, loans, ransoms, bribes, children's allowances . . . each of these involves money changing hands. None is helpfully described as simply being "about money."

Theory enables us to grasp the significance of damages payments to tort law, in turn enabling us to think about practical questions, including questions about tort reform. This should not be surprising. Adjustments to the law of damages implicate some very basic questions. Is the traditional common-law measure of damages uniquely suited to tort law, such that any legislative modification of it renders tort law less coherent or principled? Are legislatures acting within the limits of their broad authority to modify common law when they cap damages? Are they exercising that authority appropriately? Or can theory explain and justify certain modifications, as well as limits on them?

In this chapter we explore these and other questions through the lens of civil recourse theory. As it turns out, the theory equips us to explain and justify doctrines often taken to be unprincipled—including several pertaining to the special form of tort redress known as punitive (or exemplary) damages. At the same time, it suggests that some familiar reform measures are problematic because they threaten to betray the principle of civil recourse.

"Torts and Compensation Systems"

When a plaintiff prevails in a tort suit, she typically obtains a damages award. More specifically, she obtains a judgment from a court that generates for the defendant a legal obligation. With the entry of judgment, the defendant incurs a legally enforceable debt to the plaintiff equal to the amount of damages specified in the judgment. To say the debt is legally enforceable is to say (among other things) that if payment is not forthcoming, the plaintiff can gain the assistance of the state in collecting on it—for example, through a court order attaching assets owned by the defendant so that they can be sold to pay the defendant's tort debt to the plaintiff.

In a standard tort case, the money awarded to the successful plaintiff is characterized as "compensation." This language is apt: the defendant's payment to the plaintiff is compensation for what she has done to him.[1] And yet use of the word "compensate" and the phrase "compensation systems" has caused mischief.

Here is a preview of our worry. The American Association of Law Schools (AALS), which promotes the advancement of legal education, is comprised of numerous subject-related sections, such as the section on Contract Law and the section on Criminal Law. Established in 1972, tort law's section bears the name "Torts and Compensation Systems."[2] Its name is reflective of the prevailing mindset at the time, according to which tort law is properly understood as continuous with other private and public institutions that make resources available to persons who have suffered significant losses—typically physical injuries or property damage, and typically from accidents (whether "humanly created" or "natural").[3] These include first-party insurance (such as homeowner's insurance, which might provide reimbursement to a person whose home is damaged by an electrical fire); workers' compensation systems (whereby employees injured on the job are reimbursed for medical costs and a percentage of lost wages); and benefits programs (such as taxpayer-funded relief programs for disaster victims). The idea of a "compensation system" is that there are parts of our legal system that stand ready to supply financial resources to those who are in need as a result of misfortunes of various types. In conjoining "Torts" with "Compensation Systems," section members manifested their view that tort law is best understood as one such system.

To suppose that tort liability, insurance coverage, workers' compensation benefits, and disaster relief belong to the same category is not, of course, to suggest that they are identical. Indeed, proponents of the view we are describing have tended to emphasize two distinctive features of tort as a mechanism for delivering compensation. The first concerns how ample payments aim to be. Compensatory damages in tort law, it is commonly said, aspire to compensate *fully* for all tort-related losses. A consumer injured by a defective product who prevails in her suit against the manufacturer typically stands to recover damages for her past and future

---

1. For the moment, we leave aside punitive damages. They are discussed below.

2. https://memberaccess.aals.org/eWeb/DynamicPage.aspx?Site=AALS&WebKey=87e3b982 -657e-4a7c-be71-33605903d797 (last visited, January 9, 2018).

3. Imagine the AALS having a "Section on Criminal Law and Behavior Management Systems." This pairing would likewise tell us something about the perspective on criminal law brought to bear by the persons who named the section.

medical expenses, past and future lost income, and past and future pain and suffering. For a victim who suffers permanent injuries, full compensation might amount to tens of millions of dollars. First-party insurance, workers' compensation, and disaster relief do not aim to reimburse losses fully. For example, workers' compensation systems typically pay employees who suffer permanent injuries relatively modest amounts specified on a preset table or schedule. For temporary disabilities, they pay only a percentage of lost wages for a limited period of time. They also provide no compensation for pain and suffering and minimal compensation to a worker's surviving family members when a worker is accidentally killed on the job. Likewise, health insurance coverage and disaster relief are limited in various ways, including, again, the exclusion of compensation for pain and suffering. Tort compensation, for better or worse, is more individually tailored and often substantially more generous than payments provided by these other systems. On the other hand, tort plaintiffs usually have to pay their own legal fees, which means that about a third of what they obtain will be paid over to their lawyers.

Second, under the rules of tort law, the determination of a plaintiff's compensatory damages awards is largely left to juries, although judges have of late been more aggressive about reviewing and altering jury awards. With little guidance from the trial judge beyond an instruction to provide an award that is "fair" and "reasonable"—and often after gut-wrenching testimony from the victim (and friends, family, and care providers) as well as the introduction of not-so-gripping actuarial data by experts charged with estimating the plaintiff's future losses—lay jurors decide how much compensation the tortfeasor should be required to pay her victim. Again, this process is very different from the routinized, bureaucratic modes of assessment found in payment schedules or determined by insurance adjusters or benefits program administrators.

Although there is much insight to be gained by placing tort law alongside bureaucratic compensation systems, doing so also risks serious misunderstandings. It is of course true that there are choices to be made about what sort of resources will be made available, on what terms, to different classes of injury victims, such as workers injured on the job. For example, lawmakers might decide—as did state legislatures in the early twentieth century—to eliminate negligence lawsuits by employees against employers in favor of workers' compensation systems; in this instance, tort law and workers' compensation were treated as substitutes, with governments opting for one over the other. The problem resides in the suggestion that tort law and bureaucratic compensation systems are little more than *two different ways of doing the same thing*—namely, ensuring that money gets to injury victims to help them and their dependents cope with the fallout from their injuries.

Tort law, especially the law of negligence and products liability, does help get money to injury victims, and this is plainly an important fact about it, a good reason for having it, and a consideration in decisions about its design and modification. But the idea of a "compensation system" in this sense hardly captures what the common law of torts purports to do and why it purports to be doing it. Tort damages are not merely a distinctively individualized and generous mode of delivering compensation to the injured. They are a remedy granted to persons who have proven they have suffered a wrong at the hands of another. That is why there is *liability* for tort damages: liability that does not hinge on contract or government largesse. It is also why the party liable, in the first instance, is an *injurer*, not an insurance company or a government agency.[4]

Even as ways for the legal system to respond to injuries, tort law and bureaucratic compensation systems are qualitatively different. This is why, although we said above that there is a choice to be made between them (as a way of emphasizing their differences), lawmakers in fact need not choose: they can provide both without creating redundancies. Members of our society today have available to them forms of first-party insurance and disaster relief, along with tort law. One could likewise imagine a system in which workers' compensation benefits and negligence lawsuits are both available to injured workers. Indeed, other legal systems make both available.[5] The point is that the same events or phenomena can be and are addressed through distinct legal and normative frameworks.

In fairness to those inclined to describe tort law as just another compensation system, we should note that their preferred (though inaccurate) description emerged at a moment in history ripe for such a view. This

---

4. We say "in the first instance" because tort defendants' liabilities often are paid in part or in full by an insurance company under a liability insurance policy issued to the defendant. We discuss liability insurance in Chapter 9.

5. Of course, questions will then arise as to how these institutions and practices should interact. If a worker who is injured on the job can recover workers' compensation benefits and sue for negligence, should her tort award be reduced by the amount of benefits she has received?

moment—which ran from about 1945 to 1975—also marked what may prove to be the zenith of American economic and political might. In those heady, best-and-brightest days, there was a confidence that American wealth and know-how could be harnessed to solve large-scale problems on a systematic basis.[6] If we could wipe out crippling diseases with a vaccine program and send astronauts to the moon, we could also make sure that each American has the wherewithal to withstand the misfortune of suffering an injury or illness. Torts scholarship partook of this mood. Leading scholars and scholarly oriented judges took up the question of how—once it was freed from supposedly hidebound notions of duties, rights, wrongs, and redress—the tort system might operate as a "rational," systematic response to the problem of accidents and the dislocations they cause.

The focal point for these efforts at rethinking tort law was the emerging doctrine of strict products liability. The consumer goods economy was emblematic of postwar American prosperity and power. The adoption, in this important and visible domain, of a rule of strict liability was a big deal. Moreover, its adoption was canonically defended on instrumental, policy-driven grounds. It was argued that strict liability, compared to negligence, would better incentivize manufacturers to make safe products, thus reducing the incidence of product-related injuries, and better spread the costs of accidents, because manufacturers would build the cost of their liability for product-related injuries into the prices of their products. At this, the cutting edge of tort law, the notion of torts as wrongs and compensatory damages as redress was thus seen as giving way to the notion of strict (or "no-fault") tort liability as a scheme of compensation (and deterrence), with damages payments serving as a kind of first-party insurance provided to consumers by product manufacturers and ultimately the consuming public.[7]

6. John C. P. Goldberg & Benjamin C. Zipursky, *Accidents of the Great Society*, 64 MD. L. REV. 364 (2005) (discussing the "great society" mentality as it applied to traffic accidents, and how the torts scholarship of Guido Calabresi partakes of that mentality).

7. Some have argued that, taken together, the adoption of workers' compensation systems and the rise of strict products liability, along with the increasing availability of liability insurance to cover liability for negligence, have completely transformed tort law. Perhaps before these developments, the argument goes, tort law could accurately have been described as law for the redress of wrongs. Now, however, compensation is too often paid without any proof of wrongdoing—or, in the case of payments made by a tortfeasor's liability insurer, by persons other than wrongdoers—to allow for the retention of the traditional description of the field.

As is now clear, the trend that many saw in the emergence of products liability never materialized. Indeed, it never really got under way. As we discuss in Chapter 6, although instrumental reasoning about deterrence and compensation certainly played a role in convincing judges and jurists to change the rules pertaining to product-related injuries, those changes took place *within* traditional tort notions of wrongs and redress. Deterrence and compensation rationales were *not* invoked to justify loss-spreading irrespective of wrongdoing. Instead they were invoked to justify the recognition *of a new redressable wrong*—namely, the wrong of a commercial seller injuring a consumer by sending a dangerously defective product into the world. We know this because the version of strict products liability adopted by the courts was not the sort of "absolute" liability that one would put in place if one were aiming to convert the tort system into an insurance scheme or a social safety net. Rather, "strict" products liability was from the get-go based on proof of a product's *defectiveness*. (It was deemed "strict" to emphasize the difference between liability based on the presence of a product defect irrespective of seller fault, and liability based on a seller's failure to take reasonable care to prevent a product from causing injury.) A nondefective product that causes injury does not give rise to a claim for compensation—no loss-spreading occurs—even though there is as much reason to spread losses in the case of such an injury as there is in the case of an injury caused by a defective product.

The recognition within tort doctrine of strict products liability likewise cannot be said to have marked the onset of the transformation of tort law into a compensation system (or, for that matter, a system of optimal deterrence). Despite the moniker "strict," this form of liability is wrongs-based in a meaningful sense (as explained above, and more fully in Chapter 6). Those who led the scholarly charge to think otherwise were mistaken about where tort law was headed and dogmatic about the inaptness of a law of wrongs and redress to modern economic, social, and political

---

Instead, the new "lowest common denominator" of tort law is compensation for losses. Ergo, tort law is a compensation system.

There are several fallacies in this argument, including: (i) that strict products liability is not wrongs-based; (ii) that workers' compensation systems are to be treated as part of tort law when their point was to take workplace accidents out of the domain of tort law; and (iii) that payment of tort damages by a tortfeasor's insurer somehow undermines the requirement of a tort by the insured having been committed before liability can attach. We discuss the first and third of these fallacies in Chapters 6 and 9, respectively.

conditions.[8] More broadly, they were in the grip of a particularly reductive form of instrumental thinking: a Holmesian mindset impatient with the morally tinged language of the common law and a bit too eager to see the deliverables. Tort law still instantiates the principle of civil recourse, just as the notion that a person is entitled to obtain redress from a wrongful injurer remains cogent and powerful.

Making Whole and Corrective Justice

Whether awarded in a suit that sounds in conversion, libel, negligence, nuisance, or strict products liability, compensatory damages are owed by a defendant to a plaintiff by virtue of the defendant's having wrongfully injured the plaintiff. On this point, we agree with Ernest Weinrib, Jules Coleman, Stephen Perry, Arthur Ripstein, John Gardner, and other scholars who offer corrective justice theories of tort. Writing primarily in opposition to economic characterizations of tort plaintiffs as private attorneys general, and tort damages as fines and bounties paid as a reward to plaintiffs for pressing lawsuits that serve the public good, all of them have rightly insisted that there is something essential rather than contingent about a damages award being collectable, in the first instance, by a tort plaintiff from a tortfeasor. And yet we in the end reject the corrective justice account of compensatory damages.

At the center of the corrective justice account is the idea, mentioned above, of full or "make whole" compensation. The commission of a tort such as negligence generates an interpersonal injustice—in Weinrib's terminology, it involves an unjust normative gain for the injurer and a corresponding unjust loss for the victim.[9] The injurer was obligated to the victim not to injure her in the way that he did, and the victim has suffered a setback by virtue of the breach of that obligation. The injurer's breach of the primary duty to refrain from wrongfully injuring the victim thus generates a secondary duty to repair the losses associated with the injuring. Tort law, by enabling the victim to recoup her losses, sees to it that this secondary duty of repair is heeded, permits the restoration of the disturbed

---

8. Emblematic is the American Law Institute's project on "enterprise liability," launched in the 1980s, which initially sought to channel the perceived trend away from wrongs-based liability and toward loss-based compensation into concrete reform proposals. *See also* Anthony J. Sebok, *The Fall and Rise of Blame in American Tort Law*, 68 BROOK. L. REV. 1031 (2003).

9. ERNEST J. WEINRIB, THE IDEA OF PRIVATE LAW 125 (1995).

normative equilibrium, and thereby reestablishes just relations between injurer and victim. Make-whole compensation, in sum, corrects the injustice of the defendant's having wrongfully injured the plaintiff by restoring the *status quo ante*. Tort damages, to invoke Ripstein's provocative phrase, make it "as if [the tort] never happened."[10]

As we will discuss now, and also in the Conclusion, there are several problems with this account. The first might seem mundane, but is important. "Make whole" is not in fact the standard used by courts in the United States for setting compensatory damages. Juries usually determine damages and are guided in doing so by an instruction from the trial judge to set damages in an amount that constitutes "fair" and "reasonable" compensation to the plaintiff. While one might suppose that "making whole" can be a sensible way of fleshing out what counts as "fair compensation," "fair" is the more basic idea.

That "making whole" must have a subsidiary rather than primary role becomes clear when one considers the range of setbacks recognized by tort law as injuries. For convenience, we can split these into two general types: those that involve physical damage and those that do not. For libels, offensive-touching batteries, assaults, malicious prosecutions, harmless trespasses to land, nuisances, and false imprisonments, the prototypical injury is not at all Humpty-Dumpty-like. (Consider, for example a battery that involves one person unceremoniously spitting in the face of another, or a nuisance whereby one person's raucous parties constantly disrupt the sleep of his neighbor.) In these cases, there is nothing like a broken limb or a smashed or stolen object that can be repaired or replaced, and hence nothing to give traction to the idea of making whole. The injuries at issue have more to do with a notion of invasion or encroachment. Although it certainly makes sense to talk of being compensated for such injuries, compensation in this context is poorly captured by a notion of restoration. Compensation can *make up* for these kinds of mistreatment but not by putting Humpty-Dumpty back together again (nor by replacing him).

"Making whole" might seem to have more purchase for cases of bodily injury and property damage. Yet even here, the phrase tells us more about our reliance on metaphor than about the nature of a tort damages award. A payment of money—even a great deal of money—to a formerly healthy person who has been rendered quadriplegic by medical malpractice does

10. Arthur Ripstein, Private Wrongs 233–63 (2016).

not make it as if the malpractice never happened. Indeed, although not so intended, the application of the "make whole" idea to such a case verges on mockery. The problem is not simply that, in ordinary circumstances, no one would willingly trade money for being rendered quadriplegic (although this fact is relevant to the judgment that something is off in this application of the make-whole metaphor). The deeper problem lies in the supposition that money in sufficient amounts can somehow repair all manner of setbacks. Money *can* make the sheering off of a car's side-view mirror by a careless driver as if it never happened: the driver just needs to pay for the repairs. And some bodily injuries—a broken arm that promises to heal quickly and completely—might even fit this description. But others do not, and these are not limited to catastrophic injuries. Permanent loss of eyesight, disfiguring scars, and post-traumatic stress disorder are not things that can be undone. Again, money can provide *support, relief,* or *satisfaction* to persons who suffer these sorts of setbacks. This is why courts have long authorized damages in tort cases. But this is hardly to say that damages payments restore the plaintiff to her pre-tort condition.[11]

There are other problems that attend the corrective justice conception of damages as satisfying a defendant's duty to make the plaintiff whole. On the corrective justice account, once the tort has been committed the tortfeasor incurs a duty of repair. Indeed, this duty is said to be a continuation of the duty of noninjury that the tortfeasor initially owed the victim.[12] We can flesh out this idea using a hypothetical case of defamation. Suppose David owes a duty to Victoria to refrain from saying something defamatory about her to others. Victoria enjoys a corresponding right not to be slandered by David. If David slanders Victoria, Victoria's right to her good name does not somehow evaporate. But if the right persists, so too does its corresponding duty. Yet since David can no longer discharge his duty by refraining from slandering Victoria, David must do the next best thing, which is to repair Victoria's injury. Tort law, by ordering a damages payment,

---

11. Weinrib argues that the notion of full compensation is applicable even to these sorts of cases because what is being compensated is the "normative" rather than the "factual" aspects of the plaintiff's having been injured. In doing so, he all but concedes that the notion of making whole is at best metaphoric. Scott Hershovitz, *Corrective Justice for Civil Recourse Theorists*, 39 FLA. ST. L. REV. 107, 114–16 (2011).

12. Some problems with different iterations of this notion of "continuity" are discussed below.

sees to it that David performs as best he can the duty he all along owes to Victoria. Or so says the corrective justice theorist.

It seems clear, however, that a damages award often is *not* the next-best way to perform an underlying duty not to injure. In the case of David and Victoria, for example, a court order directing David to speak publicly and accurately about Victoria (say, in a newspaper ad that David pays for) is probably a better instantiation of the idea of getting David to do what he all along was duty-bound to do than is the entry of a judgment that deems him to owe Victoria a compensatory payment.[13] Likewise, where a defendant's negligence leaves the plaintiff recuperating at home for an extended period, the next best thing for the defendant to do for the plaintiff might well be to tend to the plaintiff and, for example, run errands that she is unable to run.

Ironically, as was foreshadowed in Chapter 4, the notion of "continuity" between duty of conduct and duty of repair relied upon by corrective justice theorists is more at home in legal settings *other than tort law.* Suppose A and B enter into a contract according to which B will paint A's house, but B fails to do so. Were A to prevail against B in a suit for breach of contract, the court would typically instruct the jury to award damages in an amount that would place A in the position he would have occupied had B performed. "Expectation damages" of this sort evince the continuity that corrective justice theorists misattribute to tort damages. Indeed, courts sometimes describe them as providing a *substitute for the promised performance.* The problem is that expectancy damages are a hallmark of contract law, not tort law.

This makes sense. When a contract is breached, the nonbreaching party often remains desirous of performance or its equivalent: A presumably still wants his house painted. In standard tort cases, there is no analogue to the missing performance for which damages might serve as a substitute. It is not completely out of place to talk about rights conferred by tort law as entitling right-holders to *some kind* of performance. One might say, for example, that a driver owes it to those in the vicinity of her

---

13. Nor is this notion entirely fanciful. A number of states have statutes granting limited protection to certain defamation defendants if, upon the demand of person claiming to have been defamed, the defendant publishes a sufficiently prominent retraction. *See, e.g.,* Cal. Civ. Code § 48a. And, while an order requiring a damages payment might permit Victoria to fund ads correcting David's false statement, ads run by Victoria on her own behalf might well be discounted as self-serving.

car to perform (drive) carefully. However, if the driver were to drive carelessly and strike a pedestrian, it is a mere play on words to describe the pedestrian's award of damages as delivering to her an equivalent to the safe-driving performance to which she was entitled, or that the monetary award she receives will allow her to proceed with her life as it was going to proceed had the driver heeded his duty of care. Now that the injuring has occurred, it is simply too late for performance in the relevant sense. The carelessly injured pedestrian with a permanent limp cannot retain the intactness of her body, and tort damages are not meant to deliver to her intactness that she cannot have. They instead provide redress—they aim to give her a measure of vindication, and to help her to cope with her new situation.

An examination of how two prominent corrective justice theorists—Weinrib and Gardner—have defended the continuity thesis will further reveal its shortcomings. In *The Idea of Private Law*, Weinrib offers the following argument to establish that a duty of repair flows from the defendant's breach of the primary duty:

> When the defendant . . . breaches a duty correlative to the plaintiff's right, the plaintiff is entitled to reparation. The remedy reflects the fact that even after the commission of the tort the defendant remains subject to the duty with respect to the plaintiff's right. *The defendant's breach of the duty not to interfere with the embodiment of the plaintiff's right does not, of course, bring the duty to an end, for if it did, the duty would—absurdly—be discharged by its breach.* With the materialization of wrongful injury, the only way the defendant can discharge his or her obligation respecting plaintiff's right is to undo the effects of the breach of duty.[14]

Let us begin in the middle, where Weinrib states that if "[t]he defendant's breach of the duty not to interfere with the embodiment of the plaintiff's right" brought the defendant's "duty to an end," then "the duty would—absurdly—be discharged by its breach." From this he infers that there *must* be some way the tortfeasor can still discharge his or her obligation, and the payment of reparation turns out to be that way.

14. WEINRIB, *supra* note 9, at 135 (emphasis added).

The italicized argument is unfortunately fallacious, equivocating on what it would mean to "bring [a] duty to an end." For X to act so as to bring to an end a duty owed to Y to refrain from doing A is for X to do something such that the duty owed to Y to refrain from doing A at time T_1 ceases to exist at T_2 (sometime after T_1). The first question to ask is whether it possible that some action by X could cause such a change. The obvious answer is that there is; rescinding a contract is a good example. A second question is whether the only thing that it could mean for someone no longer to have a duty is for them to have satisfied the duty. As the rescission example shows, there is no reason to believe that this is the case.

Of course, the serious question is whether the breach of a duty could make it the case that there is no longer such a duty. Why not? If one believes that ought implies can, it seems quite plausible to believe that certain kinds of actions will "extinguish" duties. Suppose X is under a duty to take care to ensure that toxins are not dumped in a reservoir that serves as a town's water supply. If X carelessly allows Y to dump toxins in the reservoir, X's breach has in fact brought *that duty* to an end. A similar or future-oriented duty might be generated, but X can no longer comply with the duty to ensure the non-introduction of toxins into the reservoir—precisely because X breached it, the thing that X was duty-bound to take steps to prevent from happening has happened. There is simply no basis for thinking that X must have discharged the duty. Similarly, imagine the publisher of a newspaper has a duty to refrain from publishing a certain fact in the paper. Once the defendant publishes it, he no longer can comply with his duty to refrain from doing so: the cat is out of the bag.

Gardner has offered a variation of Weinrib's basic idea and an argument in support of a similar conclusion.[15] On this account, the breach of a primary duty can give rise to secondary duties because the reasons giving rise to the primary duty continue to be operative, even though the earlier duty can no longer be complied with. The reason to ensure that a surgeon properly operates on a particular patient is that the patient's interest in health warrants taking care in surgery. If the surgeon engages in malpractice, the reasons for the duty of care do not evaporate, they instead turn into a secondary duty to provide compensation that will permit a

15. John Gardner, *What Is Tort Law For? Part 1: The Place of Corrective Justice*, 30 LAW & PHIL. 1 (2011).

subsequent proper treatment to occur. The same goes for other standard instances of negligence beyond malpractice. The duty of repair arises because the interest of others in physical well-being that generates reasons for care and, therefore, a duty of care in the first instance, also generates reasons for the payment of compensatory damages in the second.

This rendition of the continuity between primary duties and the duty of repair remains unconvincing for two interrelated reasons. First, the interests that generate primary duties in tort law do not consistently generate reasons for the remedies that our system provides. Conversely, there are reasons for the remedies our system provides, and they are different from the reasons for the underlying primary duties. *Ditto v. McCurdy*, a medical malpractice case, amply illustrates both aspects of this problem.[16]

Ditto sought assistance from a doctor named McCurdy in dealing with breast disfigurement that she experienced as a side effect of a prescribed medication. McCurdy performed breast implant surgery, but it went badly, causing a series of infections and further disfigurements that necessitated six subsequent surgeries. Ditto sued for medical malpractice and other torts. A jury determined that McCurdy was grossly negligent, and awarded compensatory and punitive damages, although the punitive award was vacated on appeal.

The reasons giving rise to McCurdy's duty to take care not to injure Ditto included, presumably, the value of preserving certain aspects of her physical well-being and avoiding interferences with it (such as infection), as well as the value of her being able to regain comfort with her physical appearance, and her emotional health. Once it was determined that McCurdy failed to exercise appropriate care and thus harmed Ditto physically, the court entered judgment for Ditto, and McCurdy thereupon incurred a legal duty to pay damages to her. Our question is whether this duty of repair can be understood as flowing from the breach of the primary duty, and if so, how? Are the reasons requiring McCurdy to pay Ditto the same as the reasons for him to exercise care in performing surgery on her?

In fact, the preservation of Ditto's physical well-being, the avoidance of infection, and the recovery of her self-image and emotional well-being are not the principal reasons for McCurdy's being required to pay

16. 947 P.2d 952 (Hawaii 1997).

damages. To the contrary, the liability of McCurdy constitutes *accountability* for *having carelessly interfered with her physical and emotional well-being*. That is why McCurdy ultimately incurred a duty to compensate her.

It might seem that one could reestablish the sort of symmetry sought by Gardner's version of the continuity thesis by simply expanding our understanding of the reasons giving rise to tort law's primary duties. If a patient's interest in being happy or her interest in self-esteem were the reasons for recognizing McCurdy's duty to take care not to injure her, then it is plausible that the same reasons generate a duty of repair. Compensation is supposed to increase her well-being (or diminish her lack of well-being), or her happiness or self-esteem.

The problems that lie in this direction are legion. To begin with, "happiness," "individual welfare," and "well-being" are far too generic to provide reasons grounding the specific duties of tort law. If there is a duty not to libel someone, it is presumably because of her interest in her reputation, not because of an interest in well-being per se. The entire framework for duties would have to be converted into something so vague as to approach vacuity, and in any case too vague to capture the sense in which libel, trespass to land, and negligence are distinct wrongs.

It would not only undercut an account of the wrongs of tort law to acquiesce to an overly general account of the reasons for not wronging others, it would also fail to provide a satisfactory account of why tort law results in the imposition of reparative obligations. Reparative obligations are incurred because a primary duty has been breached. In her case, it is Ditto's interest in being compensated for what McCurdy wrongfully put her through that grounds her claim to damages. And lest one think that, even if the distinctiveness of this interest from the interests underlying the duty of care owed by McCurdy to Ditto undermines Gardner's analysis, it appears finally to yield an explanation of reparative obligations, this line of analysis famously yields a whole new set of problems. For, as Coleman, Weinrib, and Perry persuasively argued more than two decades ago, this sort of interest-based analysis of reparative obligations utterly fails to capture the relational nature of tort law. Bluntly, Ditto's interest in compensation for her injuries might generate duties in innumerable persons other than McCurdy, including perhaps government officials. While there is surely normative force in that claim, we are engaged at the moment in an interpretive enterprise, and it is crystal clear that tort law does not create such general duties of repair.[17]

As an account of tort damages, corrective justice theories fail for another reason alluded to in Chapter 4, one that stands apart from problems with the continuity thesis. In short, they mistake a liability/power relation for a duty/right relation.[18] Let us concede for purposes of argument that a tortfeasor owes her victim a *moral* duty to repair losses associated with the injury.[19] Tort law recognizes no comparable legal duty. If there were such a legal duty, then, upon the commission of a tort, the plaintiff would, in principle, have a legal right to payment and the defendant would be obligated to make payment. Yet that is not the case. Suppose D is prosecuted for and convicted of the crime of aggravated drunk driving, with the aggravating factor being that he smashed into P's unoccupied car. Suppose, further that P never bothers to sue D in tort. Absent such a suit (and assuming there is no order of restitution made in the criminal case), D has no legal duty to compensate P. This even though there has been a determination in a court of law that D committed conduct that fits the definition of a tort, and even though there is no difficulty in valuing the harm

---

17. The distinction between the normative and the interpretive is highly relevant to a fair-minded evaluation of Gardner's analyses. In his 2011 article, he appears to be offering principally an interpretive account of private law. It is more perilous to attribute a particular methodological perspective to Gardner's subsequent book. JOHN GARDNER, FROM PERSONAL LIFE TO PRIVATE LAW (2018). While it is plainly interpretive at one level, it is also in important respects normative and anti-conceptualistic. It is not clear that the failure of tort law itself to match the framework he puts forward undercuts the reasons for which he advances that framework.

18. One of us made a version of this point several years ago, see Benjamin C. Zipursky, *Civil Recourse, Not Corrective Justice*, 91 GEORGETOWN L. J. 695 (2003), but Steve Smith has more recently developed and defended a very powerful account of this distinction. STEPHEN A. SMITH, RIGHTS, WRONGS, AND INJUSTICES: THE STRUCTURE OF REMEDIAL LAW (2019). Smith's work on this distinction has influenced (and shored up) our own views.

19. In fact, this seems false, in part because moral wrongfulness is not a condition of tort liability, and also because the moral duty to repair is probably sensitive to various considerations of which tort law takes no account. Suppose a single mother, through no fault of her own, is late for an interview for a job she desperately needs. In her haste, she carelessly drives into an intersection, failing to notice that a car is lawfully proceeding through the intersection toward her. To avoid being struck by that car, she swerves and strikes another car that is parked on the side of the road. As it happens, the car she strikes and damages is a new luxury car that happens to contain a valuable piece of art that is also damaged. Were a negligence suit brought on these facts, the woman could easily face liability in the tens or hundreds of thousands of dollars (in all likelihood exceeding the coverage provided by her automobile liability policy), and could be made, for example, to sell her assets to satisfy the judgment. Liability of this sort strikes us as vastly exceeding the scope of her moral duty of repair.

caused. *D*'s failure to send *P* an amount of money equal to the value of the damage might be immoral. But it is not the breach of any legal duty that D owes *to P*.

To be sure, the commission of a tort has a legal consequence. But it is not the creation of a legal duty owed by tortfeasor to victim. It is instead the creation of a legal power, and with it, a corresponding liability. To commit a tort is to render oneself *vulnerable* to being sued and to having a court authenticate the suit's demand for payment of compensation. When a court authenticates a plaintiff's claim and demand, it issues an order stating that the defendant owes the plaintiff the amount of compensatory damages determined by the factfinder, thereby adding tort debtor / tort creditor as a new aspect of the relation between defendant and plaintiff. If payment of the debt is not forthcoming, the plaintiff can then request and obtain additional relief, such as an order from the court attaching the defendant's assets, or garnishing the defendant's wages.

Fair and Reasonable Compensation as Redress

When a court issues a judgment ordering a tort defendant to pay the plaintiff compensatory damages, the court is validating the demand for redress contained in the plaintiff's complaint. A tort suit demands from the defendant a response for the defendant's having mistreated the plaintiff; a judgment for the plaintiff validates that demand and establishes that the response is owed.

Outside the tort context, the thought that victims of mistreatment are entitled to demand responsive conduct of those who have mistreated them is anything but exotic or esoteric. A woman discovers that her boyfriend of two years, who recently moved into her apartment, has cheated on her. When she confronts him, he confesses, expresses regret, and asks for forgiveness. Unmoved, the woman tells him to pack his things and leave. This is an instance of a *warranted demand for responsive conduct* addressed to wrongdoer by victim. Note that, even though there is a responsive aspect to the woman's demand, it is nowhere near the idea of wreaking vengeance. (Vengeance, in this situation, would involve something more like the woman taking a baseball bat to the boyfriend's car.[20]) Note also that the action demanded is not necessarily action that would

20. Carrie Underwood, "Before He Cheats" (2006).

be owed without the victim's demand: it is by no means clear that the boyfriend owes it to the woman to move out *sua sponte*. If anything, she might have grounds for further complaint if he preemptively left without even consulting her views on whether he should stay or go.

Now imagine two young children playing at a daycare facility. One child, aged five, grabs from the hands of another, aged four, an object that the younger child had built, and wrecks it. One would expect the younger child to be upset and perhaps even to be inclined to lash out physically. However, he will also have been instructed by adults that this way of reacting is unacceptable. If, in obedience to the rule against physical retaliation, the younger child refrains from hitting the older child, it will be natural for him to make a certain kind of appeal to an adult caregiver. In particular, the younger child might demand—and is probably entitled to receive—assistance from the caregiver in obtaining a response from the older child, perhaps in the form of an apology and assistance in rebuilding the object.

Neither of these examples involves a tort suit, but each helps convey the intuitive idea that the victim of a wrong is entitled to make and have heeded—sometimes with assistance from another—certain demands of the wrongdoer. Tort suits are, in some sense, an elaborately institutionalized variant on this general idea. The question arises as to why courts have settled on money damages as pretty much the only kind of demand a victim is entitled to receive judicial assistance in making (and having heeded) as a matter of right.

Our answer comes in two stages: a preliminary qualification, followed by a more substantive response. By way of qualification, we note that courts do sometimes order other forms of remedy. In particular, injunctive relief is commonly available to certain classes of tort plaintiffs, such as those complaining of ongoing nuisances and trespasses. In this respect, civil recourse theory enjoys another explanatory advantage over corrective justice theories. By treating the idea of making whole as hardwired into tort law, they have difficulty explaining the variety of remedies available to tort plaintiffs, including not only injunctive relief but also nominal damages, punitive damages, and declaratory relief. As demonstrated below, civil recourse theory has more to say on these topics, particularly as to punitive damages.

We don't want to overstate the present point, however. Injunctions are ordered only when the standard legal remedy of money damages is inadequate to provide redress for the wrong done, and even then the granting of an injunction is famously subject to a range of (literally and metaphorically) equitable considerations. Other forms of relief, such as nominal and punitive damages, are rarely granted. Compensatory damages (or settlement in its shadow) is the normal tort remedy. This is no accident. When it comes to setting rules for the sort of demands that tort plaintiffs can make of defendants—demands that courts must ultimately decide whether to validate—there are good reasons to limit them, in standard cases, to a demand for a monetary payment cabined by a notion of reasonableness or fairness.

As we have insisted throughout this book, one central feature of tort law is the special way in which it empowers. It enables private citizens to harness the power of the state to take action against other private citizens. Although Chapter 4 alluded to potential downsides associated with this power, we have not really had occasion to emphasize them. Until now. In fact, there are many reasons to worry about the law conferring on individuals and firms the power to redress wrongs, and hence reasons to allow it ordinarily to be exercised only in aid of obtaining a compensatory damages payment.

One worry centers around the condition that must be met for the power to be exercised. That condition, of course, is the commission of a tort. As we explain in Chapter 6, torts are defined such that they can be and often are committed by well-meaning, diligent actors. One need not be particularly culpable or blameworthy (if at all) in order to have committed a tort. This is not to back away from our claim that torts are wrongs. It is to observe that even injuries caused without malice, wantonness, or other indicia of significant culpability can be wrongfully inflicted. Tortious wrongdoing involves the failure to meet certain standards of conduct set by law. For a body of law that defines wrongs broadly, it is appropriate to limit successful claimants to redress in the form of money damages. As we note below, victims of certain more culpable torts may obtain higher compensatory awards, and can sometimes seek punitive damages separate and apart from the default remedy of compensatory damages.

Relatedly, tort defendants do not benefit from various safeguards provided in other legal processes, particularly those employed in criminal prosecutions. The decision to proceed against the defendant is an interested party's (the victim's), not that of a government official who is in principle neutral and accountable to the public for her decisions. Procedural hurdles such as grand jury proceedings are no part of tort law: the only check on the filing of a complaint—a minimal one—is the duty to refrain from filing frivolous claims. Defendants in civil proceedings enjoy no right to counsel. At trial, the standard of proof is typically preponderance of the evidence rather than beyond a reasonable doubt. And so on. These features of our civil litigation system are entirely defensible, and in noting them we do not mean to suggest that it lacks important protections for defendants, or that lawsuits are a picnic for tort plaintiffs. Instead our point is that a system of this sort should not be quick to allow plaintiffs to enlist the courts to back them in obtaining more onerous forms of redress. It is one thing for a court to validate a plaintiff's demand for money from the defendant. It is another to validate a demand for specific remedial actions. The encroachment on the defendant's liberty and the quasi-criminal stigma associated with being forced, at the behest of a government official, to engage in an atoning or redressive course of conduct are generally inapt for tort law.

Supposing that there is a convincing story about why the courts long ago settled on money damages as the standard form of redress in tort cases, we arrive, finally, at the question of the proper measure of tort damages. As noted, the prevailing legal rule calls on the factfinder (usually juries) to award compensatory damages in an amount that is fair and reasonable in light of what the defendant did to the plaintiff, and what has happened to the plaintiff as a result of the wrong. Fair compensation thus reflects not only the losses suffered by the plaintiff, but the manner in which the losses were generated.

This is perfectly intuitive. Imagine two surgical patients with identical physical injuries—each suffers permanent loss of movement in one of her hands following surgery. Now suppose that, in the case of one patient, the loss was caused by mere carelessness (a conscientious, well-trained surgeon momentarily loses control of her scalpel, in the process nicking a nerve), whereas in the other the surgeon's slip owed to the fact that he was conducting the surgery while voluntarily intoxicated. Just because the two plaintiffs suffer identical physical consequences does not entail that they ought to or will receive identical compensatory awards. A jury would be entitled to find that something different, and worse, was done to the second patient. Our point for the moment is not that the conscious-wrongdoer surgeon deserves punishment—we discuss this issue below. The point is that the wrong perpetrated against the second patient can fairly be deemed more serious or more wrongful, and hence to entitle her to more by way of compensation.

Our emphasis on fair and reasonable compensation cuts against the scholarly grain insofar as it declines to accord foundational status in tort law to the idea of make-whole damages. This is one of the points at which we part ways with Weinrib, Ripstein, and other corrective justice theorists. As we have seen, for them "make whole" is built into the conceptual fabric of tort law: the logic of corrective justice requires that damages be make-whole damages. For us, it is not. But this does not mean that our account has no place for it. The task at hand is to give the make-whole notion its due, but no more than its due.

History can shed some light here. Explicit references to "making whole" as the measure of tort damages seem to have become common only in the middle of the nineteenth century. Prior to this time, leading commentaries stated that, in personal injury cases, there was no fixed rule for damages, and instead juries had broad discretion to set damages in an amount they deemed sufficient to provide "satisfaction" to the plaintiff. As we have noted, this idea of largely unconstrained juror discretion remains intact even today in standard jury instructions. However, starting around 1850, courts and commentators began to suggest that, absent special circumstances, payment equal to the tort-related losses suffered by the victim should be regarded as the measure of fair compensation.[21] Their doing so reflected in part a desire to tie damages calculations to more observable and measurable losses (medical bills, lost wages, etc.) rather than supposedly less quantifiable normative notions of mistreatment, and, relatedly, to find a way of making tort damages somewhat more 'rational' and predictable.[22]

The genealogy of the make-whole idea is illuminating, for it suggests that corrective justice theories have mistaken what was initially developed as a *rule of thumb* guiding the application of a principle as if it were the principle itself. Making whole is neither the principle of tort damages, nor

---

21. It seems likely that notions of "making whole" first appeared in tort cases alleging only loss of (or damage to) property, as well as contract cases alleging quantifiable financial losses flowing from breach. John C. P. Goldberg, *Two Conceptions of Tort Damages: Fair v. Full Compensation*, 55 DePaul L. Rev. 435 (2006). At least absent aggravating circumstances (e.g., the willful and wanton destruction of another's property), the attraction of make-whole as the measure of fair compensation in such cases is certainly understandable.

22. *Id.*

is it irrelevant to tort damages. It is a guideline or default rule that judges use in assessing whether a jury award amounts to fair compensation for the victim. In the eyes of the law of remedies, a court that orders a tort defendant to pay the plaintiff for her tort-related losses, is (absent special circumstances) providing the plaintiff with fair compensation and thus adequate redress.

Punitive Damages and Due Process

We have offered an account of tort compensation that avoids problems that inhere in the views of corrective justice and tort-as-compensation-system scholars. But the civil recourse framework promises more than this. Among the hot button issues of modern tort law, perhaps none is more conspicuous than punitive damages. Another set of issues at the center of modern debates goes under the general heading of tort reform. In this section and the next we show how civil recourse theory sheds light on these pressing issues.

Punitive damages are by definition extra-compensatory. When awarded, they provide a plaintiff with an additional payment beyond the compensation to which she is entitled once she has proven her case. In the late nineteenth century, there was a lively debate about whether punitive damages—also known as "exemplary" or "vindictive" damages, as well as "smart money"—should be available in tort cases. Critics complained that to allow a separate award designed to punish or make an example out of the defendant introduced alien criminal-law notions into the civil litigation system. Individual victims have no business delivering punishment; that is something over which governmental officials hold a monopoly. Anything operating as punitive damages, the argument concluded, must by definition violate this principle and therefore be illegitimate.

The critics lost. The courts of almost every state have long allowed punitive damages to be awarded, albeit only in a narrow subset of tort cases. These are cases in which the defendant is proven to have acted not merely wrongfully but with a malicious purpose or with wanton disregard for the rights of the victim. Examples include gratuitous physical assaults, studied efforts to humiliate another, or conduct so recklessly dangerous as to reveal complete indifference to others' well-being. Even when a defendant engages in egregious misconduct of this sort, the plaintiff can only ask for punitive damages: she is not entitled to them. And in fact studies show that punitive damages are awarded only a tiny fraction of the tiny fraction of tort cases that proceed all the way to judgment. However, when they are awarded, they can be eye-poppingly large, which is why they have garnered a lot of attention, not only from scholars but in the media and among politicians.

Indeed, in the 1980s and 1990s, concern over punitive damages reached new heights. Advocates for the business community complained bitterly that they were running wild. A new breed of high-flying plaintiff's lawyer, they argued, had perfected the art of convincing sympathetic jurors that borderline corporate conduct—such as a car manufacturer deliberately choosing to represent its cars as new even if they have been partially re-painted prior to sale, or an insurance company with a business model that trains its agents to refuse initial requests for coverage of obviously covered losses—can be deterred from engaging in this sort of misconduct only if, when sued, they are made to pay multimillion-dollar punitive damages awards. For these sorts of actors, plaintiffs' lawyers would argue, the pay-ment of even a large compensatory award to an injured plaintiff amounts to nothing—a trivial cost of doing business. By contrast, mega-punitive-damages awards can send a message that even hugely profitable businesses cannot ignore and, in the process, vindicate the interests of the plaintiff and other victims of the same policies who perhaps lacked the where-withal or gumption to sue.

The extent to which the phenomenon just described was widespread, and the gravity of the burden it placed on businesses, have remained a source of contention among policy analysts. But, of course, the business community was not mainly interested in convincing scholars of the seri-ousness of the problem. Rather, it sought—and got—the attention of law-makers, including the Justices of the United States Supreme Court. Indeed, the outcry over punitive damages eventually led the Court to stage a re-markable intervention—remarkable because, in a landmark 1938 decision, the Court forswore any authority to make substantive rules of tort law.[23] That authority, it said, resides exclusively in state courts and legislatures (and Congress insofar as tort law raises matters of national concern).

Having disabled itself from making tort law, including rules pertaining to tort remedies, the Court thus appeared to have left itself without any legal basis to set limits on punitive damage awards upheld by state courts.

23. Erie R.R. Co. v. Tompkins, 304 U.S. 64 (1938).

Ultimately, however, a coalition of Justices concluded that the United States Constitution—in particular the Fourteenth Amendment's guarantee that no person's property may be taken without due process of law—sets procedural and substantive limits on punitive damages awarded in conformity with state-law rules. The controversial nature of these rulings—and attendant worries that the Court was being "political" in finding within a 125-year-old constitutional provision limits on liability that nobody had previously noticed—is evidenced by the fact that they have been criticized by both plaintiff-friendly "liberals" and business-friendly "conservatives," including Justices Scalia and Thomas. In scathing dissents, both accused their colleagues of granting rights to tort defendants that have no basis in constitutional text or history.

We maintain that civil recourse theory actually helps to explain why some of the Court's interventions in this area are based on a plausible understanding of "due process." The key is to appreciate that—as we and a handful of other scholars have documented over the past fifteen years—two very different conceptions of punitive damages have developed in American law, and that punitive damages awards in the great majority of states problematically fuse them.[24] Pulling the two apart— which civil recourse theory permits us to do—is critical to achieving a cogent analysis of the modern constitutional law of punitive damages.

The first conception of punitive damages is authentic to the common law of torts. On this conception they constitute a special kind of redress available to the victims of torts involving highly culpable wrongdoing. The second, by contrast, is *regulatory* in spirit and thus alien to tort law, in that it calls for punitive damages to operate roughly as the sort of fine that, in other circumstances, might be enforced by a state prosecutor or regulatory body.

The point of drawing this distinction is *not* to assert that the second type is per se illegitimate when awarded in a court judgment. It is instead

---

24. Thomas B. Colby, *Beyond the Multiple Punishment Problem: Punitive Damages as Punishment for Individual, Private Wrongs*, 87 Minn. L. Rev. 583 (2003); Martin H. Redish & Andrew L. Mathews, *Why Punitive Damages are Unconstitutional*, 33 Emory L.J. 1 (2004); John C. P. Goldberg, *Tort Law for Federalists (and the Rest of Us): Private Law in Disguise*, 28 Harv. J. L. & Pub. Policy 3 (2004); Benjamin C. Zipursky, *A Theory of Punitive Damages*, 84 Tex. L. Rev. 105 (2005); Anthony J. Sebok, *Punitive Damages; From Myth to Theory*, 92 Iowa L. Rev. 957 (2007); Dan Markel, *Retributive Damages: A Theory of Punitive Damages as Intermediate Sanction*, 94 Cornell L. Rev. 239 (2009).

to say that the imposition of quasi-criminal or regulatory punitive damages raises a set of procedural and substantive concerns that are not raised by punitive damages that genuinely amount to redress. It is precisely these concerns that are at the heart of several of the Supreme Court's punitive damages decisions. *What the courts cannot do, the Court has ruled, is employ standard tort procedures to generate a punitive damages award that can be justified only on a regulatory rationale*—to allow such an award would be to permit regulatory sanction (or punishment) without "due process" of law. One can question the particular guidelines the Court has adopted to regulate punitive damage awards, but it would be erroneous to suggest that its interventions have been unmotivated. The Justices have rightly worried that certain punitive awards, grounded in certain kinds of justifications, and awarded through certain processes, amount to regulation in the guise of redress.

In what sense might punitive damages amount to the redress of wrongs? Here it is important to recall the traditional and still-prevailing common-law rule that punitive damages are available only in cases of egregious wrongdoing, and never as of right. It is also helpful to recall that "make-whole" is a measure of full and fair compensation, not the conceptual core of what the remedy is about. For cases in which there is insult atop wrongful injury—i.e., a mistreatment that demonstrates the defendant's malice toward, contempt for, or wanton indifference to the plaintiff's rights or welfare—tort law has historically relaxed the limitation of reasonable and fair compensation. In these cases, the plaintiff is empowered to request that the court (typically through the jury) impose liability beyond what will compensate the plaintiff. In other words, some plaintiffs are empowered to be "punitive" or to be "vindictive" toward the defendant rather than simply gaining compensation geared to the losses they have suffered. This is why punitive damages were sometimes called "vindictive damages" or "smart money" (the latter referring to a monetary payment that stings or smarts). Here, in other words, the law allows the tort plaintiff *to be punitive toward a person who has very badly mistreated her.* And yet, in keeping with the "civil" nature of tort redress, there are various constraints on the exercise of this power. As is true of redress in the form of compensation, this special form of private punitiveness can only take the form of a monetary payment (as opposed, say, to retaliatory harm or incarceration). In addition, there must be proof of malicious or wanton wrongdoing. Finally, a jury whose verdict is subject to review by trial and appellate courts must choose to validate the plaintiff's demand, must set the amount of the payment, and must do so in a manner that is to some degree anchored in the actual injury the plaintiff suffered at the defendant's hands.

The regulatory conception of punitive damages is fundamentally different. According to it, there is potential value to society in having certain tort defendants pay damages beyond fair compensation to the plaintiff. Under the right circumstances, this additional quantum of damages can provide the necessary financial incentive to induce actors like the defendant to comply with their legal obligations. As noted, on this account, punitive damages operate in the manner of a fine—it is just that the fine is imposed and collected not by a government official, but by the plaintiff and her lawyer acting in the capacity of private attorneys general. Whereas on the redress model a plaintiff who obtains punitive damages receives a payment for which she is eligible by virtue of what the defendant did to her, on the regulatory model the plaintiff receives a payment principally because the system has good reason to want the defendant to make the payment; the plaintiff is allowed to keep it as a kind of bounty, akin to the bounty sometimes collected by plaintiffs under whistleblower statutes.[25]

With the distinction between the two conceptions of punitive damages in place, we can now better appreciate what drove the Supreme Court to step into in an area of law it seemed to have abandoned, and why its doing so plausibly connects to a constitutional principle of due process.[26] Insofar as plaintiffs' lawyers, with the blessing of trial courts, have convinced jurors to impose large punitive damage awards on tort defendants by appealing to regulatory arguments—by arguing that a massive award is necessary because a corporate defendant has adopted policies and practices that have probably visited harm on lots of people (not just the plaintiff be-

---

25. A clear expression of these two models is provided by so-called split-recovery statutes, according to which part of a punitive damages award is channeled to the plaintiff, and part is channeled to the state treasury, a charitable organization, or some other entity serving the public interest. *See* Catherine M. Sharkey, *Punitive Damages as Societal Damages*, 113 YALE L.J. 347, 375–80 (2003) (discussing split-recovery statutes).

26. For an elaboration of this argument, see Benjamin C. Zipursky, Palsgraf, *Punitive Damages, and Preemption*, 125 HARV. L. REV. 1757 (2012).

fore the court), and because only such an award will get the corporation to fly the straight and narrow—they have deployed an illicit, mix-and-match strategy. They have used a set of processes designed to enable victims of wrongs to obtain redress from wrongdoers as a shadow regulatory regime. This is why the Court has held that it is impermissible to award punitive damages to a tort plaintiff as a means of vindicating the interests of non-plaintiff third parties who may have suffered injury as a result of the same kind of mistreatment experienced by the plaintiff.[27] It is also why the Court has ruled that the size of any punitive award must bear a reasonable relationship to what the defendant actually has done to the plaintiff.[28]

We do not defend all aspects of the Court's punitive damages jurisprudence. Indeed, there are reasons of federalism and institutional competence that might counsel against the Court entering this area of tort reform,[29] and for declining to empower defendants to create a whole new layer of post-verdict litigation in cases where juries have found egregious misconduct. Nonetheless, it is notable that—whichever form of constitutional interpretation one favors (originalism, textualism, common-law constitutionalism, living constitutionalism, process theory, and so on)—civil recourse theory actually identifies constitutional concepts and principles that can provide guidance to courts and reason for thinking they have a role to play. This is more than can be said for corrective justice theorists, whose account ahistorically regards punitive damages as alien to tort law. It is also far superior to that of economic theorists of law, who, as theorists, acknowledge that there are probably many appropriate occasions for extra-compensatory damages, yet who, as market-oriented lawyers, tend to side with business interests committed to shearing them away.

Civil recourse theory offers a cogent account of why, for a certain kind of tort victim, it is not necessarily appropriate for the law to insist that the plaintiff be limited in her recovery to what approximates make-whole damages. For a system of *civil* recourse, this additional liability takes

27. Philip Morris USA, Inc. v. Williams, 549 U.S. 346 (2007).
28. State Farm Mut. Auto. Ins. Co. v. Campbell, 538 U.S. 408 (2003); BMW of North America, Inc. v. Gore, 517 U.S. 559 (1996).
29. Justice Ginsburg, in a dissent joined by Chief Justice Rehnquist, made the federalist and institutional competence argument in *Gore. See* 517 U.S. at 607–13 (Ginsburg, J., dissenting). To the extent that her dissent rests on Bickelian, passive-virtue grounds, we are somewhat sympathetic; to the extent it relies on there being no constitutional basis for special scrutiny, we are not.

the form of an additional payment—a payment of money that vindicates the plaintiff and castigates the defendant. It is true that this conception of punitive damages comes within built-in limits. It does not allow a plaintiff to invoke tort procedures to obtain punitive damages on a non-tort rationale. At the same time it places punitive damages on a sounder basis: one more consistent with all the other salient features of tort law. In that sense, it provides a sturdier defense of this long-standing and important feature of tort law than do more ambitious but more ad hoc efforts to defend punitive damages as ersatz regulation.

Finally, as we have demonstrated elsewhere, civil recourse theory provides guidance for courts thinking through constitutional punitive damages doctrine. It explains why the holdings of *BMW v. Gore* and *Philip Morris v. Williams* are defensible on procedural due process grounds; it suggests that certain ways of applying these cases are more justifiable than others; it helps to identify appropriate instructions for jurors;[30] it creates a foundation for other important doctrinal analyses of constitutional arguments against punitive damages; and it enables us to design regulatory regimes that would be less suspect and more effective than the award of punitive damages through tort proceedings while still recognizing the potential value of allowing plaintiffs (outside the tort context) to bring suits as private attorneys general.[31]

Damages Caps

State lawmakers—also largely in response to cries for help from repeat-player tort defendants—have been busy altering common-law rules to reduce the absolute size and variance among compensatory damages awards in tort cases. The most striking of these measures are damages caps, which set a bright-line limit on the amounts successful plaintiffs can obtain, either for one category of compensatory damages (typically pain and suffering) or for the overall amount (including both "economic damages," such as medical bills and lost wages, and "noneconomic damages," such as compensation for pain and suffering).

---

30. Benjamin C. Zipursky, *Punitive Damages after* Philip Morris USA v. Williams, 44 COURT REV. 134 (2008–09) (drawing out the implications of *Williams* for jury instructions).

31. *See, e.g.*, Dan Markel, *How Should Punitive Damages Work?*, 157 U. PA. L. REV. 1383 (2009) (examining deterrence and retribution roles that punitive damages might play under a genuine private attorney general model).

An example of the former is California's $250,000 cap on pain and suffering damages in medical malpractice actions, first adopted in 1975.[32] An example of the latter is the cap adopted by Virginia, which also applies to medical malpractice claims, and which currently limits a plaintiff to a maximum tort recovery of $2.3 million. Obviously the Virginia cap leaves room for many malpractice claimants to recover the amounts they would have recovered before the cap was put in place (those under $2.3 million). Nonetheless, the legislature clearly thought it was accomplishing something when it enacted this law, and indeed it did. The effect of a cap such as this is to limit damages in those rare cases of malpractice that cause catastrophic injuries, the damages for which can easily run into the tens of millions.

How should such damages caps be evaluated? Another development in constitutional law—this one in state rather than federal constitutional law—sheds light here. Several state high courts have ruled that flat caps on damages, whether applicable to only certain kinds of compensatory damages or all such damages, violate rights guarantees provided in their state constitutions.[33] To be sure, a number of other courts have upheld such caps against constitutional challenge.[34] However, given that modern constitutional doctrine generally accords legislatures enormous discretion to modify common law, the fact that there are court decisions striking down caps is no less remarkable than the fact of the Supreme Court's intervention in the law of punitive damages.

32. The cap is not subject to adjustment for inflation, even though $250,000 in 1975 dollars is today worth about $1 million dollars. https://data.bls.gov/cgi-bin/cpicalc.pl?cost1=250%2C000 .00&year1=201706&year2=197506 (last visited January, 28, 2018). Voters rejected a 2014 initiative to increase the cap to $1 million. https://ballotpedia.org/California_Proposition_46, _Medical_Malpractice_Lawsuits_Cap_and_Drug_Testing_of_Doctors_(2014) (last visited January, 28, 2018).

33. McCall v. United States, 134 So.3d 894 (Fla. 2014); Lebron v. Gottlieb Mem. Hosp., 930 N.E.2d 895 (Ill. 2010); Watts v. Lester E. Cox Med. Centers, 376 S.W.3d 633 (Mo. 2012); Carson v. Maurer, 424 A.2d 825 (N.H. 1980), overruled on other grounds, Cmty. Res. For Justice, Inc. v. City of Manchester, 917 A.2d 707 (N.H. 2007); Lucas v. United States, 757 S.W.2d 687 (Tex. 1988); Mayo v. Wisconsin Injured Patients and Families Compensation Fund, 901 N.W.2d 782 (Wisc. App. 2017) (following Ferdon v. Wisconsin Patients Comp. Fund, 701 N.W.2d 440 (Wisc. 2005)).

34. See, e.g., Fein v. Permanente Med. Grp., 695 P.2d 665 (Cal. 1985); Zdrojewski v. Murphy, 657 N.W.2d 721 (Mich. 2002); Adams v. Children's Mercy Hosp., 832 S.W.2d 898 (Mo. 1992), overruled on other grounds, Watts v. Lester E. Cox Med. Ctrs., 376 S.W.3d 633, 636 (Mo. 2012); Judd v. Drezga, 103 P.3d 135 (Utah 2004); Etheridge v. Med. Ctr. Hosps., 376 S.E.2d 525 (Va. 1989); Robinson v. Charleston Area Med. Ctr. Inc., 414 S.E.2d 877 (W. Va. 1991).

As was true of our discussion of punitive damages, our aim here is not to tackle head-on the question of whether the state court decisions we have mentioned are correct. Rather, we would suggest that the surprising degree to which state courts have entertained and validated constitutional objections to damages caps is evidence of the extent to which the principle of civil recourse really is a principle embedded in our legal system. Relatedly, we will suggest that there is reason to believe that, at least as applied to certain classes of tort victims, damages caps threaten to violate that principle.

Since the 1930s, federal and state courts have been reluctant to endorse constitutional challenges to legislation modifying common-law rules. Such legislation, they reason, falls within the social and economic realm, rather than encroaching on protected civil rights. Courts thus ordinarily apply highly deferential "rational basis review" to such legislation, according to which a statute will be upheld against constitutional challenge as long as it can plausibly be construed as a rational means of achieving some legitimate governmental purpose. Reform measures such as damages cap would seem easily to satisfy this deferential test, given that it is plausible to believe that they help contain the cost of liability insurance, and help promote activities—such as the delivery of medical care—that might be affected by tort liability and hence by caps on that liability.

Nonetheless, several courts have struck down caps. In so doing, some have invoked state constitutional guarantees of equal protection, jury trial rights, and separated legislative and judicial powers. Others have relied on provisions found in many state constitutions providing that "courts shall be open," such that "any person, for any injury done him, in his lands, goods, person or reputation, shall have a remedy by due process of law . . . ." (As noted in Chapter 1, these provisions trace back to rights protections provided in Magna Carta.)

Whether expressed in the language of open courts, due process, equal protection, jury trial rights, or separated powers, one intuition that seems to be driving these decisions is that a person whom the law deems to have been the victim of an injurious wrong is, *ceteris paribus*, entitled to redress in the form of fair compensation from her injurer. This is not to say that the common law of tort is immune from revision. It is instead to say that the principle of civil recourse sets a baseline, and that legislatures can only modify tort law and tort remedies in certain ways, and on certain rationales.[35]

It is one thing for courts to defer—as they usually do—to a legislative judgment that various social goods stand to be served by barring negligence suits for workplace accidents and adopting in their place a workers' compensation system. It is another for them to defer to a legislature that has simply capped the damages recoverable to a certain class of tort claimant. Workers' compensation laws, in principle, provide persons who would have had valid negligence claims with compensation. It also retains a tort-like notion of the workplace as a locus of responsibility—that is, of employers retaining some legally recognized obligation to take measures to reduce the likelihood of on-the-job injuries.[36] Caps, particularly caps like Virginia's that apply to a plaintiff's entire award, are an arbitrary and profoundly regressive mechanism for protecting a profession or industry. Under them, it is the interests of the worst-off—those with catastrophic injuries—that are sacrificed in the name of the common good. The person rendered paraplegic, with ongoing medical costs in the tens of millions, is denied what would otherwise be deemed fair and reasonable compensation, so that the general population can benefit from medical care at a lower cost. While there are many sensible and permissible ways to pursue tort reform, some courts—probably correctly, in our view—have concluded that this cannot be such a way.

Caps on pain-and-suffering damages present a more fact-sensitive question. A legislature might reasonably conclude that a plaintiff who stands to recover past and future medical bills and lost income, as well as $250,000 or $500,000 in pain and suffering damages, is receiving fair compensation

---

35. One might argue that because legislatures enjoy the authority to abolish particular torts outright without putting anything in their place—an authority many have exercised, for example, to abolish the "heartbalm" torts of criminal conversation and alienation of affections—they must have the authority to limit the damages recoverable for a recognized tort claim. It is not clear, however, that one can generalize from the authority to eliminate the heartbalm torts to a general authority to eliminate all torts. *See* John C. P. Goldberg, *The Constitutional Status of Tort Law: Due Process and Right to a Law for the Redress of Wrongs*, 115 YALE L.J. 524 (2005). Moreover, even if one could, the argument under consideration illustrates a greater-includes-the-lesser fallacy: the authority to abolish does not necessarily include the authority to limit in arbitrary ways.

36. As contrasted, say, with a taxpayer-funded social insurance scheme that lacked experience rating and other measures that maintain the idea that employers bear a special set of responsibilities with respect to workers' safety.

or something close enough to it that they perhaps can be justified (in general) as plausible measures for achieving certain aggregate social or economic goods. Yet, as other scholars have observed, such caps affect different class of potential claimants differently. In particular, they stand to operate harshly on claimants for whom pain and suffering damages would make up the bulk of their award, including, for example, the elderly (who tend not to be earners and hence do not stand to recover compensation measured by reference to lost past or future income). Moreover, while it might seem that a $250,000 award for pain and suffering damages, even if it were the plaintiff's only damages recovery, would more than suffice to redress standard-issue tortious wrongdoing, there is some evidence that, at least for certain kinds of litigation, the prospect of her client recovering $250,000 or $500,000 might actually be insufficient to induce a lawyer to take the case on a contingent fee basis.[37] If this is true, then, for these cases, damages caps are operating to deny claimants what the law purports to give them as a matter of principle: namely, an avenue of civil recourse through which to obtain redress for having been wronged.

37. *See, e.g.*, Joanna Shepherd, *Uncovering the Silent Victims of the American Medical Liability System*, 67 VAND. L. REV. 151, 165–73 (2014) (discussing modern developments that seem likely to limit the ability of certain medical malpractice claimants to pursue claims, and prior studies suggesting that they do in fact limit such claims); *id.* at 176–88 (reporting on the author's national survey of plaintiffs' attorneys and noting that a majority of respondents indicated they would not represent a medical malpractice plaintiff whose case's outcome was uncertain unless the case was expected to generate a recovery of $500,000).

PART II

The Wrongs of Tort Law

6

Moral Luck, Strict Liability, and Victim Standing

Three Features of Tortious Wrongdoing

A TORT IS A VIOLATION OF A RELATIONAL legal directive enjoining one person from mistreating another in a certain manner.[1] The tort of private nuisance, for example, contains a directive stating that a person must not use or maintain his property so as to interfere unreasonably with another's ability to use and enjoy her land. Because all tort directives address mistreatments, each tort is simultaneously a breach of a duty of non-injury by the tortfeasor and a violation of the victim's legal right against being injured. Tort law in addition confers rights of action on victims. A right of action is a legal power to make a demand upon a tortfeasor, which demand the victim is entitled to have validated by a court upon proof of claim. A tort plaintiff's demand is typically for the payment of compensatory damages.

In prior publications we have bundled the foregoing claims under the label "torts as wrongs." As slogans go, this one might seem anemic, if not pathetic. In fact, these are fighting words, at least among torts scholars

---

1. Some tort directives also enjoin a person to take steps to rescue or to protect another from being injured. When we refer to tort directives enjoining injurious conduct, we mean to encompass directives that generate affirmative duties and rights to assistance.

based in the United States, many of whom regard it as a mark of sophistication to deny that torts are wrongs, or to deny that any illumination comes with recognizing that they are wrongs. In this part of the book we therefore aim to reconstruct, restore, and revitalize the claim that tort law defines wrongs, and that it gives victims of wrongs an opportunity to respond through the court system to having been wronged.

In the present chapter we take on the skeptics directly by responding to three features of tort law that have been taken by some to undermine or render uninteresting its status as a law of wrongs. In doing so, we further isolate the distinctive structure of tortious wrongdoing, contrasting it in particular to criminal wrongdoing. We then turn from structure to substance. To understand tort law requires understanding the nature and justifiability of the process through which courts expand, curtail, and refine the rights, wrongs, and duties to which they will give legal effect. That is the focus of Chapters 7 and 8.

As a preview of the remainder of this chapter, here is a snapshot of the three arguments we will engage:

- *Moral Luck.* Actors who fail to comply with standards of conduct built into tort law's directives—for example, drivers who drive carelessly—face liability only if their failures happen to cause injury to another. Yet the consequences of an actor's conduct are often largely out of her control and hence are not a proper basis for assigning blame or responsibility. If tort liability were really liability for wrongs, it would hinge on what an actor does (or doesn't do) *not* on fortuities as to what follows from what she has done (or not done).
- *Strict Liability.* Courts have defined torts in such a way that an actor can incur liability even when she acts with good intentions and does her best to behave properly, and indeed even when she behaves reasonably. In other words, tort law recognizes "strict liability." Law prepared to impose strict liability is not law that (consistently) predicates liability on wrongdoing.
- *Improper Plaintiffs.* Even actors who violate standards of conduct contained in tort directives so as to injure another can escape liability if the misconduct that causes injury does not amount to a "wronging" of the victim herself. Law that allows actors to avoid liability when they act in a manner it deems impermissible, thereby causing what it

deems an injury, cannot be characterized as law that imposes liability for wrongs.

Although we acknowledge that each of these three features has generated puzzlement and contributed to an unwillingness among scholars to see torts as wrongs, it would be inaccurate to say that we are redefining the concept of a "wrong" so as to preserve our theoretical view that torts are wrongs. In that direction lies vicious circularity. Our basic contention in this chapter is the opposite. The concept of a wrong is by no means empty, but it is capacious and nuanced. One of the benefits of studying tort law is that doing so helps us to move beyond parochial notions of wrongs and wrongdoing that have sometimes trapped not only tort theorists but moral and political philosophers as well.

Moral Luck: Accidents That Don't Happen

The phrase "moral luck" was introduced into modern philosophical parlance by Bernard Williams and Thomas Nagel.[2] From the start, Nagel appreciated the relevance of the species of moral luck known as "causal luck" (or "outcome luck") for attributions of legal responsibility. Thus, he offered a now-familiar example:

> If someone has had too much to drink and his car swerves on to the sidewalk, he can count himself morally lucky if there are no pedestrians in its path. If there were, he would be to blame for their deaths, and would probably be prosecuted for manslaughter. But if he hurts no one, although his recklessness is exactly the same, he is guilty of a far less serious legal offence and will certainly reproach himself and be reproached by others much less severely.[3]

Legal scholars including Guido Calabresi, Larry Alexander, Christopher Schroeder, and Jeremy Waldron have pointed out that a starker version of

---

2. THOMAS NAGEL, *Moral Luck*, in MORTAL QUESTIONS 24–38 (1979); BERNARD WILLIAMS, *Moral Luck*, in MORAL LUCK: PHILOSOPHICAL PAPERS 1973–1980, at 20–39 (1981). Both book chapters are revisions of essays bearing the same titles, which were originally published in 1976 in the *Proceedings of the Aristotelian Society*. Nagel's was penned as a response to Williams's, with the latter generally credited with having coined the phrase.

3. NAGEL, *supra* note 2, at 29.

this same issue is posed within tort law, and (unlike Nagel himself) argued that tort law's differential treatment of the "lucky" and "unlucky" is indefensible.[4]

Waldron, for example, imagined two drivers, "Mr. Fate" and "Mr. Fortune," each of whom drives in an identically careless fashion on a city street, but only one of whom (Fate) hits a motorcyclist ("Hurt"), whereas the other (Fortune) hits no one. Fortune faces no liability. Fate, on the other hand, incurs liability to the tune of $5 million. Waldron grants that it is intuitive to suppose that Fate should face *some* liability. But, he continues,

> . . . [i]t is difficult . . . to go beyond this intuition and explain exactly why it is fair that Fate should be expected to come up with a sum of money this large . . . .
>
> The difficulty is exacerbated when we consider the other driver, Mr. Fortune . . . . No one would think it appropriate to require *him* to pay Hurt $5 million; yet his behavior, morally speaking, was indistinguishable from that of Fate . . . .[5]

In short, causal luck operates more starkly in tort law than it typically does in criminal law or ordinary morality because tort liability attaches *only* when there has been an injury. Moreover, tort compensation is tied to the extent of the victim's injuries, such that two persons who engage in identical tortious conduct will face perhaps significantly different liabilities depending on the severity of the injuries their respective victims happen to suffer.[6] Criminal law, because it is prepared to hold actors accountable for "inchoate" crimes (such as conspiracies and attempts), and because it less tightly links punishments to outcomes, better approximates what a genuine law of wrongs should look like. The same might seem to be true of moral notions of blameworthiness: what matters, morally (some suppose), is what one has done, not how things turn out. It seems to follow

---

4. Guido Calabresi, The Cost of Accidents: A Legal and Economic Analysis 306 (1970); Larry A. Alexander, *Causation and Corrective Justice: Does Tort Law Make Sense?*, 6 L. & Phil. 1, 12–17 (1987); Christopher H. Schroeder, *Causation, Compensation and Moral Responsibility*, in Philosophical Foundations of Tort Law 347 (David G. Owen ed., 1995); Jeremy Waldron, *Moments of Carelessness and Massive Loss*, in Philosophical Foundations, *supra*, at 387.

5. Waldron, *supra* note 4, at 388.

6. Relevant fortuities include not only the extent of the plaintiff's injuries, but the plaintiff's financial position and prospects. If it turns out that Hurt is a professional athlete who, because of the accident, is no longer able to play his sport and thus loses tens of millions of dollars in salary, Fate is in principle subject to liability for that loss.

that tort law is an indefensibly arbitrary law of wrongs, and cannot really be about the commission of wrongs after all.

Three parallel mistakes lie at the bottom of arguments such as these: one in action theory, one in moral theory, and one in legal theory.[7] In action theory, it is crucial to recognize that there are multiple available descriptions of a given act, and that choosing among them depends on the context in which, and the reasons for which, one is choosing. Consider the following renderings of an instance in which X shoots a loaded gun: (i) "X pointed the gun at Y and pulled the trigger"; (ii) "X shot a bullet at Y"; (iii) "X shot a bullet into Y's abdomen"; (iv) "X wounded Y by shooting her"; and (v) "X shot Y dead." Each of these might be an accurate description of what X did. And, while it might be tempting to think that (i) is the most basic, this is a shallow and indefensible view. It is certainly not true that (i) can claim to be the most accurate available description. "X held the gun in his hand, lifted it roughly parallel to the level of Y's abdomen, pointed it in a northerly direction and retracted the muscle of his index finger around the trigger until it snapped" might be more accurate. Nor is (i) somehow objective in a way that the others are not. Each is equally available, and hence, in choosing among them, one must consider the reasons for adopting one over the others.

In Waldron's example, there is a sense in which Fate and Fortune engaged in the same act—driving in the same careless manner. But there is equally a sense in which they did not. *Fate ran down another person, Fortune did not.* Given that tort law (in contrast to criminal and regulatory law) is fundamentally concerned with setting rules about certain kinds of mistreatment of others and about giving persons injured in the course of such mistreatments the ability to respond, it makes perfect sense for it to adopt "carelessly ran down another person," rather than "drove carelessly," as the relevant description of Fate's conduct.

The mistake in moral theory runs parallel to the mistake in action theory. Even aside from what the law requires, there is a moral duty not to drive so as to generate an unreasonably high risk of running down a pedestrian. But there is also a moral duty not to run down another user of the roads through careless driving. And it is a mistake to suppose that the

7. The analysis in this section draws substantially from John C. P. Goldberg & Benjamin C. Zipursky, *Tort Law and Moral Luck*, 92 CORNELL L. REV. 1123 (2007), and Benjamin C. Zipursky, *Two Dimensions of Responsibility in Crime, Tort and Moral Luck*, 9 THEORETICAL INQUIRIES L. 97 (2007).

former is more fundamental or basic than the latter simply because the former fits within the latter as a "lesser included" wrong (to borrow language from criminal law). The story of Fate and Fortune involves two distinct moral duties, even though these duties overlap in both requiring careful driving. The duty to refrain from driving in an unreasonable manner is a duty of *noninjuriousness*—a duty to avoid acting in a manner that generates an unreasonable *risk* of injury to another. The duty to refrain from carelessly running down another is a duty of *noninjury*—a duty not to injure others. More precisely, it is a *qualified* duty of noninjury—a duty not to injure others through a certain kind of conduct (here, careless conduct).

It is perfectly cogent to assert that both Fate and Fortune breached a moral duty of noninjuriousness by driving in an unduly risky fashion. This is why both can be blamed for behaving irresponsibly even without knowing anything about the consequences of their actions. But it is only Fate who in addition breached a duty of noninjury. And this is why, morally, the two drivers are not identically situated. Fate committed a wrong (i.e., breached a moral duty) that Fortune did not—the wrong of carelessly injuring another (breaching the moral duty not to carelessly injure others).

Finally, and most importantly (because the first two claims of "mistake" seem formal and academic without it), the skeptical critique based on the moral luck problem also evinces a mistake in legal theory. Here is a way of stating the critique that makes it about as plausible as it can be made: "Fate and Fortune rendered themselves eligible for liability in exactly the same way: by driving carelessly. Tort law is thus anomalous and unfair for imposing substantial financial liability on Fate but not on Fortune, given that they committed *the same legal infraction*." Unsurprisingly, our response to this argument is analogous to the moral-theory argument offered a moment ago. If Fate and only Fate is held liable to Hurt, it is because Fate breached a legal duty owed to persons such as Hurt that Fortune did not breach—namely, the duty recognized in negligence law to avoid carelessly injuring others. This is different from the legal duty to refrain from driving carelessly (full stop). In our legal system, violations of that duty are handled in other ways, which is why Fate and Fortune might both find themselves on the receiving end of a traffic ticket.

Readers might object that our analysis of legal duties amounts to mere wordplay. The objection is unfounded. We are providing an account of the substance of tort law's rules. Under those rules, a person is granted a right of action *only* when the defendant breaches a duty of noninjury owed to her, and (to say the same thing) only when her right not to be injured by another in a certain manner is violated. Our legal system's willingness to empower the plaintiff, and therefore to render the defendant liable, turns on the plaintiff's having been the victim of an injurious wrong and therefore of a rights-violation of this sort. Hurt has no right of action against Fortune because Hurt was not injured by Fortune and thus did not suffered a violation of the right conferred on him by negligence law. Conversely, Fortune faces no liability to Hurt, because he did not injure Hurt. Indeed, because Fortune injured no one, he violated no rights recognized by tort law, and therefore faces no tort liability.[8]

Is it illuminating to assert that Fate's vulnerability to Hurt's demand for responsive action is just a matter of luck? The assertion needs to be more fully specified before the question can be answered. If the phrase "just a matter of luck" is meant to suggest that *Fate had no control over whether he would face liability to Hurt*, then the assertion would indeed be morally illuminating, and would count as a basis for doubting that negligence law constitutes a genuine and justifiable domain of wrongs. Attributions of responsibility to an actor—and tort liability is a form of responsibility—are usually thought to presuppose an adequate opportunity for the actor to avoid doing that which renders him responsible. The problem is that this assertion, so interpreted, is simply false: Fate could have avoided liability by driving with due care.

Waldron's assertion is different. It suggests that *Fate's liability was just a matter of luck as compared to the nonliability of Fortune*, because it did not turn on anything under Fate's control. Of course, this is because the thought experiment that features them was designed to generate this answer. But we have argued above that this does not render it arbitrary or unjustifiable. Fate is vulnerable to Hurt's claim for damages because he

8. One perhaps can imagine a system with directives that generate legal duties and rights on terms that blur the distinction between duties of noninjuriousness and noninjury. For example, imagine a jurisdiction whose judicial decisions contain a directive requiring each of us to refrain from carelessly *risking* physically injury to another, and that regard such risk imposition as actionable in and of itself. In this imagined regime, the imposition of risk of physical injury on another might constitute a breach of a duty of noninjury and a violation of a right against being injured. Needless to say, as a descriptive matter, this is not our system. Moreover, it is hardly happenstance that our courts have declined to treat the imposition of risk of physical harm as an injury in and of itself. In fact, there is a host of reasons why courts have declined to go down this road. *See* John C. P. Goldberg & Benjamin C. Zipursky, *Unrealized Torts*, 88 VA. L. REV. 1625 (2002).

injured Hurt, and Fortune is not vulnerable because he did not. The fact that Fortune drove negligently and still escaped liability is neither here nor there on the question of whether Fate was given sufficient opportunity to avoid being held responsible.

There is an air of paradox at work in the Fate–Fortune parable—this is what makes moral luck problems so engaging. But the source of the discomfort is easy to locate. In ordinary discourse, we tend not to distinguish sharply among different forms of responsibility and liability. The power of the parable relies on just this sort of blurring. If we consider how the law should deal with Fate and Fortune from a criminal-law perspective, the pattern of no liability and massive liability might be hard to accept. Just as it would be facially odd for criminal law to punish actual murderers severely, but allow attempted murderers to walk away scot-free, it would also be odd to impose a criminal fine on Fate but not Fortune. But this is because the imposition of criminal liability—state punishment—is commonly understood to be designed to correlate, at least roughly, to a defendant's blameworthiness, where blameworthiness turns in large part on the extent to which the defendant's conduct was volitional and expressive of antisocial dispositions or bad character. Waldron's suggestion that there is something odd about Fate and Fortune facing different legal consequences for their "identical" acts trades on this way of thinking about wrongs. The two drivers' acts are identical *from within a framework concerned to evaluate acts by reference to the blameworthiness of the underlying conduct.*

Tort law is not criminal law. A tort plaintiff's lawsuit is not a request to the state that it impose a punishment or sanction on a blameworthy offender. Rather, it is a demand by a plaintiff to a court for assistance in holding the defendant responsible *to her* for having invaded her right. As we have explained and will continue to explain, courts apply certain control conditions in determining whether an actor has committed a rights invasion for which he can be held responsible. But requiring a defendant to have acted (or failed to act) in certain ways, then measuring liability in relation to the rights invasion experienced by another as a result—this is entirely different from assessing a defendant's conduct as an expression of his disposition or character. Although crimes and torts are both members of the genus "wrongs," they are different species. It is only when one conflates the two that the moral luck problem begins to take on plausibility as a ground to question the intelligibility or fairness of tort law, understood as a law of wrongs.

Strict Liability: The Reasonable Tortfeasor

Tort law is not about sanctioning individuals for their misconduct, but about empowering a person who has been wrongfully injured to demand redress from the wrongful injurer. This empowerment is conditioned, however, on defendant's having committed a *legal* wrong. In this respect (but not others) the wrongs of tort law do share something with the wrongs of criminal law. For reasons of justice and fairness, a defendant—whether defending against criminal charges or tort liability—can avoid legal responsibility if she does not violate applicable legal rules of conduct.

These observations lay the groundwork for the supposed problem of strict liability. Tort law hinges liability on *wrongful* injury. However, when the definitions of particular torts are scrutinized, one discovers that they offer no guarantee to actors that, by acting conscientiously, they will avoid liability. In short, tort law's definition of "wrongful" seems to include conduct that lacks the qualities that must be present in order for conduct properly to be deemed wrongful.

Take the tort of negligence. At least since the classic case of *Vaughan v. Menlove*,[9] courts have deemed its standard of care to be objective, which means that it is neither here nor there that a given defendant was naturally disposed to be imprudent (or had lesser capacity for careful conduct than most people). In Holmes's famous language: "The law considers . . . what would be blameworthy in the average man, the man of ordinary intelligence and prudence, and determines liability by that. If we fall below the level in those gifts, it is our misfortune . . . ."[10] A relatively inexperienced driver who rounds a corner clumsily, slides off the road, and causes an accident might be doing his best to drive carefully. That he was is beside the point so far as negligence law is concerned because the jury is asked to compare the defendant's conduct to that of a reasonably prudent person under the circumstances. Negligence law is also demanding in assessing carelessness in a moment-to-moment (or "snapshot") manner. A surgeon's compliance with the requirements of negligence law is determined by considering whether she competently performed *the plaintiff's surgery*. Even if the surgeon had never slipped up in a thousand previous procedures,

9. (1837) 132 Eng. Rep. 490 (C.P.).
10. OLIVER W. HOLMES JR., THE COMMON LAW 108 (1881).

if she happens to slip up during the plaintiff's surgery so as to injure the plaintiff she is subject to liability.

As we noted earlier, the demandingness of another tort—trespass to land—is even more pronounced. A person who builds a fence upon land owned by another without the owner's permission has committed the tort of trespass to land. This is so even if the builder reasonably believes that he is erecting the fence on his own land (for example, because public records contain an error as to the location of the property line). Intentionally occupying or building on a swath of land is a trespass *if in fact the land is possessed by another* and the other has not permitted the occupation or building. The occupier's or builder's having behaved prudently or reasonably does nothing to defeat liability. Indeed, as *Vincent v. Lake Erie* famously demonstrates,[11] even morally justified interferences with the property rights of another can be actionable in the law of torts.

Nuisance, defamation, battery, and other torts work in roughly the same manner. The key question for each is whether the act or conduct that constitutes the impermissible interference was in fact performed by the defendant, not whether the defendant can demonstrate that she acted in good faith and in a reasonable manner. For intentional torts such as battery, neither the intention to injure nor carelessness as to injury is required for liability. Conversely, tort law overwhelmingly rejects the whole category of excuses (as opposed to justifications).[12]

Given the demandingness of tort standards—and hence the prevalence of conscientious, reasonable tortfeasors—it seems to follow that most torts allow for a fair bit of strict liability. And once it is recognized that a great deal of tort law, even in the heartland of negligence and intentional torts, embraces strict liability, it seems necessary to reject our claim that all torts are wrongs.

The last conclusion does not follow from the doctrinal premises that precede it. The thought that it does depends on an equivocation between two senses of the phrase "strict liability." One form of strict liability—

---

11. Vincent v. Lake Erie Transp. Co., 124 N.W. 221 (Minn. 1910). We think the *Vincent* court reached the right result, but needlessly complicated its analysis by denying there was a trespass. *See* JOHN C. P. GOLDBERG & BENJAMIN C. ZIPURSKY, THE OXFORD INTRODUCTIONS TO U.S. LAW: TORTS 238–41 (2010) (explaining why *Vincent* is a straightforward trespass case that can be resolved without invoking a notion of incomplete privilege).

12. John C. P. Goldberg, *Inexcusable Wrongs*, 103 CAL. L. REV. 467 (2015).

arguably best illustrated by the famous case of *Rylands v. Fletcher*[13]— involves a court declaring that there should be liability *even though the defendant did not violate any standard of conduct, legal or otherwise*. In *Rylands*, the mere fact that loss to the plaintiff resulted from the risky enterprise for which the defendants were responsible—the flooding of Fletcher's mine that resulted from the bursting of the Rylands reservoir—sufficed for liability. Notably, *Rylands* does not suggest that the defendants did anything wrong in building and operating the reservoir, notwithstanding the risks that it posed to neighbors. Liability for damage arising from the enterprise was instead regarded as a fee imposed to cover some of the costs generated by a *permitted* activity. In other words, readiness to pay for losses caused by the enterprise, irrespective of anything that might count as substandard conduct, was treated by *Rylands* as a condition of the defendants being permitted to engage in the conduct. This form of strict liability—which we refer to as *"licensing-based"* strict liability—is quite distinct from liability based on wrongful injuring, or interferences with another's right. Licensing-based strict liability permits liability even in the absence of anything that counts as violation of a legal standard of conduct.

If *Rylands* were at the center of tort doctrine or—to say the same thing— if strict tort liability routinely took the form of licensing-based liability, there would indeed be grounds for rejecting our contention that torts are wrongs. In fact, however, *Rylands* is recognized as an exceptional case. True, it is a staple of Torts courses. But that is precisely because the terms on which it imposes liability are so distinctive as to locate it at or beyond tort law's conceptual boundaries. The form of strict liability that actually is pervasive in tort law—the one at work in the negligence, battery, and trespass to land examples provided above—is of an entirely different sort. In these domains, unlike in *Rylands*, liability *does* hinge on the breach of a standard of conduct. When courts allow for the imposition of liability on an innocent or reasonable trespasser, they do not deem the quality of the defendant's conduct irrelevant to liability. Instead, they hold the defendant to a standard of conduct that is very demanding. In these cases, liability is strict in the sense of being imposed on *unforgiving terms*, not in

---

13. (1868) 3 LRE & I App. 330 (HL). The best characterization of the basis for liability in *Rylands* has long been contested. At a minimum, it is plausible to construe the decision as we construe it here. John C. P. Goldberg & Benjamin C. Zipursky, *The Strict Liability in Fault and the Fault in Strict Liability*, 85 FORDHAM L. REV. 743 (2016).

the sense of being *unrelated to wrongdoing*. Strict tort liability is almost always strict in the unforgiving sense. To say the same thing, standard torts are, in certain common applications, "strict liability wrongs."

Some scholars will argue that this last interpretive claim is falsified by what they would describe as a huge domain of licensing-based tort liability for injuries caused by products. Until the mid-1960s, persons who sued manufacturers and retailers for product-related injuries relied primarily on negligence law (or the law of warranty). However, in the landmark 1963 decision of *Greenman v. Yuba Power Products*,[14] a unanimous California Supreme Court, in an opinion authored by Justice Roger Traynor, held that a plaintiff who sues a manufacturer can recover by proving that he was "injured while using the [manufacturer's product] in a way it was intended to be used as a result of a defect in design and manufacture of which plaintiff was not aware that made the [product] unsafe for its intended use."[15] Two years later the American Law Institute promulgated a provision in the Second Restatement of Torts that presented *Greenman's* rule as black-letter law. Penned initially by Reporter William Prosser, Section 402A emphasized that, under it, liability for injuries caused by their defective products "applies although . . . the seller has exercised *all possible care* in the preparation and sale of [the] product."[16]

Traynor, Prosser, and other proponents of the new regime of strict products liability argued for it on various grounds. The most prominent were avowedly instrumentalist. In particular, they suggested that strict products liability could operate as a kind of insurance mechanism. In an earlier concurring opinion that helped pave the way for *Greenman*, Traynor explained the insurance rationale as follows:

> Those who suffer injury from defective products are unprepared to meet its consequences. The cost of an injury and the loss of time or health may be an overwhelming misfortune to the person injured, and a needless one, for the risk of injury can be insured by the manufacturer and distributed among the public as a cost of doing business.[17]

14. 377 P.2d 897 (Cal. 1963).
15. *Id.* at 901.
16. RESTATEMENT (SECOND) OF TORTS §402A(2)(a) (emphasis added) (AM. L. INST. 1965).
17. Escola v. Coca Cola Bottling Co. of Fresno, 150 P.2d 436, 441 (Cal. 1944) (Traynor, J., concurring).

Given that products liability doctrine is prepared to hold manufacturers (and sometimes retailers) of products liable for injuries even when they exercise "all possible care," that it was adopted in part out of a desire to create a loss-spreading mechanism, and that it is a centerpiece of modern tort law, it is easy to see why many scholars regard it as Exhibit A in support of the claim that modern tort law is chock-full of liability irrespective of wrongdoing.

While understandable, the inclination to see products liability law as marking a dramatic expansion of licensing-based tort liability is misguided. Since its inception, product liability law has required more of plaintiffs than proof of injury caused by a product during ordinary use.[18] A person who, while playing tennis (and through no fault of her own), steps on a perfectly sound tennis ball, thereby breaking her ankle, has no claim against the manufacturer or retailer. To prevail, a products liability plaintiff must prove that she was injured by a *defect* in the product that rendered it more dangerous than it should have been.

The requirement of defectiveness is not an ad hoc limit on liability. Instead, it is what brings strict products liability into the domain of torts—of wrongs. Decisions such as *Greenman* certainly broke new ground. *But they did so by fashioning a new legal directive and with it, a new wrong.* Like the directives in trespass, negligence, and other torts, this directive—"Do not cause injury to a consumer by sending into commerce a dangerously defective product"—sets a standard of conduct that is unforgiving. It can be violated even if a seller takes "all possible care" to prevent a defective product from entering commerce. Thus, product sellers will sometimes find it beyond their powers to comply consistently with this directive. But of course the same is true of car drivers and doctors: they too will find it beyond their powers to comply steadfastly with negligence law's insistence on prudence. *Greenman* and Section 402A recognized a tort that imposes liability on terms that encompass conscientious and diligent actions.

We can bolster our claim that strict products liability is wrongs-based by attending to the now-familiar doctrinal distinction among three *types* of product defect: manufacturing defects, design defects, and warning

---

18. *Id.* at 440 ("[I]t should now be recognized that a manufacturer incurs an absolute liability when an article that he has placed on the market, knowing that it is to be used without inspection, proves to have a defect that causes injury to human beings.") (Traynor, J., concurring).

defects.[19] For it is widely accepted today, and perhaps has been ever since this trichotomy was introduced, that liability for injuries caused by *defectively designed* products, and by *failures to warn*, are wrongs-based. Indeed, commentators increasingly have insisted that, for these two categories, the law sets a standard of conduct that barely differs, or does not differ, from negligence law's ordinary care standard. On this view a defectively designed product *is* (or pretty much is) a negligently designed product, and an actionable failure to warn *is* (or pretty much is) a negligent failure to warn. For reasons explored in Chapter 10, we do not endorse this view, at least as applied to the idea of a defectively designed product. Although they sometimes overlap, the wrong of selling a product with a design defect can be distinct from the wrong of selling a carelessly designed product. Nonetheless, the larger point remains. There is broad agreement among courts and commentators that to injure someone by selling a product with an unsafe design or inadequate warnings is to injure them through *wrongful* conduct (even if the wrongfulness at issue is not best described as a species of carelessness).

Liability for injuries caused by manufacturing defects comes closest to imposing liability without wrongdoing of any sort.[20] It is therefore tempting to suppose that this particular branch of products liability law amounts to licensing-based liability. On this view, the law of manufacturing defects in effect says to product sellers something like the following: "Mass production inevitably produces the occasional lemon. A manufacturer who employs proper quality controls thus cannot be deemed to have done anything wrong just by virtue of sending a lemon into the world that injures a consumer. However, because mass production predictably generates occasional

19. A product is said to have a manufacturing defect if it fails to meet the safety specifications provided by the manufacturer itself—for example, a single toaster that comes off the assembly line with loose wiring that makes it prone to catch fire during ordinary use. Design defects are defects in an entire product line—for example, a drug for treating minor ailments whose chemical composition produces fatal side effects in a significant percentage of users. A warning defect involves the failure to include instructions or labels necessary to render a product safe for ordinary use—for example, a caustic chemical drain cleaner sold for household use that fails to warn users to protect against splatter that can result from pouring the product into standing water, and that may cause blindness.

20. Commentary to the products liability provisions of the Third Restatement of Torts maintains that manufacturing defect liability is strict rather than fault-based, though it also suggests that this form of strict liability may often amount to the recognition of a presumption of fault akin to the presumption generated by the negligence doctrine of *res ipsa loquitur*. RESTATEMENT (THIRD) OF TORTS: PRODUCTS LIABILITY § 2, cmt. a (AM. L. INST. 1998).

injuries in this manner, a condition of being permitted to engage in it is that a manufacturer must be ready to pay for injuries caused by its lemons."

While manufacturing defect liability certainly lends itself to being described as a form of licensing-based liability, it is important to recall once again that the mere fact that a standard of conduct is unforgiving does not establish the validity of this description. The demandingness of the rule requiring manufacturers to avoid injuring consumers through the sale of a lemon is not so different from the demandingness of the rule requiring physicians or drivers to act with ordinary prudence. (It is even closer to rules that require extraordinary care of actors such as common carriers.) Recognition of the "inevitability" of injuries caused by lemons is entirely compatible with treating the sale of a defectively manufactured product that injures a consumer as a wrong.[21] Physicians, drivers, and manufacturers are all permitted to engage in these activities notwithstanding that, even if they are careful, they might sooner or later hurt someone as a result of substandard conduct. Certainly the mere fact that the law does not prohibit conduct of a sort that generates occasional injuries fails to establish that the law in question imposes a *Rylands*-style licensing-based liability regime as opposed to a wrongs-based regime. More affirmatively, given that courts and commentators have generally treated each of the three forms of defect-based products liability as instantiations of the same concept, there is good reason to treat manufacturing defect liability as liability for wrongdoing.

Finally, what is one to make of the fact that the law of products liability was ushered in on the strength of instrumental rationales emphasizing loss-spreading, compensation, and deterrence? Does this establish that some or all of products liability law has always been a policy-driven form of licensing-based strict liability? No. The reasons or grounds that support a rule of tort law are, of course, distinct from the rule itself. One can conclude that loss-spreading, compensation, and deterrence will be served by shifting from a rule of negligence liability to a rule of strict liability without endorsing a shift to the particular kind of strict liability—licensing-based liability—that stands to maximize tort law's ability to serve those goals. Instead, attention to those goals can provide a reason for the courts

---

21. In addition, the idea that the sale of some defectively manufactured products is an inevitable by-product of mass manufacturing does not entail that dangerously defective products are inevitable. For example, defective plastic bottles do not carry the same risks as defective glass bottles.

to recognize a new strict liability wrong: that is, to complement the established wrong of negligence with the distinct wrong of injuring another through the sale of a dangerously defective product. This is what happened in the 1960s and 1970s. Traynor, Prosser, and the other founders of strict products liability never suggested that liability for product-related injuries should be irrespective of defect. Rather, they argued on various policy grounds[22] for the recognition of the new legal wrong of injuring another through the sale of a dangerously defective product.[23]

As for tort law generally, so for modern products liability law: when liability is strict, it is almost always strict in the demanding/unforgiving/wrongs-based sense, not the licensing-based sense. Nor is it mere wordplay on our part to describe tort liability as "wrongs-based, yet strict." As we have explained, even when strict liability of this sort is imposed, directives, duties, and rights are at work. Trespass to land is built around a directive that enjoins interference with others' rights of exclusive possession ("Do not enter land possessed by another without permission!"); medical malpractice enjoins interferences with a patient's right to be free of injuries caused by incompetent treatment ("Do not injure a patient by treating her with less care than would a physician with the requisite skills and training!"); and so on. In each case (apart from the few activities deemed by the courts to be "abnormally dangerous") there is a directive enjoining mistreatment and conferring on persons a right not to be mistreated. And in each case, *the question is whether the defendant failed to comply with the standard of conduct contained in the directive and thus mistreated the plaintiff in a manner that counts as a legal rights-violation.* For all of the instances we considered above—including the innocent or righteous tres-

22. It supports our interpretation that Traynor and Prosser did not rely exclusively on insurance or deterrence rationales, but also invoked considerations of procedural and substantive justice, suggesting, for example, that defect-based liability better accords with the rights that consumers ought to possess in relation to manufacturers, and better enables consumers to vindicate those rights when violated.

23. We can also offer a slightly more qualified version of this last point. Strict products liability—particularly liability for manufacturing defects—sometimes comes close to the line between strict liability wrongs and licensing-based liability without wrongdoing. It does so precisely because the standard it sets is very unforgiving. Often there will be nothing a seller can do to avoid committing the wrong of injuring another through the sale of a defectively manufactured product. It would not be surprising to find that the judges who crafted and implemented this very demanding standard of conduct took some comfort in tort law's occasional recognition of licensing-based liability for abnormally dangerous activities. They may have reasoned that, even if we are pushing wrongs-based liability to the limits, it can alternatively be justified as licensing-based strict liability.

passer, the inexperienced, well-meaning driver, and the previously per-fectly competent surgeon—the answer to this question is yes, notwith-standing that the defendant was blameless or only minimally blameworthy. Tort law is in this respect perhaps harsh, but its harshness does not under-mine its claim to being a law of wrongs.[24]

There are various reasons that render defensible the courts' use of ob-jective and unforgiving standards of conduct in tort law. Objective stan-dards tend to make the adjudication of issues of wrongdoing more straight-forward: judges and juries are not left with the difficult task of determining, for example, whether a negligence defendant really was trying to be careful, or really was doing her best. Likewise, legal standards of conduct that direct us to avoid doing something, rather than directing us to try to refrain from doing something or to make our best efforts to avoid doing something, are less qualified and hence are more easily and forcefully conveyed. For the same reason, they avoid inviting actors to rely on the prospect of being able to excuse their conduct on the ground that they meant well or tried their best.[25]

More fundamentally, the injury-inclusiveness of tort law and its strict-ness are complementary: the supposed "problems" of strict liability and moral luck are features of tort law that, to some degree, balance each other out. By virtue of the former, tort law proves to be friendlier to plain-tiffs than one might expect from a law of wrongs. By virtue of the latter, tort law is more pro-defendant. Liability is possible without proof of con-duct that is actually morally wrongful, as may well be true in the case of the conscientious, reasonable tortfeasor, but it is not possible without proof of actual interference with the plaintiff's interests.

24. We acknowledge that there is today a small pocket of licensing-based strict liability that lawyers and judges regard as part of tort law. It is the pocket that grew out of *Rylands* and is now cast as strict liability for "abnormally dangerous activities." Even though liability in these cases is not, strictly speaking, wrongs-based because liability does not require any substandard conduct—it makes a certain amount of sense for courts to have placed this very modest body of case law under the tort umbrella, much like it has made sense for courts to have folded certain expansive versions of promissory estoppel into the law of contract. See Goldberg & Zipursky, *supra* note 13, at 785 (offering reasons why courts and commentators are reasonable to stretch the category of tort to cover the marginal case of *Rylands*-style strict liability). An-other type of liability sometimes said to be licensing-based—namely, vicarious liability of em-ployers for employee torts—is wrongs-based. *See id.* at 755 & n. 50.

25. *See* Star Wars Episode V: The Empire Strikes Back (Twentieth Century Fox 1980) (re-sponding to his pupil Luke Skywalker's hedge that he would "try" to master the ways of the Force, master Yoda says: "Do, or do not. There is no try.").

Tort law is equally about duties and breaches of duties, on the one hand, and rights and rights-invasions, on the other. The fact that an actor has engaged in conduct that risks injuries to others does not mean that she actually has invaded another's right; hence the injury-inclusiveness of tortious wrongdoing. Conversely, a right can be invaded through conduct that falls below a certain standard of what is owed to others, even when the actor is conscientious and reasonable. Within a body of criminal law, such strictness would be onerous and perhaps unjust. But the violation of a tort standard of conduct does not lead to a showdown with the state and the possibility of punishment. It generates the possibility of being held liable to a private party, but only if she has actually been injured, and only if she chooses to pursue the claim.[26] The fact that tort defendants get the benefit of moral luck in the form of *outcome* luck—which greatly diminishes and narrows the range of persons to whom one might be liable—serves as a counterweight to their facing the burden of moral luck in the form of *compliance* luck, which is a byproduct of tort law's justifiable use of unforgiving standards of conduct.

Improper Plaintiffs: *Palsgraf*

Our third problem—the improper plaintiff—might seem more obscure than the other two. If so, it has been hiding in plain sight. For it is the problem at the center of the classic teaching case of *Palsgraf v. Long Island Railroad*.[27] Although *Palsgraf* is as emblematic of American tort law as any other decision, its significance has been obscured by generations of tort scholars. Overwhelmingly, they have followed Judge William Andrews's dissenting opinion in supposing that the case stands for the proposition that courts must impose limits on negligence liability under the doctrine of "proximate cause." But the key lesson of the case, as Chief Judge Cardozo's majority opinion explained, is not about proximate cause. It instead concerns tort law's *proper-plaintiff principle*, or what one of us initially described as its "substantive standing" requirement.[28] Cardozo memorably articulated this principle as follows: "[A tort] plaintiff sues in her own

---

26. In addition, as explained in the next section, the plaintiff must establish not only wrongful conduct causing injury, but conduct wrongful as to her.

27. 162 N.E. 99 (N.Y. 1928).

28. Benjamin C. Zipursky, *Rights, Wrongs, and Recourse in the Law of Torts*, 51 VAND. L. REV. 1 (1998).

right for a wrong personal to her, and not as the vicarious beneficiary of a breach of a duty owed to another."[29]

The facts of *Palsgraf* are well known to lawyers. A man leapt onto the open space at the end of a train car as the train was pulling out of the defendant railroad's station. Two conductors employed by the railroad tried to steady him by pushing and pulling him onto the train. In the process, they dislodged a newspaper-wrapped package he was carrying under his arm. The conductors did not know—and had no reason to know—that the package contained powerful fireworks, which fell onto the tracks, exploding upon impact. The explosion was powerful enough to blow away a chunk of the railway platform and to cause reverberations around the station. As a result, a large metal scale, located on the platform perhaps thirty feet away from the point where the package fell, toppled onto Mrs. Palsgraf, a ticketed customer who was waiting for a different train. She sued the railroad for negligence. A jury found for her, and a divided intermediate appellate court affirmed.

In a 4–3 decision, New York's high court reversed and held that the claim failed as a matter of law. Cardozo's analysis for the court involved three steps:

(1) Even if it was reasonably foreseeable to the conductors that, by jostling a man carrying a nondescript package as he jumped onto a moving train, they might cause harm to the man or his package, it was not reasonably foreseeable to the conductors that, by so acting, they would cause bodily harm to others at the train station not adjacent to him.[30]

(2) Because Mrs. Palsgraf was located well away from where the conductors were assisting the man with the nondescript package, it was not reasonably foreseeable to the conductors that, by helping the man,

---

29. 162 N.E., at 100.

30. It is important here to reemphasize that the conductors had no reason to suspect that the package contained explosives. *Id.* at 99 ("Nothing in the situation gave notice that the falling package had in it the potency of peril to persons thus removed.") This is why they had no reason to suppose that their actions would have any effect on Mrs. Palsgraf, even if they did have reason to suppose that their actions might cause the package-carrying man to fall, or to fall into and injure another person standing on the platform within a few feet of the point at which they contacted him. Had the man been carrying a package prominently labeled "Danger: High Explosives," then the conductors' actions might have been careless as to persons such as Mrs. Palsgraf.

they might cause bodily harm to her. Therefore, the conductors' actions, even though they could be deemed careless as to the physical well-being of the package-carrier or his package, could not possibly be deemed *careless as to the physical well-being of a person situated in the position of Mrs. Palsgraf,* and hence could not possibly be deemed a breach of the duty owed to her under negligence law.

(3) A plaintiff cannot prevail on a negligence claim unless the defendant breached a duty of care the defendant owed to her; that is, unless the defendant's conduct was careless *as to her.* The fact that the defendant's conduct constitutes a breach a duty of care owed to other, differently situated persons—that it was careless as to them—does not provide a basis for negligence liability, even if the breach of a duty owed to another results in injury to the plaintiff.

Although the first two aspects of Cardozo's analysis have generated controversy,[31] it is the third that has flummoxed most commentators.[32] Cardozo adhered to it because he believed it to be the instantiation in negligence law of a principle that runs throughout tort law. According to this principle, a tort plaintiff cannot prevail by showing that the defendant acted wrongfully toward a differently situated person yet did not act wrong-

31. It has been suggested that Cardozo manipulated the facts to make (1) seem inevitable. A more plausible challenge asserts that foreseeability, as part of breach, is an issue of fact and therefore not something for an appellate court to rule on as a matter of law. However, Cardozo quite correctly recognized that where the breach issue is completely one-sided—as it was on the question of whether the conductors behaved carelessly *toward persons such as Mrs. Palsgraf—* it is for the court to decide.

As for (2), it follows from the proposition that a breach of the duty of care owed to someone requires carelessness relative to her, combined with the premise that one cannot be careless relative to another if no injury to that other is foreseeable. The most substantial challenge to (2) concerns whether it is plausible to assert as a matter of positive law that the duty of care in negligence law is relational rather than nonrelational in its analytic structure. We have argued elsewhere that it is. *See, e.g.,* John C. P. Goldberg & Benjamin C. Zipursky, *The* Restatement (Third) *and the Place of Duty in Negligence Law,* 54 VAND. L. REV. 657 (2000).

32. Some have suggested that *Palsgraf* revealed an older and chastened Cardozo looking to close the floodgates opened by his famous opinion twelve years earlier in MacPherson v. Buick, 110 N.E. 1050 (N.Y. 1916). *MacPherson* held that product manufacturers owe downstream users, not just immediate purchasers, a duty to avoid injuring them through carelessness in the manufacture of their products. In fact, *MacPherson* presupposes the substantive standing rule made explicit in *Palsgraf.* If there were no such rule, Macpherson could have recovered merely by showing that the defendant in that case, Buick, had acted carelessly toward the car's immediate purchaser (a car dealer) so as to (eventually) cause injury to him.

fully toward her. In short, to assess accurately the third prong of Cardozo's analysis, we must understand it to rest on the broader claim that, *in general, a tort plaintiff has a right of action against a defendant only if the defendant acted wrongfully toward (committed a wrong upon) the plaintiff, rather than having acted wrongfully exclusively toward others or in general.*

As noted, in prior work we have sometimes used the phrase "substantive standing" to refer to the foregoing principle. It is a principle of *standing* because it sets limits on which persons are properly situated to prevail on tort claims. It is *substantive* because, unlike the rules for standing found in civil procedure and Supreme Court decisions interpreting Article III of the U.S. Constitution (both of which discuss "standing"), it is *not procedural* but instead is realized through an element or combination of elements in each tort (and because whether it is fulfilled is a matter of fact).[33]

In the law of negligence, the substantive standing or proper-plaintiff principle appears as the requirement that the defendant breach a duty of care owed to the plaintiff (or a person situated as was the plaintiff in relation to the defendant's conduct), instead of breaching a duty of care owed only to someone else. A comparable but distinct requirement is found in the law of trespass. A trespass plaintiff has no claim unless she has a possessory interest in the land that the defendant has entered or occupied. Even if *A* builds a hideous fence on *B*'s property that predictably and significantly reduces the resale value of *C*'s property, *C* has no "standing" to assert a trespass claim against *A*, because *A* invaded only *B*'s possessory rights, not *C*'s. As in *Palsgraf*, we here see a wrong to another generating harm to the plaintiff, which is insufficient for liability. Likewise, a fraud plaintiff must prove that the injury she suffered resulted from her own reliance on the content of the defendant's fraudulent statement. Thus, if *D* swindles *E* out of his life savings, thereby leaving *E* without the resources to continue to serve as the primary donor for charity *F*, *F* lacks substantive standing to assert a fraud claim against *D*. And a defamation plaintiff must prove that the defamatory statement that injured her was a statement about ("of and concerning") her. Even if *G* defames *H* so as to cause *I* to suffer harm, *I* has no defamation claim against *G* unless *G* actually

---

33. This is not to deny, of course, that defendants sometimes prevail because a plaintiff has not pleaded or has not plausibly pleaded this element.

defamed *I*. And so on. Each tort has a proper-plaintiff requirement built into its substantive elements.[34] Although she sued for a different tort, Mrs. Palsgraf was, legally, in the same position as *C*, *F*, and *I*—she was not among those whom tort law entitles to demand redress from a wrongdoer.

Once tort law's proper-plaintiff principle is brought into view, it is easier to appreciate why *Palsgraf* is a chestnut. It is not merely memorable for its facts. It identifies a pervasive condition of tort liability and thus speaks to the nature or character of tort law.[35] The existence of the principle supports the proposition that the wrongs of tort law have a relational form, as we claimed in Chapter 3. It also supports, if somewhat indirectly, the claim that the principle of civil recourse lies at the heart of tort law. The default position in our system is that one is not vulnerable to legal demands or claims made by others. What triggers this vulnerability is the principle that one who has been wronged by another is entitled to an avenue of redress against the wrongdoer. It is only by interacting with another in a way

34. In his *Palsgraf* dissent, Judge Andrews—who, unlike subsequent commentators, grasped the central claims of Cardozo's majority opinion—purported to identify doctrinal counterexamples to the proper-plaintiff rule. These include the allowance of wrongful death suits, in which it is not the defendant's victim who is the plaintiff, but typically a surviving family member. Similarly, Andrews noted, insurance companies have rights of subrogation that allow them, without themselves having been the victim of the tort, to bring an action for damages against an actor who has tortiously caused a person with insurance coverage to suffer covered losses. And so-called loss-of-consortium actions—typically claims by spouses to compensation for injuries to them that flow derivatively from injuries tortiously inflicted only on their spouses—plainly do not feature the victim of the wrong as the plaintiff.

These putative counterexamples actually support the structural point we are making. As we explain in the body of this chapter, it is precisely the common law's proper plaintiff principle that created the need for statutes authorizing claims by surviving family members for losses they suffer as a result of the tortious killing of their decedent. Subrogation, meanwhile, turns on the recognition by courts of equitable or contractual transfers of standing from victims to certain others. Loss-of-consortium actions originally rested on a dated and now properly rejected conception of husbands as having property interests in the services of their wives. *See* Zipursky, *supra* note 28, at 37–40 (discussing consortium and subrogation actions).

35. For most of the torts discussed in the prior paragraph, tort-specific doctrinal debates have developed among courts and commentators in connection with the particular tort's substantive standing rule. For example, the reliance element of fraud has presented long-standing puzzles as to whether it amounts to a requirement of causation, or something different. John C. P. Goldberg, Anthony J. Sebok, & Benjamin C. Zipursky, *The Place of Reliance in Fraud*, 48 Az. L. Rev. 1001 (2006). Meanwhile, the "of-and-concerning" element of the defamation torts found its way into constitutional law via the landmark case of *New York Times v. Sullivan*, 376 U.S. 254 (1964). *Sullivan* held, among other things, that the First Amendment's free speech guarantees forbid a court from deeming defamatory statements about governmental units to be statements of and concerning particular officials responsible for the actions of those units.

that the law deems a wronging of the other that one become subject to the possibility of a court-backed demand for redress.

The moral luck problem, examined above, raised the question of why it is not sufficient for a tort plaintiff to prove that the defendant acted in a manner that the law treats as generating an impermissible risk of injury. In response, we explained that the wrongs of tort law are, by design and for good reason, breaches of duties of noninjury—government does not empower persons with rights of action unless they have been injured, or until certain of their interests have actually been interfered with. Conversely, as we saw in connection with the strict liability problem, the state empowers injury victims to sue and recover when the defendant violates a norm of conduct that has been recognized in the law, even if the defendant acted in a reasonable manner. Because the legal right of the plaintiff is violated by the defendant in these cases, the plaintiff stands to recover from conscientious tortfeasors.

The proper-plaintiff principle might seem to present a further puzzle for those, like us, who insist that torts are wrongs. For because of it, persons who are injured by conduct that violates a standard contained in tort law's directives cannot always recover: conduct that falls below the legal standard and injury turn out to be necessary, not sufficient, for liability. Mrs. Palsgraf was injured by substandard conduct. The conductors were careless in acting the way that they did (albeit not careless as to her physical well-being) and thereby caused her to suffer an injury. Likewise, a person's reputation can be hurt by a defamatory statement about someone else, an investor can suffer losses as the result of intentional misrepresentations that cause a market downturn even if she never received or relied on them, and so on.

If there is wrongdoing causing injury in *Palsgraf* and comparable cases involving other torts, what's missing that must be present for liability to attach? Here is the law's answer. In improper-plaintiff cases, the claim is not valid because the plaintiff's *right* against mistreatment at the hands of the defendant, under the relevant tort norm, has not been violated, and the principle of civil recourse confers rights of action only on those who suffer a legal rights violation (the flip side of the defendant's breach of the duty of noninjury owed to the plaintiff). A plaintiff's entitlement to an avenue of recourse against another exists only if the plaintiff herself has been legally wronged by the defendant. To say the same thing, under the principle of civil recourse, only persons who can demonstrate that the defendant injured them by acting wrongfully toward them are granted a legal power to demand redress from the wrongful injurer. This is exactly what Cardozo was getting at when he said that a tort plaintiff must sue in her own right, rather than as a vicarious beneficiary of the breach of a duty owed to another.

To be clear, the claim we are making is an interpretive claim about the common law of torts. We do not mean to suggest that it is inconceivable, or would necessarily be undesirable, to have other laws or bodies of law that enable persons who have been injured by wrongful conduct to recover from wrongdoers even if those persons have not themselves been wronged. Our point instead is that such laws or bodies of law operate on principles different from that found at the core of the law of torts: the principle of civil recourse.

Consider in this regard the wrongful death statutes enacted by state legislatures in the second half of the nineteenth century. One of their main objectives was to *override* tort law's proper-plaintiff principle by authorizing surviving family members to bring claims for compensation against an actor who tortiously caused the demise of their decedent. To prevail on this sort of claim, a plaintiff must prove that a tort has been committed. But the tort that must be proven is a tort *against the decedent,* not a tort against the plaintiff. (This is why, under these statutes, legal defenses that would defeat the decedent's claim had the decedent survived and sued, operate to defeat the survivor's wrongful death claim.) It is no accident that wrongful death actions were created by legislation. The statutes that created them were not aiming to create, and did not create, new tort claims. Instead the goal was to empower certain nonvictims—persons who have suffered no rights violation (typically, a decedent's widow and orphans)—to obtain compensation from a tortfeasor whose tort against someone else had placed them in a condition of need. The hope was to provide them with economic support from a source other than governmental or charitable largesse.[36]

In short: wrongful death statutes confirm rather than call into doubt the presence of a norm delimiting the power of the state to fashion private rights of action for plaintiffs against tortfeasors, such that a plaintiff of this sort can claim a right of redress only by showing that she herself was

---

36. John Fabian Witt, *From Loss of Services to Loss of Support: The Wrongful Death Statutes, the Origins of Modern Tort Law, and the Making of the Nineteenth-Century Family,* 25 LAW & SOC. INQUIRY 717 (2000).

wronged by the defendant. Tort law, one might say, operates with a strong default against conferring rights of action, one that is surmounted only when there is a showing, not merely of wrongdoing (in some generic sense) causing injury, but of a wrongful injuring of (or mistreatment of) the plaintiff by the defendant.

One may query why there is such a strong default. If a person has breached a legal directive and thereby caused an injury, why is that not good enough to warrant the judicial creation of a legal power, even if the state is not politically obligated to provide one? As was true with regard to the moral luck problem (in the form of outcome luck), the answer to this puzzle stems in part from the vulnerability of potential defendants. Tort law is in some ways harsh. We discussed above the demandingness of its standards. We have also noted (as did Waldron) the extraordinary scope of the remedies successful plaintiffs are sometimes empowered to receive. Moreover, the state lacks discretion to decline to impose liability on a defendant when the plaintiff can prove his or her case. This is part of what it means for a plaintiff to have a right against the state to be so empowered. The consequence of this lack of discretion is that a defendant is correspondingly vulnerable to the decisions of the plaintiff about what, when, and where to make a claim, and how to pursue it. This is part of why the law is selective about who gets the power to make such a claim.

In discussing the moral luck problem, we emphasized that only a person who suffers a setback recognized by law as an injury is empowered to make a claim. The present discussion of the improper-plaintiff problem identifies an analogous limitation. A plaintiff is entitled to demand redress only if she herself has been legally wronged by the defendant. In tort law, the vulnerability of a defendant is not, in the first instance, vulnerability to a kind of taxation or loss-shifting by the state. It is vulnerability to a kind of "taking" by the plaintiff, backed by the state. A tort defendant is open to a civil attack of sorts through a lawsuit. Because, a tort claim is the embodiment of a plaintiff's right of redress, it is also the embodiment of a defendant's liability or vulnerability *to a plaintiff*.

Wrongs in Law and Morals

Too many legal scholars have for too long been too anxious to decouple torts from wrongs. In many instances they have done so on the supposed strength of arguments that we have debunked in this chapter. Moral luck, strict liability, and the proper-plaintiff principle, separately or together, do nothing to undermine the claim that torts are wrongs. Instead they help us to understand more clearly that torts are a particular species of wrong, one that stands apart from the wrongs known as "crimes," as well as from moral wrongs, or at least certain classes of moral wrongs.

Torts by definition involve injuries or failures to protect from injury. They are still wrongs. Torts do not necessarily involve conduct that is blameworthy or culpable, and do not render a person vulnerable to punishment at the hands of the state. They are still wrongs. Tort law does not allow all persons injured by conduct that is wrongful—or even all persons foreseeably injured by wrongful conduct—to pursue an action. It is still a law of wrongs. One cannot commit a tort without breaching a standard of conduct housed within a relational legal directive that identifies a duty of noninjury and a right against injury. This is the sense in which torts are wrongs.

We conclude by noting two lessons and one question that arise from our analysis. The first lesson, just now noted, is that blame—at least on a certain conception of what it means to blame—and punishment are not essential to notions of wrongdoing. As tort law demonstrates, there are blameless, bloodless (or relatively blameless, bloodless) wrongs. And there is accountability for wrongs that does not involve punishment or vengeance. Part of what makes tort law distinctive is that in many instances (though not all) it is concerned with humdrum failures or "misfires." Fittingly, accountability in this domain usually takes the form of liability to pay damages. This is not to deny the force of the observation that tort liability can be onerous and indeed overwhelming. But liability is quite different from imprisonment or even being fined, particularly in a world that often enables individual tortfeasors to obtain indemnification (and, in worst-case scenarios, bankruptcy protection).

It is one thing to emphasize, as Holmes did, that the wrongs in the heartland of modern tort law seem somewhat removed from those engraved on the tablets that Moses brought down from Mount Sinai. It is quite another to infer from this observation, as Holmes also did, that torts are not wrongs. This path leads us away from rather than toward the law. A mistaken belief that a notion of torts as wrongs leaves us with an unduly narrow, unduly moralistic picture of the field has caused all manner of mischief in modern tort scholarship. While perhaps there are conceptions of wrongdoing that can be fairly criticized on these terms, the problem with such conceptions resides in their particulars, not in the general idea. Students, judges, and scholars who wish to understand tort law cannot afford to be discomfited by the language of wrongs and wrongdoing, nor need they be. They must instead appreciate the distinctive kind of wrongdoing that is at work. Criminal law is not *the* paradigmatic law of wrongs. It is *a* law of wrongs—one that sits beside others, including the law of relational injurious wrongs that we know as tort law.

Our second lesson goes hand in glove with the first. Tort law's distinctive conceptions of wrongdoing and accountability connect in a deep way to its status as a body of common law. If tort law were on par with criminal law—if it were all about the state setting rules of conduct and then policing and punishing their violation—then one would have to worry about the way in which tort law has traditionally been made and applied. Indeed, were tort law understood on a criminal-law (or regulatory-law) model, it would seem to flout what Lon Fuller famously dubbed the "inner morality of law."[37] Publicity, notice, generality, prospectivity, and the other values that Fuller emphasized seem lacking in a system that relies on judges to articulate rules and principles on a case-by-case basis instead of stating them in canonical form in a code or statute book. (Keep in mind that decisions such as *MacPherson v. Buick*—in which Cardozo deployed his considerable analytic and rhetorical skills to locate a principle within a welter of conflicting precedents—are held out as *exemplars* of the common-law method.)

As we have emphasized throughout this chapter, tort law is quite different from criminal law. It is not about the state setting rules and punishing violations, and hence there is not the same concern to protect individuals against the power of the state in its capacity as promulgator of criminal codes and prosecutor (and punisher) of crimes. Tort law in its own way renders us vulnerable. However, the vulnerability is not to state power per se, but to other citizens who, under the right circumstances, can harness the courts to validate their claims and demands against us. While Fullerian rule-of-law protections might be necessary to protect against the abuse of criminal and regulatory law, a different set of protections is appropriate in the domain of tort law. Some of these protections are procedural and involve things such as the guarantee of an opportunity to defend oneself against a claim, the (usual) placement of the burden of

---

37. Benjamin C. Zipursky, *The Inner Morality of Private Law*, 58 AM. J. JURIS. 27 (2013).

proof and persuasion on the plaintiff, and the rule requiring plaintiffs to cover their own legal costs and attorneys' fees. Others are substantive. These include the requirement of proof of injury and the satisfaction of the proper-plaintiff principle. Others still are remedial, such as the adoption by courts of the "make-whole" measure of compensatory damages as a rule of thumb for determining what counts as fair and reasonable compensation. Finally, tort law operates against the backdrop of other practices and institutions—including the widespread (though hardly universal) availability of indemnification agreements and liability insurance—that help to mitigate the potential onerousness of tort liability.

There is another way in which tort law achieves a kind of fairness in operation by means apart from Fullerian methods. Consideration of this other way in turn leads from our lessons to our question. Part of what it means for tort law to be "common law"—and a major reason why, at a general level, tort defendants cannot legitimately complain that they are too vulnerable to being caught off guard when held liable for their torts— is that the wrongs recognized by tort law are, in their substance, drawn from everyday life rather than constructed de novo by judges in aid of some sort of social engineering project. Here we reach questions concerning the substance of tort law's wrongs. Structurally, all torts are relational wrongs, the victims of which gain a right of action against their wrongdoers. But what about the substance of tort law? *Which* wrongs have the courts recognized? Why those and not others? How are courts to think about revising—adding to, subtracting from, or modifying—the list of recognized wrongs? Chapters 7 and 8 are devoted to these questions.

7

Dual Instrumentalism

T HE PRINCIPLE OF CIVIL RECOURSE SERVES as the backbone for the law of torts. Chapter 3's account of relational wrongs, rights, duties, and rights of action, along with Chapter 5's discussion of remedies and redress and Chapter 6's articulation of key structural attributes of tortious wrongdoing, together provide a picture of its skeleton. Still, we are missing tort law's flesh and blood—its substance. We have yet to discuss in any depth the various wrongs that count as torts, as well as how courts go about defining, identifying, applying, and revising the directives at their center.

One might doubt there is much value in a theoretical account of the wrongs of tort law. Indeed, mainstream torts professors in the United States—including many who write textbooks and treatises and who draft Restatement provisions, as well as many who regularly teach the required 1L Torts course—are wont to display healthy lawyerly skepticism as to whether there is anything general to say on this subject. Tort law is predominantly made by judges. Judges typically are lawyers, not economists or moral philosophers, and they tend to see themselves as charged with the practical task of applying the law in a manner that is evenhanded and sensitive to the facts of the cases before them, as well as to the realities about what can be achieved by their decisions. The idea that law produced by officials of this sort, in this way, would lend itself to a unified field theory seems improbable.

This line of thinking seems to lead rather quickly to the conclusion that there is nothing to be said about what the wrongs of tort law are (and how they are to be adumbrated) other than that they are wrongs that judges happen to have recognized.[1] Some such thought was behind John Wigmore's mockery of the standard textbook definition of torts as civil wrongs other than breaches of contract: "As if a man were to define Chemistry by pointing out that it is not Physics nor Mathematics!"[2] Something similar might be said of a book or a Torts course that merely presents tort law as one damn wrong after another.[3] And the problem is not merely academic. It is not only professors and students but judges who look for, and stand to benefit from locating, a field's organizing ideas.

In short, tort theorists who aim to be grounded or pragmatic face a dilemma. They recognize that there is some value in theorizing about tort law's wrongs, as opposed merely to listing or cataloguing them. Yet they fear that theorizing will quickly slide into the imposition of an artificial order on a messy, worldly practice. Is there a way out of this trap?

This chapter and the next concern the foregoing questions. Alert, we hope, to the depth of the challenge presented, we offer an argument that eases our burden in two ways, one that might be called "metatheoretical," the other "dialectical." Our metatheoretical move is to explain why, although readers need not be skeptical about every effort to theorize tort law's substance, they should also have suitably modest expectations for such theorizing. The dialectical move begins by identifying a seemingly plausible candidate theory of tortious wrongdoing. This is the theory articulated in the opening pages of William Prosser's great torts treatise. As it turns out, Prosser's approach—which we label "dual instrumentalism"—suffers from irremediable problems. This leads us to consider briefly the dominant response to dual instrumentalism, here dubbed "singular instrumentalism." We then establish that singular instrumentalism is even more problematic than the dual instrumentalism it was intended to supplant. The dialectic concludes with our presentation in Chapter 8 of a theory that avoids the problems of both forms of instrumentalism—a theory that we label "dual constructivism."

---

1. John C. P. Goldberg, *Ten Half-Truths about Tort Law*, 42 VAL. U. L. REV. 1221, 1241 (2008).

2. 1 JOHN HENRY WIGMORE, SELECT CASES ON THE LAW OF TORTS vii (1912). As we suggested in Chapter 1, on a certain understanding of the phrase "civil wrongs"—one well-represented in our legal history and more robust than the placeholder that Wigmore had in mind—the standard definition is more meaningful than his criticism suggests.

3. With apologies to Toynbee. Arnold J. Toynbee, *Law and Freedom in History*, in 2 A STUDY OF HISTORY (1957).

Metatheory: Less Is More

The difficulty of finding an adequate theory of the substance of tortious wrongs naturally invites the metatheoretical question: Do we really need a theory? Tort law's basics can be found in Restatements and other treatises. So why not just rely on them to fill out the the flesh and blood of tort law by specifying which torts courts have recognized?

The problem is that tort law is neither dogmatic nor static, and that courts in the real world confront new fact patterns every day. If we could address these problem just by consulting a list of torts, then no theory would be necessary. But litigants are entitled to challenge prior decisions and categories, lawyers are required to forge such challenges (when appropriate), and judges are required to address and resolve them. Nor is tort law static; litigants often demand change, and their lawyers will demand or invite judges to engage critically with the law. Finally, even if tort law were dogmatic or static, lists would still not be adequate for the practical legal work of arguing and deciding cases. Tort law is a bottom-up affair: the law begins with the facts alleged in a plaintiff's complaint, and novel fact patterns are, to put it ironically, the staple of tort litigation.

All of the aforementioned considerations lead to the recognition that tort litigation is a forum of critical engagement and reason in the adjudication of disputes under the law. This means that a list of torts will not do, even if it is given in combination with an elaborate and sustained structural account, such as that provided in Chapters 3–6. At the same time, if it is these features of the tort system that explain *why* we need a theoretical account of the wrongs of tort law, then perhaps they also explain why the demand for theory is not quite so daunting after all. The task at hand is not to reason from first principles to a correct account of which injurious wrongs should count as torts. Rather, it is to offer a well-grounded set of guidelines for thinking critically about what does and does not count, within the law of torts, as a legal wrong, provided that the reasoning in accordance with those guidelines is suited to judges and, broadly speaking, consistent with the common law of torts that we have.

Arguably the most prominent scholar of American tort doctrine in the twentieth century—the self-consciously down-to-earth Hornbook writer and Restatement Reporter William Prosser—seems to have understood and embraced exactly these metatheoretical prescriptions (cvcn if not overtly). His work thus provides a good place to begin theorizing about the wrongs of tort law. Prosser recoiled at the thought of an essentialist theory of wrongs of tort law. Yet he did not just provide a list, either. His theory started with some homely observations. Plaintiffs bring tort suits when they have suffered harms for which they seek compensation. And courts are generally unwilling to grant plaintiffs the result they seek unless the defendant caused the harm by acting in a socially undesirable manner. From this observation, Prosser built a theory of the wrongs of tort law. Torts, he concluded, are always concatenations of compensable harms and undesirable acts. That they have this character, he further reasoned, is unsurprising, for this is what enables tort law to serve the twin purposes he deemed it to have: compensation and deterrence. We have the torts that we have, Prosser reasoned, because tort law is a way for judges to kill two birds with one stone—to compensate injuries deemed compensable and deter conduct deemed undesirable.

Some might be skeptical of our attribution to Prosser of a theory of tort law, not only because he was a doctrinalist, but also because he professed utter disdain for legal theory.[4] We would suggest, however, that Prosser was not so much an anti-theorist as a modest theorist, and indeed that the modesty of his theory was a key to his influence. In a way that proved reassuring to practical-minded lawyers, judges, and law professors, Prosser wedded an instrumentalist understanding of what tort law is good for with a methodological approach that purported to capture how courts and scholars have gone about and should go about crafting the two-ended wrongs of tort law. This is the approach we call "dual instrumentalism."

Dual Instrumentalism: Torts as Fault–Harm Pairings

Prosser's hugely influential treatise, first published in 1941, offers a window into the dual instrumentalist account of tortious wrongdoing. The book opens with the observation that "[a] really satisfactory definition of a tort has yet to be found."[5] It then briefly considers various efforts to capture the essence of tortiousness, only to dismiss them as exercises in scholasticism. The way forward, Prosser then insists, is to be practical and functional—that is, to understand tort law by reference to what is being accomplished when judges make decisions in tort cases and fashion rules

---

4. William L. Prosser, *Book Review: My Philosophy of Law*, 27 CORNELL L.Q. 292 (1942).
5. WILLIAM L. PROSSER, HANDBOOK OF THE LAW OF TORTS § 1, at 1 (1941).

of tort law.[6] In other words, Prosser thought that one must reverse-engineer an understanding of tortiousness from an account of tort law's social function(s).

In common-law systems, judges are primarily responsible for tort law's substantive rules. They fashion these rules in the course of resolving concrete disputes. In such disputes, the plaintiff comes to court seeking a remedy, typically money damages. To obtain this remedy, the plaintiff must convince the court that the defendant has done something that warrants it ordering the defendant to pay money to the plaintiff. She does this (according to Prosser) by establishing that the defendant acted in a manner that is "unreasonable, or socially harmful, from the point of view of the community as a whole . . . ."[7] While courts routinely assert that every tort case involves a claim that the defendant breached a *duty* that he owed and thereby violated a *right* of the plaintiff's, Prosser—having embraced Holmes's warning that the language of right and duty risks a conflation of law and morality—jettisoned those terms in favor of words he took to be more malleable and less freighted, such as "unreasonableness" or "fault" and "loss" or "harm." On a Prosserian view, every tort case features an allegation of harm and an allegation of fault in a legal, rather than strictly moral, sense.[8]

With these features of tort litigation in mind, Prosser arrived at a general account of tortious wrongdoing. When, based on how the defendant behaved, a court deems the defendant to have committed a tort (and thus to be subject to liability), it fashions a legal rule, whereby the defendant and others are on notice that conduct of this sort (regardless of whether it is immoral) is socially undesirable and thus renders one who undertakes such conduct eligible for judicially imposed sanctions. In addition, when a court orders a defendant to pay damages to a plaintiff because of the condition or situation in which the plaintiff is placed by virtue of what the defendant did, the court sees to it that the plaintiff receives funds to ameliorate her condition or situation. Viewed from the perspective of the social goods that it stands to deliver, tort law is a law of *deterrence and*

6. *Id.* at 10–18.
7. *Id.* at 9–10.
8. As noted below, on both the "fault" and the "harm" side, Prosser aimed for maximum capaciousness, allowing that conduct could be faulty just for being of a sort that courts deemed socially undesirable, and allowing for various forms of "presumed" harm to cover torts involving interferences with intangible or "dignitary" interests such as reputation.

compensation. This in turn explains why every tort is a fusion or pairing of two things: *an act that is faulty* (in the sense that society, through its judges or legislatures, has declared it to be undesirable, all things considered) *and a consequence that is harmful* (in the sense that society, through its judges or legislatures, has declared it a setback worthy of compensation). Thus we arrive at the core claim of dual instrumentalism: every tort is a *pairing of conduct that has been deemed appropriately sanctioned and a setback that has been deemed appropriately compensated.*

As noted, dual instrumentalism operates with broad and functionalist (rather than narrow and moralistic) notions of "sanctionable" and "compensable." Sanctionable conduct is any conduct that, for one reason or another, is appropriately discouraged by law. Accordingly, even some forms of "strict" liability—including, for example, liability for innocent trespasses or nuisances, and liability for injuries caused by products that are sold in a defective condition notwithstanding the manufacturer's exercise of care—can count as "faulty" or "socially unreasonable" and therefore tortious. The plaintiff's side of a tort case is likewise understood by reference to an expansive notion of "harm." A harm, in this context, is anything that society might plausibly deem a setback that is appropriately compensated.

Dual instrumentalism has struck generations of torts scholars as providing an appropriate account of the sort of wrong that amounts to a tort. As noted, one of its advantages is its thinness—it allows for a wide range of conduct to be deemed tortious. By adopting a functionally derived notion of fault, it also avoids excessive moralism, in that it covers conduct that is not immoral or otherwise condemnable. And it is in one sense realistic: it provides an understanding of tortious wrongdoing that sits well with the fact that tort law has been produced by judges who see themselves as problem-solvers. It also allows the theorist to be somewhat agnostic as to tort law's ultimate aims or purposes. She need not specify what ultimate goal or goals courts have been aiming to accomplish by identifying various conduct-harm pairings. It is enough to say that courts have concluded that some social value or values is or are being served through deterrence and compensation.[9]

Finally, dual instrumentalism explains how courts can claim to be working within the domain of tort law—rather than legislating in an un-

---

9. Prosser himself suggested that tort law's operation promised ultimately to promote the "'greatest happiness of the greatest number . . . .'" *Id.* at 17 (referencing Jeremy Bentham).

fettered manner—even as they innovate, sometimes dramatically. The settled substance of tort law (straightforward cases of battery, negligence, etc.) is understood to reflect past judicial determinations of the fault–harm pairings to which liability should attach. For unsettled areas—hard cases—the court's job is to articulate *what shall count* as sanctionable conduct and *what shall count* as compensable harm based on instrumental considerations (that is, on a rough assessment as to whether society stands to benefit from the provision of deterrence and compensation in the relevant class of cases). In short, judges should understand the settled rules of tort law as provisional decisions of the courts of their jurisdiction as to which acts there is reason to discourage and which setbacks there is reason to compensate. They are then to apply and, if necessary, modify those rules to achieve deterrence and compensation, while being mindful of possible undesirable side effects, such as overcrowded court dockets that might come with expanded liability. As Prosser memorably put it: when judges decide open-ended tort cases, they are thus engaged in "social engineering."[10]

In the United States the leading mid-twentieth-century tort court was undoubtedly the Supreme Court of California, and some of its leading decisions, at least at certain moments, illustrate the Prosserian, dual instrumentalist approach in action. Consider, for example, the famous *Tarasoff* case.[11] Among the defendants were psychotherapists employed by the University of California, Berkeley. A patient of theirs named Poddar had revealed in therapy his homicidal fantasies about a young woman named Tatiana Tarasoff. When Poddar later killed Tarasoff, her family sued the therapists for failing to warn Tatiana of the threat that Poddar posed to her. The therapists argued that they could not be held liable because they had no connection to Tatiana and therefore owed no duty to take steps to protect her from Poddar. In its landmark decision, the Court rejected this argument, suggesting that the therapists could be held liable for failing to warn Tarasoff of the threat.

Tarasoff—whose rule is now recognized by many American jurisdictions—expanded the domain of tortious wrongdoing by classifying a certain kind of conduct that caused harm as faulty in the sense of socially undesirable. Although different parts of the court's opinion emphasize

---

10. *Id.* at 15.
11. Tarasoff v. Regents of the University of California, 551 P.2d 334 (Cal. 1976).

different reasons for this result (and while its result might ultimately be defensible even from within a constructivist rather than an instrumentalist approach to legal reasoning), some parts quite clearly bear the hallmarks of dual instrumentalism. Thus, the court, explicitly following Prosser, suggested that legal rules about the duty of care in negligence offered no guidance on how to resolve the case before it: the question precisely was whether to impose liability and *thereby* recognize a duty.[12] Likewise, the answer to the question of whether liability should be imposed was to be arrived at instrumentally, by considering whether the social value of encouraging therapists to take steps to warn potential victims (in terms of increased safety) outweighs the social costs of doing so (including the possibility that warnings will discourage potentially dangerous patients from seeking therapy or being fully candid with their therapists). Over a dissent that was in many respects as instrumentalist as the majority opinion, the court concluded that, on balance, it would serve society better by allowing for the imposition of liability when therapists carelessly fail to warn third parties of certain risks of harm posed by patients.[13]

The same Court is equally famous for its adjustments on the harm side of tort law. In *Dillon v. Legg*, for example, a mother was severely traumatized when, from her front porch, she witnessed the defendant driver run down her young daughter.[14] To that point in time, the common-law rule held that—except for a narrow slice of "near-miss" cases reminiscent of assaults—no cause of action existed for careless conduct causing trauma not predicated on a physical injury. Denouncing prior decisions as having set arbitrary limits on liability, the Court held that there is just as much reason to compensate emotional distress as physical harm. Thus, so long as a plaintiff could prove that she was genuinely traumatized, and that her trauma was a foreseeable consequence of the defendant's careless conduct, she should be entitled to recovery. Over the past forty years, most

12. *Id.* at 342.

13. *Id.* at 347. ("Our current crowded and computerized society compels the interdependence of its members. In this risk-infested society we can hardly tolerate the further exposure to danger that would result from a concealed knowledge of the therapist that his patient was lethal. If the exercise of reasonable care to protect the threatened victim requires the therapist to warn the endangered party or those who can reasonably be expected to notify him, we see no sufficient societal interest that would protect and justify concealment. The containment of such risks lies in the public interest.")

14. 441 P.2d 912 (Cal. 1968).

American jurisdictions have, to one degree or another, recognized claims for negligent infliction of emotional distress such as Mrs. Dillon's.[15]

Notwithstanding its elegance, its resonance with a practical mindset, and its role in encouraging mid-twentieth-century courts to modernize certain areas of tort doctrine, dual instrumentalism fails to provide a theory of wrongs even remotely consonant with the contours of tort law, and fails to capture judicial reasoning about tort law. (Recall that dual instrumentalism is offered as an explanation of the tort law that we have, and as a characterization of how courts actually go about deciding hard tort cases.)

Its first and most obvious problem is that tort law should reach far more broadly than it does if each concatenation of faulty conduct and compensable harm suffices to warrant the recognition of tort liability. Many torts—fraud, battery, assault, trespass to land—require a certain kind of intentional conduct on the part of the wrongdoer. Why? The conduct in question (for example, the making of misrepresentations) would seem an appropriate target for deterrence even if done carelessly (or perhaps innocently), and the setbacks suffered by plaintiffs who allege these torts clearly count as "harms" in other settings. Yet there is no tort liability absent the requisite intent. Likewise, *Dillon* notwithstanding, it is clear that courts continue to treat certain injuries as quite serious yet choose not to render them actionable even when caused by conduct of a sort that they also deem to be appropriately deterred. Indeed—just to take *Dillon* itself—California and other jurisdictions have in the end only slightly expanded liability for negligent infliction of emotional distress, denying many claims where carelessness foreseeably causes serious emotional harm (such that liability would serve both to deter unreasonable conduct and compensate recognized harms).

Our second concern runs along similar lines and in some ways cuts deeper. Even when the law recognizes an act/harm pairing as a basis for liability, no liability will attach unless there is a causal connection between them. But if a plaintiff is genuinely injured and needs compensation, and a defendant has behaved in a manner that merits deterrence, it is not at all obvious why there must be such a connection. The point

---

15. Restatement (Third) of Torts: Liability for Physical and Emotional Harm § 48 (Am. L. Inst. 2012).

would sound trite were there not famous cases, again from the California Supreme Court, rendering palpable this very challenge.

In *Sindell v. Abbott Laboratories*,[16] the plaintiff argued that she should be able to recover damages for her illness—caused by her mother's ingestion of a generic anti-miscarriage drug known as DES—from Abbott and several others among the scores of manufactures who produced the drug while failing to warn of its potential side effects. The defendants maintained that the claim should be dismissed because Sindell could not establish that her mother had used DES made and sold by any of them, as opposed to DES sold by the many other manufacturers she did not sue. Sindell responded by arguing that this failure of proof should not matter because each defendant had engaged in identical conduct of a sort that should be deterred, and that she suffered bodily harm traceable to such conduct. In an impressive display of judicial creativity, the California Supreme Court allowed Sindell to recover partial compensation from any defendant who could not disprove having caused her harm, with the compensation owed by each corresponding to its share of the California DES market at the time Sindell's mother consumed the DES that injured Sindell.

Scholars in the grip of dual instrumentalism rightly (from within their approach) suggested that *Sindell's* notion of "market share liability" should be extended to cover vast domains of tort law. Yet nothing of the sort has happened. Tortfeasor identification has remained central to tort law. The imposition by the court of market-share liability stands as an interesting (and perhaps justified) anomaly rather than a centerpiece of modern tort law.[17]

Our third concern will have been anticipated by many readers. Whether under the rubric of "proximate cause," "legal cause," "duty," "scope of liability," "foreseeability," or some other name, negligence law insists on a certain *nexus* between a defendant's faulty conduct and a plaintiff's harm that goes beyond what lawyers call "actual cause" or "cause-in-fact." It is not enough for a tort plaintiff to show that she suffered harm of a kind that tort law generally deems compensable and that the harm was brought

16. 607 P.2d 924 (Cal. 1980).

17. The decision in *Sindell* itself may be defensible on noninstrumentalist terms but, if so, it is only because of certain features of the case that have rarely, if ever, been replicated. Arthur Ripstein & Benjamin C. Zipursky, *Corrective Justice in an Age of Mass Torts*, in PHILOSOPHY AND THE LAW OF TORTS 214 (Gerald J. Postema ed., 2001).

about by conduct of the defendant that tort law deems faulty. In addition, the harm must be of a sort that the defendant had a duty to take care not to cause, and the defendant's breach of duty must have functioned as a proximate cause of the harm. As we and others have shown, similar sorts of nexus requirements can be found in other torts.

In its heyday as a progressive leader in tort law, the California court sometimes "bit the bullet" on duty and proximate cause limitations. For example, the Court's famous decision about landowner liability in *Rowland v. Christian* left open the question of whether a burglar who is injured in the course of his crime might recover from a landowner whose poorly maintained premises contributed to the burglar being injured.[18] It is intuitive to suppose that a homeowner's duty to keep her premises in a safe condition is not owed to a burglar, and hence that she does him no wrong by failing to render her premises safe for *his* use. Yet the dual instrumentalist terms on which *Rowland* had imposed negligence liability—namely, that a homeowner is at fault for failing to maintain her premises and hence subject to a claim for compensation by anyone injured by them—offered no explanation as to why the burglar's claim should fail. Unsurprisingly, soon after *Rowland* was decided, the California legislature enacted a statute excluding recovery by persons injured by dangerous premises in the course of committing felonies.[19] As *Rowland* attests, the dual instrumentalist understanding of torts as fault–harm pairings seems to lead in one direction, while the law of torts leads in another. Proximate cause doctrine raises similar problems.

There are two stock answers to the cluster of objections that dual instrumentalist accounts cannot capture duty, proximate cause, and other doctrinal constraints on tort liability. The first, "floodgates" answer is that there will be "too much" liability if tort law allows liability for every pairing of conduct that is socially undesirable and a setback that qualifies as harm. "Floodgates" has in fact been the favorite answer of judges—particularly when confronted with a sympathetic plaintiff who argues, cogently, that a long-standing liability-limiting doctrine is "artificial" from within a dual instrumentalist framework. There is no doubt that judges sometimes reference floodgates concerns in their opinions. But that hardly solves the problem at hand. Judges face a problem that is already framed: they either

18. 443 P.2d 561 (Cal. 1968).
19. *See* Calvillo-Silva v. Home Grocery, 968 P.2d 56, 71–72 (1998) (discussing the statute).

must keep existing limits on liability or relax them and risk excessive litigation and liability. But a theorist who wishes to aid courts facing this choice must answer two different questions: (i) What, roughly, is the right level of liability and litigation?, and (ii) How do we get to that level? On the second question, dual instrumentalism allows for many more possibilities than those traditionally found in doctrine. Caps on damages, shorter limitation periods, tailoring of liability to the availability of liability insurance, excluding certain harms as categorically noncompensable—these and many other options are in principle available. Anyone familiar with tort doctrine knows that from the point of view of practicality and clarity, there are myriad ways of limiting tort liability that would be easier to conceptualize and implement than limitations based on the notions of duty or proximate cause on which courts continue to rely.

A second response to the oddity of tort law's limitations is actually more of a strategy than a definitive reply. The strategy is to explain each of the various considerations found in extant doctrine by focusing on particular kinds of policy limitations that pertain to the particular limitation. Thus, duty rules that limit recovery for emotional harm are said to be explained by the fact that claims of trauma not grounded in bodily harm are more difficult for judges and juries to verify than claims of physical harm. Limits on negligence liability set by "superseding cause" doctrine—such as decisions that decline to hold liable sellers of commercial products (for example, ammonium nitrate fertilizer) when a third-party (for example, a terrorist) uses the product to perpetrate a crime (for example, by converting the fertilizer into a bomb and then blowing up a building, killing or injuring its occupants)—are taken to be explicable as expressions of a psychological inclination to want to blame criminal offenders more than background actors whose carelessness set the stage for the offenders' crimes. Limitations on recovery for pure economic loss (lost profits) have to do with the allegedly greater efficiency of contract law, including insurance law, in handling such harms. And so on. Elsewhere we have addressed both these instrumentalist reconstructions of doctrine, and floodgates arguments more generally, and we have shown they are wholly inadequate.[20]

---

20. See, e.g., John C. P. Goldberg & Benjamin C. Zipursky, The Restatement (Third) and the Place of Duty in Negligence Law, 54 VAND. L. REV. 657, 692-723, 732-36 (2001) (discussing various senses in which courts employ the concept of duty in negligence cases, and why it is mistaken to treat all of them as instances of courts engaging in a blunderbuss balancing of policy considerations).

For now it is enough to observe that the great majority of leading tort theorists, including instrumentalist theorists, share our skepticism about dual instrumentalism. Indeed, the reason dual instrumentalism's popularity has waned since about 1970 among tort theorists is that it came in for a storm of criticism, and not only from scholars keen to emphasize tort law's relationship to notions of right and justice. The remainder of this chapter follows the path that has emerged out of skepticism about dual instrumentalism.

Singular Instrumentalism (I): Compensation Theories

Dual instrumentalism offers no convincing rationale for why tort law recognizes the wrongs that it does and why it does not recognize others. Likewise, it offers a model of judicial reasoning in open-ended tort cases that, although sometimes reflected in the language of judicial opinions, renders mysterious why courts continue to produce opinions that use the traditional language of the law, and how they have reached many of the results they have reached. Both problems, we suggest, stem from the functionalist manner in which dual instrumentalism attempts to connect what it takes to be the two sides of each tort: sanctionable conduct and compensable setbacks.

Given dual instrumentalism's weaknesses, one might have thought that when it started to come in for criticism, the critics would focus on problems posed by its commitment to the provision of an account of tort law that reasons from tort law's (supposed) functions to its substance. But what happened was quite the opposite. An initial generation of critics doubled down, arguing that dual instrumentalists such as Prosser had taken tort doctrine and concepts *too seriously* and thus were not aggressive enough in their instrumental reconstructions.

In particular, these critics maintained that it was a mistake to treat torts as two-sided—to do so was already to give too much credence to the pre-Holmesian thought that tort law is about duties and rights (even though recast in the language of fault and harm). The trick was not to explain or recharacterize the two sides of each tort, but instead to identify the one side that really mattered—the side that, functionally, was driving the law.[21] By

---

21. *See* Ernest J. Weinrib, *The Monsanto Lecture: Understanding Tort Law*, 23 VAL. U. L. REV. 485, 504 (1989) (noting that Richard Posner and other instrumentalists sought to correct the problems of prior theories that had attributed multiple goals to tort law by offering versions of "single-goal instrumentalism").

the middle of the twentieth century, scholars such as Fleming James Jr., George Priest, Morton Horwitz, and Jeffrey O'Connell, among others, were focused on the harm side.[22] Hence, they offered compensation or insurance-based theories of tort law. Then, starting around 1970, in response to these works and to the failings of dual instrumentalism, Richard Posner, Guido Calabresi, and others argued that the key was to focus exclusively or almost exclusively on the fault (or conduct) side. Hence, they offered efficient-deterrence theories of tort. Despite their evident differences, both compensation and deterrence theories share an important characteristic. Each is a version of singular rather than dual instrumentalism.

Whether in the form of compensation theory or deterrence theory, the major attraction of singular instrumentalism—not having to explain the connection between the two sides of each tort—comes with a matching weakness. As we have seen, part of what makes Prosserian dual instrumentalism appealing is its anti-reductionism and its rough proximity to certain features of legal doctrine and practice. Singular instrumentalists, by contrast, must engage in a great deal of fancy theoretical footwork. In particular they must explain why it is permissible for them to ignore or radically downplay one side of tort law—the fault/deterrence side or the harm/compensation side, and why it seems so intuitive to suppose that an account of tort law's wrongs must embrace both. Although, as we will see, singular instrumentalists have offered some ingenious responses to this challenge, the elaborateness of their responses arguably requires them to forfeit any claim to "realism" for their theories. Indeed, it is no accident that doctrinalist tort scholars who claim to be suspicious of theory tend to embrace dual instrumentalism (even though it, too, is a theory), and to regard singular instrumentalist theories such as James's or Posner's as "academic" in the pejorative sense.

For example—to step out of our chronology for a moment—consider Holmes's characteristically impressive attempt to downplay the conduct side of torts (and elevate the harm side) through an appeal to anthropology

---

22. As we discuss below, instrumentalist theories that treat tort as primarily or exclusively a scheme for compensating injury victims' losses have their roots in the work of Holmes, as well as other late nineteenth- and early twentieth-century scholars. These earlier scholars tended to be concerned with identifying the circumstances in which it would be fair or just for the law to require another person to indemnify the victim for his losses. On the whole, mid-twentieth century compensation theorists were more focused on how tort law could contribute to overall social welfare by shifting or spreading losses.

and psychology.[23] A person who brings a valid tort suit, Holmes supposed, is one who has experienced a loss traceable to the conduct of another. On that basis alone, that person shares with his "primitive" ancestors a sense of having a legitimate grievance. The unpleasantness of the loss, and the fact of its having been precipitated by another, leads him instinctively to blame the other, to call it a "wrong," and to demand redress. However, given the terms on which modern tort law imposes liability, Holmes argued, such a person would be mistaken to suppose that this is the actual basis on which he stands to obtain compensation through a lawsuit.

To be sure, Holmes was no fan of a broad regime of strict liability—he insisted that tort law generally imposes liability only upon a showing of "fault." But the fault requirement, as he understood it, was not to be construed to suggest that tort law is concerned to deter wrongful conduct. Instead it signals that tort law provides compensation only on a conditional or limited basis. In a liberal regime, he supposed, a person on whom a loss has fallen ordinarily must bear it himself. One is entitled to shift one's loss to another only if the other caused it after having had a fair chance to avoid doing so. On this *safe-harbor* understanding of the significance of the fault requirement, torts are the set of compensable losses for which the victim is entitled to demand indemnification from another person. The fault standard thus sets a fair rule for identifying those who are vulnerable to claims for indemnification, because fault, in tort law, just is the failure to take advantage of a fair opportunity to avoid causing loss to another.

Returning to the late twentieth century, an alternative to Holmes's efforts to make sense of the place of the conduct side of tort law from within compensation theory is the argument, associated most commonly with Horwitz, that the fault requirement is an artificial limit on liability that was grafted onto tort law by nineteenth-century judges eager to protect nascent industry.[24] The "true" social function of tort law, Horwitz implied, is the provision of compensation, typically by actors in a relatively good position to cover the cost of doing so. On this view, it is simply a mistake to think of torts as tied conceptually to a notion of undesirable conduct. Tort law is instead a system in which losses are spread whether or

23. John C. P. Goldberg & Benjamin C. Zipursky, *Seeing Tort Law from the Internal Point of View: Holmes and Hart on Legal Duties*, 75 FORDHAM L. REV. 1563, 1564–70 (2006).

24. MORTON J. HORWITZ, THE TRANSFORMATION OF AMERICAN LAW 1780–1860, at 63–108 (1977).

not caused by misbehavior, except to the extent judges for political reasons limit compensation.

Once one takes the view that tort law is about loss shifting and compensation, the precise position one adopts on whether there is a fault requirement becomes less important. From within compensation theory, questions as to whether or to what extent liability should be fault-based are merely questions about how to specify the conditions under which cost-shifting should take place. The more fundamental question—the question we wish to ask of compensation theory—is whether it is plausible to understand the wrongs of tort law as constituting a system for shifting losses, particularly losses caused *accidentally*, which have been the losses on which modern compensation theorists have focused.

Our framing of the question telegraphs our negative answer. If the basic domain of tort law is to be understood conventionally, so as to include trespass to land, battery, assault, false imprisonment, defamation, fraud, and so on, then it is not tenable to view it as a system of shifting losses generally, or shifting losses resulting from accidents. Many torts have nothing to do with accidents, because they can only be committed intentionally. And, as we noted in Chapter 5, some torts (like trespass to land, assault, false imprisonment, and libel) do not involve anything fairly described as a loss: nothing like a smashed car, broken limb, or lost income needs to be proven in order for the plaintiff to recover. It is true that being damaged by the conduct of another can seem to the sufferer to be a wrong, but it is simply untrue that all of those acts of others that we perceive as wrongs are fairly characterized as damaging or loss-inducing.

Some would argue, however, that our description of the field, though seemingly uncontroversial, is skewed. They would insist that the core of tort law today and for the past century has been negligence and products liability law, which concern accidentally caused losses, and that intentional torts are peripheral by an order of magnitude. Our response to this observation has several layers. One is that it is far from clear that negligence, which covers not only fender-benders but also drunk driving and professional malpractice (on the conduct side) and disfigurings and fatalities (on the setback side) is only about "accidentally" caused losses (as opposed to irresponsible decision making and non-loss-based injuries). Much the same goes for products liability, which frequently and quite plausibly comes with a rich narrative of wrongdoing and redress. A second is that it is a mistake to suppose that the criteria for what counts as the core of the field are determined by the numbers of lawsuits raising a particular theory of liability, as opposed to, for example, the impact on conduct or expectations. And a third is that—as we argued in Chapter 1—there is a sense in which lawsuits for private wrongs have a large life outside of the common law in areas such as employment discrimination and securities fraud.

Even if modern tort law is so strongly associated with accidentally caused injuries that one can say with a straight face that it is law for the shifting of accident losses (a proposition we reject), that would not change what we aim to establish at present. A substantial part of the law has to do with people suing one another for having wronged them, and this part of the law, which has traditionally been called "torts," calls out for systematic explanation and justification.

Singular Instrumentalism (II): Deterrence Theories

The late twentieth century's most influential instrumentalist rendering of tort law is a singular account that accepts the centrality of the deterrence function and thus rejects the claim that compensation lies at tort law's core. Both Calabresi and Posner—pioneers of law and economics in general and economic accounts of tort law in particular—have established elegant, single-function accounts rooted in deterrence.

Posner's is most easily grasped.[25] Tort law, he says, instructs actors who engage in conduct that risks losses to others to take cost-justified precautions against those risks being realized. Put differently, it sanctions individuals when they fail to take precautions that a cost–benefit calculus focused on aggregate welfare would call on them to take. Liability for tortious conduct, on this view, is understood as forcing the actor to internalize the costs to others of its activity. While there is no reason in principle why the injury victim, as opposed to anyone else, must actually receive the monetary sanction imposed on tort defendants, personal injury law proceeds in this manner because it turns out also to be efficient to replace a public enforcement model paid for by tax dollars with a private regulator model in which those who have suffered losses are

25. WILLIAM M. LANDES & RICHARD A. POSNER, THE ECONOMIC STRUCTURE OF TORT LAW (1987).

incentivized to sue by the prospect of keeping for themselves the "fine" imposed on the tortfeasor.

Calabresi's model is in some ways more indirect and elegant.[26] Tort liability is not a sanction as such. It is just a way that the legal system uses to counteract the traditional assumption that, prima facie, losses lie where they fall. In fact, this rule about financial responsibility for losses is purely conventional. There is no natural baseline. Just as we make up rules to allocate property rights efficiently, so we need rules to allocate accident costs efficiently. The right way to do this is to think systematically about which actors are best situated both to absorb and to reduce these accident costs. Tort law, when it is working well, assigns the accident costs to those persons. It thereby disincentivizes the kind of unsafe conduct that leads to more accident costs.

Whether one selects Posner's or Calabresi's version of singular instrumentalist deterrence theory, the connection problems that plague dual instrumentalist accounts seem to be avoided. For example, the reason that the causation requirement exists, on Posner's account, is that it is the actual costs of one's activities that are being internalized. Likewise, proximate cause and other nexus requirements are all necessary to ensure that there is neither over-deterrence nor under-deterrence (assuming the performance of the system is not skewed with contingent enforcement problems).

Before we comment on how well Posnerian and Calabresian accounts of tort law fare as interpretations or explanations of tort law's substance, we need to remind ourselves of the purposes for which we have turned to their work. We began this chapter by acknowledging the incompleteness of formal or structural characterizations of tort law. The problem is that a generic description of the wrongs of tort law—even combined with an account of the political theoretic, constitutional, and normative bases of rights of action in the *ubi jus* maxim and the principle of civil recourse—is not sufficient. Judges called upon to apply the law of torts need an understanding of why certain ways of treating others count as torts and why others do not.

To this problem, dual instrumentalism seemed an initially promising response. It proceeds on the understanding that certain kinds of conduct

---

26. Guido Calabresi, The Costs of Accidents: A Legal and Economic Analysis (1970).

can plausibly be deemed socially unacceptable, and that certain kinds of impacts on others can plausibly be considered harms, and it suggests that courts in tort cases are in the business of fleshing out these notions of "fault" and "harm." In particular, dual instrumentalism identifies two questions that courts fashioning the common law appear to be contemplating: (1) What sorts of conduct are appropriately deterred by court-ordered sanction?, and (2) What sorts of setbacks warrant compensation? By understanding tort law as simultaneously pursuing these goals through the identification of various fault–harm pairings, and observing the way that precedents have done so, the dual instrumentalist account seems to explain what courts are and should be doing in developing the law of torts.

Alas, the dual instrumentalist account was doomed to fail because tort law would have to look very different than it actually does if the account were correct. There would need to be many more fault–harm pairings that give rise to liability than those that actually do. Far less emphasis would be placed on causation. And many of the standard doctrinal tools that courts use to shape tort law would be replaced by other, very different tools.

Single function theories like Posner's may do better in matching the shape of torts and tort law, but they fail on other dimensions. The problem that led to dual instrumentalism was explaining what it is that courts are reasoning about in the common law when they are deciding what should count as tortious conduct. Posner's answer, at some level, is that courts are deciding which instances of conduct should be sanctioned in order for there to be optimal deterrence. Indeed, the whole elaborate domain of relational directives is understood as an effort by courts to set forth efficient liability rules.[27] The problem is—as Ernest Weinrib and Jules

---

27. Calabresi's account is more plainly fantastical than Posner's when considered as a positive account of the law, because his key move is to switch from the idea of specific deterrence to the idea of general deterrence. In short, it is critical to Calabresi that tort law *does not* enjoin any conduct or communicate that there is a duty not to engage in it. Tort law does not deter by saying specifically "Do not act that way or you will be sanctioned." It deters indirectly, stating "You will have to pay for the injuries that come from certain actions you take." It does not convey a duty at all. Of course, Calabresi does not assert that his is a positive account of tort law. It is an analytic framework for thinking about why tort law is able to accomplish certain goals and a normative framework for thinking about how to do so more effectively.

Posner, by contrast, did put forward his account, at least initially, as a positive account of negligence law. Indeed, he claimed to be capturing the sense in which at least one tort—negligence—incorporated an idea of wrongfulness, namely, the wrongfulness of waste.

Coleman long ago pointed out[28]—that the Posnerian theory abandons the basic understanding of what it is for tort law to be a form of private law and for torts to be relational wrongs. On his view, tort law is akin to the *qui tam* laws mentioned in Chapter 2. The wrong that defendants commit is not a wrong to anyone: from the point of view of the law, it is a wrongful act simpliciter. Tort plaintiffs have no special standing to pursue complaints and remedies. They are mere delegees of the state's power to force certain actors to incur liability in the name of deterrence.

The ingenuity of this account—the relegation of the plaintiff to the status of "private attorney general"—may indeed be part of its magnetism, and so some readers might find it odd that we are criticizing Posner for it. But recall that part of our aim here is to capture lawyerly understandings of the common law of torts. From this perspective, counterintuitiveness is a shortcoming, not an advantage. For it is preposterous to suppose that judges have fashioned the common law of torts in a manner that allows for indifference as to the identity of the person who brings a tort lawsuit. The common law claims to empower particular individuals—those who have actually been wrongfully injured—to make enforceable demands for redress against persons they claim have wrongfully injured them. It is therefore critical that, in articulating and announcing the relational directives of tort law, courts are announcing not only ways that actors must and must not behave, but announcing ways of treating others that they regard as *wrongs to* those others. And it is hardly a coincidence that courts do so in the context of lawsuits by persons who are claiming that they themselves have been wronged.

Posner's theory can escape some of this criticism if it is recast as a purely prescriptive theory instead of one that purports to make sense of the tort law we actually have. Insofar as it is meant to serve as a guide to revising the law according to certain stated metrics (efficient deterrence), it may indeed retain some force. One's view of the success of his project will thus turn in part on whether one is persuaded as to the value of the goal or goals articulated. It is no surprise that Posner to some degree shifted his focus from a positive to a more openly prescriptive account of tort law. He did so because, insofar as it seeks to capture the patterns of reasons and concepts that engage judges and lawyers, efficient deterrence theory falls short by a wide margin and in an arresting fashion.

28. *See, e.g.,* ERNEST J. WEINRIB, THE IDEA OF PRIVATE LAW (1995); Jules Coleman, *The Structure of Tort Law*, 97 YALE L.J. 1233 (1988).

The Bipolarity Critique

The shortcomings of singular instrumentalist theories as accounts of the positive law are not, in the end, surprising. Compensation theory, on the one hand, and deterrence theory, on the other, each escaped the problem of explaining the mesh between the two poles of tort law by asserting that really only one pole—one function—was principal, while the other was either to be ignored or explained derivatively. And in both cases, the account ultimately foundered because it was untenable to give up one of the two. Compensation-based tort theories understate the degree to which tort liability turns on whether the defendant has committed a wrong. Deterrence-based theories are unable to explain adequately why tort law pursues deterrence by arming victims of mistreatment, and pretty much only victims, with the power to obtain remedies from tortfeasors. It is no mere coincidence that the persons who bring tort claims seek redress for their injuries from a person who has injured them. The wrongs of tort law are injury-inclusive and relational—wrongs to another that involve injury to the other, and that generate in her a legal power to seek and obtain court-ordered redress through a tort suit.

The failures of singular instrumentalist theories suggest that giving up the defendant side or the plaintiff side of torts in constructing an account of tortious wrongdoing is misguided. Both sides matter. In this respect, Prosser was on the right track all along. *The problem with dual instrumentalism, it turns out, is not its dualism but its instrumentalism.* In Chapter 8 we therefore offer a different kind of dualistic account of the wrongs of tort law—one that is characterized not by instrumentalism but by what we term "constructivism."

Before turning to this task, however, it is appropriate to comment briefly on the relationship of our critique of instrumentalist tort theories to the well-known "bipolarity" critique developed by Weinrib and Coleman a quarter-century ago. Weinrib argued powerfully that deterrence-compensation instrumentalism cannot be correct, interpretively, because it treats certain essential features of tort law as mere contingencies. Compensation, he argued, is not rightly characterized as a "function" of tort law. For it is not as if compensation, in tort, can come from any source. In the first instance, tort law singles out the tortfeasor as the source of compensation. And it does so because the point is to hold the defendant responsible for having wrongfully injured the plaintiff—that is what tort law is doing. Likewise, the goal of deterring wrongful conduct could be accomplished by state-imposed criminal or regulatory penalties on persons who engage in antisocial conduct. In tort law, however, it is the victim (or her representative) who serves as enforcer. It is only because she is the one whose rights have been violated by the defendant that she can hold the defendant liable. Finally, in tort, the amount of the liability is not contingently or accidentally the amount of harm done to the plaintiff. Tort law, on Weinrib's account, sees to it that a wrongdoer fulfills his duty to repair the wrongful injury inflicted on the plaintiff. Its bipolar, plaintiff-defendant structure is essential, not contingent: it makes tort law what it is. Dual instrumentalism misses all of this. Coleman's important early critique of Posner's economic analysis of tort law offered a parallel structural critique of what we have called deterrence-based singular instrumentalism.

As we have acknowledged and explained elsewhere, our work builds on Weinrib's and Coleman's. Indeed, we have suggested that civil recourse theory goes an important step further, contending that more careful attention to doctrine and structure not only rules out instrumentalist renderings of the structure and function of tort law, but also rules out Coleman's and Weinrib's efforts to cast tort law as instantiating the principle of corrective justice.[29] For now, however, it is important to see that the present analysis of instrumentalism's deficiencies addresses a different set of questions than does the bipolarity critique.

We commenced this chapter by explaining that civil recourse theory is a theory of tort law's structure and the place of private rights of action within it. We noted further that the civil recourse principle does not itself provide an account of tort law's wrongs (although it does limit the range of possible accounts). We then critiqued instrumentalist understandings of tortiousness and of the reasoning judges tend to use when they apply and develop tort law. As should be apparent, the target of this critique is not the target at which Coleman and Weinrib aimed. They were concerned to rebut the claim that tort law should be understood as a means of achieving certain independently defined goods or goals. As important as it was to provide this rebuttal, it left open for instrumentalists a sur-reply, which Posner himself provided and which proceeds as follows: A successful theory of torts, Posner argued, must incorporate an instrumentalist com-

---

29. Benjamin C. Zipursky, *Substantive Standing, Civil Recourse, and Corrective Justice*, 39 FLA. ST. UNIV. L. REV. 299 (2011). We discuss corrective justice theory in Chapter 5 and in the Conclusion.

ponent, because noninstrumentalist theories have nothing to say about the *substance* of tort law. At best (on this view), corrective justice sets an abstract framework that must be filled with content from some other source. Indeed, Posner went so far as to insist that his deterrence theory *is* a corrective justice theory—one that fills the mold provided by corrective justice theory with a substantive definition of wrongfulness as the failure to take cost-efficient precautions against harming others.[30]

While Posner's sur-reply is unconvincing in several respects,[31] it does get one thing right. A theory of torts must not only constrain the possible ways of fleshing out tort law's wrongs, but also must capture and help guide judicial reasoning about what shall count as wrongs, and neither corrective justice nor civil recourse theory provides that account. In this chapter we have responded to Posner on his own terms by demonstrating that instrumentalism cannot deliver what he says it can deliver. The challenge that remains is to provide an account of tort law's wrongs, and of judicial reasoning about them, that is compatible with civil recourse theory and its notion of torts as injury-inclusive, relational wrongs for which victims are empowered to obtain legal redress.

---

30. Richard A. Posner, *Instrumental and Noninstrumental Theories of Tort Law*, 88 IND. L.J. 469, 473 (2013); Richard A. Posner, *Wealth Maximization and Tort Law: A Philosophical Inquiry*, in PHILOSOPHICAL FOUNDATIONS OF TORT LAW 99, 109 (David G. Owen ed., 1995) (arguing for "the consilience between a wealth maximizer's approach to tort law and that of an Aristotelian"); Richard A. Posner, *The Concept of Corrective Justice in Recent Theories of Tort Law*, 10 J. LEG. STUDIES 187 (1981).

31. For example, as we point out above, the bipolarity critique actually does rule out certain renderings of tort law's substance.

8

Dual Constructivism

INSTRUMENTALIST THEORIES APPEAL TO many torts professors in the United States because they seem to enable us to say something general yet grounded about the substance of tort law. Rather than conceiving of the law of torts as a random collection of wrongs, or as the law's incorporation of the requirements of morality, instrumentalism seems to provide a middle way, according to which torts are the wrongs that courts have identified in the service of deterring conduct that there is reason to deter, compensating persons who suffer certain losses at the hands of others, or both.

Unfortunately instrumentalism's promise proves to be illusory. In its dualist versions, instrumentalism fails to provide a plausible account of why courts have recognized the conduct–setback pairings that they have recognized, how conduct and harm connect to one another within each pairing, and the ways in which courts reason about tort cases. Singular instrumentalist theories—according to which torts should be understood as identifying those instances in which the law is prepared to make one person indemnify another for some loss (compensation theory) or to make an example out of someone for engaging in undesirable conduct (deterrence theory)—fare no better. Indeed, in their theoretical heavy-handedness they reproduce exactly the sort of top-down, reductionist approach to tort theory that instrumentalism was supposed to help avoid. This is why many scholars are as leery of Jamesian compensation theory and Posnerian deterrence theory as they are of Weinribian corrective justice theory.

In this chapter we offer a fresh attempt to theorize tort law's wrongs. We take seriously the desire to provide an account that is grounded and that allows tort law room to change over time. We further embrace the dual instrumentalist's recognition that tort law invites courts to deal with misconduct and setbacks as a unit. However, to avoid the problems of instrumentalism we offer a *constructivist* rather than instrumentalist account of the two-sidedness of tort law. On this view the wrongs of tort are "constructions" (or "reconstructions") of injurious wrongs explicitly or implicitly recognized in doctrine and in social norms.

In what follows, we develop dual constructivism by explaining, first, some of the ways in which it differs from more aggressively normative accounts of tortious wrongdoing. We then use an extended example— drawn, ironically, from the California Supreme Court's jurisprudence— to demonstrate our approach.

Trespass and Case

Civil recourse theory is often mentioned in the same breath as corrective justice theory. Indeed, Ernest Weinrib (among others) has questioned whether there really are differences between them.[1] As we explain at various points in this book, they do differ. One important difference is their respective approaches to the question under consideration in this chapter and Chapter 7.

As we understand it, Weinrib's version of corrective justice theory holds that a proper understanding of tort law's form and structure will go a great distance in explaining why courts have recognized wrongs such as battery, negligence, trespass to land, and the like. In other words, he seems to assert that law that is concerned to link the doer and sufferer of a wrong, and to see to it that the injustice created by the wrong is corrected, is law that will have not only the structure but also the substance of Anglo-American tort law. By contrast, other corrective justice theorists, including his colleague Arthur Ripstein, seem to suppose there is a gap between structure and substance, and seek to fill that gap by interpreting the substance of tort law in the light of moral and political theory.[2]

---

1. Ernest J. Weinrib, *Civil Recourse and Corrective Justice*, 39 FLA. ST. L. REV. 273 (2011).
2. ARTHUR RIPSTEIN, PRIVATE WRONGS (2016) (arguing that tort law's substantive rules embody the Kantian principle that no person is in charge of another).

Our approach lies in between Weinrib's and Ripstein's. We believe that civil recourse theory informs but does not determine the content of tort law, and that its content is not expressive of a particular moral or political theory, but instead derives from a set of well-established moral judgments that the courts have elaborated in both uncontroversial and controversial ways. We do not deny that the wrongs of tort law often track or resemble familiar norms of interpersonal morality. (A gratuitous punch in the nose is a moral wrong and it is a tort, and the overlap between these two domains, while by no means complete, is substantial.) Rather, we believe that understanding the wrongs of tort law requires understanding how judges have applied the common law and moved it forward by virtue of their reflective entrenchment in existing law and the social norms it embodies.

The origins of the Anglo-American common law of tort reside in a practical and political decision by medieval English officials to open the royal courts to lawsuits predicated on certain allegations of wrongdoing and injury. (Previously such allegations were heard in local or ecclesiastical courts, or resolved outside of the courts.) Thus was born the writ of trespass *vi et armis*. It enabled claims for damages by victims of forcibly inflicted personal injuries against those who injured them. It also enabled claims alleging forcible restraints on liberty, and forcible invasions or takings of property. These basic forms of injurious wrongdoing—batteries, false imprisonments, and trespasses to property—probably formed the bulk of English tort law circa 1300. Of course, they remain part of our law today.

The decision to recognize these wrongs was a political effort by the crown and its ministers to expand royal power in the name of improving prospects for civil order. Nonetheless, it would be a mistake to distinguish too sharply between the political and the moral. The injurious wrongs that were initially made actionable in the king's courts were not selected at random. They were selected *because of their widespread recognition as serious forms of mistreatment*. It is completely unsurprising that, when the royal courts began entertaining claims for redress of wrongful injury, they started with forms of mistreatment that were uncontroversially understood to warrant victims' demands for responsive actions from wrongdoers. It is equally unsurprising that these wrongs are still regarded as moral and legal wrongs today. As among Aristotle, Bentham, Kant, and Mill, as well as Nozick, Rawls, and Scanlon, there would seem to be no disagreement on the question of whether it is *prima facie* wrong to attack or kidnap another, or to occupy or possess another's property without permission.

Our point is not that there is some sort of self-evident truth to the proposition that it is wrong (for example) intentionally to confine another against his will. The point is instead that, from within a range of political-philosophical and moral frameworks—including, of course, the sort of liberal-democratic and rights-centered frameworks that have been dominant in the modern Anglo-American tradition—the recognition of this particular "doing unto another" as a wrong is easy because overdetermined. At this juncture in the argument, the question at hand is whether, in a world in which courts are open to hear complaints about, and provide remedies for, certain mistreatments of one person by another, an intentional confinement is appropriately recognized as a mistreatment of the requisite sort. That it is difficult to come up with an argument *against* its being so recognized is telling. Whatever one might think about the precise contours of tort law, the idea that it should include wrongs such as false imprisonment, battery, and trespass to land seems about as inescapable as the thought that if there is to be a criminal law, the list of crimes ought to include some version of the crimes of murder and rape.

Tort law, of course, has hardly stood still since medieval times. As was to be expected, almost as soon as royal courts started hearing trespass actions, litigants began pressing them to recognize claims for other injurious wrongs. Notably, they did so by inviting the courts to *build out, through a process of analogy, from the collection of wrongs initially actionable under the writ of trespass.* For centuries novel claims of wrongful injury were pleaded via the writ of trespass *on the case*. To allege a trespass on the case was to allege a wrongful injury that resembles yet differs from the wrongs actionable via the writ of trespass *vi et armis*. It is also notable that, under medieval pleading rules, the question of whether to recognize a claim and impose liability was to a significant extent left to the discretion of local juries. One important reason for doing so was to keep the wrongs recognized as "trespasses" (in the older sense of the term) more or less in contact with positive morality and prevailing custom.

Today's stable of torts differs from those that existed in 1400, 1600, or 1800. But it is not *that* different. The original writ-of-trespass torts are still with us. So are many of the claims that courts early on recognized under the writ of trespass on the case, including claims for professional malpractice, defamation, and nuisance. Even a quick flip through a contemporary treatise will reveal that tort law is substantively diverse. Yet because today's torts were developed primarily through a process of analogical reasoning and a process of incorporating evolving social norms, they by no means form a random collection. Instead they tend to cluster around interferences with certain distinctive but widely recognized aspects of individual well-being. Suits for negligence and products liability are referred to as claims for "personal injury" because they characteristically involve allegations of misconduct causing bodily harm. Trespass to land and chattels, along with nuisance and conversion, are routinely deemed "property torts." Battery, assault, false imprisonment, and intentional infliction of emotional distress are sometimes dubbed "dignitary torts." The defamation and privacy torts, meanwhile, concern interferences with the victim's interest in how others regard them.

Whether it is helpful to describe these different aspects of well-being in the language of interests, or protected interests, is a difficult question.[3]

---

3. The term "interest" has typically been used in a manner that is continuous with a utilitarian framework and with the language of preferences. On this understanding, a person could have an interest in the physical well-being of another, an interest in not being nauseated, and so on. Torts, by contrast, are tied to a notion of objective well-being.

We have elsewhere asserted that "[t]ortious wrongdoing always involves an interference with one of a set of individual interests that are significant enough aspects of a person's well-being to warrant the imposition of a duty on others not to interfere with the interest in certain ways, notwithstanding the liberty restriction inherent in such a duty imposition." John C. P. Goldberg & Benjamin C. Zipursky, *Torts as Wrongs*, 88 TEX. L. REV. 917, 937 (2010). It is natural but mistaken to read this language to suggest that we subscribe to an "interest theory" of rights such as Raz's (especially in light of our insistence, immediately above, that "interest" must be understood objectively).

We agree with Raz that legal rights are correlative to legal duties, and that duties are often recognized in part because important interests of others will be substantially affected by certain actions taken by the bearers of those duties. And, indeed, we are inclined to agree that it is useful to think of legal duties existing by virtue of the existence of mandatory reasons for behaving in certain ways toward others, and that certain aspects of the obligee's well-being often supply those reasons, in very significant part. Nonetheless, in our view, the rights that are correlative to these duties are not identical with the interests that warrant the imposition of the duties. Take the case of a patent right, for example. The legal duty not to interfere with another's invention has a legal right correlative to it, and it is the right of the patent owner, but it is far from clear that the core normative reasons generating this right pertain to an interest of the owner's. To the contrary, it is plausible that the interests that provide the principal grounds for having patent protection are the benefit to members of society that will inure to a system that incentivizes scientific and engineering breakthroughs by granting something akin to property rights in certain inventions.

Of course, some rights are intimately connected with an interest of the putative victim that warrants the imposition of the duty—the right against being negligently physically injured or the right against being libeled, for example. Even here, it is misleading to identify the right with the underlying interest, for there will be instances in which there is an interference with

The difficulties notwithstanding, we sometimes help ourselves to the language of interests. It is important to emphasize, however, that we do so to refer disjunctively to the various kinds of interferences with person, property, liberty, or interpersonal interaction that have been recognized as torts. Indeed, the capacity of the phrase "interferences with interests" to cover these different kinds of interactions is our principal reason for using the phrase. It would be a mistake to overemphasize the dissimilarities among the different torts. All consist of mistreatments that adversely affect an aspect of another person's individual wellbeing; all are injurious wrongs. But it would equally be a mistake to infer from the use of the term "interest" that the kinds of interferences that amount to torts boil down to a single value or idea.

Dual Constructivism and the Adjudication of Wrongs

Dual instrumentalists are correct to emphasize that the wrongs of tort law are two-sided, and that they have been defined over centuries through the adjudication of disputes over allegations of injurious wrongdoing. Where they go astray is in how they characterize the two-sidedness of torts. A more satisfactory characterization is at hand, however, and we now sketch it under the heading of "dual constructivism."

Dual constructivism's affinities with dual instrumentalism go beyond the fact that both treat torts as inherently two-sided. In particular, it shares the sensibility according to which efforts to identify and justify tort law's wrongs must be as much a matter of institutional setting, practices, and norms as moral theory. Tort law's wrongs have emerged out of a process whereby judges, in response to complainants demanding redress, have been required to make judgments about wrongdoing and civil answerability on terms that litigants can to some degree recognize. The judges who have made tort law did not start with a substantive moral principle, and have never settled on one. Rather, they started with a small collection of basic wrongs—basic in being familiar and relatively uncontroversial—and then from time to time

---

the interest even though the right was not violated. One could delimit the interest so that it always fits the relevant duty. Instead of speaking of an interest in bodily integrity, or an interest in not having one's legs crushed, or even an interest in not having one's legs crushed in an automobile accident, one might instead speak of an interest in not having one's legs crushed in an automobile accident caused by a negligent driver. This strikes us as artificial in many levels, and it stands in the way of using the term "interest" to refer to an aspect of well-being.

have refined, and revised the collection. This collection features both "classics" and important new works. One might imagine them, like artworks of similar genres, clustered together in thematically organized rooms (dignitary torts, property torts, tortious interference with one's ability to interact with others, and so on). Occasionally new rooms are added to house new wrongs. In sum, torts are neither one wrong nor a hodgepodge. Tort law is a constructed and curated gallery of wrongs.

While thus sharing some of the commitments embedded in dual instrumentalism, dual constructivism nonetheless departs from it in four fundamental and interrelated ways. The first is that dual constructivism connects misconduct and setback in a manner that is *integrative* rather than merely conjunctive.[4] This point does not admit of an easy preview, but here is the basic idea. Many of the problems that plague dual instrumentalism stem from the need to connect the deterrable/misconduct side of torts with their compensable/setback side. Dual constructivism does not face this problem because it does not regard these two sides as separate in the first instance: it does not reduce torts to undesirable conduct that happens to coincide with a compensable setback. As we discussed in Chapter 3, the relational directives of tort law generate correlative *duties and rights of noninjury*. Tort law does not instruct us to refrain from acting carelessly, nor does it protect us from being exposed to careless conduct. And it does not direct us to avoid acting with an intention to enter another's property, nor does it protect us from others acting with an intention to enter our land. Rather, it enjoins people from carelessly injuring others, and from entering or remaining on others' private property without permission. Each "act" that constitutes a tort is itself injurious. For many contemporary legal thinkers who work from within a regulatory mindset, there is something deeply counterintuitive about analyzing wrongs in this holistic manner, rather than breaking them down into what is taken to be their separate "act" and "harm" components. We shall argue that this only provides further evidence that tort law is not rightly understood as operating on the same terms as criminal or regulatory law.

Second, dual constructivism calls for reasoning about wrongs in a manner that is *direct*. To put the point negatively, it rejects the thought

---

4. On this point we are particularly indebted to Ernest Weinrib, whose insistence on the correlativity of rights and duties has led us to focus on the integrated nature of tort law's wrongs.

that a decision to deem certain kinds of injurious conduct tortious rests primarily on the social benefit that stands to be achieved by imposing liability for such conduct. A court asserting that conduct C qualifies as a private nuisance because of features x, y, and z typically is not, in the first instance, expressing the view that, in light of features x, y, and z, society will benefit from liability being imposed on those who engage in C. Instead, in treating conduct as an instance of a given tort, a court is declaring that the conduct is properly understood to fall under one of tort law's directives against wrongful injury. To say that it is in light of features x, y, and z that C qualifies as a nuisance is to point to features of C that warrant characterizing it as falling within a prohibition against causing an unreasonable interference with another's use and enjoyment of land. Dual constructivism is labeled "constructivism" because it recognizes that the law is developing. It does not deny that judicial decisions applying the law of nuisance sometimes have an element of novelty. Still, a decision that extends past or reformulates precedents and extant legal concepts need not be, and typically is not, a reverse-engineered decision about which actions it would be socially desirable to deter, and which losses it would be socially desirable to compensate.

Third, constructivist analysis is *normative* or *rectitudinal*, not reductive. According to instrumentalism, a decision to deem conduct a legal wrong reflects a judicial judgment that it is socially valuable that such conduct be so classified. Similarly, the interests whose invasion generates a claim to compensation are understood to be of value in the indirect sense that it would be socially desirable to render them compensable. The idea that torts establish something akin to moral duties to refrain from injuring and moral rights against certain kinds of interferences with interests is no part of the instrumentalist story. Constructivism, by contrast, treats torts as sharing certain features with moral wrongs, including, most fundamentally, the identification of conduct that warrants some form of censure or disapproval by virtue of being an unacceptable or inappropriate way of interacting with another.

Fourth, and finally, dual constructivist analysis is *elucidative*. On this view, courts arriving at fresh decisions on what counts as a tort—even decisions that recognize new torts—are principally engaged in elucidating the norms of tort law, rather than in positing or enacting them. Dual instrumentalists are correct to assert that appellate decisions often change tort law. But they go astray in characterizing these developments as judicial "legislation"—as courts announcing new rules so as better to achieve goals such as deterrence and compensation. Rather, as did medieval judges when they expanded the menu of actionable injurious wrongs via the writ of trespass on the case, modern common-law courts are in significant part elucidating and expanding upon norms of conduct that are already in tort law, in light of precedent and social mores, and thereby *recognizing* duties and rights that had not been clearly recognized before. Even when new torts emerge, it is usually because courts have come to realize that a pattern of liability imposed under recognized torts implicitly identifies a new wrong. In this sense, courts recognize rather than legislate wrongs.

After discussing a judicial decision that illustrates the four features of dual constructivism—integration, directness, normativity, and elucidation—we will elaborate each from a theoretical point of view and the larger framework of which they are a part.

Illustrating Dual Constructivism

Ironically, perhaps, given the California Supreme Court's historical role as a leading practitioner of dual instrumentalism, its decision in *Shulman v. Group W Productions, Inc.* provides an opportunity to see dual constructivism at work.[5] The plaintiffs, Ruth Shulman and her son Wayne, were injured when their car tumbled down a highway embankment. Ruth, whose injuries were particularly serious, was pinned under the vehicle. Both had to be cut free from the wreckage.

A rescue helicopter operated by Mercy Air was dispatched to the scene. All on board, including nurse Laura Carnahan, were Mercy Air staff, except for Joel Cooke, a videographer employed by Group W. Group W had arranged for Cooke to ride along to record a segment for its TV show entitled "On Scene: Emergency Response." For these purposes, nurse Carnahan wore a microphone that recorded her voice as well as the voices of those with whom she spoke. The video and audio recordings were eventually broadcast on a segment of the show.

At the scene of the accident, Cooke recorded footage that included images of Ruth's limbs, as well as her face covered by an oxygen mask.

---

5. 955 P.2d 469 (1998). There are multiple opinions in *Shulman*. However, our discussion relates almost exclusively to the cause of action for "intrusion"; and on virtually everything discussed below, the opinion spoke for five of the Court's seven members.

Carnahan's microphone also recorded her conversations with Ruth—including conversations in which Carnahan refers to Ruth by her first name. Ruth is also heard speaking in a disoriented manner, and twice despairingly expressing a wish to die. These images and conversations, along with footage and recordings taken from inside the helicopter as it flew to and arrived at the hospital, were featured in the broadcast.[6]

Ruth sued Cooke and Group W, claiming that Cooke had committed two torts: "public disclosure of private facts" and "intrusion." Treating the broadcast as newsworthy, and understandably displaying reluctance to impose liability for a broadcast given U.S. Supreme Court decisions granting media companies broad First Amendment protection against liability, the California Court dismissed the former claim. However, it also held that a jury reasonably could conclude that, in recording Ruth's voice and in joining and recording Ruth's air-ambulance ride, Cooke had invaded her privacy.

The Court observed that "the action for intrusion has two elements: (1) intrusion into a private place, conversation or matter, (2) in a manner highly offensive to a reasonable person."[7] Notably, in framing the issue of whether *what Cooke did* constituted intrusion, it simultaneously inquired whether *the interest of the plaintiff that was invaded was of a sort protected by the law and whether the defendant's conduct violated a rule contained in the law.* Ultimately, the Court drew on several considerations in determining that the case should go to the jury:

> Although the attendance of reporters and photographers at the scene of an accident is to be expected, *we are aware of no law or custom permitting the press to ride in ambulances or enter hospital rooms during treatment without the patient's consent.* (See *Noble v. Sears, Roebuck & Co., supra,* 33 Cal. App. 3d at p. 660, 109 Cal. Rptr. 269 [accepting, subject to proof at trial, intrusion plaintiff's theory she had "an exclusive right of occupancy of her hospital room" as against investigator]; *Miller, supra,* 187 Cal. App. 3d at pp. 1489–1490, 232 Cal. Rptr. 668 [rejecting intrusion defendant's claim that plaintiff consented to media's entry into

6. These included images of Ruth's face covered by an oxygen mask and recordings of communications between Carnahan and a dispatcher in which Carnahan reports that Ruth could not move her feet, as well as statements from Ruth about her back hurting and her feeling poorly.

7. 955 P.2d at 490.

home by calling paramedics: "One seeking emergency care does not thereby 'open the door' for persons without any clearly identifiable and justifiable official reason who may wish to enter the premises where the medical aid is being administered."].) Other than the two patients and Cooke, only three people were present in the helicopter, all Mercy Air staff. As the Court of Appeal observed, "*[i]t is neither the custom nor the habit of our society that any member of the public at large or its media representatives may hitch a ride in an ambulance and ogle as paramedics care for an injured stranger.*" (See also *Green v. Chicago Tribune Co., supra,* 221 Ill. Dec. 342, 675 N.E.2d at p. 252 [hospital room not public place]; *Barber v. Time, Inc., supra,* 159 S.W.2d at p. 295 ["Certainly, if there is any right of privacy at all, it should include the right to obtain medical treatment at home or in a hospital . . . without personal publicity."].)[8]

Included in this passage are reflections on whether extant habits, norms, and established law permit a videographer to join a private citizen in an ambulance without her consent. The Court also analogized to prior cases involving a somewhat different scenario—namely caring for a patient in a hospital room or at home. By citing those cases and quoting their disapproval of third-party intrusion in analogous settings, the Court made evident its view that prior decisions stand for a norm that applied to this case. And by invoking habit and custom, it effectively used customary expectations to circumscribe what is permissible. In effect, the Court stood in the shoes of a member of society disapproving of this conduct as wrongful when it said: "it is neither the custom nor the habit of our society that any member of the public at large or its media representatives may hitch a ride in an ambulance and ogle as paramedics care for an injured stranger." The point is that, relative to the social norms of the community, the conduct went beyond the line of what is permissible. The defendant's conduct was, in that sense, eligible to be described as *wrongful.*[9]

8. *Id.* at 490–91 (emphasis added).

9. *See also id.* at 494 ("Defendants, it could reasonably be said, took calculated advantage of the patient's 'vulnerability and confusion' . . . for the possible edification and entertainment of casual television viewers") (quoted authority omitted); *id.* at 503 (Brown, J., concurring and dissenting) (a jury could find that the defendants failed to show "fundamental respect for human dignity").

The California Supreme Court not only focused on the defendant's side of the alleged intrusion. It also considered the plaintiff's side—the question of injury:

> a reasonable jury could find highly offensive the placement of a microphone on a medical rescuer in order to intercept what would otherwise be private conversations with an injured patient. In that setting, as defendants could and should have foreseen, the patient would not know her words were being recorded and would not have occasion to ask about, and object or consent to, recording. Defendants, it could reasonably be said, took calculated advantage of the patient's "vulnerability and confusion." Arguably, the last thing an injured accident victim should have to worry about while being pried from her wrecked car is that a television producer may be recording everything she says to medical personnel for the possible edification and entertainment of casual television viewers.[10]

For much the same reason, a jury could reasonably regard a journalist's entering and riding in an ambulance with a severely injured patient to be a serious intrusion on a place of expected seclusion. Again, the patient, at least in this case, was in no position to assess who was riding with her or to inquire why each person was present and to consent to their presence. A jury could reasonably conclude that decency requires a patient's anxious and traumatic journey be taken only with those providing emergency services to her, and out of sight of the prying eyes (or cameras) of others. An anxious and vulnerable victim, the Court reasoned, may well have suffered an unjustifiable interference with her interest in maintaining her privacy by being recorded in her moments of suffering and despair at the accident scene. Similarly, it regarded the cameraman's hopping into the air-ambulance as plausibly deemed invasive, under the circumstances.

Shulman illustrates the four aspects of constructivism referred to above: the inseparability of the defendant's wrongful conduct and the plaintiff's having suffered a setback; the direct rather than derivative aspect of the court's reasoning; the rectitudinal characterization of the wrong; and the elucidative nature of the judicial decision.

---

10. *Id.* at 494 (quoted authority omitted).

First, the Court does not really set apart the riskiness, negligence, recklessness, or intentionality of the defendant's conduct from its effects on the plaintiff. Likewise, it is not as interested in the losses the plaintiff experienced as a result of this conduct as it was in whether the conduct amounted to an invasion of her privacy. The tort of intrusion is treated by the Court as uniting conduct and setback elements. Cooke's capturing of Shulman's desperate words and his observation of her while she was being transported in the ambulance—these were simultaneously actions that the Court thought a jury could deem wrongful *and* effects that the Court thought a jury could deem injurious. The question it answered was whether Cooke's actions could be found by a jury to be an intrusion— whether what he did was to invade her privacy. In words such as "intrusion" and "invasion," act and harm are joined seamlessly rather than fortuitously. They are not captured in the dual instrumentalist picture of tort cases as occasions that happen to enable a judge (and jury) to further simultaneously the goals of deterrence and compensation. To speak of an invasion of privacy is to recognize act and consequence as integrated components of a unitary, injury-inclusive wrong.

Second, although the *Shulman* Court is California's highest and although the decision of the case would unquestionably count as an important precedent, the Court did not decide the case by considering whether, in the future, such conduct should be deterred or such injuries should be compensated. Rather, the Court was interested in whether a jury could reasonably conclude that what Cooke did was too intrusive and whether the putative invasion was sufficiently offensive to warrant the recognition of an invasion of privacy claim. The application of tort law, even in cases in which extant doctrine offers support for conflicting results, is not exactly retroactive in part for this reason. Courts invite juries to ask whether the conduct of the parties *did* intrude into a private sphere and whether it *was offensive*, and courts ask themselves whether the contours of the law are such that a jury reasonably could so find. In answering this question, they are elucidating and articulating the boundaries of the tort law as it already exists. They are considering the possibility that such conduct is an instance of a recognized injurious wrong.

Third, the Court's analysis, though legal, has an obvious rectitudinal dimension. It is legal because it is rooted in California precedents, in the Second Restatement of Torts, and in a variety of other sources of law. The Court wrote: "A patient's conversation with a provider of medical care in

the course of treatment including emergency treatment, carries a traditional and legally well-established expectation of privacy."[11] Yet it also
makes references (quoted above) to the defendant's taking "calculated advantage" of the plaintiff, to what the plaintiff "should not have to worry
about" ("ogling"), to the defendant's "egregious" intrusion, and so on.

Despite the court's ample reliance upon morally tinged descriptions of
the defendant's conduct and the plaintiff's injury, *Shulman* is not a piece
of applied moral theory. There is no suggestion that the Court thought it
important to consider whether a finding of intrusion would accord with
an independently defined moral principle, and its opinion makes no reference to an aspiration for tort law to track morality. To the contrary, it is not
by virtue of a comprehensive moral theory that the morally tinged perceptions of the judges are fused with the black-letter precedents of California
into a legal holding about the scope of the intrusion tort. Instead it is by
virtue of a kind of comfortable immersion in positive morality upon which
the judges have also drawn.

The opinion in *Shulman* relies on social mores at a number of different
levels. It expressly comments more than once on the absence of a custom
according to which it was acceptable for a cameraman to insert himself
into an ambulance. Perhaps more subtly, it repeatedly expresses the view
that a jury should be able to deliver its verdict on whether the wrong of
intrusion had been committed. And most basically, the actual legal standards of the intrusion tort are articulated in a manner that plainly invites
the deployment of social norms. This is true of the requirement of "offen-
siveness" and of a "reasonable expectation of privacy."

Finally, *Shulman* is best understood as articulating or elucidating state
tort law, not as creating or positing a new rule. The Court is not formalistic or disingenuous about whether the case can be resolved by a mechanical application of precedent. Indeed, it begins its discussion of the
intrusion claim by stating candidly that "[d]espite its conceptual centrality,
the intrusion tort has received less judicial attention than the private facts
tort, and its parameters are less clearly defined."[12] Nonetheless, the Court
does not view itself as permitted to decide whether to *enact* a rule that

---

11. *Id.* at 491–92 (citing, *inter alia*, Evid. Code, §§ 990–1007 (physician-patient privilege); Civ.
Code, §§ 56–56.37 (confidentiality of medical records); *Ribas v. Clark*, 696 P.2d 637 (Cal. 1985)
(applying California criminal code provisions that prohibit the recording of any confidential
communication without the consent of all parties thereto)).

12. *Id.* at 489.

such conduct is too intrusive. Instead, it aims to clarify whether the legal category of invasion of privacy might be instantiated in the facts of the case before it.

Integrated Wrongs

Each of the four features of dual constructivism sketched in the context of *Shulman* bears elaboration. We begin with the idea that the wrongs of tort law, as understood within a dual constructivist framework, are integrated. On our account, tort law is built around norms that direct legal actors not to act upon (or to act for the benefit of) others in certain ways. The directives contained within the different torts all consist of injunctions (in the sense of admonitions) that concern interactions with others (or another): "no one shall intentionally touch another in a harmful or offensive manner," "no one shall defraud another," "no one shall carelessly injure another," "one must make reasonable efforts to aid another whom one has put in imminent peril," and so on.

Consider again battery. The basic idea is that an intentional touching of a harmful or offensive nature—a kicking, groping, or spitting upon—is *prohibited*. The dual instrumentalist here sees a legal rule that happens simultaneously to deter people from touching others offensively and that compensates those who have been harmed by being so touched: the rule is explained as having been adopted because it deters people from kicking (by imposing liability upon them if they do so) and compensates people who have been kicked (by forcing the defendant or his employer or insurer to pay compensation).

Dual constructivism offers a different interpretation. Insofar as it contains a no-kicking directive, the law of battery prohibits or enjoins kicking. A court that articulates such a directive is not itself enjoining such conduct, but is instead *recognizing* a norm that enjoins such conduct. That our system imposes liability on defendants for violation of such norms explains, in part, why a court that recognizes such a norm in the context of dealing with a battery claim would understand the system to deter such conduct.

Similarly, a court in articulating the no-kicking norm is recognizing that the law provides protection against being kicked, and recognizing individuals as having legal protection against such actions. That our system empowers those who have suffered such violations to demand compensation from violators explains, in part, why a court that recognizes the no-kicking norm in the context of a battery claim would understand our system to enable those who have been kicked to obtain compensation from those who kicked them. The norms that exist in the common law simultaneously prohibit certain interferences with others' well-being and protect certain aspects of well-being against interferences. They do this by enjoining individuals from acting upon others in certain ways. The enjoining of individuals from such injurious actions upon others is, at the same time, a validation of individuals' legal rights not to be so acted upon. Tort law is not, as the dual instrumentalist would have it, a law of deterrence and compensation. It is instead law that enjoins mistreatments of one person by another, provides redress for such mistreatments, and thereby contributes to the protection of persons from mistreatment.

The integrated quality of the wrongs of tort law is straightforward and highly intuitive in some (though not all) cases. Intentionally occupying a swath of land is a trespass if the land is not one's own (and one lacks permission to be there). Setting foot onto land that is possessed by another, when one intends to be in that location, is at once the wrongful act of the defendant and the rights-invasion suffered by the plaintiff. As we have seen, the same is true of standard instances of battery. A similar analysis applies to the torts of libel, false imprisonment, invasion of privacy, and others.

Standard examples of the tort of negligence are admittedly somewhat different. Indeed, they are sufficiently different that negligence might seem to break the mold of integrated wrongs. Careless driving, for example, seems to be misconduct that is severable from any setback it might cause, such as a broken leg suffered by a cyclist who is run down. Of course misconduct and setback are causally connected, but the integrated nature of wrongs such as trespass to land or battery seems attenuated in, if not absent from, negligence. The same seems to be true of a physician who carelessly injures a patient, an engineer who improperly designs a bridge so as to cause harm to those who use it, a grocery store that fails properly to monitor its aisles, resulting in a slip-and-fall, and so on. In each case, the plaintiff's setback appears to be separable from the defendant's misconduct. The same might be said of acts and injuries that generate claims under the law of strict products liability and other torts.

We have all along insisted that the wrongs recognized by tort law are breaches of duties of noninjury. According to this model, the tortious conduct of a negligent driver who collides with and physically injuries a cyclist *is* the careless infliction of physical harm on the cyclist. By describing this and other torts so that the injury is included in the act prohibited by the relevant legal directive, we seem to be able to sustain an integrated notion of tortious wrongdoing. Skeptics, however, will worry that this fix is merely nominal—that we are fudging through wordplay, rather than genuinely forging, a link between conduct and setback. The question at hand is whether it means something to say "*D* negligently injured *P*" beyond just saying that *D* acted carelessly, *P* suffered a setback, and the two had something to do with one another. If not, there is nothing but a question-begging verbal quip behind our claim that the wrong of negligence, like the wrongs of battery and trespass, is integrated.

In fact, there *is* much more to negligence than careless conduct and a setback connected by the happenstance of causation. Suppose a police officer spies a speeding driver and sets off in pursuit, but then, out of the blue, experiences a fainting spell and crashes his cruiser into a cyclist. If the cyclist were to sue the speeding driver (not the police officer) for negligence, it is far from clear that a court would deem this as an instance of *the driver having negligently run down the cyclist*. The defendant's lawyer certainly would argue that her client's driving, even if careless, was not a proximate cause of the cyclist's injury. The argument would be roughly this: the risk of injuries from a collision caused in the first instance by an unforeseen disability suddenly striking a pursuing police officer is not among the risks that rendered the speeding driver's conduct careless.

The meaning of "proximate cause," the appropriate standards to apply for determining whether a given instance of carelessness counts as a proximate cause of an injury, the rationales for the doctrine, the proper decision maker (as between judge and jury) to apply it, and whether it has analogues in torts other than negligence are the stuff of innumerable academic and judicial debates. For now, however, we want to invoke the doctrine of proximate cause to lay down a theoretically aggressive (although quite qualified) marker. Negligence law's proximate cause requirement, however precisely defined, helps to explain why the phrase "X negligently injured Y" is not equivalent to the phrase "X acted carelessly, and Y suffered a setback because of X's careless act." To ground a claim for negligence, the plaintiff's injury must ordinarily be a *realization* of the aspects of the defendant's behavior that rendered it careless: the plaintiff's injury must be capable of being cogently described as having been immanent within the defendant's carelessness. Negligence, in other words, contains a directive that enjoins careless injurings, not careless conduct itself, nor even harm caused (in any manner) by careless conduct.

As we noted at the outset of this chapter, our current tort system derives from the two-pronged writ system of medieval English law. The first prong, and the earliest torts, were actionable under the writ of trespass *vi et armis*. A physical attack was sued upon as a trespass. So too was an occupation of another's land without consent. The second kind, exemplified initially by, among others, cases of horses being lamed by a blacksmith's incompetent shoeing, were litigated under the heading of trespass on the case. Scholars have long debated the meaning and significance of the trespass / case distinction. We are hardly in a position to resolve that debate. Instead, we are content to note that, in many of its core applications, the trespass writ covered *per se* wrongs. If it were shown that one performed an act of the relevant description—for example, an intentional entry onto a plot of land that, as it turns out, belonged to another—liability would attach regardless of whether the actor could claim to have been behaving reasonably under the circumstances, and of whether the victim suffered tangible harm or loss. "Case" tended to be different on both sides: there usually needed to be a finding of some kind of fault and a finding of some kind of harm.

Our suggestion is that the *per se* qualities of torts such as battery and trespass to land, and the proximate cause requirement of negligence and other torts once actionable as instances of trespass on the case, achieve the same result in different ways. The result is that the injuring of the plaintiff is rendered as part of what it is the defendant has a duty not to do, according to the relevant legal directive. The wronging or breach of duty in trespass to land is per se a violation of the plaintiff's property right. The wronging of negligently injuring someone requires bodily harm or some other cognizable setback, such as serious trauma. It does so because, for purposes of the tort of negligence, carelessness is *carelessness as to an injury of that kind,* and hence the plaintiff has not suffered the wrong of negligence unless her injury counts as the fruition of the careless conduct, not simply a consequence of it.

The particular ways in which misconduct and injury arc integrated in torts such as trespass to land, on the one hand, and negligence, on the other, probably do not exhaust the possibilities. Indeed, another mode of integration is arguably at work in recognized wrongs such as tortious interference with contract and intentional infliction of emotional distress through outrageous conduct. In these torts, the integration of wrongfulness and injury is accomplished through the "targeted" way in which injury is inflicted: the defendant is held liable if his intent was to bring about an injury of the very kind suffered by the plaintiff. Arguably, both economic and emotional well-being are generally not treated in tort law as stand-alone protected interests, and it is noteworthy that in each of the two torts just mentioned, there is both an independent wrongfulness requirement (tortiousness in one, outrageousness in the other) *and* an exceptionally tight integration of defendant wrongfulness and plaintiff injury (the injury must be what the defendant intended to bring about or recklessly risked).

Direct, Not Derivative, Assessment

Once one grasps that the unit of analysis in tort is not acts taken in isolation of their consequences, but acts that are injurings, it becomes far easier to evaluate and classify them directly, rather than derivatively. The converse point is perhaps obvious. If a tort is a mere concatenation of conduct and setback, and the question is whether there should be liability for such concatenations, it is almost inevitable to ask whether such setbacks should be compensated and such conduct should be deterred. But if a tort is the cutting open of a person's abdomen, or the generation of fumes that spread into a neighbor's yard, it is far easier to see the question this way: shall individuals be protected from such injurious actions or not? When tort law responds to such questions with the answer "it depends," the dependency in question has to do with knowing more about these injurings. Was the cutting performed by a surgeon? Was permission obtained for the incision? Was enough information given to the patient prior to a request for his consent? Was the incision done competently? Was it part of a successful medical procedure? Similarly, we will want to know what kind of fumes are being spread, in what kind of neighborhood, to what effect, for how long, and so on. The point is we are judging whether persons have a right against being treated as the defendant treated the plaintiff, and we are judging whether persons have a duty to refrain from interacting with others in the manner in which the defendant interacted with the plaintiff.

Of course, there are many tort cases where it is clear that a wrong of the kind the common-law counts as a tort has been committed and, because of possible affirmative defenses, or damages questions or procedural issues, the real question is whether liability is warranted and salutary, or whether a given plaintiff should be able to recover. But the question is not whether there are cases like this. It is whether, in cases in which it is *not* clear whether there is a tort, the answer to that question can only be reverse-engineered by consideration of the effects on deterrence and compensation of allowing or denying the claim. As shown by our discussion of *Shulman* and other cases, derivative or backed-out answers are not the only ones available. And as the previous paragraph shows, understanding the wrongs of tort law as interferences with aspects of well-being, integrated as explained above, makes the structure of such analyses quite straightforward and intuitive.

Precedent, Custom, Morality, and Common Law

Once we have accepted that tort law involves direct analysis of which kinds of interactions count as wrongful injurings, we are conceding that the reasoning of courts in tort cases is at least partly normative. More specifically, it is rectitudinal in the sense of pertaining to standards of conduct. At one level, this is palpably obvious, since tort law is full of duties and rights. The question is why we should deem this acceptable, given that judges are generally not regarded as having *moral* expertise, that an ideal of the rule of law involves separating the law from what a judge happens to think is morally right, and that judges are not legislators.

The first part of the answer is that the materials with which judges begin their work are themselves legal materials and legal norms. That they are making decisions about normative matters—decisions about what one must do or may do—does not entail that they are moralizing. Instead they may be, and often are, applying or shaping the law through reasoning about *legal* norms. This sort of normative-but-legal reasoning is exactly the sort of reasoning on display in *Shulman*. Still, we have acknowledged that there is a possibility of fresh and creative adumbration of the law. We thus seem to be saying that judges are permitted to deploy non-legally-embedded normative reasoning in deciding tort cases, for what else could it mean to say that they are entitled and indeed sometimes required to rely on claims about what the law *should be* rather than claims about what the law is?

At least two qualifications are critical at this juncture. The first is that sometimes judges may be engaging in reasoning about standards of right conduct without themselves engaging either in first-order moral reasoning *or* description of settled legal standards. That is because judges might be articulating standards of conduct that are widely accepted. In these instances, they are not reasoning from an Archimedean perspective about what counts as right conduct; they are reasoning about what is right conduct from within a framework of what is *accepted or understood* to be right conduct. A second qualification is that sometimes the law itself contains concepts—such as the idea of a reasonable expectation of privacy—that are themselves underspecified and call for normative reasoning in order to be fleshed out. This too is different from first-order moralizing as such.

Finally, even when a judge's articulation of norms of conduct is not the articulation of social mores and is not the fleshing out of an open-textured moral concept embedded in the law, their reasoning may nonetheless be importantly distinct from "naked" moralizing. As jurists as different as Benjamin Cardozo, Ronald Dworkin, and Antonin Scalia have explained, the job of presenting a collection of precedents as a *body of law* sometimes calls upon courts to articulate principles that form the connective tissue of our law and allow it to stand as a coherent whole.

A candid and forthright depiction of how a good deal of common-law adjudication works, especially in appellate decisions on unsettled issues, is that the arguments and justifications brought to bear are normative at least in the sense of being about standards of conduct. Like Cardozo, we believe that the adjudication of tort claims consists of, and calls for, a mix of reasoning about history, precedent, social mores, and principles of justice. But judges undertake this inquiry in the context of fleshing out the law. Inchoate norms of conduct and inchoate expectations are, so to speak, elevated to legal status (or not) through common-law adjudication. To the extent that these norms of conduct already exist in social mores and in individuals' expectations and dispositions, common-law courts are not making them up out of whole cloth. On the other hand, it is the nature of common-law reasoning that judges possess the power to say whether such norms exist, to call upon them as extant norms and expectations, and then to decide whether to entrench them in an institutional system that generates significant practical consequences.

In the context of doing so, judges should be and typically are aware that they are making a variety of normative judgments, on at least two levels.

First, they have the opportunity to adopt a normative point of view, not simply to assert, from a descriptive point of view, that certain norms exist as a matter of sociological fact. Second, they must make what is inevitably a loaded judgment about whether the social norm being imported into the law actually does fit the precedential common-law framework that it supposedly exemplifies.

It is perhaps illuminating to see common-law decision making in torts as a "hermeneutical" activity, in which a judge utilizes her membership in a community (or set of communities) as a basis for recognizing certain norms of conduct as extant, sensible, and binding. These are not, however, simply nonlegal norms of conduct. Rather, they go along with norms of conduct that are already part of law, norms as to which there is established precedent. Because dual constructivism sees new legal norms of conduct as emergent from accepted norms, these social norms are typically perceived by judges and by litigants as having moral force. As explained below, it would be a mistake to suppose that judges grasp their moral force by virtue of a theory of morality. A judge's work is not purely prescriptive or purely descriptive. It is not her job to say what truly is the right way to treat another person. Nor is it to say what society says the right way to treat another person is. Judges deciding tort cases are neither prophets nor sociologists. Dual constructivism identifies for them a middle path.

In deciding a tort case, the common-law judge is required to declare what is and is not a permissible way to treat another person *under the law*. In doing so, she is applying and sifting through a body of precedent and principles. As virtually all legal scholars agree, the content of those principles is malleable, and, as we have argued throughout this book, many of them are morally rich. To this extent, the application of the concepts requires judgment. Nonetheless, the presence of a word or idea is not a blank check to fill in whatever the judge herself or himself believes is right. There is an understanding that the common law is built on shared customs and norms, and so it is part of what is expected of a judge *qua* judge to apply moral concepts in a manner that retains fidelity to that shared background. Some degree of fidelity to this background is important to the rule of law qualities of private law.

Cardozo struggled, as we have above, to capture the multiply intermediary role of the courts in negotiating history, precedent, tradition, social mores, and perceptions of justice in the course of articulating the common law. His rhetorical flair makes our central point more gripping. In saying what a judge must do when a case comes before his or her court, he put forward the unsurprising position that the judge must examine "the precedents," whether they be known by the judge as precedent "or hidden in the books." Elaborating, he wrote:

> I do not mean that precedents are ultimate sources of the law, supplying the sole equipment that is needed for the legal armory, the sole tools, to borrow Maitland's phrase, "in the legal smithy." Back of precedents are the basic juridical conceptions which are the postulates of judicial reasoning, and farther back are the habits of life, the institutions of society, in which those conceptions had their origin, and which, by a process of interaction, they have modified in turn.[13]

Elucidation

We are suggesting that, in cases of first impression on what counts as having been libeled, having had one's privacy invaded, having been battered, or having been negligently injured, the courts are not charged with making up what they believe is the best answer consistent with what has gone before. Rather, they are applying norms of conduct (that are contained in or supported by precedent) that inform what counts as being one of these wrongs. And they are doing so within an institutional and professional context in which it is understood that they have a (defeasible) obligation to remain faithful to the customary and traditional understanding, and to capture what is a general understanding of the law. That is why the reasoning and the directives themselves have a moral flavor, even though the judge's job is not one of deciding what is morally correct.

When a court altogether lacks precedent or when the precedent from which it is operating is plainly inadequate to push one way or another on a given issue, and, nonetheless, the court articulates a rule, it is acting like a legislature in at least one sense. Its holding becomes law by virtue of the court's having the power to adopt a rule. The opposite is the case in which precedent, while not precisely on point, is powerful, well reasoned, unop-

---

13. BENJAMIN N. CARDOZO, THE NATURE OF THE JUDICIAL PROCESS 19 (1921) (citation omitted).

posed by another line of precedent, and uncontroversially relevant. Here, one may safely say that the court is applying the law, not positing it.

Much of what garners attention in common-law tort adjudication is like *Shulman*; it is neither plainly uncovered nor plainly covered, and what appears to be a substantial precedent-based argument can be made on either side. In this case, it is tempting to say: *Judges are exercising their discretion, and because they are exercising their discretion, the product of their judgment is in the most important sense posited law or quasi-legislation. Whether or not the court dresses up the argument (as the litigating attorneys on either side will do) to appear to be an application of the law is beside the point. A court is in fact coming down on one side, and typically saying why that side is more consistent with precedent. If the court is honest, it will say that considerations of policy played a major role in its choice.*

The position rehearsed in the prior paragraph (in italics) treats a court judgment as an example of a court positing or enacting law. In some contexts, particularly constitutional law, the idea of a court acting in a legislative capacity is tied quite closely to questions of legitimacy, which in turn hinge partly on notions of judicial supremacy with respect to constitutional interpretation. In tort law, by contrast, legislatures can in principle correct judicial 'mistakes.' And typically the stakes are lower than in a case concerning, say, whether Congress has the power to enact a comprehensive regulatory regime.

For the reasons we began to elaborate above, we do not think that courts in cases like *Shulman* are enacting law. This is in part because we do not think that 'enacting versus applying' exhausts the possibilities. Courts in cases of first impression typically have the opportunity to *elucidate* the law. By this we mean that they have the opportunity to cover a range of issues that were not covered before simply by fleshing out the relational norms of conduct, customs, and precedents that are before them. The claim is not that one outcome is going to be uniquely correct, but that the articulation of the law in a new domain can accurately be understood by the court and by legal actors as a clarification of the law and a recognition of rights and duties under the law that were previously unrecognized.

Instrumentalism, Moralism, and Constructivism

Part of the reason instrumentalism has caught on in legal theory is not just jurisprudential but epistemological. This observation points us toward a potential obstacle to our emphasis on elucidation as a distinctive enter-prise. The norms or directives supposedly extant in the common law of torts need to have a certain fecundity if constructivism is going to work. If these norms or sets of them are to be cogently described as having impli-cations, then each cannot simply be a rule. Moreover, the considerations with which litigants' assertions combine in order to create putative legal conclusions must actually combine with these norms in intelligible ways.

Dual instrumentalism, a defender might argue, at least provides a model for reasoning to new results. When courts recognize certain setbacks as the basis for liability, the instrumentalist reasons, they are concluding that certain kinds of harms should be compensated. Similarly, the imposition of liability on certain conduct is analyzed as reflecting the courts' conclu-sion that such conduct should be deterred. Litigants in turn aid the courts by providing information about comparable setbacks and conduct, and information about the long-term results of recognizing certain conduct–setback pairings as torts. Absent this sort of account, it is not clear what sorts of arguments or evidence are even relevant to a judge's decision about how to fashion tort law's directives, and it is not clear that these directives entail anything at all. It seems we are, after all, left with either brute rules or a brute appeal to morality. And it is unclear why statements regarding right or duty, if not instrumentally analyzed, have a meaning or depth of the sort that will, when elucidated, yield more or more fully specified norms. That they enjoin and protect shows that they have *force*, but we need more than force.

Dual constructivism of course begins with a different view of the epis-temological options. It presumes that moral discourse about rights and duties can be coherent. In this it is hardly idiosyncratic. A wide range of scholars writing both inside and outside of philosophy assume that moral discourse or right–duty discourse is capable of being conducted rationally. That is not only because the foundationalism and logical empiricism upon which contrary views were mounted proved to be unworkable on their own terms. It is also because a range of options has been opened up within the epistemological analysis of normative discourse.

In a critique of our work, Judge Posner wrote:

> I have another question to put to civil recourse theorists: sup-posing that tort law is dedicated to providing "some sort of

redress" for people injured by "wrongful" conduct, where do we go to find out what is a "wrong"? Without an answer to that question, the theory is at risk of collapsing into a tautology: tort law provides redress for wrongful injury; injury is wrongful if tort law provides redress for it . . . . But if they are to go beyond economics, as they want to do, they have to explain how one determines whether an act is wrongful, or wrongful in a sense that requires "some sort" of redress even if not complete. I don't see that in their work. They seem to think that everyone knows right from wrong . . . . [14]

Posner's critique was wrongheaded when written and still is. But his having raised it suggests that a clarification on our part might be helpful. And so we shall do so to summarize this and the prior chapter.

Judge Posner knew full well where a judge is to look to find out what is wrongful conduct in tort law. She must examine the tort law of the relevant jurisdiction, relying both on her education and on her background knowledge to help her process what she finds. When she finds cases and principles in the law, many will indeed be selected as standing for an example of a legal wrong because the plaintiff won the case and was provided with redress, but that is not what it means for a court to have deemed it wrongful. As Posner himself has sometimes argued, courts are issuing declarations about what kinds of conduct the common law deems acceptable and what not; that is why they are willing to impose liability.

The more interesting question, which we have addressed in the past two chapters, is what to do when the precedent is not directly on point in the relevant jurisdiction, or when there is a good argument that *stare decisis* should be rejected, or when there is a case of first impression. Here is where Posner says we rely on the thought that "everyone knows right from wrong," presumably asserting that we believe judges and lawyers will simply recognize what counts as a wrong when they see it. He is correct that we think *recognizing wrongs* is what courts do, but incorrect to suppose that we think the capacity to recognize legal wrongs is some sort of unmediated intuitive capacity.

14. Richard A. Posner, *Instrumental and Noninstrumental Theories of Tort Law*, 88 IND. L.J. 469, 473 (2013).

Like Lon Fuller, and like Posner's intellectual nemesis, Ronald Dworkin, we believe that there is a morality in the law itself, and it is the job of the judge to put himself or herself "inside" that morality and recognize wrongs from that point of view, using precedents and principles embedded in the law as her principal guide. Ironically, this is what Posner himself once believed and may still believe. (After all, he has insisted that the efficient allocation of resources *is* the morality embedded in the common law of torts, and judges should therefore follow it.) Posner criticized Dworkin, with some plausibility, for erecting a moral account of law prior to seeing what was really in the legal system, and squeezing the morality into the law in strategic fashion. (Again, there is a rich irony here, given the patently anachronistic quality of the economic theory Posner once purported to find "in" the common law of torts.) In any event, we share the lawyerly sensibility—found in the early writings of both Posner and Dworkin—that judges and scholars who claim to have cottoned on to the principles and concepts that constitute the normative outlook of the law itself need to be highly attentive to the doctrinal structure and detail of the law. That is partly expressed by the idea that judges of the common law, when recognizing wrongs, are elucidating, not positing, the law. And it is largely why the great majority of our legal scholarship in torts is far more doctrinally grounded than either of theirs.

As brilliant jurists of the best-and-brightest generation, Dworkin and Posner shared a great deal, notwithstanding their differences. At least two similarities stand out as relevant here. The first is that both men, who began writing around 1970, approached the common law with a skeptical disposition toward social custom and social mores, and perhaps even with contempt for any mindset that does not share in this skepticism. And secondly, both were Harvard Law School graduates attracted to ambitious conceptions of the power and responsibility of courts to make the law what it should be.

Perhaps because we are part of a different generation, our instincts on both of these issues are quite different. To proceed in reverse order, while we hold a high opinion of courts' capacities, that does not lead us to suppose that courts are engaged in the task of crafting optimal rules or making the law the best it can be. Courts handling tort cases are answering the questions presented to them, and do so by analyzing and developing the concepts and principles that comprise the law. The task of applying legal concepts with a moral texture is simply not the same as the enterprise of turning tort law into what one thinks it should be, from a normative point of view. Only those beginning with an extraordinarily capacious conception of judicial power would think otherwise.

Something close to contempt for custom and social mores is, in our view, part of the reason that both Dworkin and Posner, especially in the later part of their careers, appeared to believe that judges will have to inject an elaborate political or economic theory into their reasoning in order to achieve a meaningful result, or one plausibly worth standing by. We do not bring to bear on tort law a Burkean reverence for custom or social mores. Our question is not whether social mores or customs tend to contain the wisdom of the ages, but what role they properly play for a judge trying to recognize the wrongs of the common law of torts. As Cardozo explained in *The Nature of the Judicial Process*, custom, precedent, tradition, and history all play a large role in the judicial process. They are part of how judges and lawyers recognize the wrongs of tort law.

The best-and-brightest disdain for custom is of a piece with the Warren Court–era embrace of judicial value-setting on many levels: judicial impatience with prejudice and small-mindedness is a civil-rights era theme that can be found in the work of both Posner and Dworkin. There is much to this perspective (to which we will return), and it certainly accounted for some of what we regard as the heroism of the United States Supreme Court during that era. But it is no way to understand the common law of torts. Here is a body of law which legislatures have great latitude to correct, if they wish. Here is a body of doctrine whose efficacy turns on its capacity to mesh well with social norms. And here is a domain of rights and duties that constitutes a kind of law only insofar as it plausibly connects with what we tend to expect of one another.

PART III

Wrongs and Recourse in Context

9

Civil Recourse in the Modern World

IN PART ONE WE IDENTIFIED the principle of civil recourse and then provided an account explaining why torts are among the kinds of wrongs that entitle victims to an avenue of civil recourse against wrong-doers. With that account in place, we then offered a justification for the principle of civil recourse and an explanation of the particular form of recourse—redress for wrongs—found in tort law. In Part Two we turned our attention to substantive tort law. Under the heading "dual constructivism," we explained how, out of precedent, custom, and positive morality, courts have applied, developed, and revised—and should apply, develop, and revise—the various two-sided (injury-inclusive) wrongs recognized as torts.

As should now be clear, though our approach has quite understandably been labeled "civil recourse theory," that label is potentially misleading. Ours is a redress-for-wrongs (or wrongs-and-redress) theory. It provides a pragmatist or constructivist account of tort law's substance: one that explains how, beginning with the recognition of claims brought via the writ of trespass *vi et armis*, courts have constructed a gallery of injurious wrongs. Our "gallery" metaphor aims to capture the thought that, even though the various torts do not express a single substantive moral principle, they are not merely an ad hoc collection either. They cluster around wrongful interferences with certain interests or aspects of human well-being, such as bodily integrity, freedom of movement, reputation, and the like. This rendering of tort law's substance is wedded, in turn, to our exposition and defense of the principle of civil recourse: the principle that victims of certain kinds of legal wrongs are entitled to a civil action through which they can obtain recourse for the wrong. Tort law is a particular instantiation of this legal and political principle, in that it allows the victim of the wrongs that count as torts to pursue and obtain redress for those wrongs.

In this part of the book, we aim to elaborate our combined civil recourse, dual constructivist framework and to provide further demonstration of its practical value. We begin by explaining more clearly how our approach cuts across dichotomies that legal academics tend either to accept on faith or to reject entirely, including alleged divides between public and private law, theory and practice, and explanation and critique.

In the remainder of this chapter we consider criticisms suggesting that an account such as ours, which takes tort law's normative concepts seriously, is nostalgic or inapt to modern conditions. Today, the criticism goes, tort law is not about a plaintiff suing and being paid damages by a defendant, is not about trials and judgments that determine whether a wrongful injury has been inflicted, and is not about the provision of redress. Instead, it is about the settlement of claims on an actuarial or aggregate basis, which settlements are often crafted and paid for not by defendants but by their insurers. What in Blackstone's time may rightly have been theorized as a law of wrongs and redress is—and for some time now has been—a decentralized, privatized, claims-processing system. Meeting our critics on their home turf, we conclude this chapter with a discussion of a recent mass tort case. It demonstrates the value of our approach as applied to pressing contemporary cases and controversies.

Public and Private Revisited

Instrumental or Realist accounts regard tort law as "public law." In other words, they treat it as a means through which government brings about goods such as improved safety, or a more desirable allocation of wealth. To distinguish our account from these, we have emphasized (as have many corrective justice theorists) that tort law is a species of private law. Some critics have suggested that, by doing so, we have disabled ourselves from giving an account of tort law's function. To cast tort law as private law is, they say, to give up on explaining what larger purposes it serves.[1] This

1. This reaction stems in part from the fact that the most prominent academic treatment to date of tort law as private law provocatively asserts that it is a mistake to assign any purpose

criticism is unfounded, as we will show. First, however, we need to be clearer about the "public" dimensions of tort law, as we understand it, and about how those relate to its "private" dimensions.

As we have stressed from the outset, tort law is, or implicates, public law because its provision is the fulfillment of a duty owed by government to victims of legal wrongs to provide them with an avenue of redress against wrongdoers. It is also public in that it involves lawmakers, typically judges, setting legal rules and standards about how one must or must not interact with others. (This as opposed to rules adopted by private actors, such as the rules contracting parties agree to observe when performing their agreement.) In this respect, tort law does indeed resemble criminal and regulatory law, a point that economic and other public-law theories have blown out of proportion when they conclude that tort law *just is* regulatory law.

While tort law is in these respects public, it is also in critical respects private. As Blackstone long ago emphasized, torts are "private wrongs": they always involve an individual (or private entity) being subjected to mistreatment by another. And, as we have emphasized throughout the book, tort law is also private law in that it confers legal powers on individuals, firms, and other private entities. Articles I through III of the U.S. Constitution are quintessentially public law because they create and confer powers on offices such as the Presidency and Congress. The same is true of legislation that creates administrative agencies. Tort law is not like these, even though it presupposes constitutional rules that have conferred adjudicative powers on courts. Instead, it empowers private persons to bring complaints and (when these are proven in accordance with relevant rules) to obtain remedies.[2] As contract law empowers us to bind ourselves and others, and property law empowers us to own and alienate land and things, tort law empowers us by enabling victims of wrongfully inflicted injuries to obtain redress.[3]

---

to tort law and other bodies of private law (other than that of being themselves). ERNEST J. WEINRIB, THE IDEA OF PRIVATE LAW 5 (1995). This is one of several important points of difference between our approach and Weinrib's.

2. Sometimes governmental actors act in the capacity of a private actor. For example, governments own land that, if trespassed upon, confers on officials a right of action to sue the trespasser for damages or injunctive relief.

3. Much greater qualification is needed for an adequate characterization of private law; this is meant not as a differentium as such but to identify a strong theme. Sometimes private

We are pleased that the phrase "civil recourse theory" has gained some traction in academic circles. However, its recognition has come with downsides. In particular, it has led certain critics to focus on the remedial side of our account to the exclusion of its structural and substantive sides.[4] So we should be especially clear on this. Ours is not a theory that aims (merely) to explain why and when certain persons are granted rights of action. Rather, it aims to explain why our legal system confers rights of actions on victims of legally recognized injury-inclusive, relational wrongs and, moreover, to explain why courts have tended to recognize the particular wrongs that they have recognized (such as battery, defamation, fraud, negligence, nuisance, and trespass). To the extent we have been laconic about substance, it is perhaps because this aspect of tort law is arguably its least mysterious feature. Few law students are surprised to learn that the law regards assaults, batteries, defamations, frauds, malpractice, nuisances, and trespasses as injurious wrongs. And this is because most of them, like the rest of the population, have been instructed from an early age to refrain from engaging in the sort of conduct that falls under the heading of these torts.

Our claim to have a theory that identifies private and public dimensions to tort law, as well as structural and substantive but also remedial components, has raised for other critics a worry that we are being squirrely. Sometimes with more than a hint of exasperation, they have asked: "You must concede that tort law, like all law, exists to serve human purposes. Whatever their problems, standard instrumentalist accounts have no trouble identifying such purposes: they tell us that tort law deters unsafe conduct or compensates injury victims. Your stance is more opaque. What do you think tort law is for?"

The snappiest answer we can offer to this question is one we have already provided: the point of tort law is to define and prohibit certain forms of mistreatment, and to provide victims of such mistreatment with the ability to use civil litigation to obtain redress from those who have mistreated them. A somewhat more fulsome version of the same answer would define

---

parties are empowered as deputies or private attorneys general (as in *qui tam* actions, for example, and more ambiguously in constitutional tort claims under 42 U.S.C. 1983).

4. *See, e.g.*, Gregory C. Keating, *The Priority of Respect over Repair*, 18 LEGAL THEORY 293, 302 n. 19 (2012).

tort law's point or purpose by reference to what we have here termed its "public" and "private" dimensions.

On the public-law, relational-directives, substantive side, tort law's immediate purpose is to articulate binding rules as to how we must treat each other. By doing so, it offers individuals partial security against mistreatment, and bolsters parallel norms of positive morality that provide similar security, thus helping to protect and preserve certain aspects of individual well-being, including physical integrity, freedom of movement, security in the possession of things, and the ability to interact with others authentically. In saying this, we do not mean to adopt the crude instrumentalist position that tort law is a tool that government uses to promote individual well-being. In part because it operates by giving legal powers to individuals who can decide at their discretion whether and how to exercise it, tort law is not designed to be, and has little hope of being, a "tool" of that sort.

On the private-law, rights-of-action, remedial side, tort law's point is related but distinct.[5] In empowering persons to seek and obtain redress, it recognizes each of us as entitled not to be mistreated and correspondingly entitled to demand accountability of someone who mistreats us. Courthouse doors are open out of a recognition of these entitlements, much like hospital emergency rooms open their doors out of a recognition of the right of each to urgently needed medical care. As explained in Chapter 4, private rights of action in tort reflect a political obligation owed by a liberal-democratic polity to its members. In this dimension, tort law offers them a form of empowerment, along with the prospects of vindication and accountability.

To be sure, in defining a certain type of wrong and providing victims with an opportunity for redress, tort law indirectly advances other values. For example, as we have previously noted at various places in this book, it sometimes promotes socially desirable conduct by identifying certain (antisocial) acts as wrongful and attaching negative consequences to them. It also sometimes provides victims with funds or a sense of vindication that

---

5. Some readers may find a similarity between our account of the public-law side of torts and the important recent work of Hanoch Dagan and Avihay Dorfman. *See, e.g.,* Hanoch Dagan & Avihay Dorfman, *Just Relationships,* 116 COLUM. L. REV. 1395 (2016). If so, the private-law side of our account counterbalances the concern we share with them to highlight the ways in which private law sets conduct-guiding norms.

enables them to get back on their feet after suffering a serious setback. Moreover, it provides a useful framework for the reinforcement and revision of social norms of interpersonal interaction, and contributes to rendering our legal and political system more just than it would be otherwise, holding the other features of that system constant. Although tort law in general advances these goals and values, and does so in a manner that is not merely coincidental or haphazard—and although any assessment of whether and how tort law is to be reformed must recognize that it does advance these goals and values—it goes too far to say that tort law is a scheme for the advancement of these goals, or that *its purpose* is to advance them. In the first instance, tort law marks off certain injurious conduct as not-to-be-done while also enabling those who are mistreated to obtain redress from, and thereby hold to account, those who have mistreated them.

Explanation and Appraisal

We have described how our theory merges tort law's structural-substantive / conduct-guidance side and its right-of-action / remedial side. We now offer an account of a different sort of merger within our theory—namely, our blending of positive (or descriptive) claims and normative (or prescriptive) claims. As in the previous section, in the interest of clarity, we will err on the side of bluntness.

Much of our work has consisted of an effort to understand and explain the concepts, rules, and structures of tort law. For example, we have offered in-depth analyses of canonical judicial decisions ranging from *Rylands v. Fletcher, Macpherson v. Buick*, and *Palsgraf v. Long Island R.R.*, to *BMW of North American v. Gore* and *Metro-North Commuter R.R. v. Buckley.*[6] We have also untied various doctrinal knots pertaining to assumption of risk, fraud on the market, duty, superseding cause, and other topics.[7] The

6. John C. P. Goldberg & Benjamin C. Zipursky, *The Strict Liability in Fault and the Fault in Strict Liability*, 85 FORDHAM L. REV. 743 (2016); John C. P. Goldberg & Benjamin C. Zipursky, *The Moral of MacPherson*, 146 U. PA. L. REV. 1733 (1998); Benjamin C. Zipursky, *Rights, Wrongs, and Recourse in the Law of Torts*, 51 VAND. L. REV. 1 (1998); Benjamin C. Zipursky, *Palsgraf, Punitive Damages, and Preemption*, 125 HARV. L. REV. 1757 (2012); John C. P. Goldberg & Benjamin C. Zipursky, *Unrealized Torts*, 88 VA. L. REV. 1625 (2002).

7. John C. P. Goldberg & Benjamin C. Zipursky, *Shielding Duty: How Attending to Assumption of Risk, Attractive Nuisance, and Other "Quaint" Doctrines Can Improve Decision-making in Negligence Cases*, 79 SO. CAL. L. REV. 329 (2006); John C. P. Goldberg & Benjamin C.

goal of these efforts has been to help make sense of this body of law. In this respect our work is positive or interpretive. It makes claims about *what the law is*. Some skeptics believe that this sort of enterprise is hopeless— that "there is no there there" because tort law is an irredeemable mess. We know of no better way to respond to this sort of skepticism than to offer and defend our account, according to which tort law, though complex, varied, and dynamic, hangs together once understood as law that identifies certain kinds of wrongs and provides victims with the power to obtain redress for them.

This said, we have not set out merely to paint a pretty picture. We aim to explain tort law in a way that enables students, professors, lawyers, judges, and legislators to think more clearly and intelligently about various problems and choices they might face. To improve one's understanding of tort law is to enable one to see how it might apply to a particular case, the roles it plays (and might play) relative to other bodies of law, when and how it should be reformed, and so forth. We can elaborate these practical aspirations by considering the multiple audiences to whom our work is addressed, starting with courts.

Tort doctrine is complex. As one look at a treatise or an ALI Restatement demonstrates, it has many moving parts that interact in complex ways. We aim to help judges navigate this sometimes daunting terrain. Different judges will do different things with this knowledge. We have a view of the judicial role that has implications for how judges ought to work with their knowledge of the law. According to it, judges deciding tort cases have a defeasible obligation to apply the law, rather than making it into something different.[8] In a common-law area such as torts, this means that settled doctrine in a given jurisdiction is entitled to deference. This default may be overcome, however, not only to prevent the operation of the law from working a serious injustice in particular cases (historically a concern of equity courts, but now a feature of the authority of law courts), but also if some part of doctrine really makes no sense or is bereft

---

Zipursky, *The Fraud-on-the-Market Tort*, 66 VAND. L. REV. 1755 (2013); John C. P. Goldberg & Benjamin C. Zipursky, *The* Restatement (Third) *and the Place of Duty in Negligence Law*, 54 VAND. L. REV. 657 (2001); John C. P. Goldberg & Benjamin C. Zipursky, *Intervening Wrongdoing in Tort: The* Restatement (Third)'s *Unfortunate Embrace of Negligent Enabling*, 44 WAKE FOREST L. REV. 1211 (2009).

8. The defeasibility of this obligation, of course, varies depending on where within the judicial hierarchy a court sits: state high courts have more of a responsibility and more authority to revise common law than does a state trial court judge.

of justification. Still, the power to override the law must be exercised sparingly: judges who too often take this path stand to lose credibility and undermine the rule of law.

This thumbnail description of how judges stand to benefit from interpretive tort theory papers over important difficulties. After all, some would say that much of tort law "makes no sense or is bereft of justification." This is because there are many different theories and principles judges might draw upon to assess a given part of the law. More importantly, at least in the common law, what the law *is*—as scholars from Holmes to Cardozo and Dworkin to Posner seem to agree—depends in part on the underlying principles that render it coherent. At least two parts of tort theory are therefore critical to our efforts to assist courts. The more basic part involves identifying what the law is so that it can be applied accurately; tort theory plays a role here because a body of common law is in part a structure of principles and concepts. But a secondary role is in understanding whether those principles and concepts hang together well enough to make sense, and even if they do, whether the justification that stands behind them really merits the deference of *stare decisis*. We readily concede that, at least as to the latter role, our theoretical offerings are not merely descriptive, positive, or analytical, but also normative. We aim to establish not merely what tort law is, but that it is an entirely defensible feature of our liberal-democratic political and legal regime.[9]

At the level of judicial law application, tort theory is relevant in ways beyond that of helping courts to identify what the positive law is. It is also relevant because, as we noted in Chapter 8, much of legal application is elucidation, and elucidation works best against the background of a larger and more detailed picture of the domain of law in question. One better understands the "reliance" element of deceit by understanding that it plays a role comparable to the "of and concerning" element of libel and slander. One better understands what is or is not meant by "strict products liability" when one understands the ways in which liability for battery, negligence, and trespass is and is not "strict." In addition, because we are not so rigid as to believe that judges typically face a binary choice between applying and ignoring the law, we recognize that applying and elucidating

---

9. John Oberdiek has been right to push us to develop further the normative aspect of our theory. *See* John Oberdiek, *Method and Morality in the New Private Law Theory of Torts*, 125 HARV. L. REV. F. 189 (2012).

the law comes with many levels of choice too. There are choices about how to shape the law, whether to clip or expand aspects of it, and so on. The significance of law's open texture expands dramatically when the nuances of facts, procedure, and institutional context are mixed in, as they are in virtually every case. We believe that a successful theoretical account of the principles in the law, how they interact with one another, and what roles they serve, should therefore inform the application of the law.

Turning, now, from the perspective of courts to that of legislators and voters, we confront the questions of which extrajudicial revisions of tort law might be warranted, and of how having a sound tort theory matters to this critical endeavor. Our message here is twofold.

First, we reemphasize that one cannot undertake intelligent reform without appreciating what tort law is and what it is not.[10] Reformers from the political right stack the deck by caricaturing tort law as nothing more than an unpredictable and heavy-handed regulatory system with big payoffs for the plaintiffs' bar. Reformers from the left depict it as a clunky and inadequate compensation system that is tilted against the little guy. For either, the case for reform—or even elimination[11]—seems nearly unassailable. While we wouldn't for a moment deny that tort law (like any complex, real-world institution) has its problems, we do deny that the question of tort law's value, and hence of its reform, can be resolved merely by attending to its ability to generate secondary benefits such as deterrence and compensation. Any such inquiry must take account of the right to redress, and must acknowledge and accommodate the role tort law plays in rendering our legal system just, and in advancing other values (by, for example, reinforcing—and providing structured, concrete contexts in which to reflect on and reshape—the relationships and responsibilities through which we live day-to-day). When assessed with due attention to these considerations, the case for sweeping tort reform looks vastly less impressive.

Second, when it comes to decisions about particular, targeted reforms, it is vital at the outset to determine if the alleged pathology in need of treatment is genuine, or whether instead a "crisis" has been manufactured from anecdotes assembled or invented out of ignorance, or for crass political

---

10. John C. P, Goldberg, *What Are We Reforming? Tort Theory's Place in Debates over Malpractice Reform*, 59 VAND. L. REV. 1075 (2006); Benjamin C. Zipursky, *Coming Down to Earth: Why Rights-Based Theories of Tort Can and Must Address Cost-Based Proposals for Damages Reform*, 55 DEPAUL L. REV. 469 (2006).

11. *See, e.g.*, Stephen D. Sugarman, *Doing Away with Tort Law*, 73 CAL. L. REV. 555 (1985).

purposes. Here the diagnostic work of legal scholars who employ social scientific methods is critical.[12] Where the problems are real, the task at hand is to fashion sensible treatments rather than a cure that is worse than the underlying ailment. Across-the-board damage caps, for example, are blunderbuss measures that can unfairly harm whole classes of injury-victims holding legitimate claims. Much more promising are targeted interventions, such as the National Childhood Vaccine Injury Act,[13] or broader reforms that take adequate account of the need to protect the interests of both defendants and plaintiffs, as did workers' compensation statutes (at least when originally enacted). Although today "tort reform" measures are understood as a one-way ratchet for limiting liability, as a matter of history and normative theory, reform has worked and must work in both directions. Just as the tort system sometimes generates excessive or inappropriate liability, so too it sometimes makes redress too difficult to obtain.

Finally, a word about theory as it relates to lawyers and legal counseling. As Holmes famously stressed in "The Path of the Law," clients often want their lawyers to provide predictions of what courts will likely do. As he also stressed (in ways his Realist successors have not), better understandings of what tort law is and how it works will tend to generate better predictions. In any event, as we noted in Chapter 3, the law of torts is filled with conduct-guiding rules, and it is very much part of the lawyer's job to inform clients what those rules are. Good lawyers will commonly phrase their advice more in practical than moral terms, and this means that they will often communicate a description of legal rights and duties neither in terms of actual predictions nor in terms of rules of conduct as such. Rather, they will inform their clients of potential liabilities associated with

12. *See, e.g.,* Nora Freeman Engstrom, A *Dose of Reality for Specialized Courts: Lessons from the VICP,* 163 U. PA. L. REV. 1631 (2015); Charles Silver, David A. Hyman & Bernard S. Black, *Fictions and Facts: Medical Malpractice Litigation, Physician Supply, and Health Care Spending in Texas Before and After H.B. 4,* 51 TEX. TECH L. REV. 627 (2019).

13. 42 U.S.C. §§ 300aa-1 *et seq.* Under the Act, victims alleging certain injuries that are known to be caused by vaccines can file a claim in the Court of Federal Claims. There, they can obtain compensation based on proof of the relevant injury without having to prove manufacturer fault. However, recoveries are limited to medical expenses and lost earnings, as well as by a $250,000 cap on pain and suffering compensation. A tax on the sale of vaccines provides the necessary funding. Claimants who are denied recovery by the Court of Claims, or who choose to reject an award from that Court, can pursue claims in ordinary courts, but such claims are subject to limitations not applicable to suits seeking damages for injuries caused by other kinds of drugs.

taking or failing to take certain actions. Lawyers and clients alike know that what is being communicated is what our legal system requires actors to do (and not to do) to others, and what it is that we have a right to expect others to do (and not to do).

Does Tort Law Survive Routinization?

The claim that a wrongs-and-redress account of tort law is at once theoretically compelling and practical runs into a seemingly obvious objection—one that we need not imagine because it has been pressed against us. The objection is that such an account is best suited to the law governing a world of horses and buggies, not self-driving cars. As emphasized with particular force by John Witt and Samuel Issacharoff, tort law today often involves the aggregation of individual claims and their resolution through settlement processes that operate on a bureaucratic model.[14] For example, when the pharmaceutical company Merck was sued on allegations that its drug Vioxx had caused some users to suffer strokes and heart attacks, lawyers for the plaintiffs and the defendant ultimately negotiated an elaborate settlement that included a schedule according to which plaintiffs were assigned different levels of compensation based on their age, their preexisting medical conditions, the injuries they allegedly suffered, and so forth. Modern tort law, Witt and Issacharoff maintain, is epitomized by this sort of procedure, which (they say) reflects little or nothing of the idea of wrongs, or a right to redress.

Relatedly, several contemporary scholars have criticized theories that cast tort litigation as occasions for courts to validate victim demands from wrongdoers. This model, they say, is patently unrealistic because it overlooks the fact that almost all tort cases are resolved prior to trial, usually by settlement.[15] In our world, litigation rarely produces an official pronouncement as to the relevant rights and duties, or an official judgment of accountability.

---

14. John Fabian Witt & Samuel Issacharoff, *The Inevitability of Aggregated Settlement: An Institutional Account of American Tort Law*, 57 VAND. L. REV. 1571 (2004).

15. Christopher J. Robinette, *Two Roads Diverge for Civil Recourse Theory*, 88 IND. L. J. 543 (2013). There is also evidence that, when trials are held, presiding judges increasingly manage the proceedings in a way that leaves less room for law application and law shaping by jurors and lawyers. Nora Freeman Engstrom, *The Diminished Trial*, 86 FORDHAM. L. REV. 2131 (2018).

A third criticism within this general rubric has a long lineage, but has recently been expressed forcefully by Steve Hedley.[16] It focuses on the fact that tort law today is bound up with liability insurance. Consider a doctor found to have committed medical malpractice, or a manufacturer held liable for injuring someone through the sale of a defective product. Hedley claims that it simply blinks reality to assert, as we do, that tort law enables the victims of wrongs such as these to hold defendants accountable to them. For in the great majority of cases, the compensation paid out to a victorious tort plaintiff is paid not by the defendant but by the company that has issued a liability insurance policy to the defendant. It is therefore a fantasy to suppose that tort law is about empowering victims to hold wrongdoers to account.

We will address these arguments in reverse order. As Jules Coleman long ago observed, the liability insurance argument relies on a false premise: namely, that if a person owes a duty to another, it is not possible for her to make a contractual arrangement with a third party to assist her in fulfilling the duty.[17] If Kit contracts with Hertz to provide her with a rental car on a particular day, but the Hertz operation at the relevant airport has run out of cars, a Hertz agent might arrange for Avis to provide Kit with the contracted-for car. Assuming that the Avis car is offered on the same terms (with respect to model, price, availability, and so on), Hertz, by making this arrangement with Avis, has fulfilled its duty to provide Kit with a rental car. Were Hertz to make advanced arrangements with Avis for this kind of situation, it would seem to be nearly identical to a case in which a company that expects, sooner or later, to be sued in tort, buys insurance to cover some of the cost of the liability the company might incur as a result of such a suit.[18]

16. Steve Hedley, *Corrective Justice—An Idea Whose Time Has Gone?*, in LAW IN THEORY AND HISTORY: NEW ESSAYS ON A NEGLECTED DIALOGUE 305 (Maksymilian Del Mar & Michael Lobban eds., 2016).

17. Jules L. Coleman, *Tort Law and the Demands of Corrective Justice*, 67 IND. L.J. 349, 370 (1992).

18. Although civil recourse theory is often lumped together with corrective justice theory, they are in important respects different. We discuss these differences in Chapter 5 and in the Conclusion. One difference worth mentioning here is their relative vulnerability to the liability insurance objection. It is not a particularly strong objection to corrective justice theory, and it is weaker still as an objection to civil recourse theory. Corrective justice theory is sometimes taken to assert that there is a kind of moral appropriateness in the legal system's visiting a duty of repair on a wrongdoer. Even assuming (as one probably should not) that this is a fair reading of corrective justice theory, and further assuming that the appropriateness of duty imposition is somehow undercut

There is a lot more to be said about liability insurance than we have room to say here. But one thing to note is that there are various ways in which it complements or reinforces the operation of tort law as a law of wrongs and redress. As we noted in Chapter 6, and will discuss again in Chapter 10, courts have historically and justifiably defined tortious wrongdoing on unforgiving terms. Moreover, because tort redress typically takes the form of compensatory damages calculated by reference to an amount that reasonably compensates the victim for her tort-related losses, liability sometimes is not commensurate to the gravity of the wrong committed: tort law contains no principle of proportional liability comparable to criminal law's principle of proportional punishment. These features are among those that have caused some of tort law's more extreme critics to call for its abolition on the grounds that it is too prone to operate unjustly.

These broad-brush objections are overstated. But they are particularly overstated in a world that features robust markets for liability insurance, as well as the ability to discharge certain tort liabilities through bankruptcy. The process and consequences of declaring bankruptcy hardly entail a pleasant experience for the bankrupted. (And the Bankruptcy Code's placing of tort victims at the back of the creditors' line—which all but guarantees that, in standard cases, they will recover nothing—may well be unjust in how it prioritizes claims among different classes of creditors.) Nonetheless, there are justice-based limits on the extent to which the state should aid victims in holding wrongdoers to account. Laws that grant tortfeasors some protection against lasting financial ruin are as much a part of a just legal regime as tort law. It is in part because we have bankruptcy laws that criticisms of the harshness and injustice of tort law carry less weight than they would otherwise. Laws that enable persons to enter into contracts for the purchase of liability insurance similarly help ease concerns about tort law's demanding aspects. Moreover, unlike bankruptcy law, they have a salutary effect so far as tort law is concerned—they enable many tortfeasors who would not otherwise be in a position to pay what they owe their victims to actually provide the redress to which victims are

---

by permitting liability insurance (which we reject), these assumptions do not generate a critique of civil recourse theory. Our theory maintains that tort law confers a legal power on tort victims that corresponds to a liability incurred by the tortfeasor, not a duty of repair. Accordingly, there is simply no reason to see tort liability as somehow undercut by its insurability.

entitled. In addition, liability insurance at times serves to reinforce tort obligations. Because insurers are often the ones who stand to pick up the "tort tab," they frequently monitor or incentivize their insureds to promote compliance with applicable tort duties.

Our point is not Panglossian: there are undoubtedly difficult and contestable questions about how to combine tort law and liability insurance in a way that leaves adequate room for tort law to do what it does without working serious injustices. We merely mean to remind readers of two obvious but often overlooked considerations. First, tort law is but one component of our legal system. It must be understood and assessed in context. Second, those charged with designing, operating, evaluating, and reforming the overall system will serve us poorly if they evade rather than address difficult questions and judgments raised by these interactions. The thought that "where there is liability insurance coverage there is no tort law" is just such an evasion. Among other things, it allows those who wish to pare down or eliminate tort law to take false comfort in the thought that tort law has, as a practical matter, already been pared down or eliminated.

Similar points bear on the settlement objection. Tort liability is not principally a symbolic process in which one person (the tortfeasor) gives up something of hers as a token that points toward the repairing of her relationship with another person (the defendant). As Scott Hershovitz has powerfully emphasized, court orders requiring damages to be paid express and reaffirm norms of conduct and the importance of victims being able to hold to account those who wrong them.[19] It hardly follows that tort law is principally "expressive." Indeed, its successful functioning does not require that tort cases consistently result in formal declarations that a wrong has been committed for which redress is being provided.

Each of us has a conditional power to have a court order that liability be imposed upon another if we can prove that the other injured us in one of various ways. In principle, it is entirely up to the holder of this power to choose to exercise it. Probably the most common thing that people do with it is . . . nothing. Reliable data are lacking, but it is likely the case that the vast majority of tort victims never bother to sue. In this respect, the rights of action conferred on tort victims are like the right to make a

---

19. Scott Hershovitz, *Treating Wrongs as Wrongs: An Expressive Argument for Tort Law*, 10 J. TORT LAW 405 (2017).

will that sets the terms on which one's assets are distributed upon death. Most people don't exercise that legal power either. Why people refrain from pursuing potentially valid claims varies enormously. A well-insured victim of a carelessly caused injury might conclude that she has no particular reason to sue. Others might not sue because they do not know their rights, or because the stakes are too small to make litigation worthwhile, or because they cannot find a lawyer, or because they don't conceive of themselves as the type of person who engages in litigation.

Among those who do commence a lawsuit, only a very few pursue their claims all the way to verdict and judgment. Instead, if the suit is not dropped or dismissed, they settle. But of course, a plaintiff's decision to settle her tort suit *is* an exercise of the conditional power conferred on her by tort law. That it is such an exercise is obscured by the fact that, in settled cases, the court never rules on whether the plaintiff is able to satisfy the condition that triggers her entitlement to redress. A system that formally empowers those who prove they have been wronged to obtain redress is also a system that empowers persons who have evidence suggesting they have been wronged to obtain compensation as a *quid pro quo* for settling.

We are offering here something more than the familiar observation that settlement happens in the shadow of the law. On our view, the primary point of supplying rights of action to those who have been wronged is *not* to facilitate the public vindication of the plaintiff's standing as a rights-bearer, or to promote public deliberation over our moral responsibilities, or to ensure that injustices are rectified. Instead, it is to provide certain legal powers to victims as against tortfeasors. The fact that victims are empowered to sue and then to settle—that their power is not binary—only underlines this point. To realize that tort law, on its remedial side, is private law, is to appreciate that its point is *not* to see to it that *justice is done*. Its point instead is *justly to empower* those who have been legally wronged; to confer on them the ability to choose whether to pursue a claim and push it through to its conclusion, or to do one of the many other things that having a claim permits, including nothing at all. Those who suppose that the tort system is "failing" when "too few" claims are brought, thus creating "missed opportunities" for compensation and deterrence—or for an expressive reaffirmation of public values—are missing the point. Tort law is not a scheme for the delivery of goods such as these. It identifies injurious wrongs and empowers victims to obtain redress for them. *If*—and of course this is a big "if" that warrants careful study (which in turn may suggest a need for reform)—most tort victims knowingly and voluntarily (in a broad sense) choose not to sue, or choose to settle, the tort system is working as it should.

Finally, we turn to the contention that our approach overemphasizes the importance of individualized justice, and underestimates the pervasiveness of claim aggregation and bureaucratic claims-processing in determining tort law's "real" substance. As we have just explained, we do not claim that tort law is a mechanism for ensuring that justice is done. It hardly follows that the point of the system is to ensure that individuals choose to exercise those powers in every case, or regardless of what others do. It turns out, as Witt and Issacharoff have noted, that in a wide range of cases the value of the formal legal power will be contingent on how others, similarly situated, might exercise it. This is a facet of our system to be taken into account by lawyers and policymakers, and sometimes by judges. As such, it does not undercut our account but complements it. And, indeed, both as lawyers and as scholars, each of us has paid close attention to a number of scenarios where aggregation calls for analysis.

Chapter 4 analogized rights of action to voting rights, and it will be helpful to do so again in this context. In a democracy, the right to vote for candidates for office is important regardless of whether it is exercised. Political actors behave with the knowledge that individuals possess the power to vote, whether or not they vote. To be sure, constituencies whose members consistently fail to vote will tend to find themselves with diminished political clout, just as any *de facto* immunity from tort liability enjoyed by manufacturers will diminish the pressure they feel to produce safer products. But at a basic level, the model captures both a formal truth and a political reality of substantial importance: the ability to hold wrongful injurers accountable changes the power structure of the world of commerce and the social world more broadly. Indeed, the complexities of modern practice, including (for example) the role of insurance adjusters, claims processors, and elaborate indemnification agreements among defendants, in no way undermines the value of having a sound account of tort law's scheme of legal rights and duties, and powers and liabilities. If anything, it only demonstrates how critical it is to get clear on what tort law is before delving into them.

Civil Recourse and Distributive Justice

Scholars who pride themselves on their "realism" bridle at the supposed distinction between distributive justice, on the one hand, and corrective justice or redress for wrongs, on the other. After all, many tort plaintiffs are individuals of modest means seeking compensation from large companies. Judges presiding over such claims, they insist, neither are nor should be blind to the redistributive consequences of a ruling for the litigants before them and all of those affected by such rulings. Tort law is as much or more about distributive justice as anything else.

We have more to say to this line of thinking in Chapter 10 and in the Conclusion, but for now we are happy to take the point and—as have John Gardner, Arthur Ripstein, and other corrective justice theorists—go one step further. Tort law's operation can have meaningful consequences for the distribution of wealth. But this actually understates the degree to which it implicates issues of distributive justice. To a substantial degree, tort law's empowerment of victims and its subjecting to liability of wrongful injurers is itself a distribution.[20] Tort law distributes powers and, in doing so, creates opportunities for the redistribution of wealth. Legal actors are and ought to be aware of this fact. However, this is a far cry from supposing that courts should decide individual tort cases or should fashion the rules of tort law based principally on a view as to the appropriate distribution of wealth in society. That tort claims today are often aggregated, such that many claimants stand to receive payment when claims prevail, does nothing to repair this particular is-ought fallacy; it merely tends to conceal it.

In closing this discussion temporarily, it will be useful to explain why we remain guarded in our approach to a certain kind of wealth-redistributivist approach to deciding tort cases or to crafting tort doctrine. Our critics tend to think it is because we are nonconsequentialists about morality and because we are formalists or conceptualists about common-law adjudication. These objections lose sight of the bigger-picture aspects of our approach. Indeed, they miss the big picture in terms of distributive justice itself. As Rawls emphasized, distributive justice is partly about wealth

---

20. John Gardner, *What Is Tort Law For?: Part 1. The Place of Corrective Justice*, 30 LAW & PHIL. 1 (2011). Whereas Gardner and others suggest that tort law is properly understood as a scheme that distributes losses, we treat it as a scheme that distributes rights and powers.

but not only about wealth. A constitutional system like ours protects individuals and respects their equality by designing institutions in a certain way. One of the key features of Anglo-American legal systems has been harnessing law to articulate and enforce norms of conduct about how others may be treated by empowering individuals to redress mistreatments through the courts. As we have noted, this empowerment is worth far more than simply the possibility of actually gaining a verdict at court, both because of what can be obtained through settlement and because actors act in the knowledge that others are so empowered, which provides them an incentive to comply with the rules.

Like a great deal of constitutional law—and, indeed, like a great deal of statutory and regulatory law—the common law is both resilient and fragile. Individuals' powers to hold others accountable remain fixed stars in the law of a jurisdiction only by the grace of legal actors, especially judges, treating them as such. Law, like language, depends on patterns of use retaining their conventional force.

It is understandable that progressives, especially over the past century, have seen the wealth-redistributive potential of the common law and sometimes sought to bend it into a tool of economic egalitarianism. In doing so, they have sometimes suffered from a kind of myopia. They have failed to see that a world in which judges read liability rules off of what they take to be a just distribution of wealth is a world in which the power of litigants to hold wrongdoers accountable is dependent on the political leanings of judges, rather than being a structural guarantee. Less contentiously put, there is reason to think a lawyerly appreciation of the structural guarantee of redress for wrongs cuts across political lines, in a way that convictions about just distributions of income do not. If that is so, then the redistributive reconceptualization of tort law favored by some progressives bespeaks a degree of political imprudence.

Vioxx Litigation

This chapter has gone in many directions—interpretive, evaluative, practical, jurisprudential, and critical. We have argued that the principle of civil recourse, when connected to the notion of torts as wrongs (including our dual constructivist account of how judges should apply and develop tort law), generates a powerful interpretive theory of tort law, and that such a theory can be useful to judges and important in enabling candid evaluations and critiques of tort law. At the same time we have argued that certain broad-brush theoretical objections to our account—for example, that it has no traction in a world featuring high rates of settlement or widespread reliance on liability insurance—tend actually to raise smaller-scale questions about how best to design the tort system: questions that require both social-scientific study and the exercise of political judgment. As to the claim that our account is unilluminating because of it presumes a simplistic picture of tort litigation, we have pushed back hard. Modern institutional realities do not supplant our theory or render it irrelevant. To the contrary they underline the need for having such an account. Finally, with regard to suggestions that tort cases should be decided by reference to their redistributive potential, we have expressed skepticism about the long-term wisdom of this approach, even for those who accept its basic political premises.

We close with an example of a contemporary tort case that illustrates many of the foregoing claims and themes. Shortly after the turn of the millennium, thousands of claims were filed against the pharmaceutical company Merck on the ground that its painkiller Vioxx had caused consumers to suffer heart attacks and strokes. Years of litigation and negotiations eventually resulted in a mass settlement that called for billions of dollars of payments issued in accordance with a schedule. As a particularly prominent and consequential event in modern tort law, the Vioxx episode is presumably one that tort scholars ought to be able to explain, and from which they ought to be able to extract some lessons. Certainly, our critics would claim that it exemplifies the complexity, multilateralism, and regulatory nature of contemporary tort law and, consequently (they would claim) the unsuitability of an approach to the subject that, like ours, focuses on wrongs and redress, rights and duties, and powers and liabilities.

The critics have things almost exactly backward. They are correct that one needs to know a lot more than our theory to claim expertise sufficient to grasp and critically assess this litigation. But the complexities that "complex litigation" adds to the basic features of tort law can be competently addressed only if one has an understanding of those features.

We begin with an overview of the facts, offering the perspective of each side of the litigation. In support of their claim that Vioxx was a dangerous drug sold without adequate warnings of its dangers, the plaintiffs pointed to the results of APPROVe, a large, double blind, placebo-controlled study performed with Merck's backing. The APPROVe study, they argued, demonstrated that patients taking Vioxx as a painkiller were more than twice as likely to have a heart attack or a stroke than patients not taking it. Because more than twenty million people had used Vioxx, and because heart attacks and strokes are a frequent cause of death, the plaintiffs contended that the drug was responsible for tens of thousands of unnecessary deaths. This claim was supported by a massive meta-analysis published in the leading British medical journal, *The Lancet*. Moreover, there was evidence that five years prior to receiving the results of APPROVe, Merck had gathered and analyzed data indicating as much as a fivefold increase in heart attacks and strokes associated with Vioxx. Merck nonetheless for years resisted the imposition by the federal Food and Drug Administration (FDA) of a required warning as to these health risks. Merck also circulated internally a document memorably titled "Dodgeball," which, as its name indicates, gave guidance to its salesforce on how to deflect questions about cardiovascular risk from physicians, nurses, and hospitals. It is likely that millions of patients would never have been prescribed Vioxx had Merck responsibly warned of these risks, and many of those who were prescribed it and suffered heart attacks or strokes would have been spared such events had they never taken the drug. Or so the plaintiffs argued.

Unsurprisingly, Merck offered a different depiction of the situation. It maintained that the APPROVe study revealed that Vioxx posed a relative risk well below 2.0, and that, in any event, the drug had to be evaluated not only in light of that risk but also in light of its positive health contributions (primarily, a reduction in morbidity and mortality associated with internal bleeding caused by other painkillers). APPROVe also did not purport to establish what the increased cardiovascular risk was for particular patients, nor how much of that risk was a function of the duration, dosage, and consistency with which Vioxx was used, as well as other risk factors, such as diabetes, heart disease, obesity, tobacco use, and age. Finally, Merck claimed it had no reason to believe there was a causal connection between cardiovascular events and its product prior to the APPROVe study, and it pulled its product from the market soon after the study came out. The supposedly worrisome data produced prior to APPROVe was from a non-placebo-controlled study, one that had been made available both to federal regulators (the FDA) and to the medical profession via a publication in *The New England Journal of Medicine*.[21]

In the end, almost fifty thousand people sued Merck on the ground that Vioxx lacked adequate warnings and thereby caused them (or a family member) to suffer injury or death as a result of a heart attack or stroke. Because Supreme Court precedents from the late 1990s limited the use of the class action device in mass tort cases, it was clear that each plaintiff was nominally required to bring his or her own tort suit. Nonetheless, procedural rules allowed for the clumping of individual lawsuits for purposes of pretrial discovery and for the resolution of certain threshold legal issues (such as which expert witnesses were qualified to testify). Although the plaintiffs' lawyers were nominally representing each plaintiff on an individual basis, many were in fact simultaneously representing multiple claimants, and thus, in their handling of the litigation, they tended to treat the plaintiffs as a group.

Some financial analysts initially predicted that Merck might face liability on the order of $15 billion to $20 billion. Merck vowed not to settle any cases, and eventually spent over a billion dollars on litigation. But, of course, defendants routinely claim no interest in settlement even as they explore that possibility. In an effort to help the lawyers value claims for possible settlement, state and federal courts held "bellwether" trials in eighteen individual cases. Although Merck lost the first of these spectacularly (a Texas jury awarded the widow of a Vioxx patient $253 million), that verdict was ultimately overturned, and Merck went on to win a large majority of the other trials. In some the jury decided that Merck had done nothing wrong. In others it concluded that Vioxx had not caused the particular plaintiff's injury.

Notwithstanding that Merck fared well in the bellwether trials, it ultimately reached a settlement with a group of plaintiffs' lawyers by which it contributed $4.85 billion dollars to a pool from which to pay a to-be-determined amount to each plaintiff who produced enough evidence to permit his or her case to go to a jury trial. How much each plaintiff would receive was to be determined based on the strength of the evidence and

---

21. During the Vioxx litigation, evidence surfaced suggesting that the data published by (and submitted by Merck to) the *New England Journal of Medicine* had deliberately been left incomplete in a manner that rendered the article misleading; the NEJM itself ultimately arrived at the view that the publication was problematically incomplete and misleading.

the plaintiff's individual risk factors. Controversially, the settlement agreement also had four important conditions built into it: (i) Merck was not obligated to adhere to the agreement unless more than 85 percent of plaintiffs agreed to settle their claims; (ii) those settling would not know how much money they would receive until after they had agreed to the settlement and thus to dismiss their lawsuits; (iii) the settlement agreement was actually with the plaintiffs' lawyers, not the plaintiffs themselves; and (iv) the lawyers were contractually bound to recommend settlement to each of their clients, to inform each client that they would cease to represent the client of he or she declined to settle, and to refuse to take any other Vioxx cases to trial. All of the courts with large numbers of Vioxx cases before them approved the settlement agreement, and over 99 percent of plaintiffs sought compensation under the settlement. In the end, more than thirty thousand plaintiffs received payments. These varied substantially in amount, but some plaintiffs received compensation on the order of several million dollars.

The settlement did not solve all of Merck's problems. Tort suits were still pending in other jurisdictions. Moreover, in the United States the company faced potential liabilities to investors for having concealed information relevant to the value of its stock, to insurance companies and others for having overpriced its product, and to federal regulators. That said, the settlement appears to have been a sound business decision, in part because Merck was able to gain favorable tax treatment for the settlement fund. The attorney largely responsible for engineering the settlement was later named the company's CEO and the company appears to be thriving.

Many of the critics whom we have been engaging in this chapter argue that philosophical tort theories, including civil recourse theory, are unable to capture what is really happening and what is really at stake in situations like the Vioxx litigation, and are unable to provide guidance in evaluating how well our system has performed in dealing with such situations. Talk of wrongs and recourse, they say, doesn't fit the reality of this important legal episode, and doesn't help resolve any of the difficult policy issues that arise in this and other mass tort litigations.

On the descriptive side, the argument continues, the plaintiffs were not exercising their legal powers but were instead passive participants. Moreover, few if any received full compensation or anything that is plausibly described as redress. Merck was not held to account: rather it avoided being held to account by paying off the plaintiffs and their lawyers. Most fundamentally, perhaps, the issue of whether Merck committed a legally recognized wrong against any of these plaintiffs received little attention from state courts of last resort.[22]

The criticisms of our approach are louder still on the evaluative side. A central lesson of the Vioxx litigation would seem to be that widespread harm cannot and will not be resolved through thousands of individual lawsuits, much less thousands of individual trials—aggregation and settlement are inevitable. The interesting policy questions are how mass settlements can be achieved as a practical matter, which settlement terms do a tolerable job of balancing the competing interests of plaintiffs and defendants, and whether and how such settlements might contribute to policy goals such as deterrence and compensation. Also of interest—and also seemingly immune to illumination from a wrongs-and-redress theory—is whether to regard the way in which the Vioxx settlement was structured and implemented as an ingenious solution to a practical problem or an instance of plaintiffs' lawyers selling out their clients.

Our envisioned critics are mistaken on both the descriptive and prescriptive fronts. Starting on the descriptive side, there are a few large questions about the Vioxx litigation that any satisfactory account would need to answer, and our approach is especially helpful in providing those answers. First, why would many of the most successful trial lawyers in the country pour their time and resources into the Vioxx litigation, but end up winning almost none of the tried cases? Similarly, given that many of the leading journals and experts in cardiovascular risk concluded that Vioxx did generate a serious risk of heart attack and stroke (and given that Merck decided to withdraw the drug from the market in light of those risks), why did juries largely side with Merck? Most pressingly, why was a publicly traded company like Merck willing to pay almost five billion dollars in settlement after it had won most of the bellwether trials?

---

22. As noted above, the Texas Supreme Court reversed the plaintiff's verdict in one of the first of the bellwether trials. Merck & Co. v. Garza, 347 S.W.3d 256 (Tx. 2011). It did so on the ground that the plaintiff—whose decedent was 71 at the time of death, who had a long history of heart disease, and who suffered a fatal heart attack after taking Vioxx for a month—had failed to offer sufficient proof that the decedent's exposure to Vioxx caused his heart attack. For its part, the New Jersey Supreme Court ruled that consumers of Vioxx with no present physical injuries could not recover for the costs of monitoring for the risks of future heart attacks or strokes. Sinclair v. Merck & Co., 948 A.2d 587 (N.J. 2008).

Various answers to these questions might be propounded. One is that, for the cases that went to trial, Merck's lawyers simply outlitigated the plaintiffs' lawyers, and would have continued to do so were the cost of litigation not prohibitively expensive. A second is that Merck was rightly worried about matters other than litigation outcomes. In particular, it was worried about its reputation among consumers, which required a meaningful settlement as a way of getting the Vioxx story out of the public eye. A third is that uncertainty over the outcome of future litigation was so destabilizing that even closure obtained at a cost of $5 billion was worth it. All of these explanations probably have some merit, but each begs a basic question. We need an explanation of what it is about these cases that made them winnable only at a very high cost, with significant risks to Merck's reputation, and in an unpredictable manner. Without it, none of these explanations adds much.

The ultimate answer to these questions lies partly in matters of procedure, evidence, medical science, and statistical analysis, but it lies above all in tort doctrine. In short, the Vioxx litigation carried a paradoxical air because of the centrality of the issue of causation to tort liability for injuries caused by products. Pharmaceutical litigation is a form of "toxic tort" litigation, a category that also includes suits for injuries caused by exposure to asbestos, solvents, lead paint, tobacco, and other substances. In toxic tort cases, a plaintiff must provide adequate evidence on two distinct questions—"general causation" and "specific causation."[23] Suppose that a worker sues an asbestos manufacturer because, after working for years at a shipyard at which airborne asbestos was present, he develops severe asthma. To prevail, the worker will have to show that asbestos exposure *is capable, biologically, of causing* asthma—this is the issue of general causation. He will also have to show that *his particular case of asthma resulted from his asbestos exposure*—this is specific causation. Each must be proved by the plaintiff by a preponderance of the evidence.

For obvious reasons, a product manufacturer facing a flood of toxic tort claims hopes to prevail on the issue of general causation. If, in the foregoing example, there is insufficient evidence of a link between asbestos

23. The specific causation issue is sometimes broken down into two sub-issues: (a) was the plaintiff exposed to a dose of the substance sufficient to cause the type of injury of which she complains?; and (b) were the plaintiff's injuries caused by such an exposure, as opposed to other possible causes?

exposure and asthma, then asbestos manufacturers have a winning argument against all would-be asthma plaintiffs. In most U.S. jurisdictions, a toxic tort plaintiff seeking to avoid such an outcome will typically need to put forward a qualified expert witness or witnesses who, on the basis of scientific studies, can testify credibly that exposure to the defendant's product at a certain level more likely than not can cause the type of injury or illness experienced by the plaintiff. For their part, defendants will not only offer contrary expert testimony, they frequently will argue that the testimony proffered by the plaintiff's expert is inadmissible, either because the expert lacks sufficient training or knowledge to opine on the general causation question, or because there is insufficient data to support the expert's opinion of a probable general causal link. In a toxic tort case, a defendant who succeeds in excluding the plaintiff's proposed expert testimony on general causation is likely to have the case dismissed entirely. This is what ultimately occurred, for example, in breast implant litigation asserting that connective tissue diseases like lupus were caused by leaking silicone breast implants.[24] By contrast, if the plaintiffs' expert evidence on general causation is deemed admissible, the case typically is deemed appropriate for resolution by a jury trial, at which the plaintiff's lawyer will have to persuade the jury that the plaintiff's expert, not the defendant's, has the better of the science on general causation, and that the plaintiff's particular injuries were specifically caused by exposure to the defendant's product.

In the Vioxx cases, plaintiffs were, with some exceptions, successful in surviving admissibility challenges to their general causation experts, and therefore were overwhelmingly successful in earning the right to get to a jury. That is because well-qualified experts relying on high-quality medical studies could attest credibly that use of Vioxx at a certain level is capable of causing heart attacks and strokes. This left individual plaintiffs with the burden of proving that their heart attacks or strokes were caused by Vioxx. Given different exposure levels (some plaintiffs had taken Vioxx for extended periods, others only briefly), and given the prevalence of preexisting health conditions (such as heart disease, diabetes, or obesity), Merck usually had plenty to work with in challenging any given plaintiff's

---

24. *See, e.g.*, Norris v. Baxter Healthcare Corp., 397 F.3d 878 (10th Cir. 2005) (affirming summary judgment for an implant manufacturer given the inadmissibility of expert testimony on an alleged causal link to systemic autoimmune disease).

ability to prove specific causation. But it would be expensive to do so, and for all the expense, Merck could not reliably predict how often it would win or lose. Moreover, prevailing in particular cases would not undermine the plaintiffs' general claim—and hence perhaps the public's perception—that Merck knowingly sold a drug that was capable of causing fatal heart attacks and strokes without warning of this risk, and probably had done so in a manner that affected the lives of thousands.

We can look at our puzzle again in terms of power or leverage: How is it that the plaintiffs' lawyers had any leverage against a giant multinational, given that so few cases that were tried actually succeeded? The answer is this. It was tort law's substantive rules and its empowering of victims of injurious wrongs, as well as the availability of qualified expert witnesses on general causation and the presence of some evidence on specific causation (in conjunction with the evidence of Merck's awareness of cardiovascular risk and its failure to disclose that risk), that enabled the Vioxx plaintiffs to obtain a significant settlement.

Of course, most torts professors—including most who reject our theoretical framework—will acknowledge the existence and practical significance of the issues of general and specific causation to the resolution of toxic tort claims. This, they would say, is a matter of black-letter law, not legal theory. However, as prior chapters have detailed, it is far from obvious why instrumentalist tort theorists are entitled to take causation so seriously, especially in a case where the plaintiffs were claiming to have been injured in a way that constituted a realization of exactly the risks that rendered the defendant's conduct wrongful. Tort law—as a law of wrongs and redress—is all about determinations of whether one person has mistreated another. Accountability, in tort, only takes place when there is proof that the person (or entity) who brings suit was wrongfully injured by the person (or entity) being sued.[25] Each Vioxx plaintiff was thus given

---

25. In so-called tortfeasor identification cases, a few courts have shifted the burden of proof onto the defendant to disprove causation. Burden-shifting of this sort is allowed, if at all, only when the plaintiff can establish that *she actually has been the victim of a tort at the hands of someone, but cannot establish who among two or more actors is the tortfeasor. See* Sindell v. Abbot Labs., 607 P.2d 924 (Cal. 1980) (adopting "market share" liability for cases in which the plaintiff could prove that one of multiple manufacturers had tortiously injured her, but, through no fault of her own, could not prove which manufacturer had done so). The Vioxx litigation was not of this sort: if there was a tortfeasor in these cases, it clearly was Merck. The question instead was whether Merck *had committed any torts.* On the distinctiveness and justifiability of burden-shifting in tortfeasor identification cases, see Arthur Ripstein & Benjamin C.

the opportunity to hold Merck accountable for having actually injured him or her, not for having engaged in risky conduct generally. This is why causation was central to the litigation, and ultimately why a settlement was crafted on the terms on which it was crafted.

Accountability is and should be part of the normative framework for thinking about the entire Vioxx episode. We have been careful not to characterize tort law as a system for doing corrective justice, and, while we think there are reasons of principle for selecting make-whole as the rule of thumb for compensatory damages, we have never said that making whole is the very point of tort law. Whatever threat the phenomenon of settlement poses to corrective justice theories—which arguably do treat tort law as aiming to restore plaintiffs to the status quo ante—it does nothing to undermine our view. According to civil recourse theory, tort law is partly about power and accountability. As a normative matter, victims of relational legal wrongs are entitled to be provided by the state with the power to commence court proceedings that aim to hold wrongdoers to account. To the extent that the law of torts remains intact and healthy, they are in fact provided with this power. As we have urged in several prior chapters, there is a significant egalitarian aspect to the empowerment of private parties to demand redress for having been wrongfully injured. But what individuals do with that power is their business.

In toxic tort cases like *Vioxx*, we see that the system of *de jure* powers to recover fair compensation if one is able successfully to persuade a judge and jury of one's claim generates a range of *de facto* abilities to recover partially if one is able to threaten a strong case. This is bargaining in the shadow of the law. But it is worth noticing that, unlike a teleological view in which tort law is about ensuring that justice is done, civil recourse theory is a structural theory in which tort law is about the respects in which a legal-political system imposes duties, vests rights, and allocates powers. Complex settlement agreements illustrate that uncertainty about rights-violations and wrongs can be dealt with by bargaining triggered by the grant of certain legal powers. In these instances, the legal entitlement to redress is being exercised, albeit in a different form than that of obtaining a judgment and court order requiring payment by the defendant to the plaintiff.

Zipursky, *Corrective Justice in the Age of Mass Torts*, in PHILOSOPHY AND THE LAW OF TORTS 214 (Gerald J. Postema ed., 2001).

In commenting upon the sense in which the Vioxx settlement agreement managed to achieve a partial reallocation of power and a right of redress, we may seem to be praising the agreement. And indeed we are, but only in part. For seeing toxic tort settlement agreements in terms of power and redress also provides us with a framework through which to assess certain features of the agreement. In fact, one of us has argued (in an article co-authored with Howard Erichson) that the plaintiffs' lawyers in *Vioxx* actually took too much power from their clients; that as a matter of legal ethics, the settlement agreement was defective because it sheared away too much plaintiff choice.[26] We mention this criticism here only to emphasize once again that civil recourse theory and dual constructivism are not a platform for apology, but for understanding and critical engagement.

Finally, there is a down-to-earth question raised by the Vioxx litigation that this book situates us well to ask. It is the now regrettably common question: Where were the lawyers? In particular, how is it that lawyers who represented a huge and generally well-regarded pharmaceutical company failed to recognize that the firm was engaging in conduct that might amount to the wrongful injuring of thousands?

We do not have the answers to this question. However, it is not completely far-fetched to suppose that decades of Holmesian thinking about tort law contributed to the problem. Sophisticated lawyers—and Merck's were surely sophisticated—have long been told that their job in the domain of tort law is to counsel their clients about liability risks, not legal rights and duties. By this we do not mean to offer the melodramatic suggestion that lawyers have lost their humanity, or their sense of what morality requires. We imagine instead that these two conflicting tendencies— alienation from a robust sense of legal responsibility to consumers and ordinary human concern for others' well-being—simply never met. Given that many of our field's most admired intellects have insisted that the key to understanding tort law is to abandon notions of rights and duties, and wrongs and responsibilities, we should not be surprised to discover that the lawyerly capacity to recognize wrongs has atrophied. To appreciate that torts are wrongs is to appreciate that legal wrongs, though different creatures, are related to moral wrongs.

26. Howard M. Erichson & Benjamin C. Zipursky, *Consent versus Closure*, 96 CORNELL L. REV. 265 (2011).

Those of our critics who harp on the supposed irrelevance of a wrongs-and-redress approach to modern tort law seem to reason as follows. Judges, legislators, and legal scholars have no hope of understanding or constructively critiquing tort law unless they appreciate that the real-world implementation of tort doctrine introduces several layers of analysis concerning the rules and realities of claims aggregation, evidence, litigation finance, and the like. To this observation they add another, which is that most tort cases today are resolved in ways that implicate these additional layers. Finally, they move from these observations to the conclusion that a functional understanding of tort law—one that casts it as a law that aims to compensate and deter—is required, and that an understanding of tort as empowering victims to redress wrongs is essentially beside the point, as are the doctrinal rules that reflect such an understanding. Plainly, this is an unsound argument from a logical point of view: the truth of the premises does not secure the truth of the conclusion. Still, a question remains: If procedure, evidence, and litigation are the layers where the "real action" is happening, where is the value in focusing on wrongs and redress, rights of action, and the like?

This chapter has answered the question. The layers that supposedly matter most are situated atop other, deeper layers. A judge, legislator, or legal scholar must understand these "lower" layers, too, if she is going to understand and critique tort law. Our efforts to explicate civil recourse and dual constructivism are first and foremost aimed at this understanding, and are far better suited to provide it than theories that treat tort law as a regulatory mechanism. Indeed, we go further and claim that interpretive depth—an appreciation of the nature of tort law's substantive, structural and remedial layers—enhances careful analysis of tort law's more visible layers.

Some of the resistance to our approach may also be predicated on the supposition that, because (in the view of our critics) a compelling theory of tort law must characterize it in terms of the aggregate good(s) it stands to deliver, our claim is that tort law aims to ensure that more wrongs are redressed. This is not our view. Tort law is not a system for maximizing redress. It is a system that, in principle (and, one hopes, in practice), empowers individuals to seek and obtain redress insofar as they are entitled to it under the law and insofar as they seek it. Done right—and of course they are often *not* done right—settlement, aggregation, liability insurance, and the like enable tort victims to obtain redress. This is why one cannot properly understand and evaluate these features of tort law except by first grasping that tort law is law for the redress of wrongs.

The critics we have engaged in this chapter understandably pride themselves on being realistic. However, claims to "realism"—even when sincerely and thoughtfully made—carry with them an inherent danger. It is all too easy to slip from asserting (accurately) that claims aggregation, liability insurance, and settlement are central to the operation of modern tort law, to asserting (falsely) that they *are* modern tort law. This sort of slippage is not merely casual overstatement; it carries with it substantial practical and political risks for our legal and political system. Specifically, it invites judges and lawyers to take massive legal change in stride (and unreflectively) by supposing that the relevant change has already happened: that the horse is out of the barn; that tort law has already ceased to be the institution that it once was. Precisely because the transformation is assumed to be a *fait accompli* rather than argued for, it is not guided by any sort of principled normative vision. A wrongs-and-redress approach, by contrast, not only provides the framework necessary to understand what is happening in modern complex litigation, it also provides a framework that aids in the determination of whether particular disputes, large and small, are being resolved in an appropriate manner and on justifiable terms.

10

Applications

The Duty of Care, Design Defects, and Internet Libel

W E HERE REVIEW A trio of torts problems to display the practical value of our theory.[1] For each of three examples—therapists' malpractice liability to patients' family members, the definition of design defect in products liability law, and the scope of federal statutory "immunity" for internet defamation—we contrast our approach with more conventional approaches, or explain why the absence of a theoretical perspective has bedeviled the area. Some of our arguments have implications for professionals and insurers, some for corporate America, and some for free speech advocates. All have potential implications for judges and legislators. In the end, we believe our analyses are more pragmatic and more institutionally sensitive than those of our Realist critics, more doctrinally nuanced than those of our "black-letter" critics, and more alive to the importance of tort theory than those of our theoretical critics.

---

1. With regard to the first and third of these, we have previously either solely or jointly offered more elaborate versions of the analyses provided here. *See* John C. P. Goldberg & Benjamin C. Zipursky, *Triangular Torts and Fiduciary Duties,* in CONTRACT, STATUS AND FIDUCIARY LAW 239 (Andrew Gold & Paul B. Miller eds., 2016); Benjamin C. Zipursky, *The Monsanto Lecture: Online Defamation, Legal Concepts, and the Good Samaritan,* 51 VAL. U. L. REV. 1 (2016).

Negligence: Therapists' Liability to Nonpatients

State courts have for decades proudly claimed to be savvy about the misleading pretensions of negligence doctrine to be concerned with "duty." As the California Supreme Court declared in a famous opinion by Justice Tobriner:

> The assertion that liability must nevertheless be denied because defendant bears no 'duty' to plaintiff 'begs the essential question—whether the plaintiff's interests are entitled to legal protection against the defendant's conduct. * * * It (duty) is a shorthand statement of a conclusion, rather than an aid to analysis in itself. * * * But it should be recognized that 'duty' is not sacrosanct in itself, but only an expression of the sum total of those considerations of policy which lead the law to say that the particular plaintiff is entitled to protection.' (Prosser, Law of Torts, supra, at pp. 332–333.)[2]

Justice Tobriner's channeling of Prosser's famous duty-begs-the-question quip is surely right as to *some* lawyerly and judicial uses of the phrase "no duty." There are judicial opinions that defend the imposition of a policy-based categorical limitation on liability by conclusorily announcing that the defendant owed no duty of care to the plaintiff. But Prosser's language goes much farther. It asserts that invocations of "duty" *can only be* opaque references to a policy judgment that liability for carelessness that causes loss cannot be allowed for policy reasons. On this basis, it calls for the adoption of a self-conscious and candid approach to duty questions, according to which they are resolved by means of a forthright "balancing" of the relevant policy considerations.

In some of our first forays into tort scholarship, we argued that Prosserian duty skepticism is ill-considered as a matter of doctrine, tort theory, and jurisprudence. We have also maintained that many tort scholars have erred badly in supposing that "taking duty seriously" is the province of regressive formalism, whereas duty-skepticism has an inherent progressive valence. The discussion that follows illustrates yet another claim we have made: that duty skepticism is unhelpful because, rather than enabling courts to clarify their reasoning, it encourages them to avoid reasoning

2. Dillon v. Legg, 441 P.2d 912, 916 (1968).

altogether. Multifactor balancing is less a matter of forthrightness than avoidance: vague talk of balancing mostly gives courts room to fudge and to speculate rather than to reason rigorously.

What we will call "the parent–therapist problem" provides an apt example of a current and controversial issue of duty in negligence law. *Roberts v. Salmi*, a Michigan case, illustrates the problem.[3] A young woman suffering from a psychological disorder received treatment from a therapist. As a result of the treatment, which allegedly involved "retrieved memory therapy," the woman came to believe that she had suppressed memories of having been sexually assaulted by her father. Eventually she confronted her father with accusations of assault, which he denied. State officials undertook an investigation and concluded there was insufficient evidence to move forward with a prosecution; in this sense, at least, the father was exonerated. Yet the allegations—which the daughter stood by—wreaked substantial filial, reputational, and emotional harm on the father.

The father sued the therapist for malpractice, asserting that her use and misuse of retrieved memory therapy caused his daughter to come to believe, falsely, that she had been the victim of abuse, and that this in turn caused him great harm. The defendant therapist moved to dismiss the case at the outset, arguing that a psychotherapist owes no legal duty to a patient's parent to be careful in the provision of therapy with respect to the possibility of injuring the parent emotionally, financially, or reputationally. According to this argument, even if there were sufficient evidence that the therapist acted carelessly in providing therapy, and that this carelessness caused the father serious harm, there could be no liability. The trial court granted the therapist's motion, ruling that the therapist did not owe a duty of care to the father.

Roberts appealed to an intermediate appellate court. As that court noted, courts from other states have split on this issue: the high courts of Illinois, Maine, Pennsylvania, and Texas had held that there is no duty of care running from therapist to parent, whereas the high courts of New Hampshire and Wisconsin had held that there is such a duty.[4] Over a

3. 866 N.W.2d 460 (Mich. App. 2014), *appeal granted*, 868 N.W.2d 911 (Mich. 2015), *vacated*, 877 N.W.2d 903 (Mich. 2016).

4. *Id.* at 470–73. A similar split exists in lower state-court decisions addressing the issue: California and New Jersey lower courts declined to recognize a duty, whereas a Washington court did recognize such a duty. The Utah Supreme Court, troubled by the close balance of policy arguments on each side, settled on a rule requiring the plaintiff to prove a substantial

dissent, the intermediate appellate court joined the minority of courts holding that there is a duty of care running from therapist to parent of patient. It therefore permitted Roberts's claim to proceed.

As indicated, the question raised by *Roberts* and other court decisions is whether, for purposes of the tort of negligence, a duty of care is owed by a patient's therapist to a close relative of the patient. Following the Tobriner-Prosser pathway—which manifests the general approach we referred to in Chapter 7 as "dual instrumentalism"—the Michigan appellate court, like most other courts to have addressed the issue, summarized its way of framing the duty question as follows: "the ultimate inquiry in determining whether a legal duty should be imposed is whether the social benefits of imposing a duty outweigh the social costs of imposing a duty."[5] Relevant social benefits include compensation for the injured parent and, because of the threat of liability, greater caution exercised by therapists in their use of questionable techniques. On the cost side of the ledger is the risk of depriving patients of beneficial treatment methods, discouraging patients from seeking therapy, and interfering with patient–therapist relations. With little explanation, the court concluded that, in this situation, the social benefits outweigh the social costs.

The list of costs and benefits invoked by the Michigan appellate court is pretty much the same as those utilized by other state courts that have addressed the issue raised by *Roberts*. Although defendants have more frequently won by convincing courts that, on balance, society is better off if no duty is owed, plaintiffs have sometimes convinced courts of the opposite, as did the plaintiff in *Roberts*. In the end, this pattern of mixed results is not surprising, because there appears to be no way to render determinate this exercise in balancing. To what extent would recognition of a duty of care to parents interfere with therapy of a certain sort? How damaging to patients is this kind of therapy? How deserving of compensation are parents who face the sort of ordeal alleged by the plaintiff in *Roberts*? Will treatment really be discouraged if there is occasional liability? Surely reasonable judges can disagree not only over the effects that are or are not likely to follow from a ruling that recognizes or refuses to recognize a duty of care, but also over the value to assign to the various costs and benefits at

---

departure from the standard of care bespeaking recklessness. Mower v. Baird, 422 P.3d 837, 863 (Utah 2018).

5. *Roberts*, 866 N.W.2d at 465 (citation omitted).

issue here. The Prosserian approach leaves judges with nothing to go on other than speculation about which decision will leave society better off, overall.

Our approach to tort law provides a very different framework for judges, one that permits a more structured form of analysis that more plausibly lies within the competency of the judiciary. The key first step is to reject duty-skepticism. In a case like *Roberts*, the duty issue *is what it seems to be*—it is the issue of whether a certain kind of obligation is owed by a therapist to certain nonpatients. To say the same thing, the immediate issue is not the Prosser-Tobriner question of whether allowing liability in a class of cases will cause more good than harm, but the question of whether the law recognizes a duty of *conduct* owed by a therapist to close relatives of a patient, such that the therapist owes it to them to be vigilant of the ramifications of his or her therapeutic decisions for certain aspects of *their well-being*.[6] The claim that there is such an obligation, looked at from within a general understanding of negligence law and of the therapist–patient relationship, has both weak and strong aspects. On the weak side, it is clear that there is something special about the relationship between therapist and patient, and whatever obligation might exist as to the nonpatient must be compatible with the nature of that special relationship. On the strong side, the prospect of harm to a parent from the incompetent inducement of false memories of abuse in a patient is entirely foreseeable.[7]

The problem is therefore not whether there are any aspects of the role of a therapist that could generate a duty of care; it is whether there is anything about the therapist–patient relationship that stands in the way of recognizing such a duty. This question cannot be answered without a

---

6. A therapist may need to take account of the effects of therapy on a third party *insofar as those effects might affect the well-being of the patient*. For example, a therapist might need to consider whether counseling a patient in a manner that is likely to cause a serious rift between the patient and a close relative will redound to the benefit of the patient.

7. The reasonable foreseeability of injury to a certain class of persons is not of itself sufficient to establish a duty to take care to avoid such injury. Indeed, in almost any case in which a tort is committed, others apart from the victim will suffer setbacks reasonably foreseeable to the tortfeasor at the time of the commission of the tort—yet many, if not most, of these persons will have no tort claim. For example, one who carelessly runs down a pedestrian can reasonably foresee that the pedestrian's relatives, co-workers, and friends will be affected adversely in various ways by the pedestrian's having been injured. With some limited exceptions, persons such as these will not have tort claims against the careless driver. Still, foreseeability, when present, points in favor of the recognition of a duty.

more thoughtful analysis of the therapist's duties to her patient. Of course, a therapist does owe a duty of care or competence to her own patient. Like medical doctors generally, however, therapists in addition owe their patients a duty of *loyalty*. As she contemplates and administers treatment, a therapist must put her patient's well-being first, prioritizing it over that of others. The trust that forms the core of the therapist–patient relationship demands such loyalty. A psychotherapist, like a physician, owes her patient fiduciary duties.

Lawyers are, of course, familiar with fiduciary duties of loyalty: they owe such duties to their clients. From these spring special obligations of confidentiality, conflict avoidance, and so on. In certain special circumstances, lawyers have sometimes been held to owe legal duties of care to nonclients. This is the case, for example, with respect to the duty that a trust-and-estates lawyer owes to a person whom her client wishes to inherit under the client's will. Her carelessness might subject her to liability if the would-be will beneficiary is harmed by the error. In other scenarios, duties of care clearly are not owed to nonclients because of the patent inconsistency of such duties with one's duties of loyalty to the client. (The lawyer for one side in a divorce proceeding owes no duty to take care to avoid distressing his client's adversary.) In a range of cases, the question of whether there is a duty of care to a nonclient is a difficult one.

Where does the parent–therapist problem sit within this sort of professional / fiduciary framework? The answer flows from a recognition that it is intrinsic to the duty of loyalty to her patient that the therapist not consider or weigh the emotional best interests of her patient against the emotional best interests of family members. A critical aspect of this duty of loyalty—perhaps a defining aspect of it—is the way in which it prioritizes the patient over others in a categorical manner. To impose on therapists a legal duty to take care against causing distress to family members is to require therapists to keep in mind how different treatment methods might upset, disorient, or dismay a patient's close family members and, in some instances, to choose the course of treatment in light of such consequences. Such a requirement is inconsistent with therapists owing a legal duty of loyalty to their patients.

To be sure, there are cases in which courts have recognized duties owed by physicians to nonpatients. Imagine a physician who prescribes a medication that the physician knows, or should know, might cause her patient to experience sudden and severe drowsiness, yet fails to inform the patient of this side effect. While taking the medication for the first time, the patient, under the influence of the drug, falls asleep at the wheel of his car, running down a pedestrian. Some courts will allow the pedestrian to recover from the physician on the ground that, by failing to warn the patient of the drug's side effects, the physician breached a duty of care owed to members of the public who were foreseeably placed at risk of injury by that failure.

These "drug warning" third-party cases are fundamentally different from therapist cases such as *Roberts*. It is not just that the negligent conduct in drug warning cases is careless to the patient as well as third parties (that was arguably true in *Roberts*, too). It is that there is nothing about physician vigilance as to the physical well-being of users of the roads that conflicts with the physician's prioritizing her patient's health. To see this, consider a variation on the example just given. Imagine that the injured pedestrian, instead of seeking to recover on the ground that the physician failed to warn the patient-driver of the drug's side effects, sued on the theory that the physician breached a duty of care owed to pedestrians by prescribing the medication in the first place. Courts have rightly rejected claims such as this precisely on the ground we have articulated. The physician's duty of loyalty to the patient precludes her from making treatment decisions that involve "weigh[ing] the welfare of [third] persons against the welfare of his patient."[8] Treatment decisions are, of course, exactly what are at issue in the therapist–parent cases, rather than the proper implementation of a course of treatment already decided upon as being in the patient's best interest.[9]

---

8. Burroughs v. Magee, 118 S.W.3d 323, 334 (Tenn. 2003).

9. Two qualifications to our position are in order. First, the duty of loyalty in question is a duty owed by a physician who is in good faith administering treatment to a patient for the benefit of the patient. A physician who engages in bad-faith treatment of his patient that also amounts to carelessness as to the physical well-being of certain nonpatients may be subject to liability for carelessly injuring a nonpatient. While recovered memory therapy of the sort at issue in *Roberts* is controversial, it is not so obviously unsound that its administration can be regarded as a form of quackery.

Second, as Scott Hershovitz has helpfully emphasized to us, to assert that a physician's duty of loyalty to her patient bars the attribution to the physician of a duty to take care with respect to the harmful effects of treatment decisions on nonpatients is not to assert that the physician owes such persons no tort duties whatsoever. For example, a course of treatment that involves a therapist encouraging her patient to harm a nonpatient might well be a breach of a legal duty owed by the therapist to the nonpatient to refrain from intentionally, knowingly, or recklessly harming the nonpatient. Our concern is exclusively with liability that sounds in negligence. *See* Goldberg & Zipursky, *supra* note 1, at 254–55.

Critics will argue that our analysis sidesteps rather than addresses the parent's clearest claim: that the therapist breached her duty of care to her patient (the daughter), and that this breach caused the parent's injury. Civil recourse theory, and more particularly its explanation of the proper-plaintiff rule (Chapter 6), answers this objection. A right of action in tort stems from one's having been wronged, not merely from one's having been injured by conduct that is wrongful in the air, or wrongful to another. The wrong alleged in the therapist cases is negligence; and negligence, as we have seen, is actionable only if the defendant's conduct is careless *as to* persons such as the plaintiff: a breach of a duty of care owed to the plaintiff rather than to others. The point is not that negligence law couldn't possibly work some other way, but rather that this *is* the way it actually works, that there are sound principles underlying its working this way, and that courts are bound by their institutional obligations to apply the law, in the first instance.

Those suspicious of our reliance on doctrinal principles will object that our analysis conflates what the duty owed by a therapist to her patient *is*, as a descriptive matter, and what it *ought to be*, as a normative matter. Our reasoning, culminating in the conclusion that no duty of care is owed to the parent, hinges on the claim that doing so would be inconsistent with the loyalty owed by the therapist. But that decision follows only if one accepts that the fiduciary duty should not be altered, and this premise, the objection maintains, has not been established.

In fact, there is no equivocation in our reasoning, for it is (and is intended to be) elucidative. The argument does indeed rely upon a normatively loaded premise that there is a duty of loyalty to the patient that forecloses the recognition of such a duty to the parent. And it is true that this premise is drawn in part from observation and articulation of extant norms within the profession. As we discussed in Chapter 8, however, common-law reasoning often proceeds (and properly so) from mixed descriptive and normative contentions to other mixed descriptive and normative contentions, and that is exactly what our argument does. The law recognizes a duty of loyalty owed by therapist to patient, and that duty is such that it is destined to be interfered with or undermined by the recognition of another legal duty, owed by the therapist to the patient's parent, to be mindful of the effects of the therapy on the parent's mental health and on the ties among family members.

A final objection bundles together the prior concerns to argue as follows: A court, if it found good enough normative reasons to override either negligence law's proper-plaintiff principle or the conventionalist recognition of the therapist's duty of loyalty to her patient, could decide the issue of therapist liability to nonpatients quite differently. To that extent, the argument proceeds, a holding that there is no duty of care to the family member is, in effect, an assertion that there are not sufficient reasons supporting a change in extant legal rules. Absent a searching evaluation of the sort that Prosser recommended (as to whether these rules promise the best outcome from an overall policy point of view), it would be mere dogmatism for a court to rule that there is no duty to the parent and therefore no liability.

There is something stunningly arrogant about this objection. It rests, after all, on the contention that common-law judges are being contemptibly dogmatic when they apply the law before them because it is the law. Our analysis in this book has argued that civil recourse theory and dual constructivism provide the best understanding of what tort law is and what it says. Nothing in our account precludes a judge from hearing an argument that the law should be changed, or even that the judge should be the one to change it. However, the first question for a judge is always how best to understand what the law is and how it applies to the case at hand. As Ronald Dworkin pointed out long ago, the plaintiff in a case like *Roberts v. Salmi* comes to the courthouse not to convince the court of the need for it to enact micro-legislation, but with an argument that, under the law as it is, he is entitled to hold the defendant accountable, even as the defendant argues that she cannot be held liable because she has not committed a legally recognized wrong.[10] Irrespective of whether one accepts Dworkin's further claims about the nature of legal reasoning (we do not), he is right that, first and foremost, the court's job is to try to ascertain which of these contentions about what the law says is correct.

Professionals' relationships with patients are deeply bound up in a variety of conventions and norms, and both the practitioners in such fields and those who utilize them rely heavily upon them. For this reason we are inclined to think—like the dissenting judge in the intermediate appellate court that decided *Roberts v. Salmi*—that if there are to be changes in the rules governing therapists' duties to nonpatients, legislatures are far better situated for this task than courts.[11] And while solemn admonitions that

---

10. RONALD DWORKIN, TAKING RIGHTS SERIOUSLY 102–03 (1977).
11. *Roberts*, 866 N.W.2d at 477 (Sawyer, J., dissenting).

judges should to defer to legislative competence and authority can amount to a kind of bad faith (when, for example, political alignments and practices ensure that no legislation will be forthcoming), that is hardly the case here. Legislatures around the country have, among other things, enacted reporting statutes requiring a range of medical care providers to act in ways that would otherwise amount to a breach of their fiduciary duty of confidentiality.

Likewise, in the area of federal securities fraud, legislatures have (commendably, in our view) weighed in on the question of how far a securities lawyer's fiduciary duties to a client should preclude the protection of nonclients. The best known, but hardly the only, example of this phenomenon is the Sarbanes-Oxley bill, passed in 2002. In the wake of the financial scandals of the late 1990s and early 2000s, it was revealed that lawyers both inside and outside of publicly held companies had failed to disclose their clients' troubling financial practices. Aware that some lawyers contended that their fiduciary duties prevented them from alerting the Securities and Exchange Commission—and aware that some elements of the bar supported this rationalization—Congress changed the law to require lawyers to disclose information under certain circumstances. More precisely, Congress delegated to the Securities and Exchange Commission the task of creating rules for lawyers appearing before the Commission specifying duties (or, in some cases, privileges) to report fraud and potential indicators thereof.[12] To reiterate our larger point, it is hardly fantastical to imagine legislative action in the face of seemingly entrenched professional norms.

Products Liability: Making Sense of Design Defect

Consumer products—vehicles, industrial machines, construction materials, household appliances, drugs, toys, packaged food, clothing, and the like—are at the center of the modern economy. They are also a regular source of injury. When product-related injuries give rise to tort suits, liability is usually governed by the doctrine of "strict products liability" (often referred to simply as "products liability").

---

12. JOHN WESLEY HALL JR., PROFESSIONAL RESPONSIBILITY IN CRIMINAL DEFENSE PRACTICE § 28.31 (3d ed. 2017).

As we explained in Chapter 6, this was not always the case. However, the middle of the twentieth century witnessed a doctrinal revolution. Writing for the California Supreme Court in 1963, Justice Traynor in *Greenman v. Yuba Power Products* held that a manufacturer is subject to liability upon proof that it sent its product onto the market in a defective condition, and that the defective product caused injury while being used in an ordinary manner.[13] Conspicuously missing from this new cause of action was negligence law's requirement of proof of failure to use due care. With a boost from Prosser's insertion of Section 402A into the Second Torts Restatement, *Greenman*'s rule of strict liability not only spread to other jurisdictions, it expanded to encompass claims against retailers, as well as to certain persons not injured in the course of using or consuming the product. In the 1960s, 1970s, and early 1980s, strict products liability was the "it" tort: an emblem of tort law's progressive potential.

Strict products liability is still with us today, though it is not the darling of progressives it once was. Within twenty years of its initial recognition, some of its most plaintiff-friendly features were being rolled back. In addition to pushing for damages caps and procedural changes (particularly with regard to class actions), pro-business organizations, along with some judges, commentators, and politicians, insisted that the revolution had left manufacturers too vulnerable to the whims of jurors, in part by failing to offer clear rules for determining what counts as a defective product. The absence of such rules was said to be particularly problematic for "design defect" claims, which allege that an entire product line—for example, a car model such as the Ford Pinto—is unduly dangerous, thus potentially exposing manufacturers to thousands of claims and billions of dollars in liability.

Disputes over the doctrinal question of how to define a design defect became particularly heated in the late 1990s, as the American Law Institute (ALI) contemplated successor provisions to Section 402A for inclusion in the Third Restatement of Torts. Indeed, critics claim that the test for design defect eventually promulgated by the ALI in 1998 (discussed further below) amounted to a betrayal of Traynor's and Prosser's vision of a progressive, consumer-protective law of products liability.

13. For simplicity's sake, our general description of products liability law will focus on its application to manufacturers. As noted at various points below, however, strict products liability from the get-go has applied to "commercial sellers" of products, which includes retailers (and distributors) that did not manufacture the product(s) at issue.

To appreciate these developments requires closer attention to the legal concept of a defective product. Since the late 1970s, courts and commentators have supposed that it is useful to identify three distinct categories of product defect—*manufacturing defects, design defects,* and *failures to warn.* A product has a manufacturing defect if it fails to conform to the safety specifications provided by the manufacturer itself for that product. Design defects, by contrast, involve an entire product line being more dangerous than it ought to be. Finally, a warning defect involves the failure to include information that is necessary to render a product safe for ordinary use.[14]

Isolating the legal standard to be used for ascertaining whether a product *design* is defective (as opposed to those used for assessing manufacturing defect and warning defect claims) is a tricky business.[15] If a plaintiff can prove that the manufacturer failed to exercise ordinary care in designing its product, the doctrine of strict products liability is not needed: a negligence action will succeed. Yet, unlike manufacturing defects— which are gauged by reference to the manufacturer's own specifications— design defects must be assessed by an external legal benchmark. In short, if a jury is being asked to ascertain whether a design is defective, a court will need to provide the jury with some external standard *other than* "reasonable care in design choice." By and large, courts and commentators have identified not one but two such standards. The first is known as the "consumer expectations test." The second is the "risk–utility test."

Consumers expect, and are entitled to expect, to use standard-issue products without undue risk to their physical well-being. A tampon design that causes women to die from ultra-high fevers when they use the product

14. In Chapter 6 we offered the following examples of each category: a single toaster that comes off the assembly line with loose wires that leave it prone to catching fire during ordinary use (manufacturing defect); a drug for treating minor ailments whose chemical composition produces fatal side-effects in a significant percentage of users (design defect); a caustic chemical drain cleaner sold for household use that fails to warn users to protect against splatter that can result from pouring the product into standing water, and that may cause blindness (warning defect).

15. Another important question is whether a nonmanufacturing seller (e.g., a commercial retailer) of a defectively designed product that injures a consumer should be vulnerable to a strict products liability claim and, if so, why. Courts and scholars who advocate for the risk–utility test have, until recent years, been content to permit liability for retailers in claims by plaintiffs who can demonstrate a design defect causing injury to the plaintiff under this test. However, a number of state legislatures have enacted statutes protecting certain retailers from being subject to strict liability for injuries caused by products they sell but do not manufacture. 1 MARSHALL S. SHAPO, SHAPO ON THE LAW OF PRODUCTS LIABILITY § 12.04 [c], at 12-87–12-93 (2013).

as instructed is an example of a product that defeats legitimate consumer expectations. The same goes for a model of lawn chair with a reclining mechanism that can snip off the fingertips of a person casually adjusting it. In each case, there is something in the design of the product that makes it much more dangerous than a reasonable consumer would have expected. This is the basic idea underlying the consumer expectations test.

The risk–utility test comes at the design defect question from a different angle. It invites judges and juries to consider whether the risks of injury inherent in the design of a product outweigh the benefits to consumers provided by that design. For example, if an industrial machine used for cutting sheets of plastic into ribbons has a feeding mechanism that can pull an operator's hands into the cutting mechanism of the machine, a court applying the risk–utility test would inquire whether, as compared to a machine with a safer feeding mechanism, the risks of injury associated with this design outweigh the benefits it offers in terms of ease of use and increased productivity.

In the last twenty-five years, litigants have pushed state high courts to choose one or the other, and many courts have done so. Although allegiances have shifted over time, the risk–utility test is today generally seen as more defendant-friendly, whereas the consumer expectations test tends to be favored by plaintiffs' lawyers. In part this is because the risk–utility test invites judges and juries to focus on trade-offs between safety (on the one hand) and cost and efficacy (on the other). The basic question is whether the added safety of an alternative design that would have prevented the plaintiff's injury was worth it, given any additional cost to consumers and any impairment of the usefulness of the product associated with the adoption of the alternative design. Relatedly, the risk–utility test sometimes carries with it a technocratic flavor, suggesting implicitly that judges and jurors should defer to expert testimony when assessing defectiveness. Given their insider knowledge of the science and methods of their own industries, and their greater resources to invest in experts, this focus on expertise probably favors defendants. By contrast, the consumer expectations test is thought to invite a more "gestalt" or commonsense inquiry that gives jurors more leeway to find a product defectively designed.

Against this backdrop, it was no surprise that when the drafters of the products liability provisions of the Third Torts Restatement opted in 1998 for a version of risk–utility as pretty much the exclusive test for design defect, they were accused of political bias. Significantly, that document's core design-defect provision—Section 2(b)—not only rejects the consumer expectations test in favor of risk–utility, it also adopts a relatively defendant-friendly version of the latter test. Under Section 2(b), a plaintiff can prevail on the issue of design defect only by proving that: (1) a reasonable alternative design was feasible at the time of design; (2) the risks of harm that were reasonably foreseeable to the manufacturer at the time of design would have been reduced by the alternative design; *and* (3) the manufacturer's failure to adopt the alternative design rendered the product not reasonably safe.[16]

The focus in prongs (1) and (2) on risks that manufacturers could have foreseen at the time of design departs not only from earlier, strongly pro-plaintiff versions of the risk–utility test, but also from others that were more balanced. The plaintiff-leaning renditions of risk–utility that some courts adopted in the early 1970s posed for judges and jurors the question of whether the design chosen by the defendant would have been adopted by a reasonable manufacturer with actual knowledge of dangers posed by the design, *including dangers that emerged after the sale of the product but prior to trial.*[17] On this approach, risk–utility was determined utilizing hindsight, not foresight. Other prior iterations of the risk–utility (and many today) are foresight- rather than hindsight-based, yet more moderate that the Third Restatement's version. Some eschew proof of an available alternative design as a *sine qua non*, treating it only as a factor.[18] Others place on the defendant "the burden of proving that the utility of the challenged design outweighs its dangers."[19]

Prong (3), meanwhile, allows for the possibility that a judge or jury could deem a product nondefective even granted the availability to the manufacturer, at the time of design, of a safer design at a reasonable cost. The idea is that, while it would have perhaps been desirable for the manufacturer to adopt the safer and not-too-costly design, the less-safe design it actually employed was still safe enough as not to reach the degree of dangerousness that marks off a product as unreasonably unsafe.

---

16. RESTATEMENT (THIRD) OF TORTS: PRODUCTS LIABILITY §2(b) & cmt. d (1998).

17. In an influential article, Dean John Wade argued for hindsight strict liability of this sort, and proposed jury instructions reflecting it. John Wade, *On the Nature of Strict Liability for Products*, 44 MISS. L.J. 825 (1973). New York arguably has adopted a version of those instructions. N.Y. Pattern Jury Instr.—Civil 2:278 (2012).

18. *See, e.g.,* Voss v. Black & Decker Mfg. Co., 450 N.E.2d 204, 208 (N.Y. 1983).

19. Soule v. General Motors Corp., 882 P.2d 298, 311 n.8 (Cal. 1994) (citation omitted).

It goes too far to suggest that Section 2(b) of the products liability provisions of the Third Torts Restatement reflects a desire on the part of the Reporters or the ALI to stick it to plaintiffs and protect defendants. (Even apart from the Reporters' well-deserved stature as serious scholars, several other features of the Restatement's products liability provisions are plainly quite plaintiff-friendly.) That said, we think Section 2(b) goes astray, and that our framework can help to explain how and why, while also providing a better way forward. The key is to adopt a dual constructivist approach that takes seriously doctrine, history, and social norms, all the while keeping an eye on the importance of the right to redress for wrongs. We start with history.

As Justice Traynor noted in *Greenman*, strict products liability was built atop two doctrinal precursors: the law of negligence and the law of implied warranty. By 1944, the date of *Greenman's* most important precursor—*Escola v. Coca Cola Bottling Co.*—each had well-known strengths and weaknesses.[20] Implied warranty predicated liability on the failure of a product to live up to the manufacturer's implicit representation of quality. A typical case was that of a consumer who purchased a prepared food item and was injured by a foreign object in it. Warranty claims were understood to sound in contract—that is, they alleged that the seller failed to fulfill *an unqualified promise* to supply to the buyer a product that was fit for consumption. There was thus no need for the warranty plaintiff to prove seller negligence—the seller's promise was *to provide* a fit product, not *to take care to provide* a fit product. This was an importantly consumer-protective feature of warranty law, given that sellers who bought and resold goods from reputable suppliers often were not negligent. Nonetheless, the seller was held liable for breaching its implicit promise to provide a wholesome product, and consequential damages for this breach included damages for the personal injury suffered by the plaintiff.

Though in the foregoing respect favorable to consumers, implied warranty claims for personal injury suffered from at least two weaknesses, so far as plaintiffs were concerned. First, because they were contractual in nature, they traditionally required privity between defendant and plaintiff. The ultimate manufacturer of the product or its distributor sometimes

---

20. 150 P.2d 436 (Cal. 1944). Of particular importance was Justice Traynor's concurring opinion in *Escola*, which, though it attracted no adherents in 1944, provided the rationales for the rule adopted nineteen years later in *Greenman*.

could not be held liable for breach of warranty if the product was purchased from an independent seller. Likewise, it was not clear that a non-purchaser (e.g., a family member with whom the purchaser shared the defective product) could recover. Second, contract law contains a variety of formal defenses, technicalities, and limitations on damages that could present serious obstacles for personal injury plaintiffs relying on a warranty claim.

With respect to its pro- and anti-consumer features, negligence law operated as the mirror image of warranty law. Because negligence liability sounded in tort, not contract, it was not bound by the limitations on warranty liability just described. Led by Cardozo's landmark 1916 opinion in *MacPherson v. Buick Motor Co.*[21] most American courts permitted an injured person to bring a negligence claim against the manufacturer of a dangerous product that had been carelessly assembled, or as to which there was carelessness in premarketing safety checks. The requirement of privity, which originated in contract law but had sometimes been applied by earlier courts to negligence claims, was eliminated. Likewise, the duty of care was deemed to extend to all users of the product, not just purchasers. Finally, negligence law contained fewer formalities than contract law.

At the same time, negligence plaintiffs faced obstacles to recovery not faced by warranty claimants. First and foremost, the plaintiff was required to prove fault—a failure to use ordinary care—on the part of the defendant. Given that the relevant information about production processes often rested with manufacturers, who tend to enjoy the advantages that come with being well-heeled, repeat-player litigants, this burden sometimes proved difficult to meet. Relatedly, even if negligence claims were more easily pursued against manufacturers than warranty claims, the same was not true for retailers and distributors, as evidence of *their* negligence in selling a prepackaged consumer item often would be nonexistent or scant. Additionally, under mid-twentieth-century tort rules, if the plaintiff's own carelessness played any part in his being injured, recovery was precluded by the defense of contributory negligence.

Each of the two famous Traynor opinions that gave birth to modern products liability law—*Escola* and *Greenman*—came to it via one of these two doctrinal streams. The plaintiff in *Escola* was a waitress who had been restocking a restaurant refrigerator when a glass bottle of carbonated

---

21. 110 N.E. 1050 (N.Y. 1916).

soda exploded in her hand. Because she was not a consumer of the product, warranty was a nonstarter, leaving her only with a negligence claim. While the bottle was demonstrably defective, it would not be easy to establish negligence on the part of the bottling arm of the massive Coca-Cola Company, both because of its ability to litigate tort claims, and because it probably employed fairly effective (though obviously not perfect) quality-control measures. The majority affirmed *Escola's* verdict by adopting an expansive version of the doctrine of *res ipsa loquitur*, according to which certain negligence plaintiffs benefit from a presumption of defendant carelessness. In his pathbreaking concurrence, however, Traynor argued that the use of *res ipsa* was circuitous and disingenuous—what was really called for was a distinct tort claim predicated on the defectiveness of the product and not the carelessness of the manufacturer.

Conversely, the plaintiff in *Greenman* was a consumer (user) of the defendant's product, though not a direct purchaser (his spouse bought it for him as a gift), and his claim had many of the hallmarks of a valid warranty action. The product in question was a power tool that, among other things, could be used as a lathe. The manufacturer of such a product is appropriately understood to warrant that its frame will not come apart during ordinary use, thereby allowing a spinning piece of wood to fly off the machine and strike the user, which is what happened to the plaintiff. However, warranty claims at the time sounded in contract, and the rules of contract law—which were designed for commercial transactions and risks of business disruption flowing from breaches of contract rather than personal injuries—did not allow product users to obtain compensation for breaches of warranty unless they had provided formal notice of the breach shortly after receipt of the product, such that the seller would have an opportunity to cure the breach. Writing for a majority of a court of which he was a senior member, Traynor maintained that a personal injury claim arising out the sale of a defective product was really a tort claim, not a contract claim, and was therefore not subject to limitations designed to be applied in disputes between businesses over the failure of one of them to live up to its side of a commercial exchange. Yet, the standard of liability would be the warranty standard: tort liability would henceforth turn on the defectiveness of the product, not the carelessness of the seller.

From within a dual constructivist framework, *Greenman* and *Escola* both mark sensible efforts to construct a new legal wrong out of existing legal materials. *Greenman* in effect grafted negligence law features onto what was basically a warranty-based tort claim, whereas *Escola* grafted warranty features onto what was basically a negligence-based tort claim.

We can start with the former. The *wrongfulness* at the core of the warranty-based tort claim recognized in *Greenman* is the marketing of a defective product. This is a breach of a duty of noninjuriousness—it is conduct that generates an unacceptable risk of injury. When that risk ripens into an actual injury, the conduct becomes a breach of a duty of noninjury. Strict products liability, so understood, took from the law of warranty the idea that there is a wrong in providing a consumer with a product that does not perform as safely as the consumer was entitled to expect, yet anchored this expectation not in an explicit or implicit promise from seller to purchaser but in a legally imposed duty. And given that this class of warranty claim is triggered by a consumer's physical injury, rather than by the lost profits typically at issue in warranty litigation among businesses, it seems to belong more in the domain of tort than contract. Hence the recognition of a design defect claim built around the consumer expectations test.

The risk–utility test has an equal claim to recognition. First, although strict products liability relieves plaintiffs of the burden of proving manufacturer fault, many product-related injuries are the result of such fault, and in this sense the two torts tend to operate in close proximity to one another. And even though the notion of a carelessly designed product is (or can be) distinct from the notion of a product that fails the risk–utility test (or some version of it), the idea of carelessness, in this context, reflects something like the risk–utility test's idea of balancing the burdens and benefits of the different precautions that might be taken by a manufacturer to prevent consumer injuries.

Second, many of the insights that have been used to craft a more plaintiff-friendly products liability law have their source in negligence law and theory. For example, bystanders who are fully outside of any version of an extended distributional chain are still *foreseeable* victims of defective products, and in *Elmore v. American Motors Corp.*,[22] an important post-*Greenman* decision, the California Supreme Court permitted bystanders

22. 451 P.2d 84 (Cal. 1969). We question below the propriety of one aspect of *Elmore*—namely, its imposition on retailers, as opposed to manufacturers, of strict liability to nonconsumers.

to bring strict products liability claims. (Similarly, products that are not being used for their intended purpose, yet are still being used in a foreseeable manner, can give rise to strict products liability claims.) Another example is liability for products that wear their defective designs on their sleeves, so to speak. Designs that create patent or obvious product dangers seem incapable of being deemed defective under a consumer expectations test: there can be no disappointed expectation of safety with respect to an industrial machine that quite evidently is capable of harming its operator. Yet courts sometimes permit plaintiffs to recover under a risk–utility conception of design defect even when the danger is patent.[23] In these cases, too, negligence—and the idea that certain dangers are unacceptable regardless of how obvious they are—is lurking in the background as the basis for liability.

Third, the shift from negligence to strict products liability was itself born in part of liberalizing instincts within negligence doctrine itself. The doctrine of *res ipsa loquitur* on which the *Escola* majority relied reflects in part a recognition that systemic asymmetries in access to evidence that favor defendants provide a reason to shift the inquiry at trial from specific evidence of defendant's careless conduct to evidence of dangerousness of the product itself. Relatedly, the objective, strict edge of negligence law's standard of care also provides a basis for looking at whether what a defendant manufacturer designed and marketed was in fact excessively dangerous. Finally, the thought that consumers rely heavily on manufacturers, who have an asymmetrical capacity to take precautions, does not just provide a theoretical reason to ratchet up the duty of care. A higher duty of care (plausibly regarded as strict) is entirely consonant with the history of elevated standards of care for common carriers and innkeepers— roles in which there is a great asymmetry of access to safety measures and greater reliance by the ordinary person on other actors attending to their duties of care.

The upshot is that, although there is indeed a basis for seeing the advent of a strict products liability action as a recognition of an implied warranty claim grafted onto a tort foundation, there is also a basis for seeing it as the recognition of a reconfigured and more plaintiff-friendly negligence claim that ratchets up the manufacturer's duty of care. For this

---

23. This is why, in the early years of products liability law (unlike today), it was often plaintiffs, rather than defendants, who favored the adoption of a risk–utility test for design defect.

reason, both the consumer expectations test and at least some versions of the risk–utility test can claim to be authentic to products liability law's origins. This point is strongly reinforced by reconsideration of the three kinds of product defects (mentioned above) that support a strict products liability claim. Manufacturing defect cases are plainly in the mold of tort-based implied warranty claims, whereas failure-to-warn cases are probably more in the mold of an expanded, product-focused idea of manufacturer negligence. It is therefore no surprise that in the middle category—design defect—there are two quite strong arguments: one for a definition based on a tort-like implied warranty claim, and one for a definition based on a product-focused variation of a negligence claim.

The question of which test to use for design defect is thus in an important sense ill-formed. The prima facie *doctrinal* answer would seem to be that both should be available. We will call this the "disjunctive model." It is by no means our creation. In post-*Greenman* decisions, the California Supreme Court has adopted different versions of it.[24] So too have the courts of New York and other states.

A pair of New York decisions helps to capture the propriety and value of a disjunctive approach. In *Denny v. Ford Motor Co.*, a motorist was injured when the car she was driving—a Ford Bronco II—rolled over after she slammed on the brakes to avoid hitting a deer.[25] The plaintiff argued that the vehicle, a compact, four-wheel-drive, sport utility vehicle (SUV), was defectively designed because its high ground clearance, when combined with its narrow and short base and its light weight, created an unduly high risk of rollover during ordinary driving. Ford countered that these design features were necessary for the Bronco to operate as an off-road vehicle, as SUVs are meant to do.

The trial court, without objection from the parties, instructed the jury that it could find for the plaintiff on either of two grounds. First, it told the jury it could find the product to have been sold in a defective condition if it concluded that a reasonable person who knew of the design's potential for causing injury and of alternative available designs, would not have marketed the product as designed. Second, utilizing a provision of New York's

---

24. Barker v. Lull Eng'g Co., 573 P.2d 443 (Cal. 1978); Soule v. General Motors Corp., 882 P.2d 298 (Cal. 1994). Neither *Barker* nor *Soule* permits what we recommend, however, which is to instruct the jury in each case that it may find liability for design defect on either theory.

25. 662 N.E.2d 730 (N.Y. 1995).

Uniform Commercial Code governing warranties, the court instructed the jury could find that the manufacturer breached its implied warranty if the product was not reasonably fit for the uses for which it was intended. The jury concluded that the design of the Bronco II was *not* such that a reasonable manufacturer would have refrained from marketing it. Yet it also concluded that the vehicle was unfit for its intended purpose, and thus found for the plaintiff. The defendant appealed to New York's high court, arguing that the jury's two findings were contradictory. If the Bronco II's design was not defective, Ford insisted, and if there were no allegations of manufacturing defect or failure to warn, then it could not possibly be true that the Bronco II was unfit for its intended purpose.

The New York Court of Appeals rejected Ford's argument. The jurors had concluded that the overall utility of the design of the Bronco II outweighed its risks. In their judgment, a vehicle of this design is the sort of vehicle that a reasonable manufacturer with knowledge of its dangers might well introduce into the market. Given the value provided by the relevant design features—enhanced off-road capability, greater maneuverability, better gas mileage, and aesthetic appeal—the increased rollover risk that those same features posed were not so grave or unmanageable that a vehicle of this sort should never have been made available to the public.

But the jurors also found—and were entitled to find—that the vehicle's design defeated the plaintiff's legitimate expectations as to the stability of a car *represented by the manufacturer as appropriate for use as an ordinary passenger vehicle*. The outcome of the case thus might have been different if Ford had marketed the Bronco II to customers specifically interested in a vehicle with off-road capabilities. But the plaintiff offered evidence that Ford had marketed the Bronco II as entirely suitable for "commuting and for suburban and city driving."[26] In other words, Ford's wrong resided, not merely in causing injury through the sale of a lightweight, compact SUV, but in causing injury through the sale of a lightweight, compact SUV that, by virtue of Ford's own representations, consumers could legitimately expect to deliver the level of safety that an ordinary passenger vehicle offers. Products liability law's warranty side (and the idea of disappointed consumer expectations), more so than its negligence side (and the idea of

---

26. *Id.* at 732 (quoting a Ford marketing manual).

a design with risks that outweigh its utilities), captured the defectiveness of Ford's design.

Another New York rollover case involving a Ford vehicle, *Motelson v. Ford Motor Company*,[27] serves as the mirror image of *Denny*. In *Motelson*, several claims were brought on behalf of persons killed or injured in a horrific crash in which a Ford Explorer rolled over multiple times. One claim—brought on behalf of the driver, who died of head injuries sustained in the crash—alleged that the Explorer's roof was defectively designed because it was not strong enough to withstand a rollover. As to this claim (as in *Denny*), there were allegations both that Ford had sold a kind of car that a reasonable manufacturer with knowledge of the roof's propensity to fail would not have sold, and that the car defeated consumers' legitimate expectations as to how the roof would perform in a crash. The *Motelson* jury concluded that the Explorer was fit for ordinary use (thus finding for Ford on the warranty claim), yet also concluded that the car was designed in a manner such that a reasonable manufacturer with knowledge of the design's dangers would not have sold it (thus finding for the plaintiff).

As in *Denny*, Ford argued on appeal that the two verdicts were inconsistent. In a terse opinion, an intermediate appellate court rejected Ford's challenge. One way to understand its ruling is as follows. Consumers might not have any particularly robust expectations as to how a car's roof will respond in a situation where a car rolls over multiple times. Nonetheless, it remains wrong for a manufacturer to sell a vehicle with a roof that is insufficiently supported and thus responds to a rollover by exposing occupants to head injuries in ways that other feasible roof designs would not. A car with a design feature that creates this avoidable hazard, with little or no corresponding benefits, is a car with a defective design.

Given the consonance of the disjunctive model with the history and nature of strict products liability, critics have been right to question the decision of the Reporters for the products liability provisions of the Third Restatement—Professors Henderson and Twerski—to recommend near-exclusive reliance on the risk–utility test for design defect and especially the incorporation into that test of a requirement that a design defect plaintiff bears the burden of proving not only that a reasonable alternative

27. Motelson v. Ford Motor Co., 20 Misc.3d 1140(A) (Sup. Ct. 2008) (unreported disposition), *rev'd on other grounds*, 101 A.D.3d 957 (N.Y. App. Div. 2012), *aff'd*, 22 N.E.3d 186 (N.Y. 2014).

design was available to the manufacturer at the time of design but also that the failure to adopt the alternative design rendered the product not reasonably safe.[28]

A close examination of this test reveals a fundamental flaw (to use a mixed metaphor) in the Reporters' formulation: its "not reasonably safe" requirement seems to come from nowhere. Recall that, by definition, it will be capable of undercutting the claim of a plaintiff who has already proven that an alternative, safer, and cost-justified design was available. Why does the plaintiff *also* need to prove that its omission renders it not reasonably safe if we already know there is a better and safer way to make the product?

The answer to this question is ironic, to put it mildly. The not-reasonably-safe requirement seems to come from the warranty roots of strict liability law. A defendant could indeed argue, plausibly, that there should be no design defect claim if the allegedly defective product was as safe as a reasonable consumer would expect. The ground of that argument would be, however, a contention that defectiveness is a matter of falling below reasonable consumer expectations. If that is the test, however, the risk–utility/reasonable alternative design portion of the Section 2(b) definition of design defect should be removed. The Reporters' test is a hybrid after all. But it is one that, in effect, requires each design defect plaintiff to satisfy *both* the risk–utility test and the consumer expectations test!

The impact of the Reporters' approach is illustrated by a recent Texas Supreme Court decision, *Genie Industries, Inc. v. Matak.*[29] Matak was killed when co-workers moved and thus accidentally tipped over the portable aerial lift on which he was standing. After being presented with evidence of a variety of alternative designs that would have prevented the injury, a jury found against the manufacturer and in favor of the wrongful-death plaintiffs, though it also assigned fault to Matak's co-workers and to Matak himself. Genie argued on appeal that none of the alternative designs proffered were properly viewed as "reasonable" and that no jury could find otherwise. A 6–3 majority begrudgingly accepted that the jury was entitled to conclude that at least one of the alternative designs identified by the plaintiff's experts was reasonable within the meaning of Section 2(b) of the products liability provisions of the Third Restatement. However, in

28. RESTATEMENT (THIRD), *supra* note 16, § 2(b) & cmt. d.
29. 462 S.W.3d 1 (Tex. 2015).

a remarkably undeferential bit of appellate review, the majority proceeded to overturn the verdict on the ground that the additional increment of safety provided by the proposed alternative design (even granting that it would have spared the plaintiff's life) was unlikely to make a difference in many other cases. Thus, in the majority's view, the manufacturer's failure to adopt the alternative design, even though it would have made the product safer, did not render the product "unreasonably dangerous." To say the same thing, the majority ruled that no reasonable jury could find (as this jury found) that the failure to adopt the safer design rendered the product not reasonably safe.

One does not have to be an unabashed cheerleader for the plaintiffs' bar to believe that something went wrong in *Matak*. Burden upon burden was placed on the plaintiff, and the burdens were not all consistent with one another. And when the *Matak* plaintiffs nonetheless ran the gauntlet, the state's high court took what appear to have been questions of fact—about the frequency with which tip-over accidents had resulted (and were likely to result) from use of a lift of this sort—and turned them into issues of law so as to support dismissal. Entirely absent from the majority opinion is any thought given to the concern expressed by Traynor, Prosser, and many others that the structure of litigation between an injured individual or his survivors and a large company already tends to favor defendants. However design defect is properly defined, it is clear that a central point of moving to strict products liability was to level the litigation playing field, or at least to render it less steeply tilted. Texas's approach, clearly inspired by the Restatement (Third)'s test for design defect, seems designed or at least destined to make life much better for defendants.

Getting to the nub of the risk–utility/consumer expectations debate requires taking a larger view of the sense in which strict products liability actions are about a particular kind of integrated wrong. We maintain that, at least as a first-cut position, both risk–utility and consumer expectations should be available for any claim of design defect, because we recognize that strict products liability law has developed by identifying two closely related wrongs, each softened a bit from its predecessor: an implied warranty claim sounding in tort, not in contract (and therefore freed from some of the commercial-law-based procedural restrictions on plaintiffs), and a higher-than-usual-standard of care negligence claim rooted in an objective focus on the product as marketed. It is true that part of what led to the softening of each of these models was an understanding of the ·plaintiff-empowering features of the other (e.g., the product focus of warranty, and the non-formal, non-privity bases of tort). But it hardly follows that courts or scholars are free to mix and match doctrinal requirements to satisfy their own preferred level of liability. As explained above, there were sound reasons for thinking that the restrictions on each of those claims were not justified by an understanding of the nature of the wrong in question.

Here we arrive at practical advantages of a dual constructivist approach over one that is dual instrumentalist. There is an *ad hoc* and unfair quality to the Texas court's willingness to overturn a plaintiff's verdict by giving the manufacturer-defendant two bites at the apple. The alleged reasons for the exactingness of the reasonable-alternative design requirement that by itself almost defeated the claim in *Matak* derive from a set of ideas that is entirely different from the reasons for the "unreasonably dangerous" requirement that ultimately did defeat it. The first rests on a commitment to a conception of design defect built on a negligence basis. The second builds on warranty notions. The Texas Supreme Court, following the Restatement (Third), seemed to pick and choose among these to design the most pro-defendant test.

Our critique of *Matak* and the Restatement (Third)'s treatment of design defects may seem to evidence a relentlessly pro-plaintiff, pro-liability outlook, but it does not. Indeed, it arguably provides reasons to be skeptical of some of the more pro-plaintiff schemes of liability that prevailed during the early years of products liability law. Consider, for example, *Vandermark v. Ford Motor Co.*, in which the California Supreme Court decided that, separate and apart from manufacturers, retailers can be held liable on a strict products liability theory.[30] It rendered this decision even though retailers typically lack any control over the design of the product that injured the plaintiff, and even though the question of retailer carefulness is often not even indirectly related to the defectiveness of the product. In our view, this was a plausible and laudatory decision, insofar as it picks up on the warranty rather than the negligence version of the wrong.

Five years later, however, the same court decided the *Elmore* case, mentioned above, which held that, despite being outside of the domain of consumers even broadly conceived, bystanders injured in a crash caused by a defective car could prevail on a strict products liability claim, not just a negligence claim. *Elmore* is sensible when understood as an aggressive

---

30. 391 P.2d 168 (Cal. 1964).

application of the negligence version of the wrong of injuring someone by manufacturing a defectively designed product, at least when the bystanders are (as in *Elmore* itself) foreseeable. However, in conformity with *Vandermark*, California tort doctrine treats *Elmore's* bystander rule as applicable to retailers and not just manufacturers. It is far from clear that a bystander should be able sue a *retailer* on a strict products liability claim that is conceived in (liberalized) negligence and foreseeability terms. Retailer liability is a warranty-driven idea. And even though the orbit of warranty obligations has expanded beyond privity, the idea of a warranty running past the class of product consumers to any person foreseeably injured by a defectively designed product is a bridge too far. The union of these two rules in one tort claim is a plaintiff's wish list, but it is far from clear that it makes any sense.

There is nothing formalistic about the foregoing criticisms. Recall that we applaud the *Greenman's* court synthesis of various doctrinal strands taken from contract and tort law. Nor are we caught up in an obsession with conceptual coherence for its own sake. Our point is principally practical and political, and, to be candid, it is advanced more as a conjecture than a conclusion. We believe that the instability of products liability law—its vulnerability to changes in the political wind, and its steady erosion—is due in part to courts' inattentiveness to the integrity of the concepts within it.

Taking a further step back, we would suggest that the attraction to relatively pro-defendant versions of the risk–utility test for design defect is as much a matter of bad tort theory as raw politics. For decades it has been standard among torts scholars to suppose that strict liability stands opposed to fault-based liability. The latter is based on a notion of deficient conduct (albeit as judged by the law's objective standard rather than a moral standard). The former, it has been thought, simply eliminates the linkage of tort liability to the failure to conform to a standard of conduct. The adoption of strict products liability in the 1960s and 1970s, on this view, was an instrumentally driven decision to provide a pro-plaintiff pocket of liability irrespective of substandard conduct that quickly became the most important exception to the general regime of negligence-based liability that applies to most other kinds of accidentally caused harm.

Starting around 1980 some courts and commentators began to question whether the instrumental case for strict products liability made by Traynor and others really holds up, at least for cases of design defect (and failure to warn). In particular, they doubted whether one could even make sense of the idea of a defectively designed product except by reference to some notion of misconduct. Because by this time U.S.-trained jurists had for decades been brought up on some version of what Holmes long ago identified as fault in the legal sense, or what Prosser referred to as "socially unreasonable" conduct, it was nearly inevitable that skepticism about the instrumental case for strict design defect liability—understood as a regime of licensing-based liability—would give way to the reintroduction of something close to a negligence rule, as is provided for by the Third Restatement.

The mistake here is twofold. One is the supposition that genuinely strict products liability can only be, and thus was, non-wrongs-based, licensing liability. The other is the supposition that the various wrongs of tort, or at least those that address accidentally inflicted injuries, all boil down to negligence—that the gist of each is unreasonable conduct in the eyes of the law. As we explained in Chapter 6, strict products liability is not (or is not primarily) a scheme of licensing-based liability. It is liability for the wrong of injuring another by putting onto the market a dangerously defective product. One can, of course, question whether a wrong so defined should be recognized, but the liability it generates cannot be dismissed on the ground that it departs from a strong presumption against "liability without fault," if by that phrase one means "liability without some form of wrongdoing." Nor can one presume that, if liability for product-related injuries is to be wrongs-based, it must in the end be liability for negligence or something quite like negligence.

The Reporters and many courts have failed to recognize that a firm that sells a defectively designed product that injures a consumer during ordinary use has *wrongfully* injured the consumer. This is so regardless of whether the design is defective because it defeats consumers' safety expectations or because it fails the risk–utility test in a foresight- or hindsight-based version. An insistence that tort liability is and must be wrongs-based, rather than a "naked" redistribution of losses from consumers to manufacturers and retailers, provides no basis for insisting that the idea of a defectively designed product must be cashed out by reference to a notion of negligent design selection.

Libel: The Internet, Good Samaritans, and the CDA

This final section differs from its predecessors in that it analyzes the interaction of state tort law and federal statutory law, and because it concerns the tort of libel. The statute in question, the Communications Decency Act (CDA), was enacted in 1996. Among its provisons is Section 230(c). Section 230(c) limits the liability of internet service providers (ISPs)— persons and firms that provide internet access to subscribers, and those that provide online bulletin or message boards, search engines, and the like—for content appearing on sites that they host or to which they provide access. Evocatively, Section 230(c) bears the title: "*Protection for 'Good Samaritan' blocking and screening of offensive material.*"

Those not in the habit of associating Facebook, Google, and other internet companies with the teachings of the famous biblical parable might find this language odd. And there is indeed something puzzling about it. The puzzle, however, does not reside in the use of the phrase "Good Samaritan." As we will see, that phrase refers to a familiar tort doctrine. Rather, it concerns the way in which courts and commentators have misread Section 230(c). Nor has theirs been a mere technical error. The prevailing misreading has created a legal accountability deficit for ISPs, one that arguably has contributed to the problems of internet incivility and fake news that now plague us.[31]

Section 230(c) was enacted to deal with two related concerns expressed by ISPs such as America Online, Prodigy, and Compuserve, as well as by the internet industry more broadly.[32] The first was straightforward: they worried that if someone posted a defamatory statement online, the person defamed might bring a libel suit against the ISP (instead of or in addition to the person who posted the statement) on the theory that the ISP played a role in causing third parties to be exposed to the defamatory statement, either by transmitting the statement or by failing to remove it.

The second concern of the internet industry, related to the first, was (astutely) highlighted by the ISPs in lobbying Congress for statutory protection from liability. It was this concern that generated Section 230(c)'s reference to the Good Samaritan. Even if courts were unwilling to hold ISPs liable simply for transmitting or failing to remove defamatory con-

---

31. *See* DANIELLE KEATS CITRON, HATE CRIMES IN CYBERSPACE 170–81 (2014) (arguing that CDA immunity from liability has contributed to widespread online misogyny, which is now a basic civil rights issue for women).

32. Entities such as AOL function as online service providers (OSPs), in that they not only transmit packets of data but also host content on their servers. Jonathan Zittrain, *Internet Points of Control*, 44 B.C. L. REV. 664, 653 (2003). Although the CDA's limits on liability discussed below were probably crafted by Congress primarily with OSPs in mind, they apply *a fortiori* to ISPs that do not function as OSPs. We will therefore refer in this chapter to "ISPs."

tent, they might do so on a more nuanced theory. According to it, any ISP that *voluntarily undertakes to screen and monitor bulletin boards and websites* for inappropriate content would thereby incur a legal duty to remove defamatory postings and would face liability for failing to perform that voluntarily assumed duty. Borrowed from negligence law, the idea that a voluntary decision to filter or monitor content generates a duty to curate pointed to the ironic result that a website or internet provider that touts itself as "family friendly" for taking steps to protect against the spread of vulgar, obscene, or defamatory content—the Good Samaritan ISP—would end up facing liability, while its unconcerned, laissez-faire competitors would not.

As it turns out, both of these concerns—that the mere provision of access to defamatory content, or that the failure to fulfill an undertaking to filter such content, would serve as a basis for liability—had some basis in reality, though it is far from clear that a parade of horribles would actually have come to pass if Congress had not stepped in. To appreciate the ISPs' potential vulnerability requires a brief excursus into the common law of libel, as well as of negligence.

Publication and Republication

Libel consists of publishing, through a writing or broadcast, a statement about another of a sort that tends to prompt condemnation, ridicule, or ostracism. In this formulation, "publishing" is a term of art. To "publish" a defamatory statement is to communicate it to at least one person other than the victim. For example, if Spencer sends a hardcopy letter to Ted that describes Ursula as a someone who has stolen money from her church, Spencer has "published" the statement about Ursula, and is a "publisher" of the statement, so far as the common law of libel is concerned.

While defamatory statements frequently are published by their authors, they are as or more frequently published by nonauthors. Indeed, the bulk of American law's most famous libel cases, including the landmark case *New York Times v. Sullivan* (as well as many garden-variety libel suits that have resulted in judgments for plaintiffs) involve the imposition of liability on publishers who did not author the statements in question. A newspaper or book publisher (in the lay sense of the term) is a paradigmatic example of such a publisher. Deliberately selecting a statement written by another and then circulating it to readers counts as publication, so far as libel law is concerned. Thus, if Spencer sends the letter containing the statement about Ursula to a newspaper for publication in its Op-Ed section, and the newspaper prints it, Ursula may be able to recover from both Spencer and the newspaper as publishers of the libelous statement.

Small-potatoes versions of publishing someone else's libelous statement also count as libels. Indeed, under the venerable *republication rule*, various actors who repeat another's defamatory writing are subject to liability as if they were the original authors and disseminators of the defamatory material. Suppose in the above example that Ted, after receiving Spencer's letter, writes his own letter and sends it to Vincent. Suppose further that Ted's letter includes the following passage: "Hey Vincent! I just received a letter from Spencer stating that Ursula has stolen church funds!" According to the republication rule, even if Ted's letter to Vincent merely repeats Spencer's original statement, Ted counts as a publisher of the defamatory remark about Ursula.

The idea behind the republication rule—that one who chooses to repeat a statement that is defamatory cannot avoid liability merely by pointing out that someone else said it first—is perfectly sensible. Repetition is the lifeblood of defamation. The harm done by republication is often equal to or greater than that caused by the original statement. Moreover, a republisher often has substantial control over whether, and how widely, to circulate the statement. And there is enormous potential for opportunistic evasion if one can avoid liability merely by attributing one's words to another. In the most visible and important part of defamation law—libel law—it has thus long been standard for the defendant to be a person or entity entirely distinct from the original creator, writer, speaker, or author of the statement. Indeed, although there are some categorical exceptions to the republication rule (as when a newspaper produces a neutral news report of what was said in a town meeting), the basic republication rule is well settled.

In contrast to these well-settled rules stand more esoteric notions of publication, two of which found their way into the Restatement (Second) of Torts and garnered the attention of lawyers in the 1990s, as the internet was growing in importance. One of these esoteric notions addresses "distributors" such as mail deliverers, newsstands, libraries, and bookstores. It is clear that the mere act of delivering a sealed letter containing a defamatory statement does not render a mail delivery service a publisher of the letter. The same goes for a bookstore that happens to have in stock a book containing a libel. However, Section 581 of the Restatement (Second) of Torts, relying on a few pre-1964 authorities, maintains that distributors can count as having "published" another's defamatory speech *once they are on notice that they are distributing defamatory content and yet continue to distribute it.*[33] In a similar vein, Section 577(2) of the same Restatement and a few lower-court opinions suggest that when a defamatory message is posted on a person's property so as to be visible to the public, the property owner or possessor—if she is on notice of the presence of the defamatory message and does nothing to remove it—publishes that message. On this latter theory, the owner of a bar who learns that someone has scrawled a defamatory statement in one of the bar's bathroom stalls, yet fails to remove it, might face liability to the victim of the libel.[34]

These aggressive (and questionable) extensions of defamation law's concept of publication helped set the stage for the adoption of Section 230(c). So, too, did a legal stretch of a different sort. That stretch involved not an extension of libel doctrine but the transplantation into it of a doctrine whose original home is the law of negligence.

Negligence, Rescue Doctrine, and Good Samaritan Statutes

As we have seen, the tort of negligence subjects to liability persons who carelessly injure others. In doing so, it draws a sharp distinction between "misfeasance" and "nonfeasance." "Misfeasance" refers to a careless course of conduct, whereas "nonfeasance" refers to a careless failure to undertake action. To drive a car carelessly, to make one's premises available to guests without taking care to ensure it is safe for their use, to render professional services in an incompetent manner—each of these is misfeasance. Nonfeasance, by contrast, involves standing by and do nothing in a situation where one could, by acting, save another from injury.

The long-standing (though controversial) default rule of negligence law states that there is no liability for nonfeasance. Generally speaking, one owes no duty to others to make reasonable efforts to protect or rescue them.[35]

---

33. Following a leading treatise, we doubt whether the holdings of these cases—which were decided before the Supreme Court's landmark opinion in *New York Times v. Sullivan*—would survive First Amendment scrutiny today. DAN B. DOBBS, PAUL T. HAYDEN, & ELLEN M. BUBLICK, THE LAW OF TORTS § 522 n. 5 (2d ed. 2011).

34. Hellar v. Bianco, 244 P.2d 757 (Cal. Ct. App. 1952).

35. If the person played a role in placing the other in peril, he may incur a duty to take steps to rescue him or her. Thus, the rule applies mainly to perils brought about by natural causes, a third party, or the imperiled person herself.

However, the rule has well-established exceptions, including for persons who *voluntarily undertake* to protect or rescue another. A person who chooses to rescue or protect another, the courts have said, must exercise reasonable care in effecting the rescue. More to the point, where actors undertake action aimed at saving or protecting another, the common law of negligence regards such undertakings as creating a duty of care, thus surmounting the default no-duty rule that would otherwise be applicable.

To see how the no-duty-to-rescue rule and the undertaking-to-protect exception interact, imagine an off-duty physician who, while driving on a quiet road on a frigid night, happens to pass by the aftermath of single-car crash and observes that the driver has been seriously injured. Under the no-duty rule, if the physician merely drives by, she faces no liability to the crash victim. This result holds even if the physician could have easily rendered assistance that would have prevented the victim from suffering further injuries (for example, even if she could have provided a blanket that would have prevented the victim from suffering frostbite). However, under the undertaking-to-protect exception, if the physician chooses to intervene, and then provides help in a manner that is careless (such as failing to splint an arm properly), she is deemed to have assumed a duty of care to the crash victim, for the breach of which she faces liability.

For reasons that will become clear, we must mention one last aspect of this corner of negligence law. As it turns out, state legislatures have been sufficiently bothered by the common law's treatment of persons such as the imagined physician who chooses to rescue that they have exercised their authority to modify this aspect of negligence law. Specifically, they have enacted statutes—unsurprisingly known as "Good Samaritan" statutes—that shield from negligence liability those who undertake good-faith rescue efforts in emergency situations. By virtue of these statutes, judges and juries no longer have the authority to impose liability on a well-meaning person who chooses to help another in peril. In other words, these statutes largely eliminate the common-law undertaking-to-protect exception that, paradoxically, had left the Good Samaritan in a legally more vulnerable position than her coldhearted fellow citizen.

Cubby, Stratton Oakmont, and the CDA

We said above that at the time the CDA was enacted, ISPs claimed to be at risk of defamation liability based on materials that they themselves did not author. We are now in a better position to understand why. By the early 1990s, lawyers representing defamation plaintiffs had begun to invoke the esoteric publication doctrines mentioned above, as well as an analogue to the undertaking exception to negligence law's no-duty-to-rescue rule, as bases for ISP liability.[36] Two trial judges located in New York—one a federal district judge and one a state trial judge—penned decisions on these issues that helped to set the stage for Section 230(c).

The first was *Cubby v. CompuServe*.[37] CompuServe charged subscribers for access to information via its website, which included a newsletter whose content was provided by a separate company. CompuServe had no employment or contractual relationship with that company, and exercised no control over the newsletter's content. The plaintiff, claiming to have been defamed in the newsletter, argued that CompuServe was subject to liability for having "published" the newsletter. Although the court rejected Cubby's claim, it entertained the possibility that an ISP might be subject to liability if a plaintiff could prove—as Cubby had not proved—that the ISP was on notice of a defamatory comment in a newsletter it made available to its subscribers, yet did nothing to remove it. At that point, the court said, CompuServe could be deemed to have published the defamatory content contained in the newsletter.

The second and more significant decision came in the case of *Stratton Oakmont v. Prodigy*.[38] Prodigy hosted a bulletin board that, according to the plaintiff brokerage firm, defamed the plaintiff by describing it as a corrupt, criminal enterprise.[39] Prodigy had emphasized to subscribers that it was a family-friendly ISP that removed or blocked inappropriate content on its bulletin boards. In certain marketing materials, it had also expressly likened itself to a newspaper whose editors exercise active control over content. The plaintiff, Stratton Oakmont, argued that Prodigy's undertaking

36. Plaintiffs' lawyers also argued for ISP liability on less esoteric grounds, but these arguments seemed destined to fare badly, given courts' consistent refusal to find the publication element of libel satisfied merely by virtue of an actor's having transmitted another's defamatory statement. *See, e.g.,* Lunney v. Prodigy Servs. Co., 723 N.E.2d 539, 542 (N.Y. 1999) (under New York common law, the mere transmission by defendant ISP of an email is akin to transmission of a call by a telephone company and hence not a publication of the email's content).

37. Cubby, Inc. v. CompuServe Inc., 776 F. Supp. 135 (S.D.N.Y. 1991).

38. Stratton Oakmont, Inc. v. Prodigy Servs. Co., 1995 WL 323710 (N.Y. Sup. Ct. May 24, 1995).

39. This characterization turns out to have been true. The activities of the firm and its key executives were later memorably depicted in the film "The Wolf of Wall Street."

to protect users served as a basis for distinguishing this case from *Cubby*, and that Prodigy could be subjected to a libel claim for postings that it failed to take down. The state trial judge, noting that Prodigy had (at least for a period of time) compared itself to a newspaper publisher, held that Prodigy would face liability if the plaintiff were able to show that the bulletin-board posting defamed it, thus applying in libel an analogue to the voluntary rescuer exception to negligence law's rule of no duty to rescue. In sum, *Stratton Oakmont* created an undertaking-to-monitor doctrine to get around the fact that Prodigy itself had not posted the allegedly defamatory statement about Stratton Oakmont.

Rather than continuing to litigate these issues in the courts, ISPs and other players in the emerging internet industry turned to Congress for preemptive statutory protection. As noted above, in doing so they expressed concern about a variety of theories plaintiffs and jurists were generating to support their contention that the publication element of libel claims against ISPs should be deemed satisfied. These theories included the theory of failure-to-remove-upon-notice liability entertained but not adopted by the federal judge in *Cubby*. Primarily, however, they emphasized the bind in which a decision like *Stratton Oakmont* placed ISPs that aimed to monitor for obscene, offensive, or defamatory content. And this, of course, is why the phrase "Good Samaritan" appears in 230(c)'s title. In relevant part, the statute reads as follows:

> **(c) Protection for "Good Samaritan" blocking and screening of offensive material**
> (1) Treatment of publisher or speaker
> No provider or user of an interactive computer service shall be treated as the publisher or speaker of any information provided by another information content provider.
> (2) Civil liability
> No provider or user of an interactive computer service shall be held liable on account of—
>> (A) any action voluntarily taken in good faith to restrict access to or availability of material that the provider or user considers to be obscene, lewd, lascivious, filthy, excessively violent, harassing, or otherwise objectionable, whether or not such material is constitutionally protected; or

(B) any action taken to enable or make available to information content providers or others the technical means to restrict access to material described in paragraph (1).[40]

Quite clearly, Section 230(c) constitutes Congress's effort to do for ISPs in the realm of libel law what state legislatures have done, through their Good Samaritan statutes, to protect persons (such as our imagined off-duty physician) who might otherwise face negligence liability based on voluntarily undertaken rescues. In particular, subsection (c)(2)(A) provides a direct federal analogue in the domain of libel law to the state statutes that have modified the common law of negligence. In doing so, it overrides *Stratton Oakmont's* ruling that ISPs, by voluntarily monitoring content, incur a duty to use care in monitoring. Under 230(c)(2)(A) an ISP's good-faith effort to monitor does not generate such a duty, and hence its careless failure to fulfill that undertaking cannot provide the basis for holding it liable on the ground of having published the material it failed to remove.[41]

This leaves us to make sense of (c)(2)'s predecessor provision, (c)(1). Unfortunately, it is not immediately clear how this subsection relates to the rationales for (c)(2). It is this lack of surface clarity that explains why subsection (c)(1) is at the center of subsequent judicial misinterpretations of the CDA's liability-limiting provision.

Armed with an understanding of the legal and commercial lead-up to *Stratton-Oakmont*, however, the point of subsection (c)(1) can readily be grasped. Some ISPs (like Prodigy) had maintained that they were akin to newspaper publishers, apparently without appreciating the legal perils of doing so. More generally, plaintiffs' lawyers—harnessing borderline theories of publication (such as the theory that on-notice property owners are subject to liability for failures to remove libelous graffiti)—had argued that ISPs should be regarded as having published defamatory statements

---

40. 47 U.S.C. § 230(c) (2018).

41. *Cf.* Olivier Sylvain, *Intermediary Design Duties*, 50 CONN. L. REV. 203 (2018). Sylvain argues that, in light of the ways in which ISPs commercially exploit user data and shape user experiences, ISPs should face liability for enabling users of their services to engage in wrongful conduct such as racial or gender discrimination. In making this argument, he rightly rejects the thought that the CDA entitles ISPs, so far as the law is concerned, to be indifferent to all of the various harms caused by the use of their services, and rightly emphasizes the Act's aim of encouraging Good Samaritan monitoring.

simply because they own the medium through which third parties communicate those statements, and thus have the power to remove the defamatory content from their sites, at least once they are made aware of the problematic content. If this argument were allowed, (c)(2)'s protection against Good Samaritan liability would be for naught. By decreeing that "[n]o provider or user of an interactive computer service *shall be treated as the publisher or speaker* of any information provided by another information content provider," (c)(1) blocks the argument that the publication element of a libel claim against an ISP can be established on any of the esoteric grounds mentioned in the Restatement (Second) of Torts, and advanced by plaintiffs' lawyers in cases like *Cubby*.[42]

The interaction between the common law of defamation and Section 230(c)'s provisions thus closely resembles the interaction, described above, between the common law of negligence and state Good Samaritan statutes. Just as the latter ensure that an undertaking to rescue will not alter the baseline rule that there is no duty to take care to rescue strangers in emergencies, so Section 230(c)(2) ensures that an undertaking to protect users from defamatory or otherwise objectionable third-party postings will not alter the baseline rule that there is no affirmative duty to screen, filter, or remove such postings.

There is, however, a subtle but significant difference between these two areas of tort law. In negligence, the baseline rule of no liability for failure to rescue strangers, as well as its exceptions, have long been well settled,

---

42. Readers will note that Section 230(c)(1) offers its protection not only to "provider[s]" of interactive computer services but also to any "user" of such services. The inclusion of this term has caused some mischief. On first glance it seems to suggest, absurdly, that anyone who is a user of the internet—presumably nearly all persons living in the developed world and many living elsewhere—face no defamation liability, at least if the defamatory content in question is somehow connected to their use of the internet. Directory Assistants, Inc. v. Supermedia, LLC, 884 F. Supp.2d 446 (E.D. Va. 2012) (deeming persons who retrieve defamatory content from websites and then forward it via email to be "users" who, as such, cannot be held liable for that content).

In fact, the addition of the term "user," like Section 230 as a whole, was largely driven by perceived problems associated with *Stratton Oakmont*. In that case, the plaintiff had sued not only the ISP (Prodigy) but also the individual whom Prodigy had hired, as an independent contractor rather than an employee, to monitor the bulletin board on which the allegedly defamatory statement was posted. Statutory protection that applied merely to ISPs and not to others such as the contractor in *Stratton Oakmont* would have done little to spare ISPs from the problems for which they were seeking congressional assistance. By granting immunity to "user[s]" of an ISP, Congress thus aimed primarily to ensure that both the ISP itself and those it hires cannot be held liable merely for rendering others' defamatory statements accessible on the web. See *Zipursky, supra* note 1, at 34.

and the Good Samaritan statutes have helped to ensure that these settled rules will not discourage the provision of assistance to persons facing imminent peril. As compared to negligence law, defamation law, as it existed prior to the CDA's enactment, was clearer in some ways and less clear in others. In the real world of libel litigation, there were no analogues to the established exception to the no-duty-to-rescue rule of common-law negligence for those who choose to undertake a rescue. In practice it was nearly unheard of for a court to recognize an affirmative duty to remove another's defamatory statement. Moreover, mere transmitters of information, such as telephone companies and mail deliverers, faced almost no failure-to-remove defamation liability. Yet there was a paucity of case law on the topic and, as indicated above, some plaintiffs' lawyers and policy wonks had proposed that there should be affirmative duties imposed on ISPs to remove objectionable material, with corresponding liability. Thus, ironically, in order for Congress to *shut down the undertaking-based exception* to the rule of no liability for failure to screen or remove—the shutdown achieved through the enactment of Section 230(c)(2)—it first needed to *solidify the more basic, underlying no-duty-to-screen-or-remove rule*. This is exactly what Section 230(c)(1) does.

Post-CDA Case Law

More than two decades after the CDA was enacted, it is clear that ISPs and website owners and operators got what they wanted from Congress, and then some. In an early, landmark opinion, *Zeran v. America On Line, Inc.*, the federal Court of Appeals for the Fourth Circuit held that Section 230(c) completely protects ISPs from libel claims predicated on the failure to remove a defamatory statement posted by another, no matter how irresponsibly the ISP behaves, and no matter how serious the consequences for the victim of the posting.[43] Although—for the reasons stated above—we believe *Zeran* was correct to construe the CDA as barring notice-based duty-to-remove liability even in extreme situations such as the one facing the plaintiff in *Zeran*, courts have subsequently interpreted Section 230(c) in a much more expansive manner, so as to provide defendants with protections that far exceed the text or purpose of 230(c).

---

43. Zeran v. America Online, Inc., 129 F.3d 327 (4th Cir. 1997), *cert. denied*, 524 U.S. 937 (1998).

Among the most striking misapplications of 230(c) is the courts' use of
the statute to eviscerate the well-established and well-justified republication rule (described above) for internet libels. *Batzel v. Smith*, decided by
the United States Court of Appeals for the Ninth Circuit, is an early and
influential opinion illustrating this point.[44] Batzel, an attorney, sued Cremers, an expert in museum security, alleging that Cremers had sent defamatory statements about her through a listserve and had posted them on
a widely read website that Cremers hosted. The statements in question
were not authored by Cremers, but instead by one Smith, a handyman
whom Batzel had previously employed. In an email to Cremers, Smith
claimed to have proof that Batzel was a descendant of the Nazi Heinrich
Himmler, and that she was in possession of art stolen from Jews during
World War II.

When Batzel sued Cremers for having posted Smith's defamatory statements, Cremers invoked CDA Section 230(c). Specifically, Cremers argued against liability on the basis of subsection (c)(1)—which, again, states
that a "provider or user of an interactive computer service" may not be
"*treated as the publisher or speaker*" of a defamatory posting authored by
someone else. According to this argument, Batzel's claim was barred
because it was predicated on "treat[ing]" Cremers—an internet service
"user"—as a "publisher" of defamatory statements about Batzel that had
been "provided" to Cremers by "another information content provider,"
namely, Smith. In response, Batzel argued that, while Section 230 was
meant to shield defendants from liability for *failure to remove* statements
posted by others, it has no application where a website operator *chooses to
post* a defamatory statement authored by a third party. In such a situation,
Batzel argued, a user such as Cremers has published the statement, notwithstanding the fact that the statement was authored by another, just as a
newspaper is deemed to publish content created by others that its editors
decide to include in its pages.

Over a dissent by Judge Gould, the majority sided with Cremers. The
key passage in the majority opinion is written as a response to the dissent:

> [The dissent] simultaneously maintains that 1) a defendant who
> takes an active role in selecting information for publication is

---

44. Batzel v. Smith, 333 F.3d 1018, 1020 (9th Cir.), *reh'g denied*, 351 F.3d 904 (9th Cir. 2003),
cert. denied, 541 U.S. 1085 (2004).

not immune; and 2) interactive computer service users and providers who screen the material submitted and remove offensive content are immune. These two positions simply cannot logically coexist.

Such a distinction between deciding to publish only some of the material submitted and deciding *not* to publish some of the material submitted is not a viable one. The scope of the immunity cannot turn on whether the publisher approaches the selection process as one of inclusion or removal, as the difference is one of method or degree, not substance.[45]

The panel remanded Batzel's case for further proceedings, but Cremers ultimately prevailed.[46]

Batzel's interpretation has taken root.[47] In case after case involving ISPs and website operators posting content created by others, courts have treated both individuals and entities as entirely at liberty to choose to circulate defamatory statements, even ones they know to be defamatory, and even if out of pure malice, so long as the statements were initially authored by someone else. For example, the New York Court of Appeals has held that the CDA blocks the imposition of liability on a website operator who re-posted statements that the plaintiff was an anti-Semite and a racist who slept with prostitutes and beat his wife.[48] Meanwhile, the California Supreme Court extended the CDA's protections to a defendant who

45. *Id.* at 1032 (citation omitted).

46. Batzel v. Smith, 372 F. Supp. 2d 546, 547 (C.D. Cal. 2005) (entering summary judgment for Cremers against Batzel on procedural grounds). The Court of Appeals remanded for a determination of whether Smith had sent the emails to Cremers intending or expecting them to be posted on Cremers's website. If not, the majority supposed, Cremers's actions would fall outside the scope of Section 230's protections. The Court offered no textual basis for its distinction between a website operator's posting of emails meant by their author to be posted and the operator's posting of emails not meant to be posted. Instead, it claimed (questionably) that this distinction would best serve the CDA's goals of promoting free speech and the development of the internet. *Batzel*, 333 F.3d at 1034–35.

47. With respect to claims against website operators for forms of wrongdoing involving communication apart from defamation, some of the most shockingly expansive invocations of the CDA have been rolled back. For example, the Ninth Circuit reversed a decision that had read Section 230(c) to insulate from legal liability a roommate-matching website that operated in a manner that facilitated discrimination on the basis of race, gender, and sexual preference. Fair Housing Council v. Roommates.Com, LLC, 521 F.3d 1157 (9th Cir. 2008) (en banc). Also, the so-called FOSTA-SESTA package—CDA amendments removing immunity for websites that knowingly facilitate child prostitution (which immunity, remarkably, had previously been recognized by some courts)—was signed into law by President Trump in April 2018.

48. Shiamili v. Real Estate Grp. of N.Y., Inc., 952 N.E.2d 1011 (N.Y. 2011).

posted statements falsely claiming that the plaintiff had been arrested and convicted for stalking.[49] And the Sixth Circuit has ruled that, even if the owner of a website recklessly posts another person's false statement that the plaintiff—identified by name and photograph—suffered from gonorrhea, there could be no liability as a matter of law simply because the statement was authored by someone else.[50]

Batzel's reasoning is deeply flawed. Its core claim is that it would be incoherent to read Section 230(c) to deem a website operator who selects information for publication to be subject to liability yet then to deem immune one who screens and removes defamatory content. This framing of the central issue actually begs the question. The problem can be seen (in the passage quoted above) in the parallel phrases: "deciding to publish only some" and "deciding *not* to publish some . . . ." Neither Batzel nor the dissenting judge was arguing for this distinction. Instead, they pressed a distinction between one who *decides to post certain material* authored by another (while declining to post other of the author's materials) and one who *declines to remove, or block access to, material* posted by another (while deciding to remove or filter other posted material). Under ordinary rules of libel law, a person who posts defamatory material authored by another counts as having published the material in the post. However, it is a mistake to assume that failure to remove, or block access to, certain material posted by others is itself publication. Indeed, the main point of Section 230(c) is *to entrench a rule stating that there is no duty to remove or block someone else's posting,* regardless of whether or not an ISP or user took affirmative steps to remove or block others' postings. Shifting back to the language of defamation doctrine, Section 230(c)'s point is that a failure to remove or block a statement that another person has posted shall not be treated as a case of publishing that statement. Yet the *Batzel* majority—doing what the Section actually forbids—analyzes postings of statements and failure-to-remove posted statements equally as publishings, and then reasons that the provision creates immunity for a website that hosts any content penned originally by someone else, at least if the original author meant for her statement to be posted.

The Ninth's Circuit's crucial oversight highlights a larger point: courts have taken Section 230(c) to repeal a long-standing, well-settled, and fun-

---

49. Barrett v. Rosenthal, 146 P.3d 510 (Cal. 2006).
50. Jones v. Dirty World Entm't Recordings LLC, 755 F.3d 398 (6th Cir. 2014).

damental rule of defamation law—the republication rule—for defamatory statements posted on internet sites. On first blush, the reason behind this extremely pro-defendant interpretation of Section 230(c) is the text itself. Once again, Section 230(c)(1) states as follows:

> No provider or user of an interactive computer service shall be treated as the publisher or speaker of any information provided by another information content provider.

One way to read this text is that if a libel defendant is the user of an interactive computer service who has written, posted, texted, or uttered a defamatory statement, the court must rule for the defendant as soon as it determines that the statement was originally provided to the user by some other person or entity. Cremers was a user of an interactive computer service, and the content of the statement he posted came from an email written by Smith. Thus, on this reading of the statute, Cremers could not be deemed to have published the statements about Batzel and could not be held liable.

Tempting as it might be, this "first-blush analysis" of 230(c)(1), as we will call it, is untenable for several reasons. The most obvious is that this reading of the language would yield extraordinarily broad results. In the United States, almost everyone above a certain (young) age is a "user" of an "interactive computer service." As to any such person, there would be no liability for communicating information provided to him or her by another content-provider. Even if one narrowed the reading to say that there is never liability for *using the internet* to communicate information one has learned from someone else (and this narrowing would already deviate from the more straightforward reading contemplated in the paragraphs above), it would still be bizarrely broad.

Consider the following hypothetical:

> Fortune 500 company F hires a private investigator PI to run a background check on job candidate C for a highly visible managerial position. F receives PI's report on C via a confidential email. In the email, PI asserts that C has had several extramarital affairs, and has twice filed for personal bankruptcy. Although F has learned from other sources that PI's investigative work is highly unreliable and that his statements about C are almost certainly untrue, F nonetheless decided to post PI's

statements on a portion of the company's website accessible to its investors and the financial press. *C* sues *F* for libel.

On the first-blush reading of 230(c)(1), this suit should be dismissed because it calls for *F* to be held liable for the posting of information provided to *F* by another content provider (*PI*). Obviously, this is but one of innumerable examples. Anytime an online journal publishes information that came to it first from some other source it would be free of liability. Indeed, each of us would be free to rebroadcast on the internet—on Twitter, Facebook, or anywhere—any information given to us by someone else. As Judge Gould said (here writing in dissent from the panel's denial of a rehearing en banc in *Batzel*):

> I do not believe that Congress intended to make, or ever would consciously make, the policy choice made by the panel majority. Human reputations, built on good conduct over decades, should be not so easily tarnished and lost in a second of global Internet defamation. Under the panel majority's rule, there might be a remedy against the initial sender, but there is no remedy against the person who willingly chooses, with no exercise of care, to amplify a malicious defamation by lodging it on the Internet for all persons and for all time. Unless this result was commanded by Congress, we should not create such a system.[51]

There is not an ounce of support (other than the superficial appeal of the first-blush reading) for supposing that this wholesale abandonment of the republication rule, only for the internet, was what Congress enacted when it passed the CDA. Needless to say, this reading of the statute is both wildly in derogation of the common law and stands largely to undermine the civil recourse principle as it applies to a basic and long-recognized legal wrong: the wrong of libel.

---

51. Batzel v. Smith, 351 F.3d 904, 910 (9th Cir. 2003) (Gould, J., dissenting from denial of rehearing en banc), *cert. denied*, 541 U.S. 1085 (2004). Judge Gould is not the only federal judge to have identified problems with the overbroad reading of the CDA provided in decisions such as *Batzel*—though none, to our knowledge, has explained precisely where and how courts have gone wrong, or how properly to interpret Section 230(c). *See* Fair Housing Council v. Roommates.Com, 521 F.3d 1157 (9th Cir. 2008) (en banc) (Kozinski, C.J.); Chicago Lawyers' Comm. for Civil Rights Under Law, Inc., v. Craigslist, Inc., 519 F.3d 666 (2008) (Easterbook, C.J.).

Ironically, the first-blush reading is especially untenable on textualist grounds. For one thing, it renders an entire portion of the statute—subsection (c)(2)—superfluous. As construed by *Batzel* and other similarly minded courts, the CDA is akin to a statute containing one provision stating that all persons ages eighteen to forty must register for the military draft, then a second provision stating that all persons ages twenty-eight to thirty-two must register. After all, on the first-blush reading, subsection (c) (1) already tells us that there will be no liability for *any* internet provider or user for content provided to it by another. Necessarily this includes ISPs who engage in filtering. Yet the latter providers receive separate statutory protection under (c)(2)!

This difficulty with the first-blush reading complements another obvious problem posed for it by the plain language of the Act. Recall that the title for the entire Section—not just for Section 230(c)(2)—is "Protection for 'Good Samaritan' blocking and screening of offensive material." On the account favored by the *Batzel* majority and other courts, Section 230(c) provides vastly broader protection from liability than is contemplated by its title.

Finally, and most fundamentally, the broad reading of the Section favored by *Batzel* and other courts ignores or misconstrues Section 230(c) (1)'s use of the phrase "shall be treated as." To see why this is so, consider the following discussion of a hypothetical statute adopted by a state legislature in response to developments in the common law of tort.

Modern products liability law holds *commercial product sellers*—in particular, product manufacturers and retailers—strictly liable for injuries caused by defects in their products. In doing so, it confers certain advantages on plaintiffs, including relieving plaintiffs of the burden of proving fault that they would bear were they instead suing for the tort of negligence. Against this backdrop, suppose creative lawyers representing persons injured while driving rental cars have argued to trial judges, with occasional success, that rental car companies should be subject to the rules of products liability law. Suppose further, however, that in reaction to these developments, the state's legislature enacts a statute titled the Rental Car Fairness Act (RCFA). It contains two substantive sections, as follows:

(1) Treatment of Rental Car Companies as Commercial Sellers.
   No company that rents cars for use on public roads shall be treated as a commercial seller of such cars.

(2) Civil Liability.
    No company that rents cars for use on public roads shall be held strictly liable for injuries caused by a defective rental car on account of any action voluntarily taken in good faith by the company to inspect rental cars for defects.

Section (2) of this imagined statute, like CDA Section 230(c)(2), blocks courts from ruling that a certain type of undertaking by a certain kind of actor that might otherwise generate a tort duty actually generates such a duty. What about Section (1)? Like CDA Section 230(c)(1), it blocks courts from conferring a certain legal status on an actor just by virtue of it being a certain kind of entity: an entity cannot be deemed a "commercial product seller" merely because it is a rental car company. For a court to confer such status on such grounds would be to *treat rental car companies, qua rental car companies, as commercial sellers* of cars. That is exactly what RCFA forbids courts from doing. Yet it hardly follows that, under RCFA, rental car companies are somehow incapable, ever, of selling cars commercially. For example, if a particular rental car company were to diversify its business by creating a division that sells new cars directly to consumers, its status as a rental car company surely would not prevent it from being deemed to have sold commercially the cars *that it in fact sold qua commercial seller* and therefore subject to products liability law.

    The same point holds with regard to the language of Section 230(c)(1) of the CDA. The statute does not provide a blanket immunity for ISPs or internet users for defamatory content authored by another content-provider. Instead it blocks them from being *"treated as"* publishers—that is, from being held to have published a defamatory statement *simply by virtue of being the service or medium through which another's defamatory statement is transmitted* (or simply by having control over the service or medium through which it is transmitted). It says that courts shall not treat internet service providers *qua internet service providers* as publishers (and the same with regard to ISP users). By contrast, the imposition of liability on an ISP for having *actually posted* another's defamatory statement is not forbidden. That would be treating an ISP *qua poster of another's content* as a publisher. Liability in such a case would attach on the ground that the ISP *is* publishing—is a publisher of—that statement.

    All of the foregoing interpretive problems are avoided once one grasps that 230(c)(1)'s rule is not a general provision concerning the permissibility of imposing liability on ISPs or internet users for content created by others, but is instead about preventing courts from treating them as if they have published content provided by another simply by transmitting such content, or by failing to remove it after being on notice of its presence in their systems. Once we see that (c)(1) is only meant to ward off this particular—and particularly aggressive—argument for treating ISPs as having engaged in publication, we can in turn appreciate the necessity for Section (c)(2) as a separate, nonredundant rejection of an undertaking-based exception to the general no-duty rule. As our discussion above indicates, (c)(2) thus operates exactly as do state Good Samaritan statutes with respect to the common law of negligence.

It is ironic that *Batzel's* radical expansion of Section 230(c) stemmed from its rejection of a distinction between posting, on the one hand, and failing to remove, on the other. Section 230(c) was put into place with the goal of preempting plaintiff-friendly applications of the esoteric libel doctrines discussed above, which would have softened the posting/failure-to-remove distinction. The whole point of the statute, in other words, is to *harden* that distinction by preempting state tort law that would recognize a duty to remove content created by others irrespective of any undertaking to filter by the ISP—Section (c)(1)—or based on such an undertaking—Section (c)(2). It is thus striking that, with the no-liability-for-failure-to-remove rule already firmly in place as a matter of federal law, federal courts would read the statute to extend immunity to *active posting* cases as well. This, after all, amounts not to a hardening of the posting/failure-to-remove distinction but instead to its evisceration.

Tort Theory's Contribution

Faced with the foregoing deep dive into libel law and the CDA, readers may wonder what any of this has to do with civil recourse theory, dual constructivism, and tort theory more generally. A lot, in fact.

To begin with, the courts' willingness to abandon, with surprisingly little thought, huge swaths of private actionability for defamation (among other wrongs) plainly belies a rather dim view of a person's right to recourse for wrongs done to her. The courts' propensity to describe the effect of Section 230 by use of the term "immunity" (which nowhere appears in the relevant provisions of the CDA, but instead is a gloss offered by defense lawyers) makes clear that they are content to avoid entirely the question of whether, in a given case, the plaintiff has suffered an injury because of conduct by the defendant that was negligent, reckless, knowing, or even intentional. It is one thing to say that ISPs should be able, at an early stage of litigation, to have dismissed suits against them based on their failure to remove postings by others. It is quite another thing to misread a statute to have effected a wholesale repudiation of the republication rule for internet postings. Doing so manifests a bizarre lack of regard for a person's right to vindication in the face of even deliberate and malicious attacks by others. Civil recourse theory calls attention to this dimension of tort law, which courts seem simply to have ignored or forgotten in their haste to render the internet open and free. In this respect, judicial and scholarly treatments of the CDA capture vividly our claim, made at the end of Chapter 1, that lawyers today are losing their sense of the centrality of the civil recourse principle to our legal practices and traditions.

The skewed reading of Section 230(c) also reflects an impoverished way of thinking about legal wrongs in statutory (and constitutional) interpretation. Defense lawyers have understandably tried to persuade courts that the point of this provision is to ensure that the internet is not overregulated and to promote free speech. Emphasizing these policy rationales has led courts to expand the level of protection it provides. We are seeing, here, the pro-defendant face of dual instrumentalism, now in statutory interpretation. It is easy to dismiss the compensatory needs of plaintiffs in defamation cases; on average, reputational harms strike many as less tangible and less grave than physical harms. From a free speech perspective, moreover, deterrence concerns are downgraded or even rejected in light of worries about "chilling effects." The statute is thus analyzed as establishing a massive "immunity" blocking the operation of tort law, understood as a scheme of deterrence and compensation, whenever an allegedly defamatory statement is communicated via the internet.

A dual constructivist perspective of the sort articulated in Chapter 8 provides judges and lawyers with a better grasp of the meaning of Section 230(c) precisely because it takes seriously the judicial predicament that led to the adoption of this provision. This Section was not enacted on the presumption that the normal operation of state defamation law would generate ISP liability for others' statements, such that a federal immunity was necessary to block such liability. Rather, it addressed a much more specific problem, namely, what courts should and should not do in determining whether the publication element of a libel claim is satisfied if an

ISP hosts someone else's defamatory statement or fails to remove a posting when it is equipped to do so.

Congress has instructed courts that they cannot treat an ISP or user as a publisher simply by virtue of being on notice of another's defamatory posting. It has further instructed them to reach the same result even if the ISP or user chooses generally to filter or remove postings. To be sure, policy reasons led Congress to create this protection, but the problem it was addressing, and the means it chose to address it, can be understood only when one appreciates the common law's long-standing concern for the misfeasance/nonfeasance distinction, and how state legislatures have gone about modifying this aspect of the common law of negligence.

Finally, two aspects of pragmatic conceptualism are displayed in our treatment of this pressing issue of contemporary law. One relates to the problems that tend to arise when courts fail to engage basic tort doctrine. A major driver of *Batzel*'s misinterpretation of the CDA was the Ninth Circuit's dismissiveness of the posting/failure-to-remove distinction. In fact, variants on this distinction are all over tort law, and are crucial to understanding it descriptively (regardless of where one stands normatively).[52] Disregarding them all but guarantees interpretive mistakes.

The second aspect was addressed in Chapter 9. Judicial crafting of common law is but one way in which law is made. Legislative bodies and other political decision-makers play an important role in revising parts of the common law in need of reform. Indeed, legislatures have and should have the capacity to anticipate problems that may arise and as common law develops. Properly understood, this is what CDA Section 230(c) did.

---

52. *Cf.* Benjamin C. Zipursky, *Thinking in the Box in Legal Scholarship: The Good Samaritan and Internet Libel*, 66 J. LEGAL EDUC. 55 (2016) (suggesting that academics' failure to properly interpret CDA Section 230 stems in part from the legal academy's undervaluing of serious descriptive analysis).

Conclusion

Recognizing Wrongs

"WHERE THERE'S A RIGHT, there's a remedy." We began our book by arguing that this ancient legal maxim stands for an important principle of law and political morality—the principle of civil recourse. According to it, when the law recognizes a wrong that involves one person violating a legal right enjoyed by another, it must (ordinarily) grant the victim of the rights-violation an avenue of recourse against the wrongdoer.

Under the heading "the conduct rule theory of rights," we next offered an account of the type of wrong that triggers the civil recourse principle. We also explained why torts exemplify this type. In Anglo-American law, torts are violations of legal directives that simultaneously identify duties not to injure others and rights against being injured by others. Directive-violations of this sort thus generate for victims a claim to recourse in the particular form of redress from wrongdoers.

Shifting from analytic and interpretive to normative claims, we demonstrated that tort law, understood as law for the redress of relational, injury-inclusive wrongs, is a readily justifiable feature of a liberal-democratic regime, akin in many respects to law that provides individuals with the right and the power to vote. Finally, we completed our account of tort law as an instantiation of the principle of civil recourse by demonstrating that compensatory damages awards of the sort to which successful tort plaintiffs are entitled, as well as some punitive damages awards, are cogently and correctly understood as redress, and hence qualify as instances of civil recourse.

Having established that torts are a certain type of wrong, and also that courts and legislatures, by specifying such wrongs and enabling victim-redress, fulfill a political obligation owed by government to members of the polity, we turned to the task of accounting for the particular torts that have tended to be recognized by Anglo-American courts. After first clearing away objections to the treatment of familiar torts such as negligence, nuisance, products liability, and trespass as genuine wrongs, we provided a "constructivist" account of tort law's substance. Rather than treating the various torts as instantiations of a foundational moral principle, this account links their substance to the process of judicial recognition through which they have emerged. Long ago, courts invited individuals to bring before them allegations of "trespass"—of wrongful, injurious conduct. For centuries now, English and American judges, with the aid of juries, have assessed these allegations for their plausibility as measured against prevailing norms. This process of assessment has generated and has increasingly been guided by, a body of decisional law that reflects these norms but also refracts them, in part to accommodate special institutional considerations applicable to legally enforceable norms.

Judicial deployment of this dual constructivist method has been and is the engine through which the various torts have been identified, refined, and revised. In tort cases, courts typically set about identifying duties of noninjury and rights against injury, and they perform this task by fastening on readily recognizable forms of wrongful behavior that interfere with important aspects of individual well-being, including bodily integrity, psychological stability, possession of property, decisional autonomy, and the ability to interact with others on terms that are not distorted (either by misinformation or by true information that others are not entitled to know). This explains why we have the torts of battery and negligence, intentional and negligent infliction of emotional distress, trespass and conversion, and fraud, defamation, and invasion of privacy.

Dual constructivism not only describes the manner in which courts have gone about defining the wrongs of tort, it describes the way that they should do so. The law-articulation and law-application it involves are, after all, well suited to officials whose primary job qualifications are legal training and experience with dispute resolution. Moreover, as we demonstrated in Chapters 9 and 10, a constructivist approach, as compared to instrumentalist alternatives, promises to enable judges better to apply tort law even in today's settlement-dominated, insurance-driven, big-data world.

By way of conclusion, we revisit and amplify our account of the way in which tort law's two basic aspects—its provision of redress and its specification of wrongs—together embody critically important values. We note, first, that the common law of tort is particularly, perhaps uniquely, well-positioned to reinforce and clarify, but also to prompt and guide the revision of, norms of interaction that are crucial to the maintenance of civil society. Second, we consider the relationship of tort law to justice. Specifically, we explain how, notwithstanding our rejection of the corrective justice theorists' contention that tort law aims for the doing of justice between plaintiff and defendant, there is a deep connection between a law of wrongs and redress and the maintenance of a just social and political order.

Finally, having emphasized from the outset that tort law is fundamentally about duties, rights, and wrongs, we consider further what it does and does not mean for courts to be in the business of recognizing wrongs. Here we repair once again to the contrast between two titans of American law: our perennial foil, Oliver Wendell Holmes, and his disciple and fellow pragmatist, Benjamin Cardozo. For Holmes, being a pragmatist went hand in hand with a commitment to skepticism about concepts of right and wrong. Cardozo, by contrast, demonstrated how a judge could adopt a pragmatist approach to legal reasoning while crediting such concepts. Cardozo's path—once so clearly marked and still readily available—is the path forward.[1]

---

1. Although we here emphasize tort law's contributions to certain values or goods, this is not because we believe that it is properly characterized in instrumentalist terms, as a mere means of achieving them. An accurate appreciation of tort law's overall worth must take into account the extent to which it helps maintain an evolving civil society, contributes to the justness of our political arrangements, and allows for the articulation and crystallization of notions of interpersonal wrongdoing, among other things. However, none of these is rightly characterized as tort law's *telos* or purpose.

Duties, Rights, and Civil Society

Suppose one is prepared to accept that there is value in having law that identifies correlative duties and rights of noninjury and that provides some form of enforcement mechanism to discourage breaches, as well as some form of relief to those who suffer rights-violations. Even with this assumption in place, a certain kind of skeptic will argue, we have not made the case for tort law. For we have not explained why this body of law should be developed primarily in a constructivist fashion by judges and juries, nor have we explained why enforcement should involve rights of action, liability, orders to pay damages, and the like. Perhaps instead there should be a Ministry of Deterrence and Compensation staffed by bureaucrats who issue regulations defining socially undesirable conduct, who collect fines for rule violations, and who issue payments to persons who prove they have suffered losses of the sort typically risked or caused by such violations.

In fact, we have said quite a bit about this topic already. We have argued that giving judges the job of reasoning in a constructivist fashion about rights and wrongs helps keep the law in touch with social norms and positive morality. So too does the use of lay jurors to resolve disputes about how legal rules apply in particular cases. And we have argued that the provision of rights of action gives individuals a power to which they are entitled as a matter of liberal-democratic theory, and that they would not enjoy from within a bureaucratic scheme for the provision of deterrence and compensation. Here we aim briefly to build upon these arguments by pointing out a related set of values that are served by having tort law that operates more or less as ours does.

Law is concerned with the maintenance and improvement of the social order. As H. L. A. Hart famously emphasized, it does this as much by enabling as by constraining behavior.[2] Contract law, for example, plays a crucial role in allowing people to engage in mutually beneficial transactions. Property law permits and encourages people to undertake and invest themselves or their assets in certain kinds of activities and projects. In a different way, tort law—even though it is largely a law of proscriptions— underwrites certain valuable modes of social interaction. It does so both by setting the terms on which they must occur and by standing ready to hold each of us responsible to those with whom we interact.

2. H. L. A. HART, THE CONCEPT OF LAW 27–28 (2d ed. 1994).

As we observed in our first co-authored work, and as John Gardner has more recently emphasized, a good deal of the value in everyday life is bound up with various kinds of relationships.[3] These range from familial relations and friendships to commercial dealings and even to the sort of transitory relationships that sometimes obtain between total strangers. Various bodies of law matter to these relationships. Obviously, for example, family law and property law play a crucial role in shaping family dynamics. Tort law plays a comparable role in defining and supporting a range of relationships. Consider one such relationship: that of doctor and patient. It is governed by certain norms and expectations that find expression in, are reinforced by, and at times are revised under the influence of, medical malpractice law.

Medicine is a heavily regulated profession, both internally (through professional licensing regimes) and externally (through law enforcement). Tort law has a particular role to play in sustaining and shaping it. As we observed in Chapter 10, insofar as courts have been cautious about identifying duties of care owed by physicians to nonpatients, they have done so in recognition of, and to reinforce, the physician's duty of loyalty to her patient. In addition, the fact that doctors owe their patients a tort duty of competent treatment—one largely immune to contractual waiver—contributes to the maintenance of professional norms and the meeting of patients' expectations about the quality of the care they will receive. In some instances, courts have shaped tort law in ways that have probably altered the terms of the doctor–patient relationship. For instance, the well-known line of "informed consent" decisions growing out of the D.C. Circuit's 1972 decision in *Canterbury v. Spence* have likely induced physicians to adopt a broader understanding of their duty to disclose to patients information about the risks and benefits of alternative courses of treatment.[4]

The fact that tort law contains rules of conduct is only part of the story. Perhaps one could just as easily have such rules issued and enforced by a state's Board of Medicine, or some other regulator. The fact that these rules have been developed and applied by judges charged with deploying constructivist methods of reasoning has meant that they have been crafted with sensitivity (though not complete deference) to professional norms, as

---

3. John C. P. Goldberg & Benjamin C. Zipursky, *The Moral of* MacPherson, 146 U. PA. L. REV. 1733 (1998); JOHN GARDNER, FROM PERSONAL LIFE TO PRIVATE LAW (2018).
4. 464 F.2d 772 (D.C. Cir.), *cert. denied*, 409 U.S. 1064 (1972).

well as social norms more generally. In other words, the articulation of the substantive law of medical malpractice has not been a technocratic effort to engineer rules that achieve appropriate levels of aggregate welfare. Instead it has been a matter of lawyers, juries, and judges reasoning about extant legal rules, the legitimate expectations of patients, and applicable norms. Thus, in *Canterbury* and its progeny, courts both detected and advanced a revised understanding of the doctor–patient relationship that rendered it less paternalistic than it historically had been by requiring physicians to enable patients to have more of a say about certain treatment decisions.

Tort law's linkage of substantive norms and liability also gives those norms a particular, "directed" character. The fact that malpractice goes hand in hand with potential liability conveys in a concrete and vivid way that the norms in question involve relational duties and corresponding rights. Doctors who commit malpractice do not merely behave badly: they mistreat their patients. And doctors who commit malpractice do not merely face sanctions: they face liability to their patients at the demand of their patients. Responsibility in this domain takes the form of answerability to particular persons, and answerability of this sort reinforces the notion that doctor–patient is a salient relationship.

There is another distinctive aspect of tort law as a body of recognized wrongs to which liability attaches. Its rules and standards, one might say, occupy a space between the more-or-less voluntarily assumed obligations of contract, on the one hand, and state-imposed obligations of criminal and regulatory law, on the other. As a body of law that tracks, refines, and revises norms of interpersonal interaction, tort law is neither voluntarist nor statist, but instead an outgrowth of what is sometimes called "civil society." It builds on and reinforces rights and duties that people tend to recognize when they deal with each other, in part by announcing that each of us is vulnerable to being held accountable to others for violating those rights and breaching those duties. We don't meant to suggest that other bodies of law have nothing to do with the recognition and maintenance of civil society. At least in some respects, criminal law exists to respond to particularly serious threats to the social order.[5] But tort law's less "vertical" and more

---

5. For a recent articulation of this idea, see Joshua Kleinfeld, *Reconstuctivism: The Place of Criminal Law in Ethical Life*, 129 HARV. L. REV. 1485 (2016).

"horizontal" character—its emphasis on what we owe each other and the ways in which we are accountable to each other—makes it distinctively a law of civil society.

Nothing in the foregoing is meant to offer or rely on a starry-eyed picture of tort law. Like any institution, and certainly any body of law, tort law not only can misfire in particular cases, it can misfire more generally. Often the problem is that its rules and structures have come to sit poorly with the realities of the interactions to which they are meant to apply, a phenomenon that in turn frequently results from changes in practices and social norms. This is why, at various times, in various settings, legislatures have rightly adopted reforms that promise to handle certain interactions better than tort law is handling them. Workers' compensation laws, enacted in the early twentieth century to supplant negligence law as applied to employee injuries caused by unsafe work conditions, are one salient and important example of salutary tort reform. In the doctor–patient setting, various sensible reforms (along with many ill-considered reforms) of both substantive and remedial tort rules have likewise been adopted or considered.[6]

The discussion in this section has relied heavily on the example of the doctor–patient relationship. Other relationships that have been central to the development of tort law would have served just as well, including carrier–passenger, hotel–guest, school–student, and so forth. Some critics might find problematic our invocation of "special" relationships such as these. Indeed, they might say that it is emblematic of the "retro" nature of our approach. Modern mass industrialized polities are heterogeneous and dominated by anonymous interactions. A discussion of tort law's importance as a sustainer and reformer of civil society is thus out of touch and out of place. Law in modern industrialized societies can only be a top-down, technocratic affair. (So the critique would go.)

---

6. This is not to deny that workers' compensation systems have problems of their own. One example of a possibly salutary (or at least facially plausible) bit of tort reform is Florida's Birth-Related Neurological Injury Compensation Association ("NICA"), enacted in 1988. Among physicians, obstetricians are particularly vulnerable to huge damage awards in malpractice cases. NICA seeks to address this problem as follows: if a child suffers permanent neurological injuries during childbirth, and the obstetrician who delivered the child is a participant in NICA, the child is eligible to obtain compensation for certain medical expenses on a no-fault basis, without pursuing litigation. This compensation scheme is funded by tax dollars and by contributions from participating physicians.

These objections carry little weight. Centuries ago, tort law may have been predominantly concerned to articulate norms governing "thicker" relationships. Yet even back then, stranger–stranger interactions were hardly unknown and hardly went unaddressed by tort law.[7]

Moreover, the notion of "anonymous" interactions needs careful unpacking. Stranger-to-stranger encounters are themselves norm-governed, in part thanks to tort and other bodies of law. The relation of a manufacturer of a mass-produced product to users of the product might be rightly described as anonymous and impersonal. Yet the very point of decisions such as Cardozo's in *MacPherson v. Buick Motor Co.*[8] and Traynor's in *Greenman v. Yuba Power Products, Inc.*,[9] is to identify the rights and responsibilities that attend this relation. Hence both, albeit on different terms, recognized the wrong of a manufacturer causing injury to a user through the sale of an unduly dangerous product. Manufacturer–consumer, no less than doctor–patient, is a salient relationship in modern civil society, and the terms of that relationship have been set in part by tort law. The same is true for an array of stranger–stranger interactions.

Understanding the relation between persons matters even where there is no personal relationship between them. Consider the anonymous interactions that many take to be the hallmark of modern tort law—the automobile accident. Users of the public roads are no less aptly described as bearing a relation to one another than are manufacturer and consumer. A driver on the road does not need to have met, or know anything about, the driver next to him in order to appreciate that, because they "share the road," they owe various obligations to one another, including an obligation to take care against colliding. Our interactions with one another as drivers, consumers, and the like take place within, not apart from, civil society.

It is also worth emphasizing that the tort process—which empowers claimants to file complaints of having been wronged, and thereby invites courts to consider what has counted as a legal wrong and what should so count—is well-designed to serve as a mechanism of revision, not just reinforcement. We have long held out *MacPherson* as exemplary. We have

---

7. J.H. BAKER, AN INTRODUCTION TO ENGLISH LEGAL HISTORY 409 & n. 40 (4th ed. 2002) (noting fifteenth-century English court decisions holding property owners liable for injuring passersby).

8. 111 N.E. 1050 (1916).

9. 377 P.2d 897 (1963).

done so because it clearly instantiates a wrongs-and-redress conception of tort law and negligence in particular, and because Judge Cardozo's landmark opinion deftly deploys dual constructivist methods. But it is also a prototype of the common law's capacity for critical engagement and revision. And it is hardly alone. Many widely heralded modern decisions—including *Canterbury*, *Escola v. Coca Cola Bottling Co.*, and other opinions discussed in this book—can be understood on similar terms. Much the same can be said of the scholarly analysis famously provided by Warren and Brandeis, as well as Prosser (notwithstanding his instrumentalist proclivities), that recognized in the interstices of case law previously unrecognized wrongs involving invasions of privacy.[10]

We close this section with an analogy designed to emphasize, as we did in Chapter 10, the contemporary relevance of our approach. As many have noted, the digital revolution has changed the way we relate to one another, sometimes for better, sometimes for worse. Downsides have included the ways in which social media distorts and disrupts various forms of discourse, including public political discourse, as well as the discourse we know best from our professional lives—that of academic communities. Because popular platforms enable speech that is anonymous and untraceable, and because they reward bombast and snark, they threaten to undermine certain ways of communicating, even as they create new ones. To be clear, it is not the refined metaphors of white-glove civility we worry about losing in the internet era. The dismantling of such barriers is, to our way of thinking, all to the good. (Our references to "civil society," like our references to "civil recourse," are not meant to evoke some sort of refined, aristocratic notion of "civility.") Rather, it is reasoned and respectful exchange that we—along with a gaggle of aging baby-boom pundits—see as imperiled.

The troubled commerce of internet discourse is the tip of the iceberg in 2020. It is possible that, as we noted in our discussion of the Communications Decency Act, tort law's lack of applicability to the internet has been part of the problem. That, however, is not our present point: our reference to social media in the prior paragraph was offered by way of analogy. The suggestion instead is that a world without tort law would in

---

10. Samuel D. Warren & Louis D. Brandeis, *The Right to Privacy*, 4 Harv. L. Rev. 193 (1890); William L. Prosser, *Privacy*, 48 Cal. L. Rev. 383 (1960).

some respects be a world that might suffer from some of the problems associated with discourse that takes place through modern social media. Tort law helps to construct relations of various kinds, and to preserve accountability and expectations associated with them. In the absence of tort law, we may have a harder time establishing and maintaining such relationships. It is, potentially, a place in which we will find it more difficult to recognize each other as fellow members of the same civil society. Such a world, of course, will still have law. But it will be law more in the voice of Hobbes and Austin than Cardozo and Traynor—state-issued commands about how each of us must behave, rather than rules reflecting norms of interaction.

Tort law is all about recognizing wrongs. It is equally about recognizing each other. Each of us has a claim on others, just as others have claims on each of us. In this respect, tort law stands both to reinforce and revise an important moral dimension of social life—the dimension sometimes expressed through the idiom of civil society.

Justice: Distributive, Corrective, Dynamic, and Constitutive

We maintain that our reconstruction of tort law, though grounded in history and tradition, is neither dated nor nostalgic. Today's courts—no less than those of the past—articulate rules and standards of right and wrong, make themselves available for claims of redress, and apply the method of dual constructivism in doing so. By so proceeding, they fulfill a basic political obligation and deliver various goods, including, as we have just argued, support for civil society and its reform.

Some readers will notice that we have not emphasized a concept or value often associated with approaches to tort law that give prominent place to rights, duties, and the like. This is the concept of *justice*. Indeed, in Chapter 9 we suggested that, while understandable, scholarly calls for courts to treat tort cases as opportunities to pursue distributive justice have been misguided. In this section, after a quick dip into intellectual history, we explain the ways in which our wrongs-and-redress account of tort law is or is not correctly understood as a justice-based theory of tort.

Neglected by academics in the first half of the twentieth century, justice reemerged as a central topic in political and legal theory with the publication, in 1971 and 1974, respectively, of John Rawls's A *Theory of Justice* and Robert Nozick's *Anarchy, State, and Utopia*. Against the backdrop of the civil rights movement and Great Society ideals, these works fomented lively debates, particularly with respect to questions of *distributive* justice. Law professors were not reluctant to join in. George Fletcher adapted Rawls's ideas to tort theory in a prominent 1972 article titled "Fairness and Utility in Tort Theory."[11] The next year Richard Epstein published his equally famous "A Theory of Strict Liability." The opening pages of that piece emphasized the widespread acknowledgment "of certain questions of 'justice' or 'fairness' rooted in common sense beliefs that cannot be explicated in terms of economic theory," and that hence required explication.[12] In sum, by the early 1970s justice and fairness were back—both were regarded as concepts suited to serious philosophical analysis.

Notwithstanding Fletcher's early Rawls-inspired intervention, as well as the work of important successors, including Gregory Keating,[13] the reanimation of justice-oriented theory among torts scholars has tended to focus less on distributive justice and more on *corrective* justice. Three figures in North America are principally responsible for this focus: Epstein at Chicago, Jules Coleman at Yale, and Ernest Weinrib at Toronto. Epstein was and remains a libertarian, enchanted by Locke and schooled in classical legal thought. Coleman is a nonlawyer moral and legal philosopher who came of age as a scholar in the 1970s and who brought to bear a Calabresian understanding of tort law as fundamentally concerned with loss distribution, but also a broader rights-oriented perspective on normative questions.[14] Weinrib is a law professor, classicist, and legal theorist immersed in both Aristotelian and Kantian thought.[15]

Epstein, Coleman, and Weinrib all started from the premise that tort law is not profitably analyzed as a system of distributive justice. All saw that there was something "localized" and "private" about it, given its focus on interpersonal interactions rather than on institutions and policies that aim directly to address the distribution of wealth and opportunities. Yet they also recognized that tort nonetheless could plausibly be linked to some notion(s) of justice. Weinrib in particular was drawn to

11. George P. Fletcher, *Fairness and Utility in Tort Theory*, 85 Harv. L. Rev. 537 (1972).

12. Richard A. Epstein, *A Theory of Strict Liability*, 2 J. Legal Stud. 151, 151–52 (1973).

13. *See, e.g.,* Gregory C. Keating, *Rationality and Reasonableness in Tort Theory*, 48 Stan. L. Rev. 311 (1996).

14. Jules L. Coleman, Risks and Wrongs (1992); Jules L. Coleman, *Corrective Justice and Wrongful Gain*, 11 J. Legal. Stud. 421 (1982).

15. Ernest J. Weinrib, Corrective Justice (2012); Ernest J. Weinrib, The Idea of Private Law (1995).

Aristotle's discussion in the *Nicomachean Ethics*. Aristotle treated distributive justice as a somewhat geometrical concept employed in the ascertainment of who gets which fraction of some good. Corrective justice, by contrast, pertains to the undoing of a transaction between two parties, and in that way is arithmetic. Given the choice of characterizing tort law in terms of distributive justice or corrective justice (understood more or less on Aristotelian terms), almost any philosophically oriented tort theorist would have to have chosen corrective justice. And that is what each of these scholars did.

From our vantage point, it was a good thing that these scholars and others (unlike some of their predecessors) were willing to speak the language of justice when analyzing tort law and private law more generally. Nonetheless it is arguably unfortunate that they latched on to corrective justice as the perceived best alternative to distributive justice. Particularly on Aristotle's rendition, corrective justice—the justice of undoing a matching wrongful loss and wrongful gain—is ill-suited to torts, which often involves losses with no corresponding gains. Perhaps it would have been better (though obviously less gripping) for these scholars to have written of "justice, but not primarily in the distributive, goods-allocation sense."[16]

Many scholars have observed that our tort theory resembles corrective justice theory, and they are reasonable to do so. Like Weinrib, we take tort law to be a scheme of legal rights and duties, and we think it is crucial that those duties are relational in analytic structure (as discussed in Chapter 3). We also share his rejection of reductive and instrumental accounts of tort concepts, insisting that they be interpreted rather than ignored, dismissed out of hand, or run roughshod over. On our account, too, tort law is in certain respects private law. Tortfeasors are held to account because they have wronged others and they bear responsibility for the wrongful injuries they have inflicted. Courts respect the rights of individuals not to be legally wronged, and their rights to use the courts to remedy wrongs done to them.

These overlaps are no accident. We have been deeply influenced by Weinrib's work, as well as by the work of other corrective justice theorists, including Coleman, Stephen Perry, Arthur Ripstein, Scott Hershovitz,

---

16. *Cf.* Richard W. Wright, *Liability for Possible Wrongs: Causation, Statistical Probability, and the Burden of Proof*, 41 LOY. L.A. L. REV. 1295, 1296 & n. 6 (2008) (suggesting that "interactive justice" would better fit tort law than "corrective justice").

and others.[17] But overlap is not identity, and it is important to see both points of agreement and points of divergence. We see Weinrib's corrective justice theory as making at least two distinct claims about the justice of tort law. At the risk of terminological overload, we will deem these to be claims about *constitutive justice*, on the one hand, and claims about *dynamic justice*, on the other.[18]

To speak of constitutive justice is to speak of the structural features of a polity that contribute to making it just. Ironically (given that he is frequently miscast as exclusively being a theorist of distributive justice), Rawls's own theory has a lot to say about constitutive justice. After all, as others have emphasized, his "difference principle" figured in his theory as the second principle of justice, ranked lexically below the first.[19] The first holds that "each person is to have an equal right to the most extensive scheme of equal liberties compatible with a similar scheme of liberties for others."[20] While this principle is patently egalitarian in spirit and in this sense might be called a principle of distributive justice, to call it this would be misleading. It is not about the distribution of goods or wealth. It states that the only restrictions on liberty that are permissible are those that are necessary to preserve the equally important basic liberties of others. Much of Rawls's work pertains to what sorts of structures and constitutional safeguards would—in a manner commensurate with self-interested rationality, with our sense of justice, and with our natural duties—properly implement this scheme of basic liberties. In these respects, at least, Rawls offered a theory of constitutive justice.

Though not a Rawlsian in other respects, Weinrib's account of tort law (and private law more generally) as a scheme of legal rights and relational duties among private parties seems implicitly to treat it as an element of a just political order, and thus seems to offer an account of tort

17. ARTHUR RIPSTEIN, PRIVATE WRONGS (2016); ARTHUR RIPSTEIN, EQUALITY, RESPONSIBILITY AND THE LAW (1999); Stephen R. Perry, *The Moral Foundations of Tort Law*, 77 IOWA L. REV. 427 (1992); Scott Hershovitz, *Treating Wrongs as Wrongs: An Expressive Argument for Tort Law*, 10 J. TORT L. 405 (2017).

18. Benjamin C. Zipursky, *Integrity and the Incongruities of Justice: A Review of Daniel Markovits's A Modern Legal Ethics: Adversary Democracy in a Democratic Age*, 119 YALE L.J. 1948, 1987 (2010).

19. *See, e.g.*, ROBERT B. TALISSE, ON RAWLS 44 (2001) (observing that the difference principle applies to institutions that distribute wealth, status, and authority—but not liberty, which is governed by Rawls's first principle of justice).

20. JOHN RAWLS, A THEORY OF JUSTICE 53 (Rev'd ed. 1999).

law as constitutive justice.[21] When one person does a wrong and another suffers it, an injustice arises. A legal system that makes no attempt to recognize such episodes for what they are—that has no enforceable rules or standards that give expression to the duties we owe one another and the rights we have against one another—is a legal system that is unjust (even if just in other respects). Conversely, the incorporation of such rules and standards contributes to the justness of such a system.

At the same time, like certain versions of retributive justice theory in criminal law, Weinrib's corrective justice theory offers an account of how tort law's operation achieves justice in individual cases. Here we find a notion of dynamic justice at work. Dynamic justice is the sort of justice that is invoked when prosecutors, judges, and victims'-rights advocates say things like: "Justice must be done; the killer needs to go to prison for a long time!" Of course, Weinrib's theory is a theory of private law, not criminal law—it has nothing to do with retribution or punishment. Instead he maintains that private law, by connecting primary rights and duties of conduct to secondary rights and duties of repair, allows for the restoration of a "normative equilibrium" between the "doer" and "sufferer" of the wrong. On his view, tort law is like criminal law in that it provides a mechanism through which an injustice is undone, rectified, or corrected. When Weinrib claims that private law instantiates the principle of *"corrective* justice," he is asserting that courts in tort cases (and other private-law cases), by imposing liability and thus seeing to it that wrongdoers perform their duties of repair, *do* justice.

The theory offered in this book can be understood as a constitutive justice theory of tort law. This much is evident in our argument in Chapter 4 that tort law's instantiation of the political principle of civil recourse helps render justifiable the exercise of political and legal authority in a liberal democracy. More generally, we believe that our system's incorporation

---

21. Ripstein's *Private Wrongs*, which was self-consciously written, in part, in defense of his colleague Weinrib's views on private law, makes this claim of constitutive justice even more clearly. Scholars writing outside of the corrective justice framework have also argued that tort law makes a crucial contribution to the justness of the regime of which it is a part. *See, e.g.*, Hanoch Dagan & Avihay Dorfman, *Just Relationships*, 116 COLUM. L. REV. 1395 (2016) (arguing that the central value of tort law and other departments of private law is that they help ensure that individuals interact with one another on just terms); Mark Geistfeld, *Compensation as a Tort Norm*, in PHILOSOPHICAL FOUNDATIONS OF THE LAW OF TORTS 65, 84 (J. Oberdiek ed., 2014) (arguing that law that enables injury victims to obtain compensatory damages is "essential for implementation of a liberal egalitarian scheme of distributive justice").

of a body of law that identifies relational duties of noninjury and rights of noninjury, and that enables those who suffer violations of those rights to obtain recourse in the form of redress, contributes to its being a just system.

Where we have previously parted ways with Weinrib, and continue to do so, is in our rejection of the idea that tort law is about doing dynamic justice.[22] "Rejection" is perhaps an overstatement. As Andrew Gold and Arthur Ripstein have (independently) stressed to us, it is common for judges and lawyers to connect tort law to the capacity of courts to restore what was wrongfully disturbed and, in so doing, to do justice. There is nothing inapt about such comments, so long as they are placed in proper context. It is surely the case that the law of torts *sometimes* succeeds in moving things from a less just to a more just state of affairs. Moreover, unlike functions often imputed to tort law by instrumentalists, such as "deterrence" and "compensation," the doing-of-justice through tort litigation is not haphazardly connected to the latter's core features. When a more just state of affairs is brought about through tort litigation, that outcome is achieved through an institution provided by the state in the name of justice (in the constitutive sense). Thus, when a tort plaintiff exercises the right of action that is provided to her as a matter of constitutive justice, and is thereby compensated, the system sometimes noncoincidentally serves the function of rectification, or dynamic justice.

This connection notwithstanding, Weinrib and others err in positing a deep connection between tort law and dynamic justice. In fact, three features of tort law—the nature of private rights of action, the strict or unforgiving terms on which tort law defines wrongs, and the realities of tort litigation—ensure that there will often be a gap between them.

Part of what it means for a plaintiff to have a right of action is for her to have near-complete discretion to choose to bring a claim: it is the plaintiff's

---

22. As noted in Chapter 5 and elsewhere, we have other differences with corrective justice theorists, particularly on the question of how to characterize tort liability. Specifically, we reject the notion that a tortfeasor, by committing a tort, incurs a legal duty of repair, as opposed to a legal liability corresponding to the victim's right of action. Relatedly, whereas many corrective justice theorists seem to regard the tortfeasor's duty of repair as linked analytically to her primary duty of noninjury, we treat the connection as substantive. An unprivileged violation of a right against noninjury recognized by tort law does not generate a right of action because the latter is somehow inherent in the former. Rather, it does so by operation of the principle of civil recourse.

power, the plaintiff's right, the plaintiff's choice. Thus, to have a right of action is to be able to press it even when doing so is selfish, heartless, or unjust (though not when it is abusive in certain senses).

The opposite is the case in criminal law. Prosecutors not only have the liberty to decide which charges to press, in part by reference to considerations of justice, they have a duty to do so. Tort law and other bodies of private law recognize no counterpart to this prosecutorial obligation. To offer a variant on a familiar example in the torts literature, a wealthy and well-insured business mogul might well have a right of action for damages against a cyclist of modest means who carelessly scratches the mogul's luxury car. A decent person in the mogul's position would let it go. However, thanks to tort law, it is open to her to sue and to recover, in principle, thousands of dollars in compensatory damages. If the mogul were successfully to press her claim, forcing the cyclist to hand over $5,000, in turn preventing the cyclist from obtaining valuable services for her special-needs child, there would be little reason to suppose that justice was being done.

This problem—call it the problem of the overreaching plaintiff—is deepened by the unforgiving nature of the standards of liability in tort law. Individuals and companies face substantial vulnerabilities to potential plaintiffs, and these vulnerabilities are on terms that do not necessarily connect with culpability in a moral sense. Add to this that there are plenty of opportunists in our world, and there is every reason to think that many potential tort plaintiffs might have little concern about what will happen to those whom they sue. Moreover, it is not the job of a judge or a jury to figure out what the just outcome will be when overreaching plaintiffs do sue. It is their job to impose liability if the plaintiff proves her case. In such instances, it seems disingenuous to say that tort law delivers justice in the dynamic sense.

In emphasizing the problem of the overreaching plaintiff, our point is *not* to trash tort law as a haven for sharks or leeches. Nor is to deny that justice is sometimes—perhaps often—done in tort cases. Rather, we mean to stress a more basic point: the only way that tort law will see to it that justice is done is if plaintiffs' choices systematically conform with what dynamic justice requires (whatever that might be), and we see no reason to believe that they will.

There is another, equally important reason to reject the thought that tort law is an institution of dynamic justice. Among lawyers and law professors it is today trite to observe that civil litigation is overwhelmingly not about trials and verdicts. Settlements are the order of the day. As we argued in Chapter 9, this phenomenon is not particularly threatening to the idea of tort as a law of wrongs and redress. It is more threatening to the idea of tort law as a mode of dynamic justice. The conferral of rights of action generates a power to force a settlement in a larger number of cases, even when justice, as measured by the corrective justice ideal of making whole, is not being done. And in more cases still, an enforceable system of rights and duties provides no grounds for liability because of the absence of a plausible allegation of a tort inflicted upon the plaintiff, even though a body of law committed to implementing a fair or just reallocation of losses might dictate liability.

Again, we do not mean to reject the value of doing justice among private parties, or to deny that tort law's capacity to do justice might be among the reasons it is worth having. The doing of justice—like deterrence and compensation—is something that tort law can sometimes deliver. But this is quite different from saying tort law is a system for the doing of justice. It is not. Tort law is a system of relational directives, rights and duties, and powers and liabilities. Interpretive fidelity to the common law of torts requires that these features be acknowledged as central to it. Tort law's capacity to deter, to compensate, or to do justice merit consideration in an overall appraisal of it, but none carves at its joints.[23] (A

---

23. Principles of corrective justice might have a substantial role in guiding our thinking about the maintenance, transformation, or revision of tort law. Legislators and voters no doubt think that a company that has lied about the efficacy of safety devices in its cars should compensate those who bought the cars and were injured because the devices were unsound. Partly this is out of a belief that the company should take responsibility for what it did. But it may also reflect a belief that it is just for a company that has wrongfully caused harm to be forced to compensate those it has harmed.

Conversely, consider the skepticism that sometimes is expressed about recoveries in less straightforward cases. Some members of the public would bridle at the thought of a young adult recovering from a perfume manufacturer for burns she suffered after spraying the perfume on a lit candle. Insofar as critics object to recoveries of this sort, they do so in part based on the perception (apt or not) that recovery would be *unjust*—that the failure to warn users against the obvious risk of igniting the perfume did not constitute a wrongful injuring of the victim.

In our view, lawyers, legislators, judges, and citizens are right to build corrective justice considerations (among others) into their evaluation of the merits of the common law of torts. Concepts of corrective justice, like concepts of fairness, responsibility, civil recourse, deterrence, efficiency, compensation, equality, social harmony, and many others, have a place in thinking critically about the various aspects of the law of torts facing possible legislative revi-

professional baseball team might at times be a source of civic pride. But professional baseball is a sport, not a civic pride delivery system.)

It is unclear to us how Weinrib might respond to the foregoing discussion. Perhaps he would disclaim that his theory incorporates a notion of "dynamic" justice. (It is, after all, our term, not his.) He might indeed insist that he has always used the term "corrective justice" to refer to constitutive justice—the scheme of rights and duties as among private parties, at least so long as the rights in question include the right to obtain compensation for having been wronged, and the duties include the duty to provide such compensation. The question of the appropriateness or inappropriateness, virtue or vice, justice or injustice of actually bringing the claim, he might say, is simply outside of the scope of his theory. If this were so, then he would have been correct all along to claim that there is little space between corrective justice theory and civil recourse theory. However, we would then insist—as we did in Chapter 5—that the label "corrective justice" is misleading, and that the language of "civil recourse" and "redress for wrongs" is truer to the phenomena being described.

As we have explained here (building on Chapter 4), at the core of the union of civil recourse, wrongs, and dual constructivism lies the recognition of duties not to mistreat and rights against mistreatment, of an entitlement to hold others accountable, and of the state's responsibility to provide law for the redress of wrongs. By institutionalizing in civil law a domain of rights and duties and empowering individuals to hold others to account, the law of torts both promotes our capacity to treat one another as we are obligated to and constitutes one important respect in which our society is a just polity.

Two Paths of the Law

Tort law has links to justice. But it is most immediately about rights, wrongs, and redress. This is in part why we have chosen to call our book *Recognizing Wrongs*. Yet we have acknowledged from the get-go that talk

---

sion. As we emphasized in Chapter 9, this broader domain of critical assessment also requires critics to incorporate the best information available on how various aspects of the law actually play out in the real world.

of rights and wrongs raises problems of its own. In particular, as we noted in Chapters 1 and 2, it sticks in the craw of many modern legal academics. In this, our final section, we return to that topic and, with it, to the remarkable but in many ways unfortunate legacy of Oliver Wendell Holmes.

Though it was published when the horse and buggy had yet to give way to the motor car, Holmes's essay "The Path of the Law" remains a staple for American law students.[24] It does so because it gives voice to a sentiment that is still widely shared and deeply felt among legal academics in the United States: that lawyers, judges, and scholars must resist the temptation to adopt an easy or self-satisfied moralism about their subject. Clients don't look to lawyers to be schooled about their moral rights and duties. And the notion that law is about the state holding us to the requirements of morality seems off. Of course laws often set standards of conduct. But lawmakers are not philosophers, priests, or prophets. The standards *they* adopt reflect practical and policy considerations, not rarified notions of right or justice.

Some of our fiercest critics have contended that our tort theory runs afoul of Holmes's injunction. In particular, Judges Calabresi and Posner have accused us of inviting judges to rely on unvarnished moral intuition.[25] Anyone who has worked through our doctrinally focused writings (including Chapter 10 of this book) would know that we are, if anything, prone to overemphasize the degree to which judges can find the guidance they need in decisional law and statutory language. It is true, though, that our first co-authored works feature the words "moral" and "duty" in their respective titles, and we have insisted here and elsewhere that torts are wrongs. We have also aligned ourselves with Cardozo and Dworkin, two jurists who in different ways posited a deep if complicated connection between law and morality. And we have offered an account of normative reasoning in law that is noninstrumentalist, while contending that tort law (in some version) is an element of the basic structure of a just society.

These indications notwithstanding, we are not moralists about law, or at least not moralists in a way that leaves us vulnerable to criticisms of the

---

24. Oliver W. Holmes, *The Path of the Law*, 10 HARV. L. REV. 457 (1897).

25. Guido Calabresi, *Civil Recourse Theory's Reductionism*, 88 IND. L.J. 449 (2013); Richard A. Posner, *Instrumental and Noninstrumental Theories of Tort Law*, 88 IND. L.J. 469 (2013).

sort that have been levelled against us. It is important to see why not. The nearer we come to moralism, some might say, the more tenuous our claim to being pragmatists. And there is a huge risk for our project if it is understood to advocate for the view that judges facing hard cases should first decide what is morally right and then import those conclusions into the law. Holmes-inspired Realists and instrumentalists have made a lot of hay by painting their adversaries as vastly too sanguine about the competence of judges properly to deploy notions of right, fairness, or justice.

So we will here address some lingering questions about our understanding of the relationship of tort law to morality. Those questions include "How are answers to legal questions about rights and duties related to reasoning about moral rights and duties?" and "What are you saying, if you are not saying that judges should read moral rights and duties into the law of torts?" In responding to these queries, we draw once again on our contrast between Cardozo and Holmes.

The two men agreed on many things, which is why Cardozo considered himself a disciple of his great predecessor. Both saw themselves as pragmatists. Both regarded common-law courts as tasked with the difficult but vital job of mediating among past, present, and future—of following the inherited law yet keeping it current and enabling it to grow. Both layered onto this already difficult assignment an additional complexity: namely, the need to account for law's institutional dimensions, which requires courts to be mindful of (among other things) the respective roles of judge and jury, differences across jurisdictions, and the deference owed to legislatures.

These commonalities notwithstanding, Holmes and Cardozo held very different views of the common law, and of law more generally. Like Austin before him, Holmes had trouble coming to terms with common law and common-law reasoning. He rejected the thought that it is merely applied morality. Indeed, he famously (and correctly) observed that morality takes greater cognizance than law of character, excuses, and the like. Nor is the common law a matter of the state issuing commands, or of officials exercising the power to confine or kill those who fail to heed its commands. Instead, as evidenced most familiarly by negligence law's tying of liability to an objective fault standard, the common law operates in a space somewhere between the aspirational normativity of natural law and the brute coercive force of a Hobbesian sovereign. In Holmes's time and today, to be subject to the rules of common law is, overwhelmingly, to be subjected to legal standards of conduct at the peril of being held liable to those one injures by failing to conform to those standards. For all of his deep historical and doctrinal learning, Holmes seems never to have fully reconciled himself to an institution of this sort. He insisted on giving common law an Austinian cast—hence his famous pronouncement that the common law is not "a brooding omnipresence in the sky, but the articulate voice of some sovereign or quasi sovereign . . . ."[26] But neither judges, nor the rules articulated in their decisions, nor the phenomenon of liability really fits the picture of a sovereign commanding his subjects.

Cardozo also embraced the common law, and also perceived it as betwixt and between other domains of normativity. But whereas Holmes saw common-law liability as a watered-down version of a scheme of commands and sanctions, Cardozo saw it as a beefed-up version of social mores, customs, and conventional norms of interpersonal interaction.[27] On his understanding, the common law is an institutionalized and state-backed system for the recognition and enforcement of these mores, customs, and norms (or a subset of them). With an eye on basic fairness, and relying on both precedents and their own judgment to keep legal rules democratically in touch with everyday beliefs and expectations, judges and juries are charged with adjudicating disputes and determining liability for violations of common-law rules. Liability, on this understanding, is not "punishment lite." Rather, it is a formalized version of informal, everyday practices of people holding themselves and each other responsible. As one holds oneself and is held by others to certain basic obligations—such as the obligation to take care against injuring others—so too does the common law, albeit on somewhat different terms, and with different consequences.

Near to the core of the intrafamilial dispute between Holmes and Cardozo are distinct conceptions of the way in which law goes about setting rules and standards of conduct. The law of negligence again illustrates the difference. Holmes—and later Judge Andrews in his famous *Palsgraf*

---

26. S. Pac. Co. v. Jensen, 244 U.S. 205, 222 (1917).

27. John C. P. Goldberg, *Book Review: The Life of the Law*, 51 STAN. L. REV. 1419 (1999); John C. P. Goldberg, *Note: Community and the Common Law Judge: Reconstructing Cardozo's Theoretical Writings*, 65 N.Y.U. L. REV. 1324 (1990).

dissent—saw in the "reasonably prudent person" a standard of conduct imposed by the state on each of us.[28] It is government's way of directing all of us to refrain from acting in a way that generates unreasonable risks of harm. This standard generates a duty of sorts, but it is a nonrelational duty. It is not owed to anyone in particular, but simply owed.

Cardozo understood the common law, including the law of negligence, as relational—that is, as articulating obligations running from one person to another or others. In this respect he took it to mimic morality (or certain basic branches of morality) in that it involves conceptions of what one owes to others and what others owe to one. The common law is legal, not moral, but it shares a great deal of morality's content and structure. It is not fundamentally about a state or a sovereign commanding people to behave the way it wants them to behave so that it can achieve its purposes. It is about how a person is obligated to interact or refrain from interacting with others, whether they are known or unknown to her, and whether individually or as members of a class.

Needless to say, Cardozo was perfectly well aware that judges sometimes are required to exercise discretion, and cannot simply look up answers in cases or statutory text. And he plainly thought that, on these occasions, judges would and should be drawing from positive morality. All this is stated forthrightly in *The Nature of the Judicial Process*.[29] Yet he believed that the judicial reliance on positive morality, like judicial reliance on legal precedent, was constructive rather than mechanical or descriptive. The goal was to fashion answers to legal questions that will stand up to critical scrutiny. Unlike instrumentalists, for him, scrutiny in this context was not wholly or even primarily concerned with estimating the extent to which the net social impact of adopting one rule rather than another will be positive. As a self-consciously pluralistic judge, Cardozo was open to hearing arguments about social impact. But the form of reasoning he saw on display in judicial decisions (and approved of) was not consequentialist. It was constructivist.

The title of our book, and of this conclusion, is meant to capture the various dimensions of a Cardozoan conception of common law in a do-

---

28. Palsgraf v. Long Island R. Co., 162 N.E. 99, 102 (N.Y. 1928) (Andrews, J., dissenting) ("Due care is a duty imposed on each one of us to protect society from unnecessary danger, not to protect, A, B, or C alone").

29. BENJAMIN N. CARDOZO, THE NATURE OF THE JUDICIAL PROCESS (1921).

main such as tort law. The term "recognizing" is, in some contexts, performative. Relatedly, it connotes practical conduct that carries with it institutional significance. A head of state might recognize the leader of one parliamentary party as the prime minister, just as a committee chairperson might recognize a speaker when it is the speaker's turn to be heard. Likewise, the act of recognizing a wrong, duty, or right, especially when it is the act of an appellate court, is itself partially constitutive of there being a legal wrong, duty, or right. The recognition by the New York Court of Appeals of a duty to take care not to injure that was owed by Buick Motor Company to Donald MacPherson was itself partially constitutive of Buick's owing such a duty not only to MacPherson, but to those whom it was aware (or should be aware) might face serious risks to life and limb as a result of carelessness in the manufacture of its cars.

The performative aspect of the phrase "recognizing wrongs" does not exhaust its meaning. The term "recognizing" obviously also relates to cognition, and alludes to something like "noticing," "seeing," or "perceiving." To recognize someone as a scoundrel, a sensitive soul, or an able lawyer is to apprehend that she is someone with the characteristics of such a person. Similarly, consider what it means to recognize that an uninvited shoulder massage in the workplace might be a battery, or what it means to recognize that calling someone a "son-of-a-bitch" is more an insult than a slander. In these cases, to "recognize" means to apprehend these acts as instances (or not) of a certain category, one that has both a moral flavor and legal significance.

Cardozo believed that judges (and juries) have the capacity to recognize wrongs—to apprehend which kinds of conduct and which kinds of injury can and do qualify as torts. Grasping, observing, apprehending, and articulating wrongs is a matter of appreciating the duties and responsibilities that are owed to others. It goes hand in hand with grasping what we expect of ourselves and others. The word "expect" is both fruitfully and dangerously ambiguous, having both a predictive and a normative dimension (as does the word "we" in the phrase "we expect of ourselves and others"). Judges deciding common-law cases are empowered and obligated to decide the dimensions of duties, rights, and responsibilities, and they do so in part by consulting their own understanding of what the law, properly understood, expects of us and what we expect of one another.

In the process just described, judges draw from legal precedent, positive morality, and critical morality at one and the same time. Skeptics complain that this amounts to trickery—an illicit slipping back and forth among different modes of analysis. This complaint, however, presupposes that these different forms of normativity have clear boundaries, and that knowledge is available *of them* and *in them*, but only so long as their boundaries are respected. The validity of this presupposition is doubtful, to say the least. Indeed, as much work in twentieth-century jurisprudence has shown, it is optimistic to the point of recklessness to suppose that it can be established.

At the risk of trying to squeeze too much from a phrase, we repair yet again to our title. It is not only judges and lawyers who interact with the law of torts, directly or indirectly. Everyone does. We all need to know what to expect of the persons, businesses, offices, and organizations around us, and we all need to know what is expected of us. This is why the wrongs recognized by courts as torts cannot be the wrongs that Judge Hercules would endorse for being those whose recognition would make the law the best it can be from the perspective of aspirational political or moral theory. Torts must be *recognizable* wrongs.

"Recognizing" and its cognates carry other connotations that we find apt and illuminating. Our effort to describe and reinvigorate modes of legal analysis that fall between crude instrumentalism, on the one hand, and sanctimonious moralism, on the other, is in large part an effort to invite legal scholars to re-cognize (rethink) conventional wisdom—to recognize that discourse about law can be rigorous and grounded even when not partaking of the methodologies of economics or statistics. Another variation: in identifying relational legal wrongs, and in empowering victims of such wrongs to make demands on wrongdoers via the courts, tort law recognizes each of us as a person: as someone who "counts" and who thus cannot fairly be made to sublimate her individual interests entirely in the name of some larger good. Yet this same body of law simultaneously invites us each to recognize our responsibilities to others—that, as we go about our lives interacting with others, we owe it to them to take various measures against injuring them.

More than a century ago, Holmes proclaimed that legal rights and duties in the common law cannot properly be understood without abandoning the moral connotations they carry on their surface. In this book we have rejected Holmes's path in favor of the alternative charted by Cardozo. Though no less practically oriented, Cardozo's path starts from a very different place. It supposes that, *unless* we see that legal rights, wrongs, and duties have a normative structure and content similar to their moral counterparts, we will fail to produce a workable account of the law for judges, lawyers, and others who want to know the law. We are confident that, for all their differences, Holmes and Cardozo would have agreed on one thing: the selection of a framework and a method for analyzing tort law, or law itself, is not a matter of a priori reasoning. Who can better explain the law? Who can ferret out its strengths and weaknesses? Who can offer detailed and constructive ways of thinking about why we need it and how to work with it? On these questions and others, the path that calls on us to recognize wrongs will serve us better than the path that would lead us to ignore them.

ACKNOWLEDGMENTS

This book has been long in the making. We took the first, unknowing steps toward its creation in the fall of 1988, when, as 1L section-mates at NYU Law School, we struck up a conversation that continues to this day. Work on the manuscript would not commence until twenty years later and has proceeded, well, slowly. While perhaps not ideal, this tempo reflects our conviction that a theory of tort law must rest on a broad and deep knowledge of the field at the level of practice, doctrine, history, and jurisprudence. It also reflects our having benefited from opportunities to publish our work in the form of journal articles and book chapters. Although this book builds on those prior writings, which began with the 1998 publication of Zipursky's *Rights, Wrongs, and Recourse in the Law of Torts* and Goldberg and Zipursky's *The Moral of MacPherson*, it has been written afresh. The upshot, we hope, is a clear and systematic presentation of a mature theory.

A work with this sort of gestation period generates a lot of debts: far more than we can possibly acknowledge. We continue to benefit from the wonderful legal training we received at NYU, including from our Torts professor, Sylvia Law (with whose views we stubbornly but respectfully continue to disagree), as well as our mentor in Jurisprudence, Ronald Dworkin, and a wonderful group of advisors including Rochelle Dreyfuss, Chris Eisgruber, Lewis Kornhauser, Bill Nelson, and Larry Sager. We are grateful as well to the judges for whom we served as law clerks—Judge Kimba M. Wood, and Judge Jack B. Weinstein and Justice Byron R. White. To the extent our work expresses confidence in the abilities of the judiciary, it reflects our having seen first-hand the work of these remarkable jurists and public servants.

Throughout our professorial careers, we have been blessed with input from extraordinarily patient and thoughtful colleagues at Fordham, Vanderbilt, and Harvard. They include: Brooke Ackerly, Bill Alford, Aditi Bagchi, Oren Bar-Gill, Michael Baur, Chris Bavitz, Helen Bender, Susan Block-Lieb, Gabriella Blum, Mark Brandon, Lisa Bressman, Rebecca Brown, Jim Brudney, Glenn Cohen, George Conk, Nestor Davidson, Debby Denno, Charlie Donahue, Paul Edelman, Jim Ely, Howie Erichson, Dick Fallon, Nita Farahany, Noah Feldman, Martin Flaherty, Jim Fleming, Sheila Foster, Jody Freeman,

Charles Fried, Barry Friedman, Jake Gersen, Bruce Green, Chris Guthrie, Gail Hollister, Morton Horwitz, Clare Huntington, Howell Jackson, Bob Kaczorowski, Sonya Katyal, Andy Kaufman, Duncan Kennedy, Andrew Kent, Nancy King, Mike Klarman, Joe Landau, Richard Lazarus, Jae Lee, Tom Lee, Ethan Leib, Dan Meltzer, Frank Michelman, Richard Nagareda, Jackie Nolan-Haley, David Partlett, Mark Patterson, Russ Pearce, Todd Rakoff, Bob Rasmussen, Joel Reidenberg, Bill Rubenstein, Ben Sachs, Aaron Saiger, Tim Scanlon, Steve Shavell, Suzanna Sherry, Jed Shugerman, Joe Singer, Rob Sitkoff, Holger Spamann, Kevin Stack, Carol Steiker, Matthew Stephenson, Linda Sugin, Cass Sunstein, Olivier Sylvain, Bob Talisse, Steve Thel, Mark Tushnet, Mike Vandenbergh, Ian Weinstein, Nick Zeppos, and Jonathan Zittrain.

For their unwavering and generous support, we are immensely grateful to Deans Matthew Diller, John Feerick, Elena Kagan, John Manning, Michael Martin, Martha Minow, Ed Rubin, Kent Syverud, and Bill Treanor.

One of the great pleasures of writing in the fields in which we write is that it has introduced us to an array of gifted scholars working in overlapping international communities. As our text and citations attest, whether at conferences, by email, or in the quiet of a library or office, our interactions with them and their work have been hugely enriching. Among them are: Ken Abraham, Larry Alexander, Emad Atiq, Ahson Azmat, Tom Baker, Shyam Balganesh, Charles Barzun, Avi Bell, Peter Benson, Anita Bernstein, Brian Bix, Vince Blasi, Sam Bray, Curtis Bridgeman, Jacob Bronsther, Alan Brudner, Ellie Bublick, Guido Calabresi, Alan Calnan, Peter Cane, Jonathan Cardi, Martha Chamallas, Vincent Chiao, Danielle Citron, Eric Claeys, Jules Coleman, Nico Cornell, Hanoch Dagan, Stephen Darwall, Nestor Davidson, Mihailis Diamantis, Avihay Dorfman, Antony Duff, Avlana Eisenberg, Richard Epstein, Howard Erichson, Chris Essert, Kim Ferzan, John Finnis, George Fletcher, Stephen Galoob, John Gardner, Mark Geistfeld, Mark Gergen, Maria Glover, Andrew Gold, Patrick Goold, James Goudkamp, Mike Green, Jeff Helmreich, Jim Henderson, Scott Hershovitz, Ori Herstein, Heidi Hurd, Andy Hurwitz, Keith Hylton, Dmitry Karshtedt, Larissa Katz, Greg Keating, Erin Kelly, Leslie Kendrick, Greg Klass, Josh Kleinfeld, Dennis Klimchuk, Jody Kraus, Alexi Lahav, Brian Lee, Jed Lewinsohn, David Luban, Paul MacMahon, Nick McBride, Gabe Mendlow, Tom Merrill, Paul Miller, Michael Moore, John Murphy, Liam Murphy, Tom Nagel, Jason Neyers, Donal Nolan, Ken Oliphant, Nate Oman, David Owen, Gideon Parchomovsky, Dennis Patterson, Stephen Perry, Jeff Pojanowski, Richard Posner, Gerald Postema, Bill Powers, Dan Priel, Robert Rabin, Andrew Robertson, Chris Robinette, Tanina Rostain, Chaim Saiman, Fred Schauer, Steve Schaus, Sam Scheffler, Lauren Scholz, Scott Shapiro, Cathy Sharkey, Emily Sherwin, Ted Sichelman, Ken Simons, Zoë Sinel, Steve Smith, Jason Solomon, Jane Stapleton, Rob Stevens, Martin Stone, Rebecca Stone, Steve Sugarman, Victor Tadros, Zahra Takhshid, Will Thomas, Lynne Tirrell, Aaron Twerski, David Waddilove, Jeremy Waldron, Ernie Weinrib, Robin West, Ted White, Trish White, John Witt, Richard Wright, and Katrina Wyman.

Over the life of this project, our friends Abner Greene, Michael Martin, Arthur Ripstein, Tony Sebok, and Henry Smith have served as constant sources of helpful feedback and guidance. And for their scrupulous and hugely helpful comments on this manuscript, we are beyond grateful to Don Herzog, Daniel Markovits, and John Oberdiek.

Too many years ago to mention, it was Lloyd Weinreb who encouraged us to undertake this project, and Michael Aronson at HUP who worked with us to develop an initial proposal. Many thanks to them, to our editor Lindsay Waters, and to Joy Deng and the members of the HUP editorial and production team, for guiding this project to completion.

Finally, we would like to acknowledge the scores of enthusiastic and brilliant students whom we have had the pleasure of teaching and working with. We thank them for pressing us to clarify, rethink, and justify our views of tort law and law generally.

INDEX

wrongful death statutes, 61 n14, 204

wrongs: blame and, 206; civilly actionable, 26; criminal law and, 184; equitable wrongs distinguished, 56; injurious, 4, 26, 28, 30; judicially recognized, 5; legally recognized, 26; private, 40, 41–42, 54–55; punishment and, 206; recognizing, 21, 257, 290, 343, 363–365; relational, 4, 26, 28–29, 30 (*see also* relationality; relationships); torts as, 3–5, 17, 181–182, 205–208

Zeran v. America On Line, Inc., 329